RENEWING CATHOLIC FAMILY LIFE: EXPERTS EXPLORE NEW DIRECTIONS IN FAMILY SPIRITUALITY AND FAMILY MINISTRY

GENERAL EDITOR: GREGORY K. POPCAK, PHD

Our Sunday Visitor Publishing Division
Our Sunday Visitor, Inc.
200 Noll Plaza
Huntington, IN 46750
1-800-348-2440

ISBN: 978-1-68192-677-3 (Inventory No. T2544)
LCCN: 2020938927

Cover and interior design: Lindsey Riesen
Cover art: Adobe Stock

PRINTED IN THE UNITED STATES OF AMERICA

Contents

INTRODUCTION

11

PARTICIPANTS

19

PART ONE

Understanding the "Catholic Difference" Family Life:
The Family as Domestic Church

Chapter One

De-Romanticizing the Domestic Church:
The Liturgical-Sacrament Vocation of the Christian Family

———————

TIMOTHY O'MALLEY
McGrath Institute for Church Life, University of Notre Dame

29

Chapter Two

The Population Balm: How the Church Taught the
World to Welcome Children

———————

MIKE AQUILINA
Saint Paul Center for Biblical Theology; Contributing Editor,
Angelus News

47

Chapter Three
Without a Vision, the People Perish:
Biblical Foundations for Renewal of the Family

———

Dr. Joseph C. Atkinson
*Pontifical John Paul II Institute for Studies on Marriage and Family
at The Catholic University of America*
63

Chapter Four
"The Nearest Hospital": Exploring the Domestic Church
as a Place of Healing

———

John Grabowski
*The Catholic University of America, Pontifical Council
for the Family (emeritus)*
Claire Grabowski
Pontifical Council for the Family (emerita)
79

Chapter Five
Focusing on Families: Nurturing Catholic Identity and Promoting
Social Change through Family Practices

———

Julie Hanlon Rubio
Santa Clara University
95

PART TWO

Catholic Family Life and the Social Context: Who Are We? What Are We Up Against? How Must We Respond?

Chapter Six

Early Twenty-First Century American Catholic Families

MARK M. GRAY, PH.D.

Center for Applied Research in the Apostolate, Georgetown University

119

Chapter Seven

Sex, Marriage, and Parenting: Culture versus the Catholic Difference

HELEN M. ALVARÉ

Antonin Scalia Law School, George Mason University

149

Chapter Eight

Marriage: The Sacrament of the Fulfillment of the Sexual Nature of Man

PAT FAGAN

Marriage and Religion Research Institute, The Catholic University of America

165

PART THREE
Parents Matter More Than They Think:
What Does It Take to Pass on Catholic Faith and Values?

Chapter Nine
Millennials, Parents, Grandparents: Are Catholic Families
Still Passing on Their Faith?
—
VERN L. BENGTSON
University of Southern California
MERRIL SILVERSTEIN
Syracuse University
195

Chapter Ten
Parents: The Decisive Agents in the Religious Outcomes
of American Youth
—
JUSTIN BARTKUS
Institute of Design
Illinois Institute of Technology
213

Chapter Eleven
Raising Virtuous Children: Children's Basic Needs and the Evolved
Nest
—
MARY S. TARSHA AND DARCIA NARVAEZ
University of Notre Dame
235

PART FOUR
Catholic Family Life and the Multicultural Context

Chapter Twelve
Black Families Are Holy and Worthy!

ANDREW AND TERRI LYKE
Arusi Network
271

Chapter Thirteen
Hispanics and Family Life in Twenty-First Century America:
A Catholic Call to Action

HOSFFMAN OSPINO, PHD
Associate Professor of Theology and Religious Education at Boston College, School of Theology and Ministry | Director of Graduate Programs in Hispanic Ministry
299

Chapter Fourteen
Challenges of Cultivating Catholic Family Spirituality in Interfaith Households

JOMON KALLADANTHIYIL, CSC
Director of Pastoral Ministry, Saint Joseph's Oratory, Montreal
313

PART FIVE

The Building Blocks for a New Vision of Catholic
Family Life and Spirituality

Chapter Fifteen

The Domestic Church and the Pilgrimage to the Father's House

———————

Dominic Lombardi, STL
*Executive Director: USCCB Secretariat of Laity, Marriage,
Family Life, and Youth*
337

Chapter Sixteen

The Divine Pedagogy and the Family

———————

Joseph D. White, PhD
*Family Psychologist, Director of Catechetical
Resources — Our Sunday Visitor*
353

Chapter Seventeen

A Spirituality of the Home

———————

Tim and Sue Muldoon
Authors of Six Sacred Rules for Families, The Discerning Parent, *and*
Reclaiming Family Time, *and frequent speakers on the spirituality of
family life.*
373

Chapter Eighteen
The Gospel Still Works, Right?
So What Have We Been Missing in American Families and Parishes?

Dr. William Keimig
Catechetical Institute, Franciscan University
391

Chapter Nineteen
They Will Know We Are Christians by Our Joy

Damon and Melanie Owens
JoyTOB.org
415

PART SIX
Putting It All Together:
A New Vision for Family Spirituality and Family Ministry

Chapter Twenty
Come and Be Formed! The 3R's in the Liturgy of Domestic Church Life

Gregory K. Popcak, Lisa A. Popcak, David McClow
Pastoral Solutions Institute
445

Chapter Twenty-One
The Rite of Relationship/Attachment:
A Formation Program in the Priestly Mission of Baptism
457

Chapter Twenty-Two
The Rite of Rituals of Connection:
A Formation Program in the Prophetic Mission of Baptism
467

Chapter Twenty-Three
The Rite of Reaching Out:
Ongoing Formation in the Royal Mission of Baptism
477

INTRODUCTION

GREGORY K. POPCAK, PhD

Imagine being asked the following questions. How would you respond?

1. Are Catholic families called to relate differently to one another than our non-Catholic counterparts? If so, how?
2. What does an authentic "domestic-church-based spirituality" (i.e., one that doesn't simply try to shoehorn monastic practices into family life) look like in practice?
3. How can Catholic parents be more effective at practicing intentional discipleship at home and be equipped to raise the next generation of intentional disciples?
4. How can Catholic families be empowered to become the primary outposts of evangelization and positive social change that the Church calls them to be?

These are remarkably important questions that speak not only to the heart of Catholic family life, but also to the future vitality of the Church itself. For instance, what is the experiential case for Catholicism if our families are unable to experience, much less articulate, what difference the Catholic faith makes in our homes?

Likewise, because so much of what we think of as "Catholic spirituality" is drawn from the clerical and religious tradition, much of it doesn't easily fit into messy family life. How many people have we encountered who say, "I *used* to have a great prayer life, until I got married and had kids"? The lack of the development of an authentic, ecological, domestic-church-based spirituality has created a dynamic in which familes are all but forced to view their vocation as an impediment to living a grace-filled, holy life.

Similarly, how much of our pastoral ministry resources and efforts are spent chasing after sheep that should never have been lost in the first place — children raised in Catholic households? Why do so many Catholic parents and pastors assume that Catholic children are *supposed* to fall away as a matter of course, when so much solid research offers parents — and the Church — real hope for being able to raise adult children who are passionate about their faith?

Finally, almost forty years since *Familiaris Consortio* said that families should be viewed as partners in the salvific mission of the Church, why do so many of our pastoral ministry and educational efforts continue to treat families as incidental at best, or a hindrance at worst? Why do we continue to treat families solely as one more group that needs to be ministered to, instead of equipping families *to be the ministries* (i.e, "the domestic churches") Catholic teaching says they are meant to be?

UNASKED AND UNANSWERED

As important as these four critical questions are, there is a good chance you have never encountered them before. Remarkably, in the history of the Church, these questions have never been explored in a systematic way.

There are many reasons for this. The short version is that, historically, it was felt that the priesthood or religious life was the preferred and normative path for anyone who felt called to live a holy life. Everyone else was more or less expected to follow the example set by their spiritual betters as best they could. The Second Vatican Council challenged this historical — and frankly, clericalist — view by promoting the "universal call to holiness," which asserted that all of God's people — lay and religious alike — were called to live lives of heroic virtue.

Saint John Paul II, the first pope whose pontificate was entirely in the post-Vatican II era (except, of course, for Pope John Paul I, who only lived a month after his election), made it his business to lay a foundation for what the universal call to holiness might look like. In his pontificate, he arguably wrote about two-thirds of all the theology the Church had ever produced up to that point on marriage and family life. He proclaimed Saint Thérèse of Lisieux to be a Doctor of the Church largely because her "little way" of holiness was the most relevant model for a lay path to holiness. He canonized more lay and married saints than anyone before him, providing the faithful with clear examples of heroic virtue as lived in everyday life. Perhaps most importantly, he developed his *Theology of the Body* to give the laity their own unique lens through which to view salvation history, the Gospels, the sacraments, and the spiritual life.

Many Catholics in academia and even the hierarchy have struggled to relate to the significance of the *Theology of the Body*. It is often treated as the odd pet project of a man who was overly concerned with the sexual teachings of the Church. This view misses the point entirely. It could be argued that the *Theology of the Body* was intended to serve as the philosphical and theological foundation for the new spiritual approach demanded by the universal call to holiness. How? As I already indicated above, historically, the predominant lens through which salvation history, the Gospels, the sacraments, and spirtuality in general were viewed was that of "Christ the High Priest." This, of course, is the lens that is most relevant to clerical and religious life. By contrast, the *Theology of the Body* explores what happens when Christians view all the essential elements of our faith through the lens of "Christ the Bridegroom." This view does not conflict or compete with the insights produced by the Christ the High Priest model, but complements it — like the complementary relationship between man and woman, or that of the "Church of Peter" and the "Church of Mary."

Considering that, by age seventy-five, 96 percent of all lay people will have been married at least once (Yau n.d.), the idea of developing a model of lay spirituality rooted in the image of Christ the Bridegroom would, when properly unpacked, have almost universal resonance for the laity.

Brilliantly, the lens of the *Theology of the Body* changes absolutely nothing about Catholic faith and spirituality while simultaneously changing everything that is viewed through it. It provides lay people with the tools required to build a robust, ecological, dynamic, authentically Catholic spirituality — *rooted firmly in the lay experience* — from the ground up. Because of Saint John Paul II's gift of the *Theology of the Body*, the laity are no longer required to beg spiritual scraps from the clerical table. Both priest and lay person may now carry their own complementary spiritual dishes into the Heavenly Feast.

Of course, since this original body of work was developed by Saint John Paul II, Pope Benedict and Pope Francis have made their own contributions to the Catholic theology of marriage and family, the latter especially with his promulgation of *Amoris Laetitia*. Likewise, in the last several decades, many other academic theologians have made their own important contributions to this topic.

Unfortunately, very little of this work is what one might consider accessible to the average rank-and-file Catholic. For various reasons, despite the existence of this compelling body of higher-level theology on the Catholic vision of marriage and family life, there has been very little work done to answer the questions each of us at least unconsciously asks when we encounter so-called big ideas; namely, *So what? Who cares?* and *What's in it for me?*

The four critical questions that I presented at the beginning of this Introduction, questions that served as the basis of the Symposium on Catholic Family Life and Spirituality, are ultimately ordered to address these practical concerns.

THE SYMPOSIUM ON CATHOLIC FAMILY LIFE AND SPIRITUALITY

Working closely with Jason Shanks, president of the OSV Institute, as well our cosponsors, Holy Cross Family Ministries and the McGrath Institute for Church Life at the University of Notre Dame, my organization, the Pastoral Solutions Institute, organized a historic gathering of more than forty social scientists, theologians, pastoral counselors, and pastoral ministry professionals, internationally recognized for their research and work with families. By design, it was an ethnically, ideologically, and academically diverse group of professionals. Better still, virtually all of the participants were also religiously engaged parents (both biological and adoptive) and grandparents with a very personal stake in finding answers to the questions we were exploring.

The participants shared research and insights from our respective disciplines. We prayed and reflected together on the four critical questions. We debated what practical answers to those questions might look like. This book is the result of these efforts. Of course, thanks to Family Theater Productions (a ministry of Holy Cross Family Ministries), you are also welcome to view the presentations yourself at www .PeytonInstitute.org.

We do not presume to have the final answers to the questions we have proposed in this volume, but we sincerely hope that both the symposium and this book will serve as catalysts for a much wider, global conversation on new approaches to family spirituality and family ministry. As neglected as the development of a practical theology of Catholic family life has been, nothing speaks to the everyday lives of rank-and-file Catholics — as well as the future vitality of the Church — as do these issues.

HOW TO USE THIS BOOK

The contributors took pains to avoid overly academic language so this work could be as accessible as possible to as many people as possible. Even so, we admit that this is a rather hefty tome. Fear not! To make the information easier to digest, each chapter begins with "Five Quick Takes," enumerating what the authors considered to be their most important points. I would invite readers to begin by reviewing the quick takes for each chapter, and then doing a deeper dive into the chapters that pique their interest or speak to their specific concerns. Fair warning: There is a lot of inspiring and eye-opening material in this book. You may find yourself reading more than you expected to.

Also, because we hope to ignite a much larger conversation about the renewal of Catholic family life and Catholic family ministry, we have included discussion questions at the end of each chapter. We want to offer you an opportunity to reflect on how the material applies both to your own family life and to your efforts to minister to other families. We hope these discussion questions will help make the material in this book more immediately relevant to parents, pastors, and family life ministers at both the diocesan and parish level.

THE LAY OF THE LAND

Like the Symposium on Catholic Family Life and Spirituality that inspired it, this book is divided into six sections, each with about three or four chapters exploring the topic at hand from the perspective of the various disciplines represented at the symposium.

Part One: Understanding the "Catholic Difference" Family Life: The Family as Domestic Church, unpacks the historical, biblical, and theological understanding of the term "domestic church." What does that phrase mean? What doesn't it mean? What hints can it give us about how Catholic families are called to live and relate to each other differently than our non-Catholic counterparts?

Part Two: Catholic Family Life and the Social Context: Who Are We? What Are We Up Against? How Must We Respond? examines what the social sciences can tell us about what today's Catholic family looks like, what challenges we face in promoting the Catholic vision of family life, and ways we might rise to those challenges.

Part Three: Parents Matter More Than They Think: What Does It Take to Pass on Catholic Faith and Values? presents some incredibly exciting new research describing factors that enable parents to successfully pass on their faith and values to the next generation. The picture is much more hopeful than conventional wisdom might have us believe, and the action items the authors suggest are simple, practical, and doable for almost every family who cares about their faith.

Part Four: Catholic Family Life and the Multicultural Context illuminates the unique concerns we must keep in mind as we minister to African-American and Hispanic Catholic families, as well as those Catholics struggling to celebrate their faith in interfaith households.

Part Five: The Building Blocks for a New Vision of Catholic Family Life and Spirituality offers new and eye-opening insights into how Catholic families can create a dynamic prayer life, spirituality, and path to holiness that is both considerate of our Catholic spiritual inheritance and respectful of the unique challenges of family life.

Part Six: Putting It All Together: A New Vision for Family Spirituality and Family Ministry draws from the insights of all our contributors as well as other research to present a practical framework for constructing an authentic domestic-church-based spirituality. In addition to this big-picture framework, the chapters in this section also offer many simple, practical suggestions families can use to experience God as an actual member of their households and encounter their faith as the source of warmth in their homes. This framework also proposes a new vision for Catholic family ministry; one that enables the Church to not simply minister *to* families, but also empower familes *to be* the ministries (i.e, the domestic churches) our Catholic faith calls them to be.

THE PEYTON INSTITUTE FOR DOMESTIC CHURCH LIFE

Finally, the Symposium served as the launching point for the Peyton Institute for Domestic Church Life. Named for our patron, the Venerable Father Patrick ("the family that prays together stays together") Peyton, CSC, the Peyton Institute is a collaboration of the Pastoral Solutions Institute and Holy Cross Family Ministries dedicated to promoting the conversation about family spirituality and family well-being through original research, professional training, family events, and creative resources supporting domestic church life.

One of the first initiatives of the Peyton Institute is a cooperative effort with the National Association of Catholic Family Life Ministers to train diocesan family life directors across the United States in the model of family spirituality and family ministry we propose in Part Six of this book. We hope that this training will serve as the next step in a much larger movement to renew both Catholic family life and Catholic family ministry.

To that end, we want to know what you think about both the four critcal questions and what the Peyton Institute can do to support your family and the families to which you minister in experiencing a more meaningful, dynamic, and grace-filled domestic church life. Please feel free to write to us at Institute@hcfm.org.

With that, I sincerely hope this book, and the larger conversation we hope to spark with this book, will be a blessing to you, your family, and your ministry. May God bless you abundantly. Holy Family, pray for us!

GREGORY K. POPCAK, PHD, BCD, FAAPC
General Editor
Organizer/Host: Symposium on Catholic Family Life and Spirituality
Codirector: Peyton Institute for Domestic Church Life

REFERENCE

Yau, Nathan. "Percentage of People Who Married, Given Your Age." Accessed September 9, 2019. https://flowingdata.com/2017/11/01/who-is-married-by-now/.

SYMPOSIUM ON CATHOLIC FAMILY LIFE AND SPIRITUALITY PARTICIPANTS

(*These participants contributed a chapter to this book. Those without an asterisk actively contributed to the symposium discussions. Their input was instrumental in the revisions of the symposium papers, which became the chapters in this book, hence their inclusion in this list.)

ORGANIZERS/HOSTS

***Dr. Greg and Lisa Popcak** are the directors of the Pastoral Solutions Institute (CatholicCounselors.com), a prominent Catholic tele-counseling practice serving clients around the world. The authors of more than twenty books on Catholic spirituality, marriage, family life, and parenting (including *Parenting with Grace, Discovering God Together,* and *For Better … Forever!*), they are the hosts of *More2Life,* a call-in program airing weekdays on EWTN Radio and SiriusXM 130. They also serve as the directors of the Peyton Institute for Domestic Church Life, a collaborative ministry effort of the Pastoral Solutions Institute and Holy Cross Family Ministries. They are the parents of three children.

PARTICIPANTS

***Joseph Atkinson, PhD,** is an associate professor of Sacred Scripture at the Pontifical John Paul II *Institute for Studies on Marriage and Family* at Catholic University of America. Specialization: biblical foundations of the family. He is a primary authority on the concept of the domestic church, which explores the ecclesial structure and meaning of the family.

*Helen Alvaré, JD, is a professor of law at Antonin Scalia Law School, George Mason University, where she teaches Family Law, Law and Religion, and Property Law. She publishes on matters concerning marriage, parenting, non-marital households, and the First Amendment religion clauses. She is faculty advisor to the law school's *Civil Rights Law Journal* and the Latino/a Law Student Association. She has been a consultor for the Pontifical Council of the Laity and continues to advise the U.S. Conference of Catholic Bishops. She cooperates with the Permanent Observer Mission of the Holy See to the United Nations. Her most recent book is *Putting Children's Interests First in U.S. Family Law and Policy: With Power Comes Responsibility* (Cambridge 2017).

*Mike Aquilina is the author of more than fifty books on Catholic history, doctrine, and devotion. He is executive vice president of the Saint Paul Center for Biblical Theology.

*Justin Bartkus is a graduate learner at the Illinois Institute of Technology. He was the lead author, with University of Notre Dame sociologist Christian Smith, of "Parental Cultures and Practices of Intergenerational Transmission of Religious Faith."

*Vern L. Bengtson, PhD, is a research professor in the Edward R. Roybal Institute on Aging at the University of Southern California's Suzanne Dworak-Peck School of Social Work and AARP/University Professor of Gerontology Emeritus. A past president of the Gerontological Society of America, he has published nineteen books and 260 research articles on aging, families, and intergenerational relationships. His most recent book, *Families and Faith: How Religion Is Passed Down across Generations* (with Norella Putney and Susan C. Harris), recently received book-of-the-year awards from the Gerontological Society of America and the American Sociological Association's Section on Sociology of Religion, and was featured in *The New York Times, Wall Street Journal, Washington Post,* and *USA Today,* and on National Public Radio.

Mike Day is the president of the National Association of Catholic Family

Life Ministers. He is the director of the Office of Family Life for the Diocese of St. Augustine, having served in marriage and family life ministry for twelve years with the diocese. (Discussant)

*Pat Fagan, PhD, is founder and director of the Marriage and Religion Research Institute (www.MARRI.us) at The Catholic University of America. Pat has been a therapist specializing in child, family, and marital issues, a Senate staffer, the Deputy Assistant Secretary for Family and Social Policy at the U.S. Department of Health and Human Services under President George H. Bush, and a Senior Fellow of Family and Culture at the Heritage Foundation. He is publisher and editor of Marripedia.org and the weekly *Faith and Family Findings,* has authored more than thirty synthesis papers, and has commissioned from others dozens of original research projects in marriage, family, child development, and religious practice. His work has appeared in or been covered by *Time* magazine, the *Washington Post,* the *Washington Times,* the *Globe and Mail, USA Today,* and the *Guardian.* He and his wife, Theresa, have eight children and thirteen grandchildren.

Julia Dezelski, STD, is the assistant director of Marriage and Family Life, Laity in the U.S. Conference of Catholic Bishops Secretariat of Laity, Marriage, Family Life, and Youth. (Discussant)

*John and Claire Grabowski: John (PhD, Marquette University) has taught moral theology at The Catholic University of America for the past twenty-six years. He has three times been appointed as a theological consultant to the U.S. Conference of Catholic Bishops. In 2015 he was appointed by Pope Francis to serve as an auditor at the Synod of Bishops on the Family. His books include *A Catechism for Family Life* (with Sarah Bartel). Claire has been a Catholic educator and active in a variety of lay ministries for many years. Together, they have been in marriage ministry for more than twenty-five years, served as a member couple on the Pontifical Council for the Family, and are the authors of several books on marriage and family life, including *Raising Catholic Kids for Their Vocations.* They have five children and several grandchildren.

*Mark M. Gray, PhD,** is the director of CARA Catholic Poll and a senior research associate at CARA. He has a doctorate in political science and a master's in social sciences from the University of California, Irvine.

*Father Jomon Kalladanthiyil, PhD, CSC,** is the director of pastoral care, Saint Joseph's Oratory — Montreal, Quebec. His specialization is Christian spirituality in interfaith households.

*Bill Keimig, PhD,** is the assistant director of the Catechetical Institute at Franciscan University. For fifteen years, he served as the director of religious education at St. Mary's of Piscataway Parish in Clinton, Maryland. He served for nine years as the director of the Association for Catechumenal Ministry. He is the father of six.

Tim and Lara Kirk have five children ages sixteen to twenty-four and live near Canberra, Australia. Together they have directed their pastoral energy over three decades into evangelization and Church renewal. Lara works for the Catholic Archdiocese of Canberra & Goulburn managing the Marriage, Family, and Relationships office. Tim sits on the senate of Australian Catholic University, which serves thirty-five thousand students across eight campuses, including a campus in Rome. Tim's training is in theology, and he formerly taught New Testament at a Jesuit secondary college. He has just completed six years as the international leader of the Disciples of Jesus Covenant Community. (Discussants)

*Dominic Lombardi, STL,** is the executive director of the U.S. Conference of Catholic Bishops Secretariat of Laity, Marriage, Family Life, and Youth. Prior to coming to the USCCB in 2018, he served the Diocese of Harrisburg as secretary for Catholic life and evangelization, and the Archdiocese of Philadelphia as the director of family life. Dominic also has taught theology for more than two decades at Saint Joseph's University in Philadelphia. He and his wife, Melanie, are the blessed parents of six children.

*Andrew and Terri Lyke** are the authors of *Marriage on a Lampstand: Exploring a New Paradigm for Modern Christian Marriage,* published by Visual Dynamics Publishing. They are the founders of Arusi Network Inc., an organization that educates African-Americans on the skills and benefits of Christian marriage. Together they served as advisors to the U.S. Conference of Catholic Bishops' Committee on Marriage and Family.

*Tim and Sue Muldoon: Tim (PhD, Catholic Systematic Theology, Duquesne University) is a pastoral theologian, author, and professor. He is co-editor, with Cynthia Dobrzynski, of the award-winning *Love One Another: Catholic Reflections on Sustaining Marriage* (Crossroad, 2010), and the co-author, with Sue Muldoon, of three books on the spirituality of family life: *Six Sacred Rules for Families* (Ave Maria Press, 2013), *The Discerning Parent* (Ave Maria, 2017), and *Reclaiming Family Time* (The Word Among Us Press, 2017). He serves as the director of mission education at Catholic Extension. Sue (MA, counseling, Franciscan University) is a therapist and religious educator with many years of experience in clinical, academic, and pastoral settings. She is the director of family ministries at Good Shepherd Parish in Wayland, Massachusetts.

*Tim O'Malley, PhD, is director of the Notre Dame Center for Liturgy at the McGrath Institute for Church Life. He engages in scholarship that seeks to retrieve biblical, catechetical, and liturgical insights that facilitate a renewal of the Church's liturgical imagination. He is also founding editor of the McGrath Institute for Church Life journal, *Church Life: A Journal for the New Evangelization*. The McGrath Institute was a cosponsor of the Symposium on Catholic Family Life and Spirituality and hosted the Symposium at their facilities.

*Darcia Narvaez, PhD, is a professor of psychology at the University of Notre Dame who focuses on moral development and flourishing from an interdisciplinary perspective. Dr. Narvaez's current research explores how early life experience influences societal culture and moral character in children and adults. She integrates neurobiological, clinical, developmental, and education sciences in her theories and research about moral development. She publishes extensively on moral development, parenting, and education. She is a fellow of the American Psychological

Association and the American Educational Research Association. One of her recent books, *Neurobiology and the Development of Human Morality: Evolution, Culture, and Wisdom,* won the 2015 William James Book Award from the American Psychological Association as well as a 2017 Expanded Reason Award.

*Hosffman Ospino, PhD,** is an associate professor of theology and religious education at Boston College, School of Theology and Ministry, where he is also director of graduate programs in Hispanic ministry. Dr. Ospino was the principal investigator for the National Study of Catholic Parishes with Hispanic Ministry (2014) and co-investigator for the National Survey of Catholic Schools Serving Hispanic Families (2015). He is currently advancing a national study on Latino Catholic vocations. He has authored/edited thirteen books and dozens of essays.

*Damon and Melanie Owens** are founders of JoyTOB (joytob.org). Since 1993, Melanie, a full-time homeschooling mother of eight, and Damon, the first executive director of the Theology of the Body Institute, have trained more than twenty thousand couples in marriage, NFP, and *Theology of the Body.* Melanie earned her MSW from UC Berkley. In 2018, Pope Francis awarded the Benemerenti Medal to Damon for his service to the Church in support of marriage and family life.

Father Willy Raymond, CSC, is the president of Holy Cross Family Ministries, a major cosponsor of the Symposium on Catholic Family Life and Spirituality. HCFM continues the legacy of the Venerable Father Patrick ("the family that prays together, stays together") Peyton, CSC. It serves as the umbrella organization for several ministries promoting family spirituality and family well-being, including the Museum of Family Prayer, Family Theater Productions, Family Rosary, the Father Peyton Family Institutes, and CatholicMom.com. HCFM has a presence in sixteen countries. Following the Symposium, HCFM teamed up with the Pastoral Solutions Institute to create the Peyton Institute for Domestic Church Life. (Discussant)

David Scott is the vice chancellor of communications for the Archdiocese of Los Angeles. He is the former editor-in-chief of the Catholic News Agency and the editorial director for the Saint Paul Center for Biblical Theology. (Discussant)

Jason Shanks is the president of the OSV Institute and former CEO of Catholic Charities of Southeast Michigan. The OSV Institute was the major sponsor of the Symposium on Catholic Family Life and Spirituality, and the idea for the symposium evolved out of conversations with Jason related to the OSV Institute's Catholic Parents Project. (Discussant)

*****Julie Rubio, PhD,** is a professor of social ethics at Jesuit School of Theology of Santa Clara University in Berkeley, California. She writes and lectures nationally about Catholic social thought as it relates to sex, gender, marriage, and family. She is the author of four books, including *Family Ethics: Practices for Christians* (Georgetown University Press, 2010), and *Hope for Common Ground* (Georgetown University Press, 2016). Her essays have appeared in academic journals such as *Theological Studies,* the *Journal of the Society of Christian Ethics,* and the *Journal of Political Theology,* as well as *America,* the *Washington Post,* and *Catholicmoraltheology.com.* Her current project is titled *Gender, Catholicism, and the Family.*

*****Joseph White**, **PhD,** is the director of catechetical resources for Our Sunday Visitor Publishing and Curriculum and is in part-time practice as a child and family psychologist. Dr. White has written ten books and numerous articles about catechesis, family life, and ministry. He is co-author of the *Allelu* and *Alive in Christ* religion series.

Carolyn Woo, PhD, served as the president and chief executive officer at Catholic Relief Services from 2012 to 2016. Dr. Woo joined CRS in January 2012 after a distinguished academic career. From July 1997 to December 2011, she served as dean at Mendoza College of Business at the University of Notre Dame. Prior to the University of Notre Dame, she served as associate executive vice president for academic affairs at Purdue University. She serves as a director on several corporate and non-profit boards. (Discussant)

PART ONE

Understanding the "Catholic Difference" Family Life: The Family as Domestic Church

I n this opening section, we explore the unique historical, biblical, and theological foundations for the Catholic understanding of family life.

In the first chapter, Tim O'Malley, a theologian at the University of Notre Dame, director of the Notre Dame Center for Liturgy at the Mc-Grath Institute for Church Life, and academic director of the Notre Dame Center for Liturgy unpacks the concept of "the domestic church." He encourages readers to avoid an over-romanticized view of the domestic church and offers suggestions for applying this concept in a manner that is truly respectful of the hard realities and genuine struggles facing Catholic families.

Next, Mike Aquilina, executive vice president and trustee of the Saint Paul Center for Biblical Theology, provides a bracing overview of the ways the Christian vision of family life challenged classic views of family in the early centuries of the Church. Drawing from the writings of ancient historians, early Church Fathers, and modern sociologists of religion such as Rodney Stark, he asserts that it was, in large part, the Church's unique vision of family life that allowed it to grow from a backwater religious offshoot of Judaism to the prevailing religion of the Roman Empire in the short span of a few hundred years. The parallels between the ancient and modern challenges to the Catholic view of the family may surprise you.

Then John Grabowski, a moral theologian at the Catholic University of America, and Claire Grabowski, who served with John on the Pontifical Council for the Family for many years and coauthored *Raising Catholic Kids for Their Vocations,* explore the underappreciated role of the family as the "nearest hospital"; that is, the best opportunity Christians have for experiencing the hard-won — but ultimately healing — power of Christian love.

Finally, Julie Rubio, professor of social ethics at Jesuit School of Theology of Santa Clara University and author of several books, including *Family Ethics*, reviews the surprising role the Catholic theology of family plays in the development and application of Catholic Social Teaching and the ordering of a just society on both micro and macro levels. She also offers simple suggestions for family practices that enable all families to act as engines of positive social change.

CHAPTER ONE

De-Romanticizing the Domestic Church: The Liturgical-Sacrament Vocation of the Christian Family

Timothy O'Malley

McGrath Institute for Church Life, University of Notre Dame

FIVE QUICK TAKES

1. The Christian family must primarily be rooted in communion and kinship rather than experiences of affinity.
2. Family life is that space where the divine drama of love becomes present amid the mundane.
3. The domestic church as a communion of kinship makes God's love present in the world — visible to the family and to the entire of society.
4. De-romaticizing domestic church life (i.e., eschewing an affinity-based view) allows a sacramental mysticism of the mundane to flourish.
5. A properly ordered romantic view of the family is not rooted in affinity, but in a romantic view of a God who has entered into relationship with humanity, daring to transform every relationship through the art of self-giving love.

In his *Letter to Families*, Saint John Paul II describes the domestic church's vocation to cultivate a civilization of love.[1] There is a public vocation to the Christian family. The family is to become a space of self-giving love within a modern context that often reduces the human being to a utilitarian end. The family must learn to fulfill its prophetic vocation, functioning as a counter-witness to a hyper-individualism that has created a culture of exclusion rather than hospitality. The domestic church refers, as Saint John Paul II writes, "to the civilization of love as a possible system of human life and coexistence: 'to be together' as a family, to be for one another, to make room in a community for affirming each person as such, for affirming 'this' individual person."[2] The Christian family thus offers a vision of human flourishing as related to communion, a communion revealed in the Christian doctrine of the Trinity.

Saint John Paul II's description of the domestic church is prophet-

---

1. Saint John Paul II, *Letter to Families* (Manchester, NH: Sophia Institute Press, 2015), no. 13.
2. *Ibid.*, no. 15.

ic. It is thus ironic that some contemporary appropriations of the term "domestic church" often fail to take into account the public and thus prophetic vocation of the family within the world. In popular accounts of the domestic church, the family becomes a perfect nuclear society of husband, wife, and children. The Catholic family has lots of kids, drives a big van, and lives in a suburban enclave. The home is idealized as a space of harmonious unity, existing apart from the rest of society and culture. The family is a place to escape from the workaday world and the social dysfunction evident in both culture and politics. There are pleasant meals shared in the company of obedient children. Husband and wife enjoy near-perfect communion with one another, their sexual lives bearing fruit in the gift of children. The family celebrates each feast of the liturgical year with appropriate reverence, as parents and children alike delight in the mysteries of Jesus Christ. The romanticized domestic church enjoys leisure time including trips to the zoo, vacations, and other opportunities to delight in one another's presence.

This romanticized account of family life tends to bypass the experience of actual families. It is an almost idolatrous vision of family life that passes over the difficulties that a family will experience in becoming a civilization of love. There are families suffering from the plague of domestic violence. Some couples are unable to have children, experiencing the agony of infertility rather than the communion that leads to a large brood of Catholic children singing along to the *Salve Regina*. In the United States, migrant families are separated, attempting to make a life apart from each other — sometimes by choice and sometimes because of political policy. Families in the United States suffer from poverty, unable to keep a roof over their heads let alone enjoy a meal together. Parents agonize as their children are arrested, struggle with alcohol and drug addiction, experience divorce, and even die prematurely. If the term "domestic church" is to function prophetically within society, it must take into the fullness of the human condition — not only an idealized, upper middle-class account of Christian life.

For the domestic church to serve its public vocation, to speak to the lived reality of families today, there is a need to de-romanticize how we understand the Christian family. The liturgical and sacramental vocation of the family is essential to this process of de-romanticization. The family is not a communion apart from the rest of society, but a place where men and women learn the logic of self-giving love in day-to-day life. The Christian family is not a haven apart from the world, but an immersion of men and women into the sacramental mysticism of the mundane lived within the kinship of the family.

TEMPTED BY ROMANCE

A romantic account of the family pervades our cultural world. Think about advertising. The celebration of Christmas consists of a harmonious gathering of the generations. We see these happy families in commercials selling luxury cars, smartphones, and even puppies. In a Christmas commercial produced by Apple, we meet a young man whose attention is permanently affixed to his iPhone. This late teenager — as it turns out — is not an inattentive Millennial, addicted to checking his most recent notifications via Snapchat. He is producing a film documenting the intergenerational family Christmas, employing technology for reasons of virtue rather than addiction. The iPhone becomes an engine for family harmony — pulling on the heartstrings of the reluctant parent to give his or her child the newest device for Christmas. The iPhone won't separate the teen from the family but will mediate experiences of affinity, bringing everyone closer together.

Advertising is not the only engine of romanticization of family life in the United States. Family vacations are meant to function as experiences in which we escape from normal life, spending a life-changing week in Hawaii or traveling to the fantasyland of Disney World. There, children and adults discover a previously unimaginable happiness, fusing anew the bonds of family life that are relentlessly fraying as time passes. The hardened teenager, regularly annoyed by her parents, will return to her once childlike self after a week of riding Space Mountain or spending time on a pristine beach on the island of Maui. In both cases, family bonds are renewed through undergoing experiences of transcendence. Family intimacy is something that has to be cultivated, either through documenting an intergenerational Christmas getaway to Vermont or through leaving behind the everyday world for a vacation.

The assumption of both these narratives of "happy" family life presumes that families exist to have experiences with one another. These experiences become the affective glue that holds the family together. Without vacations, without consumer products that intensify experience, without a happy hearth, the family is in peril of falling apart.

This romanticization often infects the Church's own description of the domestic church, especially in catechetical settings or blogs. Families experience the gift of Mass together on Sunday mornings, afterward enjoying a pleasant brunch spent in the company of other happy families. The home becomes a space of leisure often connected to the experience of consumption. There becomes something almost religious to watching a movie together on a Friday evening or heading to the mall on a Saturday. The love of husband and wife within the family must be cultivated through romantic experiences like dates apart from the children, opportunities to "renew" love through sexual intimacy.

This understanding of family and romantic love alike would be weird to previous generations, including our great-grandparents. I know from experience. Romantic love and family life are held together in our own age through powerful experiences that take place apart from the objective bonds of kinship that are part of day-to-day life. We need the experiences to testify to the bonds of love, and it is precisely the normalcy of daily life that threatens this love. The exotic experiences testify that this love is true. It is really real, because I feel it. I know my mother loves me, my father loves me, and my spouse loves me because I "know" this love through experiences of mutual affinity. It's not enough that you're there each day, making sure that I get to school on time or that I have my lunch packed. How can we really focus on our relationship, on the intimacy that brings our family together?

The Polish sociologist Zygmunt Bauman has analyzed this perilous transition from kinship to affinity in the context of both romantic and familial love. He writes:

> Affinity is born of choice and the umbilical cord is never cut. Unless the choice is restated daily and ever new actions are taken to confirm it, affinity will wilt, fade and decay until it falls or crawls

apart. The intention of keeping affinity alive and well portends a daily struggle and promises no rest to vigilance. For us, the denizens of the liquid modern world that abhors everything that is solid and durable, that is unfit for instant use and allows no end to effort, such a prospect may be more than one would willingly bargain for. Establishing a bond of affinity proclaims that intention of making the bond like that of kinship — but also the readiness to pay the price of the avatar in the hard currency of day-in, day-out drudgery. When the willingness ... is missing, one would be inclined to think twice before acting on the intention.[3]

If families are founded on the basis of affinity rather than kinship, then there is nothing that holds the family together except for the romantic experiences that produce feelings of harmony in hearth and home. If these feelings dissipate (and they often do in the course of normal life), then what remains? Is there an objective bond that transcends the affections, or is the family just a stronger version of a voluntary association of those who happen to share common, powerful experiences? Must we eventually grow apart from our mothers and fathers, from our siblings when we find ourselves in new, stronger relationships of affinity?

If the domestic church as a description of the family is influenced by this preference for affinity over kinship, for powerful experience over obligatory bonds, then one can see why so many families fail to hit the mark relative to becoming images of the domestic church. Much of family life — as any dad, mom, grandparent, or kid knows — is the commitment of a person to obligation. Moms and dads rarely want to wake up in the middle of the night to soothe their child suffering from a stomach bug — a comforting that will inescapably result in illness on the part of the parent. It's not pleasant to care for a dying parent suffering from dementia, incapable of expressing even an iota of gratitude. No one wants to leave their homeland, taking their children on a perilous journey, hoping that the next generation will be raised in a land without the threat of constant violence. Siblings experience genuine diminishment when they

---

3. Zygmunt Bauman, *Liquid Love: On the Frailty of Human Bonds* (Malden, MA: Polity Press, 2003), 29.

have to learn to share space and stuff with another, often compulsorily learning that obligatory love is a good worth pursuing. Families participate in radical hospitality, opening their door the neighbor in need, not because they want to host everyone in the neighborhood for dinner — instead, they recognize their obligation to share the return gift of love they have received.

Perhaps, this emphasis on obligation seems coldhearted to the reader. It often does to my undergraduates. When I tell them that I am obliged to love my wife — having vowed to do so — they're shocked. They want love to consist of rainbows and bunnies, a desire to sit in one another's presence and experience love pangs until the end of time. They struggle to understand that obligation is a binding, a fastening of one's life with another. The family is obliged to love one another because they share a common narrative that is not dependent on their individual affections. I am bound, obliged to love my spouse, because of a promise that has come to define me. This obligation, this bind, has reshaped every other relationship that I have, every decision that I make.

In conclusion, the romanticization of the family — focusing on powerful experiences of affinity within the nuclear family — risks neutering the prophetic vocation of the family. That is, the family just becomes another optional place to have experiences, easily replaceable by other relationships defined by affinity. I'll be a dad when I want to be a dad, and I'll do something else when I want that! I'll love my spouse as long as I feel attracted to her, but when that's over, it's time to move on. I'll love my child when it's easy, but if he or she is in prison or addicted to drugs, surely there's another creature (perhaps a pet) that could become the source of my affection.

Of course, the Church can respond to this romanticization of the family through a theological account of the domestic church. That is, the domestic church is not ultimately about placing a Catholic coating on the romanticized family. Instead, the domestic church as a term acknowledges that the family exists because of a bond of love that transcends the individual experiences of its members. Here, the liturgical and sacramental vocation of the family enables a re-narrating of the domestic church as existing within a mysticism of the mundane rather than transcendent experiences of affinity.

THE LITURGICAL-SACRAMENTAL VOCATION OF THE DOMESTIC CHURCH

In his *Divine Likeness: Toward a Trinitarian Anthropology of the Family*, Marc Cardinal Ouellet points to the incarnational nature of the domestic church. In that which is most mundane, that which is most human, that which is most "normal," the salvation of humanity. For Ouellet, the family comes about through participation in the sacrament of marriage. In the sacrament, the couple comes together, vowing to love one another unto the end of their lives. Importantly, this vow of love is not dependent on a disposition of affinity, of powerful experiences that enable the couple to always "feel in love." This vow is not the result of their own hard work, a sense that they have earned love through becoming good people, worthy of such love. Instead as Ouellet writes:

> When theological doctrine affirms the spouses to be the 'ministers' of the sacrament of matrimony, it does not mean that they are the principal agents of the sacrament. The principal agent of the sacrament is Christ, who acts through the mediation of the couple. Of the 'human act by which the partners mutually surrender themselves to each other (GS 48), one must say in fact that it is an act of Christ who receives them and gives them to each other. In this way, marriage becomes a sacramental reality, that is, a 'divine gift' hidden within a 'human gift'; this gift of Christ is an act of spousal love which blessed the couple and entrusts them with a sacramental mission.[4]

It is Christ's own act of obligation, of self-giving love as mediated to the human family that makes possible the nuptial commitment. Even in situations where the couple has not entered into a sacramental marriage within the Church — having contracted a civil marriage — the Church's

---

4. Marc Cardinal Ouellet, *Divine Likeness: Toward a Trinitarian Anthropology of the Family* (Grand Rapids, MI: Eerdmans Publishing, 2006), 90.

vocation is to invite the couple to see the "primordial" love that has made possible this union, especially if that union involves the gift of children.[5] The religious orientation of the natural ends of marriage — including the presence of children — is taken up in the sacrament of marriage.[6]

In this sense, the love of the family is not the result of experiences of mutual affinity, the work of mutual affection. Instead, family life is that space where the divine drama of love becomes present amid the mundane. It is God's love, including the mystery of the Trinity and Christ's life, death, and resurrection, that is the origin of married love and the family alike. In the spouse's concrete commitment to one another, in the bond of love that has come to unite them in Christ, and through the task of educating and caring for children, God acts in the world through the kinship of the family.[7] When a parent wakes up in the middle of the night to care for a sick child or an immigrant father works long hours to send money home to his wife and kids, divine love becomes present. The mystery of the Church as the gathering of all humankind in praise of God is played out in these concrete relationships, these bonds of love that transcend individual affections. The mystery of salvation unfolds not apart from the mundane, not through an escapism of transcendent experiences in Hawaii or Disney World, but through the delight of duty.

The domestic church does not involve placing a religious veneer upon a secular community of affinity. Instead, the family — by its very nature, abiding in a space of obligation — becomes the domestic church. The husband and wife who pledge to love each other until death become a communion of love, shaped through the supernatural work of the Holy Spirit, for the world to see.[8] One cannot "see" the bonds that bind together communities of affinity, because they are exclusively subjective. You can gaze upon an image of a family at Disney World, but what are you really looking at? A moment of single happiness, an "experience" that brought the family closer together. One can see the enduring bonds

5. Pope Francis, *The Joy of Love* 297, https://w2.vatican.va/content/dam/francesco/pdf/apost_exhortations/documents/papa-francesco_esortazione-ap_20160319_amoris-laetitia_en.pdf.

6. Matthias Joseph Scheeben, *The Mysteries of Christianity*, trans. Cyril Vollert, S.J. (New York: Crossroad, 1946), 595.

7. Cardinal Ouellet, *Divine Likeness*, 55.

8. *Ibid.*, 99–100.

of kinship taken up in Christian marriage and family life. One can see the relationships between siblings who love one another even when it is difficult. One can perceive the witness of a mother who loves her child who is prison, praying for him, longing for his redemption. One can gaze upon the witness of a husband or wife who remains faithful to a spouse who has left the relationship.

Because the domestic church is based on an objective bond of love, on kinship rather than affinity, the family can assume a public vocation within the world. This does not mean, according to Cardinal Ouellet, that the family must run political campaigns. Instead, simply by existing as a family, as a communion of love within the world, the family becomes a sacramental sign to the world of divine grace. He writes:

> … what is essential for the witness of Christian spouses is not a social or political activism, but the very presence of the Christian family in the world and the peaceful and silent strength of its communion. What can better edify youth in need of help but the beauty of a united and open family who knows how to share its material and spiritual goods through hospitality.[9]

The family has a vocation of hospitality that is connected to its very identity. Because the communion of love made present in the love of husband and wife, of grandparents and siblings, is part of God's own pedagogy of love for the human family, the existence of this love must be shared with the world. Here, the love of the Christian family is not akin to the love of the closed family that turns inward, seeing no obligation to contribute to the renewal of society.[10] The family practices solidarity among each other, a solidarity of love that extends outside the obligation of kinship to the neighbor.[11]

The domestic church extends the language of kinship to each mem-

---

9. *Ibid.*, 200.

10. David Matzko McCarthy, *Sex and Love in the Home: A Theology of the Household*, 2nd ed. (London: SCM Press, 2004), 93–97.

11. Julie Hanlon Rubio, *Family Ethics: Practices for Christians* (Washington DC: Georgetown University Press, 2010), 152–153.

ber of the human family. Because every husband and wife learns to delight in the obligation of kinship — a kinship made possible through Christ — they may extend this kinship to their biological children. Their children also learn to extend this kinship to siblings. A family will then extend this kinship even further, discovering the gift of kinship with neighbor, with those on the margins, and with every member of the human family.

In conclusion, the domestic church is not therefore a "spiritualized" version of the romantic family, seeking "religious" experiences rather than trips to Disney World and Hawaii. The domestic church is the profession of faith that the family through the bonds of kinship — established through marriage and lived out within the obligatory relationships of family life — is a space of divine renewal in the world. The family is taken up in the mystery of divine love not apart from, but within the context of mundane life.

Of course, this is very good news — especially for those of us who come from families that are more likely to appear on the late-night news rather than in the latest family friendly movie or Catholic mom book. I come from one of these complicated families — one that experienced poverty, domestic abuse, violence, drug use, divorce, and remarriage. Even here, in the midst of what looked like tragedy, divine love was present. Not always through relationships of affinities, of exotic vacations together each summer, but through the hard-fought commitment to love one another to the end.

FORMING THE DOMESTIC CHURCH

As Julie Rubio points out in her work *Family Ethics*, the family may function objectively through the sacraments as a domestic church, a space of divine love that brings the ecclesial communion to every corner of the world. But the family may not always actually live out this vocation either among one another or the rest of the world.[12] There are plenty of families that are not civilizations of love, places where the objective bonds of love are denied. A husband who abuses his wife and a dad who

---

12. Rubio, *Family Ethics*.

cheats on his wife is not manifesting the deepest identity of the family as a communion of love grounded in kinship. Of course, we don't even need these extremes. It's hard to love your brother and your sister, your grandma and your grandpa, your alcoholic aunt or uncle because they belong to you. It takes formation. In this way, the family must become the domestic church, to understand how the relationships of obligation may become spaces of divine hospitality in the world.

This formation is even more important when considering the romanticized vision of family life that is so prominent in the United States. Families may spend little time contemplating the theological language of the domestic church. But they spend a lot of time watching television, dreaming about vacations, and experiencing FOMO (fear of missing out) by pondering other "seemingly" perfect families in their neighborhoods. If the Church is to successfully form the domestic church in a communion of kinship rather than affinity, it will need to be explicit. Here are four places where the Church can re-form the imagination of women and men to think anew about the domestic church.

1) Cultivate a Sacramental Mysticism of the Mundane

In a later book, Cardinal Ouellet describes the transformation that takes place in the sacrament of marriage. The transformation of the couple is not reserved simply for the moment of marriage, but extends throughout the life of the couple, into their very flesh-and-blood commitment to each another. He writes:

> The mutual 'yes' expressed verbally in the liturgical celebration is then translated into the 'language of the body,' that is to say, not only into the conjugal encounter (consummation), but also into the spouses' shared life, daily fidelity, friendship, reciprocal forgiveness, fecundity, education, etc. The sacramental sign prolongs itself in time. The spiritual act of self-gift 'in the Lord,' enriched by the redemptive power of Christ and the salvific action of the Church, establishes the couple as a permanent sacrament and transforms its history into salvation history — in

other words, into a sign that bears the gift of God to his people.[13]

A sacramental mysticism of the mundane will underline for the couple, from the moment that they enter into the nuptial bond, that divine grace will operate in the relationship not only in moments of transcendent delight but in the day-to-day commitment of abiding together in love. The couple does not need to pursue a mystical life that takes them apart from their families, from their commitment of sharing life with each other. Instead, it is the history of abiding together in obligation that enables the family's own history to enter Christ's history.

I suspect that one of the problems of marriage formation in the Church at present is an overemphasis on such transcendent moments. Sex becomes a total, almost euphoric participation in Trinitarian communion. The pair are invited to reflect on their love as unique and remarkable. Perhaps, there is a gift in inviting these couples toward an apprenticeship into the mundane. Do you do the dishes together? Who takes out the trash? What do you talk about when you're talking about nothing in particular? These are the kind of dispositions that will sustain a married couple as they move from the transcendent, early days of nuptial life to year fifteen.

2) The Efficacy of Family Prayer and Blessings
The domestic church exists because of the gift of kinship, the bonds of love that exist objectively within the family. A regular, liturgical, and ritualized practice of family prayer will better enable the family to express these objective bonds to God and to one another. Liturgical prayer within the family is not just an occasion for a romanticized family life, in which perfect children express their perfect desires to God. Sometimes during night prayer at our house, the kids will pray for dinosaurs (or as dinosaurs). They might interrupt the Our Father through smacking each other in the face. We don't stop praying because no one is feeling it. We

---

13. Marc Cardinal Ouellet, *Mystery and Sacrament of Love: A Theology of Marriage and the Family for the New Evangelization*, trans. Michelle K. Borras and Adrian J. Walker (Grand Rapids, MI: Eerdmans Publishing, 2015), 70.

don't stop because the prayer seems ineffective. We engage in these concrete practices of prayer because they establish in our family the ultimate objective bond that unites us to God. Prayer is formative of the human personality, but it is first oriented toward the glorification of God. Simply by committing ourselves to a regular practice of prayer, we reestablish ourselves as a family based in kinship, the kinship of the kingdom, rather than pure affinity.

Likewise, these moments of liturgical prayer should involve blessings. A sacramental mysticism of the mundane is not learned in the abstract. Rather, as we bless our children, as we bless the food in our home, our travel to school, even blessing one another in our sorrows, we come to see the various ways that God can become present in our day-to-day life. We don't need transcendent experiences to perceive God's activity in our midst. We often need simply to attend to the signs that exist before our very eyes. Blessing invites us to slow down and attend to these signs. We learn to be grateful merely for the existence of the person in our presence, the one who is our mother, our father, or our child.

3) Theological Reflection in the Family

Theological reflection is a process whereby we engage with human experience through the lens of the Gospel, learning to read every dimension of human life as related to the mystery of salvation. In his audiences on the family, Pope Francis invites us to apply this kind of theological reflection to the very roles and responsibilities within the family. In reflecting on children, he writes:

> Children have the capacity to smile and to cry. Some, when I pick them up to embrace them, smile; others see me dressed in white and think I am a doctor and that I am going to vaccinate them. … Children are like this: they smile and cry, two things which are often 'stifled' in grown-ups, we are no longer capable. … Children smile spontaneously and cry spontaneously. It always depends on the heart, and often our heart is blocked and

loses this capacity to smile, to cry.[14]

Children don't just provide us with a series of transcendent experiences. Instead, they cause us to wonder, to ponder what it means to be a human being in Christ. Why are children capable of expressing their affections so clearly? What is wrong with us adults that often leads us to deny our affections? To live as robots, incapable of true communion? Children fulfill a prophetic office for the entire human community, even if the child is (blissfully) not aware of it.

Through looking at concrete roles in families (children, grandparents, the hungry and thirsty in our towns), Pope Francis allows the Church to think about the domestic church less as a romanticized "thing" than a series of salvific signs, given by God to the entire human family, that we might journey toward salvation. Inviting families to read this text in their neighbors with one another, to reflect together on what it means to belong to a family, could be important for forming members of the domestic church to recognize their vocation through kinship rather than affinity. It is my identity as father, as mother, as brother and sister, as child that shapes my identity, my very sense of what it means to be a man or a woman in Christ.

4) The Charism of the Family in the World
It is not enough for every individual family to experience affection for each other within the home. The domestic church must move beyond the walls of hearth and home to offer hospitality to the world. The charism of the family is to embody the sacramental love of the Word made flesh not in experiences of affinity, but in kinship offered to everyone who hungers and thirsts for meaning. As Pope Francis notes in his reflections on the family:

> Indeed, the family's covenant with God is called today to counteract the community desertification of the modern city. But the lack of love and smiling has turned our cities into deserts. ... The

14. Pope Francis, *On the Family* (San Francisco: Ignatius Press, 2015), 42–43.

smile of a family can overcome this desertification of our cities. This is the victory of family love. No economic and political engineering can substitute for this contribution of families. ... We must come out of our towers and from the armoured vaults of the elite to spend time again in the homes and open spaces of the multitudes, open to the love of families. ... Wherever there is a loving family, that family with its witness of love is capable of warming of the heart of an entire city.[15]

The romantic family seeks only to cultivate affection among each other, becoming closed to the needs of the world. Parishes cannot just get moms and dads to spend time with their kids and vice versa. The task is to awaken in each family an understanding of their vocation, to sanctify the entirety of the created order through the mundaneness of committed love.

Parish formation of families, thus, can't just get families to show up to the parish. Instead, it must recognize that families have a particular vocation in their neighborhoods, in their cities to be spaces of divine hospitality. If the family takes up this vocation, aware of the dignity of kinship, the domestic church may once more become an agent of fostering a civilization of love.

CONCLUSION

At the beginning of this essay, I suggested that Saint John Paul II's account of the civilization of love within the domestic church risked being co-opted into a narrative of the domestic church that erased its prophetic quality. The family becomes a pleasant place to experience religious affections, rather than a sacramental sign to the social order that divine love has become manifest, even in this mundane relationship between husband and wife, child and parent, grandparent and grandchild. Further, this romanticization reduces the family to a consumer community, who enjoys transcendent experiences of affinity. This romanticization,

---

15. *Ibid.*, 112–113.

even when applied to Catholic religious practice, risks stripping the family of its sacramental vocation to reveal divine love.

Of course, one could accuse the Church in the end of remaining inexplicably romantic. After all, is it possible that divine love could really be seen in something so messy as family life? Is this not a naïve hope, a failure to recognize that families are places (in the end) so screwed up that our only hope is to escape them?

I suppose, in the end, the Church remains a kind of romantic around families. This romanticization is not because we adore at the altar of experiences of affinity. Rather, it is a romantic view of a God who has entered relationship with humanity, daring to transform every relationship, every aspect of creation through the art of self-giving love.

If a civilization of love will be built, it requires a bit of romance. Just the right type.

DISCUSSION QUESTIONS

1. The romantic family is based primarily around experiences of affinity. Where have you seen this in culture? Where have you seen this in your own parish?
2. The domestic church is not a community of affinity but of kinship. How would you explain this to parents within your parish? How might it be good news to families to learn this?
3. What other practices for forming the church in its liturgical-sacramental vocation would you suggest?

CHAPTER TWO

The Population Balm: How the Church Taught the World to Welcome Children

_____

MIKE AQUILINA

Saint Paul Center for Biblical Theology; Contributing Editor,
Angelus News

FIVE QUICK TAKES

1. The Roman Empire was collapsing under the weight of a demographic winter due to the widespread practice of contraception, abortion/infanticide, and the weakening of marital fidelity/family life.

2. Augustus failed in his attempts to encourage childbearing, strong marriages, and stable families by law and political pressure.

3. The Church "conquered" the Roman Empire and experienced remarkable growth by opposing contraception and abortion and promoting childbearing, the dignity of women, and the value of marriage and family life.

4. The Church's teachings on sexuality, marriage, and the sanctity of human life were revolutionary, but these teachings were viewed by both Church Fathers and modern sociologists as central to the Christian message and key to the Church's ability to evangelize the ancient world.

5. The Christian message promoting the gift of children, the sanctity of sex, and the dignity of marriage and family life remains key to evangelizing the culture today.

"Bliss it was in that dawn to be alive."

I'm writing not (as Wordsworth did) of the French Revolution, but of the first century, when a savior had arrived on the world scene, and the savior's name was Augustus Caesar. He called himself *Princeps Civitatis* (First Citizen), but everyone knew he was emperor.

During a long and astonishing reign, he unified lands and peoples stretching from Great Britain to Egypt, from Morocco to Georgia. He suppressed rebellions and practically eradicated piracy on the high seas. He developed a system of roads for easy transport — and a postal service for worldwide communication. He inaugurated a period of relative peace in the world. Commerce was unimpeded, and Romans were the great beneficiaries. Taxes and tribute flowed into the capital from as far away as India, where Roman settlements were raising temples to Augustus's genius.

"Bliss it was to be alive" in an age of such prosperity.

Yet Augustus, at age seventy, saw clearly that all his achievements were destined to crash. The reason was simple: Romans were not reproducing. They weren't even marrying. Over the decades of ease, they had come to enjoy an unmoored, leisurely lifestyle, drifting from pleasure to pleasure without the encumbrance of children. Now, in the year we call A.D. 9, Augustus observed that there was not much that he could call a younger generation.

Rome was heading for demographic winter, and the First Citizen was alarmed. It was a desperate situation, as he saw it. Who would man the armies? Who would run the institutions? The stopgap solution was to job the tasks out to foreign mercenaries and slaves. But increased immigration brought other problems. Who would carry forward the Roman legacy? How would armies of mercenaries affect homeland security?

Augustus, unfortunately, was almost alone in his concern. Everyone else, it seems, was having a good time. Bliss it was in that dawn to be alive. To be male, and noble, and single, and childless was very heaven.

But Augustus was in charge, and so that year a new law went into effect to promote marriage. It outlawed bachelorhood and spinsterhood, punishing both by fines and taxation. It criminalized adultery and homosexual acts, prescribing penalties as severe as flogging and death. Childbearing, on the other hand, was rewarded by state grants and subsidies.

This legislation is known to history as the *Lex Papia et Poppaea*. It was named for the two consuls who introduced the law at the behest of Augustus. They were Marcus Papius Mutilus and Quintus Poppaeus Secundus. Both men were bachelors.

So the law seemed doomed from the get-go. The nobles who could afford it paid the fines and went on living as they wished. But they weren't pleased with the expense, and they complained bitterly at every opportunity. Nothing changed except the level of discontent.

Augustus was distraught. Rome itself was doing a slow fade, and he was the only one who cared.

The historian Cassius Dio preserves for us a strange and pathetic moment that took place in spring of that year.[1]

Augustus found himself in one of those meet-and-greet moments that define the life of all heads of state. The day was to consist of ceremonies and games — a light celebration to welcome home Tiberius, Augustus's adopted son and heir.

But throughout the day the equestrians made known their bitterness about the new taxes.

So Augustus pulled a stunt that looks almost Solomonic. He asked the men to divide into two camps: those who were married on one side, and those who were unmarried on the other. The scene, Dio tells us, was ridiculously lopsided, with the singles vastly outnumbering the marrieds. Augustus was "filled with grief" at the sight.

From his heart he delivered two anguished speeches, one to each group, and in the process left us a kind of pagan "theology of the body."

He began by praising the married men; because, he said, "you have shown yourselves obedient and are helping to replenish the fatherland." They were fulfilling a divine purpose.

> It was for this cause most of all that that first and greatest god, who fashioned us, divided the race of mortals in twain, making one half of it male and the other half female, and implanted in them love and compulsion to mutual intercourse, making their association fruitful, that by the young continually born he might in a way render even mortality immortal. Indeed, even of the gods themselves some are accounted male and others female; and the tradition prevails that some have begotten others and some have been begotten of others. So even among those beings, who need no such device, marriage and the begetting of children have been approved as a noble thing.

He told the married men that they had "done right, therefore, to imitate the gods and right to emulate your fathers, so that, just as they begot you,

---

1. Cassius Dio, *Roman History* 56.1-10.

you also may bring others into the world."

It's poetry. It even dips, as I said, into theology.

But then Augustus turned toward the single men, and all he had for them was contempt.

> [W]hat shall I call you? Men? But you are not performing any of the offices of men. Citizens? But for all that you are doing, the city is perishing. Romans? But you are undertaking to blot out this name altogether. ... For what seed of human beings would be left, if all the rest of mankind should do what you are doing?

Alas, there was no happy ending for Augustus. No one listened. The laws were a joke, and Augustus himself was hardly a model of the kind of citizen he was trying to encourage. He had been married three times before he ascended to the throne. He had only one child, a daughter, and her life was scandalous and rule-breaking.

Three generations later, the historian Tacitus observed that — in spite of the penalties and in spite of the incentives — "marriages and the rearing of children did not become more frequent, so powerful were the attractions of childlessness."[2] His contemporary, Pliny the Younger, spoke of the "burden" of having even one child and the "rewards of childlessness."[3]

In times of prosperity, people looked at the fines and decided that they could afford them. They were lifestyle expenses. Various emperors after Augustus tried to encourage childbearing through legislation, but their efforts uniformly failed. The law makes a lousy aphrodisiac, and not even the emperor could require citizens to transcend their most immediate desires for the sake of the common good.

The empire, for all its marvelous achievements, could not compel its citizens to trust in the future. Lacking that hope, Romans didn't want children, and so they didn't have them.

What they had instead was electively sterile sex. They used contra-

---

2. Tacitus, *Annals* 3.25.
3. Pliny the Younger, *Letters* 4.15.

ceptives. They practiced perversions. If they happened to conceive, they procured abortion. The satirist Juvenal observed that childbearing was an occupation for the lower classes. He writes:

> Poor women … endure the perils of childbirth, and all the troubles of nursing to which their lot condemns them; but how often does a gilded bed contain a woman that is lying in? So great is the skill, so powerful the drugs, of the abortionist, paid to murder mankind within the womb.[4]

Failing to abort, a woman could commit infanticide — having the midwife drown the baby at birth or abandon it at the town dump. And they did. Most of the infants drowned or exposed were female. Just in the last two decades archeologists have turned up at least three baby dumps, all very large: one in Athens, another in Ashkelon, and yet another in Scotland, all from roughly the same time period. (The Scottish site held the bones of more than a thousand children.) So the practice was geographically widespread and very common, as the written record suggests.

It was almost universal. *Almost.*

Jews, throughout antiquity, had set themselves apart from other peoples in many ways, and one was their condemnation of infanticide.

And in the ancestral land of the Jews, in the first century, there was a religious movement rising, which would soon gain adherents in all the cities of the Roman world. In Antioch the movement was first called Christian.

At the heart of Christian life was a Savior far different from Augustus. Indeed, Christian authors would later observe that Virgil's consciously vatic *Fourth Eclogue* — which hailed the birth of a divine leader strongly resembling Augustus — should more appropriately be applied to Jesus.

Both were hailed as saviors, but the ideals of Jesus and Augustus seemed to be at cross-purposes. Augustus penalized celibacy, for example, while Jesus praised it. Augustus absolutized national and family

4. Juvenal, *Satires* ("The Ways of Women"), 78.

bonds, while Jesus relativized them. In Christianity all familial and social relationships were reordered, now made subordinate to the relationship with Jesus.

Jesus said: "If anyone comes to me and does not hate his own father and mother and wife and children and brothers and sisters, yes, and even his own life, he cannot be my disciple" (Lk 14:26).

And Saint Paul declared: "There is neither Jew nor Greek, there is neither slave nor free, there is neither male nor female; for you are all one in Christ Jesus" (Gal 3:28).

Jesus and the apostles were hardly strong advocates for the Roman idea of family or national piety. And yet the relationship with Christ was itself cast in familial terms, and it carried strong implications for family life. "Husbands, love your wives, as Christ loved the church and gave himself up for her" (Eph 5:25). "Husbands, love your wives, and do not be harsh with them" (Col 3:19).

These were radical statements in a world where playwrights referred to women as "odious daughters," and where women were not permitted to give testimony in courts of law — and where female offspring were often drowned at birth.

Still more radical were Christian statements about children. The Roman upper classes did everything in their power to ward away the little ones. But Jesus said:

"Let the children come to me, and do not hinder them; for to such belongs the kingdom of heaven" (Mt 19:14).

He also said, "Truly, I say to you, unless you turn and become like children, you will never enter the kingdom of heaven" (Mt 18:3).

The Christian converts of the earliest generations came mainly from the Greek and Roman religious traditions. Their conversion certainly involved a revaluation of children, women, and the marriage bond.

We see almost immediately a more welcoming attitude toward children — though we find it expressed negatively in the Christian prohibition of contraception, abortion, and infanticide. The earliest Christian documents are univocal in their condemnation of these practices. Both the *Didache* and the *Letter of Barnabas*, produced in the mid- to late first century, speak of contraceptive and abortifacient potions (*pharmakeia*) in their discussions of "the Way of Death." *Barnabas* also includes a rather blunt denunciation of those who practice oral sex, a common way to evade conception.

Clear condemnations — of contraception, abortion, and infanticide — continued from Christian authors in the second and third centuries: Saint Athenagoras of Athens, Minucius Felix in Rome, Tertullian in North Africa, and Clement of Alexandria in Egypt. The geographic diversity of the authors, and the consistency of the teaching over time, show us that this was hardly a local quirk or passing fad. The later authors were increasingly more specific in their critique. They condemned not only the general category of "potions of sterility," but also particular methods. Most mention drugs. Clement of Alexandria mentions withdrawal during intercourse, saying: "the seed is not to be vainly ejaculated, or damaged, or wasted."

The second-century *Letter to Diognetus*, an anonymous plea addressed to a governmental official, puts the matter in positive terms. It speaks of the Christians' "wonderful and striking way of life." They were set apart, he continued, by their lifelong fidelity in marriage and their welcoming of children.

If these were indeed peculiarly Christian characteristics, then it's not a great leap for us to assume a higher level of satisfaction in Christian home life. If you eliminate infidelity and child-murder, you've removed two major stressors from a marriage.

The Roman jurist Minucius Felix seems to intimate that Christian homes reflected a recognizable stability and happiness: "In our heart," he said, "we gladly abide by the bond of a single marriage; in the desire of procreating, we know either one wife, or none at all."

The Christians' attitude toward sex and family often proved an irritant to their tradition-minded Roman neighbors and overlords. Some stories of the martyrs begin with a wife's conversion to Christianity and her subsequent refusal to cooperate with immoral bedroom practices. From there the narrative proceeds to the woman's denunciation, trial, sentence, and execution. Other stories begin with a young consecrated virgin's refusal of a marriage proposal. They end the same way.

The very idea of consecrated virginity was a provocation to tradition-minded Romans. Why, when marriageable women were in short supply, would the Church remove so many young lovelies from the market? It seemed cruel and senseless — and, by the standards of Augustus, downright unpatriotic.

Christian standards were hardly mainstream in the Roman world. Yet the Fathers seemed eager to highlight the differences. In the late second century, Clement of Alexandria argued, for example, against the common practice of child marriage, in which girls of eleven or twelve were married off to much older men. Clement said this was a sin equal in gravity to fornication, and he laid the blame with the girl's parents as much as the husband.

Such condemnations seem calculated to alienate the people who practiced these customs.

But Clement was onto something. Behind his prohibition was an assumption: that women deserved vocational freedom. Perhaps there was another assumption: that child marriage was not a psychologically healthy situation for the child, and it didn't make for happy homes.

In any event, Christian doctrine on family life appears to have worked — and on many different levels. Rather than drive people away from Christianity, it seems to have drawn them into it. The sociologist Rodney Stark argues that the Christian population increased steadily during this period, in spite of persecution and other challenges. He concludes, in fact, that the Church grew at a steady rate of forty percent per decade over the course of its first three hundred years — and that this growth is attributable, in part, to the Christian view of marriage. Christianity held out more appeal for women, because it respected their dignity and freedom (not to mention their childhood), and so women made up an outsized share of converts. The outsized number of women, then, made Christianity more attractive to men who wanted marriage. Moreover, since Christianity emphasized mutual respect and service, Christians who married were probably much more likely to find themselves in a happy spousal relationship — which would itself, in many cases, lead to increased fecundity.

When homes are happy, the population grows.

Outside the Christian Church, however, the Roman population

was still failing. As the second century turned to the third, the emperors were still alarmed by the population implosion, but still powerless to change the situation. *Dulce et decorum est pro patria mori.* "It is a sweet and lovely thing," said Horace, "to die for the fatherland."[5] But very few people were willing to bear a child for it. Instead, they made do with pets. Clement of Alexandria observed that his neighbors who killed their newborns nevertheless lavished attention and money on their animals: "They expose children that are born at home, and take up the hatchlings of birds, and prefer irrational to rational creatures."[6] The wealthy who put their children out with the trash sometimes buried their dogs and cats in elaborate tombs.

By the rise of the Severan Dynasty, it was clear that the laws of Augustus didn't work. At the same time, it was equally clear that Christians were succeeding where traditional Romans were failing. Christians were having babies.

So the emperors crafted a new and interesting kind of legislation. They fashioned laws that imposed select tenets of Christian morality upon the entire Roman populace.

Under Septimius Severus (193–201), Roman law, for the first time in history, criminalized abortion and the use and sale of abortifacients. In his survey of ancient attitudes toward abortion, American New Testament scholar Michael Gorman finds this development remarkable. All of the revered thinkers of Greco-Roman antiquity — Socrates, Plato, Aristotle, Seneca — had found no moral problem with abortion or infanticide. What had changed with the Severan emperors — and changed so suddenly?

Gorman believes it was the influence of Christianity, which had just reached a critical mass in the wider population. Gorman asks:

> Is it only coincidental that the apologetic writings of Athenagoras and Tertullian immediately preceded the first Roman laws against abortions? … It seems quite possible that a growing

5. Horace, *Odes* 3.2.13.
6. Clement of Alexandria, *The Instructor* 3.4.

Christian populace influenced public and government opinion toward punishing abortion and promoting life. Perhaps the Romans merely needed ways to counteract the decrease in their population and took advantage of the Christian moral perspective. Whatever the Roman motives may have been, it is difficult to resist the conclusion that Christians contributed to the third-century anti-abortion statutes.[7]

Here's a surprise for you: The laws of the Severans failed just as surely as the earlier laws of Augustus had failed. All failed because they had no coherence with the rest of Roman law. In the name of preserving Roman tradition, they broke with longstanding Roman custom.

The Fathers of the Church could point out (and they did) that Greco-Roman custom was debased because it had deviated, centuries before, from the laws of nature inscribed upon the heart. It should have been unnatural to kill one's own child. Yet, to the Romans, it had become second nature.

Similarly, it should have seemed unnatural to make an individual's childhood miserable through the practice of pederasty. Yet this, too, was considered an acceptable recreation by the Roman upper classes.[8] Quintilian tells us that parents who sent small boys to school *assumed* that the tutors would molest them.[9] The ancient historians praised the Emperor Trajan because he was a *moderate pedophile* and tried not to harm the boys with whom he dallied.[10] Nero, on the other hand, had no such delicacy and insisted on having his young sex slaves surgically altered.[11]

The Fathers, who had little patience for child marriage, condemned child sex without exception.

Saint Cyprian pointed out what should have been obvious, but never

---

7. Michael Gorman, *Abortion and the Early Church: Christian, Jewish, and Pagan Attitudes in the Greco-Roman World* (Downers Grove, IL: InterVarsity Press, 1982), 61–62.
8. See Christian Laes, "Desperately Different? Delicia Children in the Roman Household," in David L. Balch and Carolyn Osiek, eds., *Early Christian Families in Context* (Grand Rapids, MI: Eerdmans Publishing, 2003), 317–324.
9. Quintilian, *Institutio Oratoria* 1.3.16–17.
10. Cassius Dio, *Roman History* 68.7.
11. *Ibid.*, 57.28.

is. He said that unchastity had made people miserable. "In fact, we must say that adultery is not pleasure, but mutual contempt. It cannot be delightful, because it kills both the soul and modesty."[12]

A century later, Saint Basil noted that humans alone, of all the animals, will cause themselves harm and pain by making choices that run contrary to their nature.

> If the lioness loves her cubs, if the she wolf fights to defend her little ones, what shall man say who is unfaithful to the precept and violates nature herself; or the son who insults the old age of his father; or the father whose second marriage has made him forget his first children?[13]

Among the Romans, patterns of vice had settled into custom, making individuals unhappy, families brittle, and society sick unto death.

It would be easy, I suppose, to exaggerate the change produced by Christianity. We could read selections from the Fathers and conclude that Christian families were fairly sinless and free of sorrow. That was, of course, not the case. Christians committed adultery, used contraceptives, visited prostitutes, and pursued sexual perversions. Otherwise we would find no exhortations against these practices in ancient homilies; nor would we find penalties for them in the canons of ancient councils. It grieves me to report that the ancient Church even suffered from the sexual abuse of minors by clergy.[14]

Christians failed then, as they do in every age. No one can deny, however, that Christians held themselves accountable to a high standard of sexual purity that was alien to Greek and Roman society in their time — and, in having children, they succeeded to a degree unmatched by that society.

By stabilizing marriage, Christianity reversed the long downward demographic trend. Gillian Clark, in her study of childhood in the ear-

---

12. Saint Cyprian, *Of the Discipline and Advantage of Chastity* 11.
13. Saint Basil the Great, *Homilies on the Hexaemeron* 9.4.
14. Aline Rousselle, Porneia: On Desire and the Body in Antiquity (Cambridge, MA: Blackwell, 1988), 147–148.

ly Church, concludes that "Christianity made a difference to children's lives in much the same way as it made a difference to women's lives."[15] She emphasizes the unprecedented vocational freedom enjoyed by both children and women.

We need to remind ourselves also of the dignity of both — a dignity recognized and revealed by Jesus Christ.

That dignity made an enormous difference for young people in late antiquity. Plato had considered children to be like animals, only worse because they were more intractable. Aristotle had taught that young people, like women and slaves, lacked sufficient reason to participate in society. Roman law treated minors as property, to be disposed of as their fathers wished. A father had the authority (though rarely exercised) to condemn a child to death for misdeeds. Fathers also had the right to reject a newborn baby and demand its death. To the poor in the Roman world, children were useful as laborers. To the upper classes, they were admired as sex objects.

Christian youth, however, were prized not for their usefulness or their physical beauty, but because they were people, created in God's image and likeness. As such, they were children of God and not the property of men.

This had very practical consequences. Children and adolescents were full members of the Church, and they could participate in Christian society in ways unimaginable in old Rome. An adolescent named Origen taught adults in the intellectual capital of empire. Saint Agnes exercised more influence in the Roman Church than even adult females could muster in wider Roman society. Young women had a voice in the Church; outside the Church, women and children were confined to silence. Christian children chose to submit themselves to martyrdom, and their parents respected their choice.

Ordinary young people were welcome to participate in the central mysteries of the Christian faith. The Church encouraged parents to baptize their sons and daughters as babies, and some churches even admit-

---

15. Gillian Clark, "The Fathers and the Children," in Diana Wood, ed., *The Church and Childhood* (Oxford: Blackwell Publishers, 1994), 26.

ted infants to Holy Communion.

In recent decades we have been the beneficiaries of several extensive studies of childhood in the early Church. One speaks of the Christian difference in the strongest terms, summarized in the book's title: *When Children Became People: The Birth of Childhood in Early Christianity*.[16] Another, more cautious study bears as its title the saying of Jesus: *Let the Children Come to Me*. Though the language in this latter work is more guarded, it arrives at similar conclusions:

> We should not underestimate the advances in the lives of children which Christianity brought: the opportunity to share in life itself and the opportunity to be free of sexual violence. Nor can we omit the most significant spiritual reality: that children as children were seen to be valid partakers of the kingdom of heaven.[17]

Such basic doctrine made all the difference, not only in the lives of the children who were loved this way, but in the lives of the parents who loved them.

Without the coercion of laws — and seemingly without effort — Christianity achieved what the imperium found perpetually elusive: population increase, with its attendant advances in economy and culture and happiness. Beginning with homes that welcomed children, Christians established societies more welcoming toward children. Grace restored nature, built upon it, and began the work of healing and perfecting it.

DISCUSSION QUESTIONS

1. In what ways was pre-Christian Rome like our current culture? In what ways was it different?
2. Why were the values of the emperors so different from the values of

16. O. M. Bakke, *When Children Became People: The Birth of Childhood in Early Christianity* (Minneapolis, MN: Fortress Press, 2005).
17. Cornelia B. Horn and John W. Martens, *"Let the Children Come to Me": Childhood and Children in Early Christianity* (Washington, DC: The Catholic University of America Press, 2009), 351.

their aristocrats?

3. How did Christianity succeed where the emperors had failed? What made the difference?

4. Who benefited most from the shift in attitudes on marriage and family? What might the specific benefits have been for wives? Husbands? Children? The state?

5. What can we learn from this episode in history? What can we apply to our own times?

CHAPTER THREE

Without a Vision, the People Perish: Biblical Foundations for Renewal of the Family

———————

DR. JOSEPH C. ATKINSON

Pontifical John Paul II Institute for Studies on Marriage and Family at The Catholic University of America

FIVE QUICK TAKES

1. The Christian vision of marriage and family life is prophetic. God has given us the vision of who we are and the meaning of our lives. If we reject the vision of reality, grounded in creation, we end up fractured and alienated from truth. We create a culture of death. If we embrace and live out God's truth of who we are, we will flourish, creating a culture of life. We do theology with our bodies. Without this vision, our world perishes.

2. The Christian vision of marriage and family life is rooted in the order of creation (i.e., objective reality) and affirmed by revelation. To defend this vision is to stand against the meaninglessness and nihilism of our secular world.

3. In acknowledging the essential goodness of our created nature, the complementary gender differences between men and women as the true basis of human sexual relationality become a profound sign of the basic truth of human existence: We are created not as automonous, self-created individuals, but we fulfill our humanity specifically in communion with others.

4. The intersecting relationships of love within the family between the man and woman, given concrete form in children, manifest and reveal in the created order the relationship of Christ with his Bride, the Church (Eph 5:32), and image forth the inner love and life of God.

5. In the Old Testament, the family (as described above) was the carrier of the covenant, so much so that without the family there is no covenant. In the New Testamant, through baptism, the family now fulfills this mission and *becomes a critical place*, a sphere where the Holy Spirit is actively bringing about the salvation of the world through these familial relationships.

I am going to rely on two quotes to frame this presentation so that this reflection on family life, its anthropological meaning, and its theological purpose is grounded in the reality of our present historical moment. The first quote comes from Saint John Paul II, written in 1981:

> At a moment of history in which the family is the object of numerous forces that seek to destroy it or in some way to deform it, and aware that the well-being of society and her own good are intimately tied to the good of the family, the Church perceives in a more urgent and compelling way her mission of proclaiming to all people the plan of God for marriage and the family. (*Familiaris Consortio, 3*)

Forty years have passed since these words were written, and the forces antithetical to family life have expanded exponentially on every level. The attacks are worldwide, coordinated in a manner inconceivable forty years ago, regularly backed by political and legal force to bring to heel any dissenters from the new secular orthodoxy. We have only to think here of *Masterpiece Cakeshop v. Colorado Civil Rights Commission* or Netflix's threat to move out of Georgia when it decided to become a pro-life state.

The second quote that will frame our discussion comes from Sister Lucia, the last seer of Fatima. The background to this quote starts with Cardinal Caffarra of Bologna, who was the first president of the Pontifical John Paul II Institute. He stated in a 2017 interview that the new Institute for Studies on Marriage and Family begun by Saint John Paul II "was not wanted within and outside of the Church, because of the vision it was proposing." During these difficult times, Caffarra decided to write Sister Lucia of Fatima asking for prayers, but not expecting a reply as Lucia's communication with the outside world was restricted. Yet, surprisingly, she wrote back. Caffarra has given sworn testimony of what the letter contained, and stated that Sister Lucia wrote:

"Father, a time will come when the decisive battle between the kingdom of Christ and Satan will be over marriage and the family. And those who will work for the good of the family will experience persecution and tribulation. But do not be afraid, because Our Lady has already crushed his head."[1]

Now, almost thirty years later, Caffarra realized "Sister Lucia's words are taking place." As he sees it, at this moment, Satan is constructing an anti-creation.[2]

All through the history of the Church, God has caused prophetic voices to arouse His people to action, to return to Him before it was too late. There is always an urgency in these prophetic voices, for they remind us poignantly that each and every human person is part of the divine cosmic battle begun at the Fall and that our own personal choices determine the final outcome of our particular historical reality. That final reality is determined by the degree that we either join our own particular history with the history of the divine Son or our refusal to do so. These quotes show the urgency and depth of the current crisis in the family. Within this context, I want to establish what I believe to be the indispensable *foundational principles* if the recovery of the family and the faith is to take place. This primary issue has to do with *identity*.

Currently, there are numerous books and programs (Protestant, Catholic, and secular) that purport to help one construct a better self and a better family, how to have balanced children, etc. They provide chapters and checklists of how to improve rituals in the home, have a better prayer life, assure family integration with the sacraments (if Catholic), provide mealtime discussion questions, etc. They clearly serve some purpose, but are they actually addressing what is at the center of the crisis in family life today? At a recent meeting of the US Conference of Catholic Bishops, Word on Fire Catholic Ministries founder Bishop Robert Barron stated that 50 percent of Catholics thirty years old and younger have left the church. On top of this, Barron also stated that, "for every one person joining the Church today, 6.45 are leaving" and most are leaving at young ages, primarily before age twenty-three. The median age of those who leave is thirteen.[3]

---

1. Diane Montagna, "Cardinal Caffarra: 'What Sr. Lucia wrote to me is being fulfilled today'," *Aleteia*, May 19, 2017, https://aleteia.org/2017/05/19/exclusive-cardinal-caffarra-what-sr-lucia-wrote-to-me-is-being-fulfilled-today/.
2. *Ibid.*
3. Matt Hadro, "What's going to bring the 'nones' back to the Church?" *Catholic News Agency*, June 14, 2019, https://www.catholicnewsagency.com/news/whats-going-to-bring-the-nones-back-to-the-church-46276.

Given the statistical evidence provided by Bishop Barron, it is clear that the Church and the family (which are called to be prime evangelizers and disciple-makers), are manifestly failing at this primary task. At the heart of the problem is that in the West, the Christian faith has largely been evacuated of its radical nature. Authentic Christian faith re-creates man such that in every dimension of his life, he is called to be conformed to the person of Christ. As theologian Dietrich Bonhoeffer said, when Christ calls a man, he calls him to die. We must die to all that would separate us from the Father. Faith in Christ in not some extra we add to our current lifestyle, like getting a degree or taking on a new hobby. Rather, Christ illumines life, is life and truth itself. One would rather die for Him than deny him. But this sense of radical faith has simply been deracinated from our modern lives and our secular consciousness. Faith is something privatized, reduced to a personal opinion. The sense of transcendence is systematically being obliterated in the modern world. As a consequence, man is left de-rooted. Like characters in Sartyr, he finds himself in a meaningless world. This truth provokes both a crisis and a response. We either reject this nihilism and begin to seek out the roots of our being and the proper framework that helps us interpret our lives, or we sink deeper into the oblivion.

In the religious sphere, when genuinely radical faith is no longer present, when the radical decision for Christ is absent, a crisis emerges. Religion becomes empty, and people no longer are committed. Rather than looking at root cause, "solutions" are proffered, but they can only superficially fill the need. These solutions take many forms, but are all equally ineffective. They impose *forms* of religious life, ones that may even resemble the spiritual fruit of a once-living faith, but no longer have transformative power, as there is nothing within people to which these forms of religious life can speak to. Without the radical commitment to Christ, these remain mute to the onlooker.

With a diminished sense of transcendence, modern man has little sense of his own alienation or the need to commit himself to someone or something beyond himself. Rejecting the truth of his own creature, he is rootless; he is empty. This *existential emptiness* is often filled by secular psychological forms that appeal to people because they speak of self-affirmation, of empowerment, and assert values that are lived out in a materialistic and relativistic framework. But this, eventually, is discovered to be hollow as well and empties man of meaning.

This way of thinking has become dominant in our culture; it is the operative anthropology underlining modern society that sees man as an isolated, self-determining individual. Based on fiction, it is ultimately so fragile that nothing is allowed to contradict or transgress its dictates; rational discourse is not tolerated. Objective reality (for example, saying there are two genders, or that marriage and sexual activity is only proper between a man and woman) now becomes hate speech that must be eradicated at all costs. To speak of objective truths is to become an enemy of the state and its new social order. Just as the early Christians, people of faith today will be persecuted for speaking truth.

If this deeply entrenched understanding of human nature is not directly confronted, then any solution we proffer to the crisis of the family will fail. The crisis has been provoked by this false anthropology and is grounded in it. As Catholics we need to deal directly with the question of who man is. The question of human nature is the question of human identity. Without addressing this primary question, solutions offered to deal with the crisis in the family are merely a form of arranging deck chairs on the Titanic, but with one difference: This old cliché refers to useless activity in the face of an *approaching* disaster. Culturally — and ecclesially — the ship named family has already hit the fatal iceberg and is tipped halfway out of the water, half-submerged. A daunting image to be sure, but it accurately portrays the sense of urgency that is needed in the present moment.

At this point any observant person is aware of the litany of attacks on the family and on Catholic truth within modern society. As Sister Lucia foresaw, we are in a pitched battle for our own souls, the souls of our children, and the soul of the Church. The more the Church and Catholic families look to the modern world for its clues, the more they accept false values, its anti-creation categories, as Caffarra said, and its deceptive stratagems, such as politically correct language, the absolutizing of inclusiveness, and apologizing for the truths of the Gospel that contradict the current totalitarian viewpoint. Unless the falseness of this modern anthropology is demonstrated, the loss of faith is inevitable, regardless of what programs or approaches we use.

This loss of faith within the culture and within the Church is, in fact, a loss of identity.

To make this relevant, we need to wrestle with two major questions that will bring these abstract ideas into the concrete.[4]

1. How can Catholic families be equipped to be more effective forges of intentional discipleship?
2. How can Catholic families be equipped to fulfill their mission as primary outposts of evangelization and positive social change?

These two questions can be rearticulated into the following: How can the family (1) fulfill its *ad intra-mission* of passing on the faith to those within the family and (2) fulfill its *ad extra-mission* of bringing others into the experience of Jesus Christ? "Family" here is understood to be the family baptized into Christ and desiring and adhering to the Catholic faith. It is critical that "answers" to these two key questions not be formulated until the question of the "identity" is securely addressed.

As Saint John Paul II wrote in *Familiaris Consortio*:

> The role that God calls the family to perform in history derives from what the family is; its role represents the dynamic and existential development of what it is. Each family finds within itself a summons that cannot be ignored, and that specifies both its dignity and its responsibility: <u>family, become what you are.</u> ... Accordingly, <u>the family must go back</u> to the "beginning" of God's creative act, if it is to attain self-knowledge and self-realization <u>in accordance with the inner truth</u> *not only of what it is* but also of what it does in history (17, emphasis added).

---

4. During the Catholic Family Life Symposium at the McGrath Institute for Church Life at the University of Notre Dame in July 2019, these questions, along with several others, were developed to help focus what needs to be addressed in the current situation regarding family life and the faith.

Put simply: Being precedes doing. Therefore, the fundamental question that needs to be answered first is: *What is it to be baptized in Christ Jesus? How does that give a form / an ontological shape to my person and to those with whom I am united; i.e., my family? How does baptism affect my relationship to the world outside of me?*

As Saint John Paul II has stated, it is only by "going back to the beginning" that any authentic going forward can be achieved. We will not be able to recover and restore the family and the fullness of faith unless we first lay the theological foundation for our true identify given by God. This requires going back to the revelatory truth about creation in Genesis. The issue is fundamentally not what methods or programs or approaches we use. The issue is the recovery of our twofold identity as created and redeemed beings.

To do that, we need to engage in the following work:

1.   the recovery of an authentic theology of creation, *and*
2.   the recovery of an authentic understanding of baptism

THE THEOLOGY OF CREATION

The narrative of creation (Gn 1–3) provides the God-given framework by which we can interpret human experience. Specifically, it provides the antidote to the false anthropology of radical subjective individualism.[5]

In the creation narrative, we see first that God alone is creator and that everything that comes into being (see Jn 1:2)[6] comes to be through the speaking of God's Word. It is He alone who gives the structure, the meaning, and the end (the telos) to each created reality. This, of course, belies the efforts of our modern culture to proclaim that we are our own creators. We have a given nature, written into our very being, with which we either cooperate and flourish, or reject and end up in a state of disintegration.

---

5. See Joseph Atkinson, *Biblical and Theological Foundations of the Family: The Domestic Church* (Washington, DC: The Catholic University of America Press, 2014).
6. "All things came to be through him, and without him nothing came to be," Jn 1:3, NAB.

Biblical Concept of History

Even the first phrase of Scripture, *be-ra'shith*, "in the beginning," points us to the fact that there is also "an end" toward which we are all moving. In other words, unlike the dystopia of Sartre, we cannot create our own meaning. Our meaning, our end, is given within our created nature. Our task, like the first primordial man, is to discover and live out this meaning.

Genesis 1:1 gives us the first revelation of the concept of history. History, in the Biblical sense, is the proposition that human actions in time move toward an end. What this means is that human action matters. Each choice we make either moves us toward our properly defined end, or moves us further away from it. Human will and human action matter and are intrinsically tied to our becoming, and determine the final state we will arrive at. Consequently, our faith cannot simply be an experience. It has to determine the actions in our lives. *We do theology with our bodies.* Hence, to contracept, to abort, to commit adultery, to break up our families, to reject the given purpose of gender, etc., are all to reject our true nature and our God-given final end.

Principle of Differentiation

Creation, in popular imagination, is often thought of as the bringing together of numerous entities that had been discreetly and separately created elsewhere. But this is not the Biblical vision. Rather, Scripture shows that God first creates an original unity (called in Hebrew the *tohu vevohu*) **from which** all other forms of terrestrial life are separated out. The plants, the animals emerge from the soil. They are not made separately and then brought together to form the world. First there is the original unity *from which* emerge earthly creations. This is the principle of *l'havdil*, or differentiation. This is critical for understanding human nature and how it works. We are not bound contractually; we are bound ontologically. We are not a set of discreet individuals, created in isolation and then brought together. Rather, in the terrestrial creation, there is the original unity (the *tohu vavohu*) from which the many emerge. Individual things only exist because of a preceding original unity.

For man, this means that to understand human nature, one has to account for the positive relationship between the many and the one, be-tween being a personal being that, at the same time, is *already* grounded in a corporate reality. In other words, I cannot simply exist as an individ-ual. My individuality is always rooted in the corporate reality of human-ity. As the African saying goes, "I am because we are."

It can be considered a theological heresy to affirm that man lives in isolation and is self-creative of both his bodily and existential reality. If not a heresy, it is certainly a psychosis and can only lead to a disintegrat-ed personality.

Being Made in the Image

But in this mystery of the profound relationship of the one to the many, we also see a mystery that lies at the heart of man's being. In Genesis 1:26–27, man is said to be made *in the image of God*. At this point, we know little of God except that He is creative, and that He is a being of communion. He speaks to Himself and says, "Let us make man in our image" (v. 26). If we are made in the divine image, and God is a being of communion, then man cannot exist in isolation. He is, by his created nature, ordered toward communion for his fulfillment. Man's flourish-ing, both individually and corporately, is grounded in this need for, and living out of, existential communion, both with God and with others. To create a society based on the primacy of the isolated individual is ceasing to live in reality and inevitably leads to a culture of death and nihilism.

Theological Meaning of Marriage

This truth is taken to an even higher key in the second movement of the narrative of creation in Genesis 2. Here, Scripture takes on the task of exploring the specific nature of the man-woman relationship. As before, there is an original unity (the 'adam, the first man) and from this pri-mordial one comes the second, the woman. Then, from this primordial pair emerges the rest of humanity. But here in Genesis 2 we discover that sexual differentiation in man is not only ordered to procreation. There is a sub-theme that is discernible with the narrative, which points to the theological meaning of the human sexual union. A thorough study of Genesis 2 shows that the text is replete with covenantal and Temple imagery. The gold reminds the reader of all the gold that overlaid the instruments and furnishings of the Temple in Jerusalem; the onyx stone recalls the breastplate of the high priest, which carried these stones with the names of the twelve tribe of Israel; the bdellium connotes the manna that God had given to Israel and that was contained in the Ark. The eastward position of the Garden, the Tree of Life, the command to guard and keep are all profoundly connected to the world of God's Temple. With study, it becomes clear that the Garden is, in fact, the prototypical, the blueprint for the Temple that will be built in Jerusalem.[7]

The question now emerges: Why, when the Torah deals specifically with the man-woman relationship, does it take place within a text that is replete with covenantal imagery and language? The conclusion is that this context points to the fact that the differentiated human sexual relationship has a greater depth of meaning than originally appears on the surface. Marriage is tied intrinsically to God's salvific covenant and His way of bringing salvation into the world. This truth is embedded in the text, but it will take a key, a hermeneutical key, to finally unlock the mystery of this text.

Marriage: The Great Mystery Revealed

It is with Christ that this mystery of the man-woman relationship is finally revealed. As Paul shows in Ephesians 5:22–32, the one-flesh union of man and woman expressed in Genesis 2:24 is, in reality, a participation in the sacrificial love of Christ for His Church. Throughout the earlier parts of Ephesians, Paul had been talking about the mystery of Christ's love and our redemption in Him. Then, beginning in chapter five, he shifts his focus to the nuptial relationship of man and woman and the family. Finally, he concludes by quoting from Genesis 2 about the two becoming one flesh. But then, suddenly piercing through this mystery, he unequivocally states that "this is a great mystery, but I speak in reference to Christ and the church."

---

7. To see an analysis of this text, see Atkinson, *Biblical and Theological Foundations of the Family*, passim; G. J. Wenham, "Sanctuary Symbolism in the Garden of Eden Story" in *I Studied Inscriptions Before the Flood: Ancient Near Eastern, Literary, and Linguistic Approaches to Genesis 1–11* (Winona Lake, IN: Eisenbrauns, 1994) 399–404.

Simply put, the relationship between man and woman and the differentiation of mankind into a binary sexual reality is grounded in, and participates in, the love of Jesus and the Church, which is perfectly revealed in Christ's' sacrifice on the Cross. This is the awe-filled vocation of marriage. Human marriage is meant to be an icon representing and participating in the divine nuptials of the Cross. As von Balthasar explained, this divine cruciform love of Christ is the *theological form of marriage.*[8]

Only in this way can we begin to understand the ecclesial nature of marriage and family — or, as we prefer to call it, the nature of the domestic church. Without this theological grounding from both creation itself and from the narrative of creation in Genesis, the concept of the family and domestic church becomes merely a theological tag that can be filled with any content one desires. To recover the truth about marriage and family, we have to take seriously creation itself and the revelation of its truth in Scripture.

Baptism as Foundational

The second foundation for identity is baptism. We are not only created but also redeemed, re-created. In looking at baptism, we are faced with the fundamental question that all humanity must answer: Will we be Lord, or shall Christ? As mentioned earlier, Bonhoeffer said that when Christ calls a man, he first calls him to die. This is the invitation of baptism: to cease living in sin-created isolation, and to allow one's old adamic nature to be united to Christ on the Cross and die (cf. Rom 6).[9] There is simply no other way to salvation. There is no other way to wholeness. "No one can enter the kingdom of God without being born of water and Spirit" (Jn 3:5).

This is the radical call of the Gospel. In the Fall we usurped the place of the Father and tried to become gods. The invitation of Christ is to return sovereignty to Christ so that our wills may be aligned with the

---

8. Hans Urs von Balthasar, "Ephesians 5:21–33 and Humanae Vitae: A Meditation" in *Christian Married Love*, ed. Raymond Dennehy (San Francisco: Ignatius Press, 2018).
9. "All of us who have been baptized into Christ Jesus were baptized into his death," Rom 6:3, RSVCE.

Father. That is why the first creed of the Church was "Jesus is Lord," with the subtitle (as it were) "and we are not."[10] The kingdom of God means precisely that. The kingdom is the place where God rules; that is, we seek His sovereignty over us. We seek to have this mind in us that was also in Christ Jesus.[11] How different this Biblical truth is from the secular attempts at self-actualization and self-determination. These are only variations on the first original sin.

Baptism is a revelation of the true corporate nature of man originally seen in the narrative of creation. Baptism moves us out of alienation from God (existential isolation) and exchanges our fallen adamic nature for that of Christ's. As Paul will say, "it is no longer I who live, but Christ who lives in."[12] This incorporation into Christ is meant realistically.

What the New Testament is showing us is that man properly begins to fulfill his telos — his end — when he becomes part of the Body of Christ and a functioning part of it. Biblically, it is not a question of being saved and then later deciding to join a Christian community. For Paul this is impossible. Salvation and being reborn and grafted into the Body of Jesus are one and the same thing. Hence, the truth of man as a communal being can only be manifest and properly lived out in the Church as Christ's Body.

The Power and Realism of Baptism

We see the dynamic effects on baptism within the family in Paul's discussion in 1 Corinthians 7. Here, Paul is dealing with a family in which one spouse is baptized in Christ and the other is a pagan. By virtue of Christ living within one spouse (because of baptism), the whole organic unity of the family (the one-flesh unity) is made holy — even bringing the pagan spouse into this realm of holiness (1 Cor 7:10ff). Paul writes to the Corinthians: "For the unbelieving husband is made holy through his wife, and the unbelieving wife is made holy through the brother [*i.e.*, her Christian husband]. Otherwise your children would be unclean, whereas

---

10. "And no one can say 'Jesus is Lord' except by the Holy Spirit." Cf. 1 Cor 12:3, RSVCE.
11. Phil 2:5.
12. Gal 2:20, RSVCE.

in fact they are holy" (1 Cor 7:14). This dynamic effect of baptism is only present in the family and in no other relationship. The unity of the family is so organic that the members are really one flesh, one psychosomatic unity. When Christ is present in one, He affects all members. This is a result of the corporate reality that we saw in Genesis 1 concerning creation. The singularity of a person is always grounded in a preceding unity.

The Theological Purpose of the Family

In the Old Testament, it is clear that the family is the carrier of the covenant; so much so that without the family there is no salvific covenant with God. The life of faith and its manner of being passed from one generation to another is through the family. The key festival of Passover was primarily lived within the context of the family. The three main rituals of circumcision, redemption of the firstborn, and Passover were father-led rituals.[13] The legislation of Israel had a preponderance of laws concerning the observance of family life essential to the covenant within the home. In the Old Testament, without the family, there is no covenant. The family is, in fact, the carrier of the covenant.

In the New Testament, this theological task of the family is brought to its ontological conclusion in baptism. Baptized in Christ, the family plays a key role in the sharing of the grace and power of Christ's death and resurrection and of the power of the Holy Spirit. The family now *becomes a critical place*, a sphere where the Holy Spirit is actively bringing about the salvation of the world. The one-flesh union of the family becomes the means by which the Holy Spirit brings all the members into the sphere of Christ's holiness. Christ, now present in the baptized family members, enables the family to reach its teleological purpose. It now takes on, and is called to fulfill, its ecclesial nature. Family becomes a living part of the Church, infused and animated with the life of the Spirit, where the true theological form of marriage with the husband as icon of Christ and the wife as icon of the Church takes on a concrete form in the nuptial relationship. Hence, in Christ, through baptism, marriage and family become key to God's salvific redemption of the world.

---

13. See John W. Miller, *Calling God "Father"* (Mahwah, New Jersey: Paulist Press, 1989).

This is borne out and confirmed, as we have alluded to, in Paul's letter to the Ephesians. In the first five chapters, Paul goes to great lengths to explain the theological implications of salvation in Christ. Then, suddenly, toward the end of chapter five and then in chapter six, Paul begins to speak of the way a person, reborn into Christ, is to live out his marriage. Paul's advice is not mere good counsel of how to be kind, communicate, or organize one's home. Rather, Paul shows the theological depths of the relationship between husband and wife. He shows how the man must, as head, lay down his life for his wife. He shows how the wife takes on the ecclesial role, the role of Church, in how she relates to her husband. These are not culturally conditioned roles; in fact, they are decidedly countercultural. This is the theological form of marriage — to which all marriages are ordered. It is only on this basis that one can begin to think of how to prepare people for marriage or explain the purpose and meaning of family life. Anything less is a simple superficial response, which ultimately cannot bear lasting fruit.

Marriage is a covenant, an iconic participation in Jesus' love for the Church. Like His love and His covenant, it cannot be broken. What we do within our marriages is either a reflection of, or a rejection of our acceptance of this theological truth. Again, we need to remember that we do theology with our bodies and what we do determines our final relationship with God. This participation of Christ's love for the Church is the vocation of marriage. It is the inner meaning of the family now seen as a domestic church. It is only once this primary identity is secured and the radical commitment to Christ realized that we can begin to authentically recover marriage and family within our society and within the Church.

————————————

DISCUSSION QUESTIONS

1. It is not easily self-evident that our homes and families are a form of Church. Do you see aspects of your home that are like the Church or that help build up God's kingdom in this world? Do you conceive of one of the purposes of your family as to help make followers of Jesus?
2. What does the phrase "we do theology with our bodies" cause you

to think about? Do you connect your faith in God with what you do with your body?

3. Do you believe that God has given a specific nature to us as men and women, as husbands and wives, or is it up to us to decide how we think about our bodies, our sexuality, and the roles we live out in our families? Is how we think about this important or just our own personal preference?

CHAPTER FOUR

"The Nearest Hospital": Exploring the Domestic Church as a Place of Healing

———————

JOHN GRABOWSKI

The Catholic University of America, Pontifical Council for the Family (emeritus)

CLAIRE GRABOWSKI

Pontifical Council for the Family (emerita)

FIVE QUICK TAKES

1. In addition to Penance and the Anointing of the Sick, Baptism, Marriage, and the Eucharist have healing dimensions that are important for family life.

2. The grace communicated in the sacrament of Marriage is not a one-time infusion, but an ongoing source of strength and power for couples in living out their vocation as spouses and parents.

3. The healing effects of Baptism and Marriage are fruitfully received and extended through the life of a family by regular practices of love, prayer, reconciliation, acknowledgement, and service.

4. The Eucharist is the "source and summit" of the life of the domestic church, and its healing effects are extended in the life of a family by time spent together — especially at the family dinner table.

5. The healing effects of these sacraments empower and equip Christian families to answer the call to be active agents of the New Evangelization in ministering to others.

Pope Francis has repeatedly described the Church as a "field hospital" and has called the Christian family "the nearest hospital."[1] This description invites reflection on how the Catholic family founded in Marriage is called to be a place of healing. A primary source of this healing comes through the grace of the sacraments. While Penance and Anointing of the Sick are those sacraments that are traditionally associated with healing,[2] other sacraments that are central to the life of families also have healing dimensions. Baptism, the Eucharist, and Marriage itself all communicate grace, which restores the members of families and their ability

---

1. *Amoris Laetitia* 321. All citations of Church documents are from the Vatican website: http://w2.vatican.va/content/vatican/en.html unless otherwise noted.
2. See the *Catechism of the Catholic Church* (hereafter CCC) 1421.

to love and care for one another as well as to fulfill their Christian mission outside the walls of their home.

Of course, families do not fulfill this call to be places of healing automatically. They can also be places of brokenness and dysfunction that actually wound their members and pass on patterns of destructive behavior across generations.[3] Furthermore, families who live in situations of poverty, violence, persecution, or homelessness face profound challenges to their human functioning — let alone their Christian flourishing.[4] Likewise, sacraments are not magic, and the grace they offer does not take effect without active cooperation on the part of those who receive them.[5] We have to work to dispose ourselves to be receptive to this grace and to take steps to allow this grace to permeate our lives and relationships. In families this means that regular formative practices are key to enabling members to draw effectively on the grace that they receive in the sacraments and fully experience their healing effects. In this essay, we argue that Baptism, Marriage, and the Eucharist, joined to regular practices within the life of a family in the context of the liturgical year, offer pathways to healing so that that the domestic church can indeed be "the nearest hospital." This can, in turn, ground a Catholic spirituality of the family and highlight the role of its members as "the principle agents of the family apostolate" of the Church.[6]

We will proceed by highlighting some of the healing effects of Baptism

---

3. This is one way to understand biblical warnings about the sins of parents being visited on their children (cf., e.g., Ex 20:5–6; 34:6–7; Nm 14:18; Dt 5:9–10). It should be noted that other biblical texts affirm individual responsibility for one's own sins (cf., e.g., Dt 24:16; Jer 31:29; Ez 18:2; Jb 21:19). But Scripture does make clear that sin impacts families and their histories. The sin of Adam and Eve is followed by the murder of their son Abel by Cain (Gn 4:1–16). David's adultery with Bathsheba and blood guilt in having her husband Uriah killed results in a history of violence in his family (2 Sm 12:10 — cf. Absalom's rebellion and death in 2 Sm 15–18). Contemporary social science tells us that cycles of brokenness and dysfunction in families (e.g., abuse, addiction, violence, divorce) are often passed down. On the specific impact of childhood trauma on mothers, see Christina G. McDonnell and Kristin Valentino, "Intergenerational Effects of Childhood Trauma," *Child Maltreatment* 21, no. 4 (November 2016): 317–326. On strategies for breaking such negative patterns for social workers, see Briana Woods-Jaeger, Bridget Cho, Chris Sexton, Lauren Slagel, and Kathy Goggin, "Promoting Resilience: Breaking the Intergenerational Cycle of Adverse Childhood Experiences," *Health Education and Behavior* 45, no. 5 (October 2018): 772–780.

4. Cf. *Familiaris Consortio*, 85; *Amoris Laetitia*, 44, 46, 49.

5. Even in the case of the Baptism of infants in which parents and godparents consent on behalf of the child, the infused theological virtues of faith, hope, and love that form the capacity of the baptized to relate to God will not grow and develop without the active cooperation of the child as he or she matures. Cf. CCC 1266 and 1270.

6. *Amoris Laetitia*, 200.

and Marriage as foundational to the identity and mission of the family, as well as specific practices that dispose parents and children to draw on the grace they communicate. We will then discuss how these foundational sacraments and their associated practices are ordered to and perfected by the family's participation in the Eucharist. A final section will briefly consider how the healing effected in these sacraments and their associated practices equips families to live their mission in the world.

A couple of disclaimers are in order. First, this brief treatment is meant to be suggestive — rather than in any sense exhaustive — of the topics considered. Second, in what follows we presuppose that families are engaged in basic practices that flow from and express their reality as domestic churches: prayer and catechesis (priesthood), witness in word and action (prophecy), and service in and outside their homes (kingship).[7] The specific practices we mention here are intended to highlight dimensions of those basic forms of activity or to further supplement them. Third, the term "family" as used here refers not just to the "nuclear family" of parents and children, but also to the richer multigenerational reality of grandparents, uncles, aunts, cousins, and other relations.[8] Fourth and relatedly, even the strongest and most vibrant of Christian families are not meant to be "islands" of Christian life and practice — they need the support of the Church's ministers, other families, the parish, and other forms of Christian community to genuinely flourish.

THE FOUNDATION: BAPTISM AND MARRIAGE

The ecclesial identity and mission of the family is founded in Baptism. The healing effects of Baptism are well-enumerated in the Catholic tradition. The sacrament forgives sin (both original and actual), incorporates a person into the body of Christ, and brings the recipient into a new re-

---

7. Obviously, this is to the degree that they are able to do so within their specific social, economic, and life circumstances.

8. This is a point frequently made by Pope Francis. See, for example, *Amoris Laetitia*, 187. Recent Church teaching has also recognized the multiplicity of forms in which "family" is found and lived — e.g., single-parent families, blended families (due to remarriage after divorce or the death of a spouse), or families headed by grandparents. Pope Francis is not the first to acknowledge such complexity. For a study of this theme in magisterial teaching through the pontificate of Saint John Paul II, see Donald Miller, OFM, *Concepts of Family Life in Modern Catholic Theology* (Bethesda, MD: Catholic Scholars Press, 1997).

lationship with God. As the *Catechism of the Catholic Church* explains:

The Most Holy Trinity gives the baptized sanctifying grace, the grace of justification:

- enabling them to believe in God, to hope in him, and to love him through the theological virtues;
- giving them the power to live and act under the prompting of the Holy Spirit through the gifts of the Holy Spirit;
- allowing them to grow in goodness through the moral virtues.

Thus, the whole organism of the Christian's supernatural life has its roots in Baptism.[9]

Less well known is the relationship between Baptism and Marriage in the Latin Church and the synergy between these sacraments in providing healing within the life of Christian families.

Unlike the Christian East, which regards the priest as the minister of the sacrament of Marriage in administering the nuptial blessing to the couple in the liturgy, the Western Latin churches have a different view. As Pope Francis explains in *Amoris Laetitia*: "In the Church's Latin tradition, the ministers of the sacrament are the man and woman who marry."[10] The ontological priesthood conferred on the couple in their Baptism empowers them to confer the sacrament on each other through their exchange of mutual consent. This sacrament is not a "thing or a power," but an encounter with Christ, who then accompanies the couple in their life together.[11] This grace takes up and extends the effects of Baptism. As Saint John Paul II noted:

The sacrament of marriage is the specific source and original means of sanctification for Christian married couples and families. It takes up again and makes specific the sanctifying grace

---

9. CCC 1266.
10. *Amoris Laetitia*, 75.
11. Cf. *ibid.*, 73.

of Baptism … "This love the Lord has judged worthy of special gifts, healing, perfecting and exalting gifts of grace and of charity."[12]

The bond created by their exchange of consent (i.e., the *res et sacramentum*) is not a one-time infusion of grace, but an ongoing source of power for the couple over the whole of their life together, enabling them to love, serve, forgive, and care for each other and their children.[13] The grace of the sacrament, which unites Christian spouses across their years together, in turn pervades the whole life of their family. As Pope Francis notes: "More generally, the common life of husband and wife, the entire network of relations that they build with their children and the world around them, will be steeped in and strengthened by the grace of the sacrament."[14] This is a vital point. The grace of the sacrament of Marriage pervades the whole life of a Christian family. This includes the specific healing effects of Marriage.

Though Marriage is typically described as a sacrament "at the service of communion," the notion that it also serves as a vehicle of healing has deep roots in Scripture and in the Catholic theological tradition, especially when considered together with Baptism, which is its foundation. Among such healing effects highlighted in recent Church teaching and Catholic theology are: indissolubility as a gift of grace,[15] the mutual submission of husband and wife to one another in Christ (cf. Eph 5:21),[16] and Marriage as a *remedium concupiscentiae* (remedy for concupiscence), or-

12. *Familiaris Consortio*, 56, quoting *Gaudium et Spes*, 49.

13. In his mature teaching on sacraments, Saint Thomas articulates the view that each sacrament communicates the grace to achieve the end for which it is given (see *Summa Theologica*, III, q. 62, a. 2). Applying this position to marriage (which he did not because the work was unfinished), we can draw the conclusion that the grace of the bond empowers couples to live out all of the duties of their state as spouses and parents.

14. *Amoris Laetitia*, 74.

15. See *ibid.*, 62.

16. See Saint John Paul II, Apostolic Letter, *Mulieris Dignitatem*, 24. For an analysis of this teaching as a development of the Catholic doctrine of marriage, see John S. Grabowski, "Mutual Submission and Trinitarian Self-Giving," *Angelicum*, 74 (1997): 489–512. In *Amoris Laetitia*, Pope Francis echoes this teaching and applies it specifically to the sexual relationship of a married couple (see 156). For an examination of the living out of this teaching in the daily life of a couple, see John and Claire Grabowski, *One Body: A Program of Marriage Preparation and Enrichment for the New Evangelization* (Steubenville, OH: Emmaus Road Publishing, 2018), 105–17.

dering the couple's sexual relationship to life and love.[17] These healing effects serve to overcome the "hardness of heart" (Mt 19:8), the desire to dominate (cf. Gn 3:16), and propensity to use one another (cf. Mt 5:27–28), unleashed in the relationships of men and women by the Fall.

One of the primary effects of Marriage is to perfect the natural love of the married couple.[18] As Saint John Paul II characteristically described it, the communion of love between husband and wife is the basis of the community of parents and children in the family.[19] The mutual love of husband and wife and their shared fertility expressed in sexual self-gift capacitates them to receive the gift of a child and generously welcome her or him into their lives and home. It is in the love of their father and mother through which children have their first experience of the unconditional love of God and begin to understand their own dignity and that of others as human beings made in His image and likeness. It is also the foundation of the family's practice of hospitality in welcoming others into their home and engaging in service outside of it.

The perseverance of parents in love in spite of the inevitable suffering and trials that are the part of the life of every family "East of Eden" is a powerful witness to children of the possibilities for human faithfulness when supported by the faithfulness of God.[20] The grace of indissolubility that flows from the sacrament is watered in the regular practice of reconciliation within families. In *Amoris Laetitia,* Pope Francis challenges families to make the words of Saint Paul a daily practice in their

17. The fullest articulation of the profound interconnection between life and love, its anthropological foundation, and application to the Christian life is provided by Saint John Paul II in his catecheses known as the *Theology of the Body*. The best available English version of the work is *Man and Woman He Created Them: A Theology of the Body*, translated and edited by Michael Waldstein (Boston: Pauline Books and Media, 2006). For recent applications of this vision to marriage and sexual ethics, see Janet E. Smith, John S. Grabowski, J. Budzinski, and Maria Fedoryka, "Self-Gift: The Heart of Humanae Vitae," *The National Bioethics Quarterly* 16, no. 3 (Autumn 2016): 449–74; Janet Smith, *Self-Gift: Humanae Vitae and the Thought of John Paul II*, Renewal Within Tradition (Steubenville, OH: Emmaus Academic, 2018); Cormac Burke, *The Theology of Marriage: Personalism, Doctrine and Canon Law* (Washington, DC: The Catholic University of America Press, 2015), esp.181–240.
18. See *Amoris Laetitia*, 89.
19. See *Familiaris Consortio*, 18, and the Letter to Families, *Gratissimam Sane*, 7. For an extended treatment of this theme, see John S. Grabowski, "Marriage as a Unitive and Procreative Partnership," available on the USCCB website at http://www.usccb.org/issues-and-action/marriage-and-family/upload/Grabowski-NPIM.pdf.
20. For a thoughtful treatment of the bond of marriage as God's offer of faithfulness sustaining human freedom, see Walter Kasper, *Theology of Christian Marriage*, trans. David Smith (New York: Crossroad Publishing Co., 1991), 21–24, 49.

household: "'Be angry but do not sin; do not let the sun go down on your anger' (Eph 4:26). My advice is never to let the day end without making peace in the family."[21] Following the practice of the Liturgy of the Hours, many families do a nightly examination of conscience in which they ask forgiveness of one another and of the Lord for the hurts and offenses that they gave to one another during the day — including parents asking forgiveness of their children when necessary. This practice then forms the basis for the family's regular participation in the penitential rite in the Mass and in the sacrament of Reconciliation. Christian perfection means facility in seeking and granting forgiveness.[22] This praxis of daily reconciliation is extended into a family's patterns of communication by habituation to simple phrases, as Pope Francis frequently observes: "In the family, 'three words need to be used. I want to repeat this! Three words: "Please," "Thank you," "Sorry." Three essential words!'"[23]

If the grace of the sacrament makes possible "the mutual submission out of reverence for Christ" (cf. Eph 5:21) of husband and wife in the form of practices such as regular and effective communication, collaboration in household tasks, and shared decision-making, this too has a counterpart in the relationship between parents and children. While underage children are called to "obey your parents [in the Lord]" (Eph 6:1b) and to "honor your father and mother" (Eph 6:2a; cf. Ex 20:12; Dt 5:16), Saint John Paul II points out that parents owe a certain "honor" to their children as well by acknowledging their value as persons and seeking their good above the parent's own interests.[24] After all, children of whatever age belong first and foremost to God rather than their parents. Parents, as "the first teachers of their children in the faith" are entrusted with forming them and fostering the gift of faith infused in them at

---

21. *Amoris Laetitia*, 104.
22. The Gospels themselves make this point in various ways. For example, in the Sermon on the Mount, Jesus' challenge to his disciples to "be perfect, just as your heavenly Father is perfect" (Mt 5:48) follows upon his exhortation to forgive and love even one's enemies. This is reinforced by the petition of the Lord's prayer, "and forgive us our debts, as we forgive our debtors" (Mt 6:12), as well as Jesus' explicit teaching that his disciples must forgive not "seven times but seventy-seven times" (Mt 18:22c). In this last case, the teaching introduces the dramatic parable of the unforgiving servant, which provides a grim illustration of the dangers of unforgiveness (Mt 18:21–35). All biblical citations are from the NABRE.
23. *Amoris Laetitia*, 133.
24. *Gratissimam Sane*, 15.

baptism.[25] This faith, along with the other infused theological virtues, deepens and matures in the family's daily practices of mutual prayer, witness, and service. These activities of the domestic church are aimed at enabling children to encounter the Lord, not as a one-time event but on an ongoing — even daily — basis.[26] It is then that children can hear and respond to the Lord's call to them — to their primary baptismal vocation to holiness and later to a specific state of life.[27]

The healing graces communicated in the sacrament of Marriage with the daily praxis of service and mutual care in the household effect "an apprenticeship in self-mastery" in which the virtue of chastity orders a couple's sexual drives and relationship toward the goods of life and the gift of self in love.[28] Sexual intimacy serves as a mirror for the other forms of intimacy needed in a healthy marriage — verbal/emotional, physical (but not genital), and spiritual; and the interplay among these aspects of closeness is facilitated by chastity.[29] The lived witness of a couple's mutual love expressed through tenderness, affection, and daily service in turn aids their children in acquiring the virtue of chastity and, through it, the freedom to respond to God's call to make a gift of themselves in marriage, consecrated single life, religious life, or priesthood. The couple's generosity in welcoming children as gifts, whether through birth

---

25. See the blessing of the father in the Rite of Baptism: "God is the giver of all life, human and divine. May he bless the father of this child. He and his wife will be the first teachers of their child in the ways of faith. May they be also the best of teachers, bearing witness to the faith by what they say and do, in Christ Jesus our Lord." The text is from the Catholic Liturgical Library and is available at: http://www.catholicliturgy.com/index.cfm /fuseaction/Textcontents/index/4/subindex/67/textindex/7.

26. See Pope Francis' words at the beginning of his Apostolic Exhortation, *Evangelii Gaudium*: "I invite all Christians, everywhere, at this very moment, to a renewed personal encounter with Jesus Christ, or at least an openness to letting him encounter them; I ask all of you to do this unfailingly each day" (3).

27. On the universal call to holiness and the parallels in the way this is lived out in the family and in the monastery, see Kent J. Lasnoski, *Vocation to Virtue: Christian Marriage as a Consecrated Life* (Washington, DC: The Catholic University of America Press, 2014), esp. 35–87. For a theological reflection and practical guide to the mission of parents in this regard, see John and Claire Grabowski, *Raising Catholic Kids for Their Vocations* (Charlotte, NC: TAN Books, 2019).

28. Among the most profound philosophical treatments of the transformative effects of love is that of Karol Wojtyla, *Love and Responsibility*, trans. H. T. Willetts (New York: Farrar, Straus, and Giroux, 1981; rpt. San Francisco: Ignatius Press, 1993), esp. 45–210. The same process is treated through the lens of Scripture in the *Theology of the Body* catecheses. For an overview, see Burke, 181–240; and Thomas Petri, O. P, *Aquinas and the Theology of the Body: The Thomistic Foundations of John Paul II's Anthropology*, Thomistic Ressourcement Series (Washington, DC: The Catholic University of America Press, 2016), 127–97.

29. For a practical look at the interplay between the various forms of intimacy and the virtue of chastity in the life of a couple, see John and Claire Grabowski, *One Body*), 121–57.

or adoption, and caring for life — especially in its vulnerable stages (in the very young, the disabled, the elderly, or those without the support of a family) in and outside the family's home — reinforces the connection between the love and the family's mission to serve life.[30]

The synergy between Baptism and Marriage in forming the foundation of the family as a domestic church and effecting the ongoing healing of its members is reinforced by the subsequent initiation of their children through Baptism and, later, Confirmation.[31] These sacraments ensure that each member of the family has the same wellspring of grace upon which to draw — a wellspring refreshed in the Sacrament of Reconciliation. However, all of these sacraments ultimately draw their efficacy from and point families toward the Eucharist, "the source and summit" of their life as a domestic church.[32]

THE EUCHARIST: HEART OF THE DOMESTIC CHURCH

Recent Church teaching has highlighted the close relationship between the Eucharist and the family founded in marriage. Saint John Paul II taught: "The Eucharist is the very source of Christian marriage. The Eucharistic Sacrifice, in fact, represents Christ's covenant of love with the Church, sealed with His blood on the Cross. In this sacrifice of the New and Eternal Covenant, Christian spouses encounter the source from which their own marriage covenant flows, is interiorly structured and continuously renewed."[33] This recalls the Council's teaching that the marriage covenant comes into being through the couple's "conjugal covenant of irrevocable personal consent" in which they give themselves to each other.[34] Hence the self-gift of couples draws its life from and is "continuously renewed in the self-gift of Christ the Bridegroom to the Church in the meal of the New Covenant. Receiving the Body of Christ together, the members of the Christian family are formed into one body with one another and joined to the larger body of Christ. Commenting

---

30. On "manifold service to life" as the heart of the family's mission, see *Familiaris Consortio*, 41.

31. Of course, the Eucharist is also one of the sacraments of initiation, but because of its import it will be treated separately in the next section.

32. See *Lumen Gentium*, 11; cf. *Catechism of the Catholic Church* 1324.

33. *Familiaris Consortio*, 57.

34. *Gaudium et Spes*, 48

on this insight into the nuptial character of the Eucharist, Pope Benedict XVI states: "The Eucharist inexhaustibly strengthens the indissoluble unity and love of every Christian marriage. By the power of the sacrament, the marriage bond is intrinsically linked to the eucharistic unity of Christ the Bridegroom and his Bride, the Church (cf. Eph 5:31–32)."[35]

To these theological insights, Pope Francis appends some further considerations. Especially relevant to our focus here is his insistence in *Evangelii Gaudium* and in the famous footnote of *Amoris Laetitia* chapter eight (note 351) that "the Eucharist … is not a prize for the perfect, but a powerful medicine and nourishment for the weak."[36] It is worth recalling that even classical sacramental theology has recognized this medicinal quality of the Eucharist. Reception of the Body and Blood of the Lord forgives venial sins and helps to heal our attachments to sin.[37] Hence the sacrament to which the whole of a Christian family's life is ordered is also a key source of its healing. Furthermore, building on the insights of his two predecessors on the socially formative nature of the Eucharist, Pope Francis insists that participation in the Eucharist makes concrete demands of us in regard to charity and solidarity with others. He observes that Saint Paul's warnings to the Corinthians about discerning the Body of the Lord and receiving it worthily (1 Cor 11:17–34) had to do with the scandal of divisions in the community based on distinctions of wealth and class. Instead, Christians are called to a different praxis; he writes: "For their part, open and caring families find a place for the poor and build friendships with those less fortunate than themselves."[38] Fed and formed by the Body of Christ they receive, Christian families can be the Body of Christ in the world through their solidarity with the poor and the vulnerable. Practices of witness, hospitality, service, and simplicity of life in resistance to the "throwaway culture" around them

---

35. Apostolic Exhortation, *Sacramentum Caritatis*, 27.

36. *Evangelii Gaudium*, 47; cf. *Amoris Laetitia*, 305, m. 351.

37. Thomas Aquinas preached in a homily for the feast of Corpus Christi (which was instituted during his lifetime): "No other sacrament has greater healing power; through it sins are purged away." The Church includes an excerpt of the homily in the Office of Readings for the Feast. A fuller version of the text can be found at: https://www.crossroadsinitiative.com/media/articles/wonderfulbanquet/. Furthermore, Preface I of the Most Holy Eucharist in the Roman Missal says, "As we drink his Blood that was poured out for us, we are washed clean."

38. *Amoris Laetitia*, 183.

are sustained by their regular participation at the table of the Lord.[39]

But there is a second table at the center of the Christian family's life, intimately connected to the first in numerous ways. This is the family dinner table. This table, too, feeds and forms those around it as parents, children, extended family, and guests come together to share faith, food, and fellowship. The family dinner is a time of celebration where those around it can open their hearts and lives to one another in conversation. Time spent in conversation around the dinner table is never wasted — it builds and enriches relationships between spouses, siblings, parents and children, grandparents and other relatives, and visitors to the family's home. Enriched by the rhythms of the liturgical calendar, it can be a coming together in either feasting or fasting in the quality and amount of food that is shared.[40] Penitential days and seasons reinforce and give liturgical momentum to a family's decision to opt for simplicity of life in solidarity with those who have less. During special seasons of the liturgical year (Advent, Christmas, Lent, Easter), families might add extra prayer around the table by adding a Scripture reading or devotional practice such as lighting a candle on an Advent wreath or placing an ornament on a Jesse tree. Such practices around the dinner table concretize the liturgical seasons within the home and imbue a family's calendar with the bright hues of the liturgical seasons. They also draw this table closer to the Eucharistic table at the center of the family's life.

Making it a point to attend church together serves to underscores the centrality of Eucharist in the family's life and weekly calendar. As Pope Francis notes: "The family's communal journey of prayer culminates by sharing together in the Eucharist, especially in the context of the Sunday rest. Jesus knocks on the door of families, to share with them the Eucharistic supper (cf. Rev 3:20)."[41] The pause in the hectic schedules of many families afforded by both of these tables is vital. Not for nothing

---

39. On ways in which families can live the vow of poverty, which parallels that made in monastic life, see Lasnoski, 179–88.

40. On the formative nature of a family's eating practices, see Julie Rubio, *Family Ethics: Practices for Christians* (Washington, DC: Georgetown University Press, 2010), 128–63. For a deeper look at practices of eating shaped by the rhythms of the liturgical year, see Siobhan Benitez, "Table of Sacrifice, Table of Plenty: Toward a Sacramental Family Food Ethic" (PhD diss., The Catholic University of America, 2019).

41. *Amoris Laetitia*, 318.

does Pope Francis observe that the Sunday liturgy is celebrated in the context of a day of rest. From the earliest parts of the Church's history, Christians celebrated the Lord's Day as a day of rest from work as well as a day to come together in worship very much like the way in which our Jewish brothers and sisters observe the Sabbath. Far from a mere legal requirement, the third commandment corresponds to a basic anthropological need for leisure, festal celebration, and worship.[42] In giving the commandment, the Decalogue itself recalls creation, which culminates in the worship of the seventh day (see Ex 20:8-11; Dt 5:12-15; cf. Gn 2:1-4). Families are thus freed from the cycle of empty busyness created by the oscillation between work and endless scheduled activities, none of which quite qualifies as genuine recreation.[43] When families pause from their hectic schedules at the two tables, they acknowledge the centrality of God in their lives and truly discover the source of their life as a domestic church.

In addition to claiming space within a family's calendar and daily life, nourishment at the dinner table and the Eucharistic table make a further claim upon Christian families. They remind those gathered of the need to make a space for silence within their lives and homes in a noisy world filled with the clamor of media and technological distractions.[44] Even the conversation around the family dinner table trains members of a family to listen as the conversation passes between and among persons. But even more, without this silence in our homes we cannot hear the "still small voice" (1 Kgs 19:12d) of the Lord who speaks

---

42. This is a recurring theme and focus of the great twentieth-century Thomistic philosopher Josef Pieper. See especially *Leisure, the Basis of Culture*, trans. Gerald Malsbary (Random House, 1963; rpt. San Francisco: Ignatius, 2009); *In Tune with the World: A Theory of Festivity*, trans. Richard and Clara Winston (South Bend, IN: St. Augustine's Press, 1999); and *Happiness and Contemplation*, trans. Richard and Clara Winston (South Bend, IN: St. Augustine's Press, 1998).
43. This cycle is what Pieper referred to as "the workaday world" to which liturgical celebration is the antidote; cf. *Leisure, the Basis of Culture*, 90-91.
44. See the insightful work of Robert Cardinal Sarah and Nicolas Diat, *The Power of Silence: Against the Dictatorship of Noise*, trans. Michael Miller (San Francisco: Ignatius Press, 2016).

within our hearts, our homes, or wherever we pause to pray.[45] In praying within their families, it is important for parents and children to recall that prayer is not just about talking to (or at) God — it is listening for His voice and discerning it from among all of the other voices we hear within ourselves and in the world around us. This spiritual capacity forms the members of a family to fully enter into the Liturgy in which the Lord speaks in Word and Sacrament.

CONCLUSION

This paper has asserted that Baptism, Marriage, and the Eucharist, joined to regular practices within the life of a family in the context of the liturgical year, offer pathways to healing to its members. This is not to deny the healing offered in the other sacraments, such as Reconciliation or the Anointing of the Sick. Certainly the latter can be an opportunity to encounter Jesus the Healer for those in a situation to receive it.[46] The sacrament of Reconciliation is an underutilized and sometimes unrecognized resource for Christians seeking to respond to their fundamental baptismal vocation to holiness and to grow in virtue.[47] Our contention is that these are not the only sacraments that are capable of communicating healing grace to families seeking to live out their call to be communities of prayer, witness, and service as domestic churches.

But this healing is not an end in itself, so that families can withdraw from the world and flourish within the walls of their homes.[48] The fam-

---

45. The Hebrew phrase ḍaqqāh dəmāmāh qōw, sometimes translated "a light, silent sound," is paradoxical. How does one understand — or hear — a "silent sound" or a "still voice"? The phrase points to the mysterious nature of God's communication to us in prayer. It also contrasts with the great signs that had heralded God's revelation of himself to Moses and the Israelites on the same mountain in Exodus — "a strong and violent wind," "an earthquake," and "fire" (see 1 Kgs 19:11–12; cf. Ex 19:16–19; 33:18–23).

46. Such persons are not simply the terminally ill or those in the process of dying, but can include persons dealing with chronic physical or mental health issues or those undergoing surgery.

47. See the insightful collection of essays edited by Jana Bennett and David Cloutier, *Naming Our Sins: How Recognizing the Seven Deadly Vices Can Renew the Sacrament of Reconciliation* (Washington, DC: The Catholic University of America Press, 2019).

48. This is a not infrequent reading of the book by Rod Dreher, *The Benedict Option: A Strategy for Christians in a Post-Christian Nation* (New York: Sentinel, 2017) as applied to the situation of families in an increasingly post-Christian United States. This is not an entirely fair characterization of Dreher's work, modeled as it is on the Benedictine Rule lived in early medieval monasteries, which were not enclosed islands of prayer, work, study, and virtue, but centers of evangelization for the Barbarian people who occupied the territory of the western half of the Roman Empire after its fall.

ily is indeed called to be "the nearest hospital," ministering to persons and families outside of itself. In this way, Christian families can themselves be "the principle agents of the family apostolate" of the Church.[49] The active involvement of families and indeed of all of the baptized is surely part of what is "new" in the "New Evangelization."[50] Encountering Christ in the "field hospital of the Church" and its nearest iteration in the domestic church, the members of families, though they themselves are convalescent sinners, can invite other wounded persons to encounter the same healing touch of the Great Physician.

DISCUSSION QUESTIONS

1. What are four effects of the grace of the Sacrament of Marriage according to the *Catechism of the Catholic Church* (1641–1642)?
2. Can you identify a time when you experienced healing through your reception of a sacrament? What was the sacrament, and what was the fruit of this healing?
3. Identify three regular practices within your household that help its members draw on the healing effects of the sacraments. What are two additional practices you believe you should add to these?
4. In *Evangelii Gaudium*, Pope Francis teaches that: "Every Christian is challenged, here and now, to be actively engaged in evangelization" (120). How are you responding to this challenge in the daily life of your household?

---

49. *Amoris Laetitia*, 200.
50. On the need for all of the baptized to be actively engaged in the New Evangelization, see *Evangelii Gaudium*, 120.

CHAPTER FIVE

Focusing on Families: Nurturing Catholic Identity and Promoting Social Change through Family Practices

JULIE HANLON RUBIO

Santa Clara University

FIVE QUICK TAKES

1. Catholic family life is an unjustly overlooked focus of theological and even pastoral inquiry.
2. Catholic social teaching cannot be properly understood unless it is rooted in an understanding of both the family's role in the social order and its socially transformative mission.
3. Family life is not merely ordered to the personal good of the members; it is a social reality ordered toward the common good of society.
4. The consistent focus on families in the documents comprising the Catholic social thought "canon" suggests their fundamental importance as sites where identity is formed and society is shaped from the ground up.
5. Simple family practices such as eating, tithing, and serving are powerful, if underappreciated, engines of social transformation.

I have spent most of my twenty-plus years as a Catholic social ethicist focusing on the family. This makes me something of an anomaly in academic theological circles. In 1991, when I decided to write my dissertation on Catholic social thought (hereafter CST) and the family, I did not anticipate that this choice would be controversial. It turns out, however, that Catholic theologians who lean "liberal" tend to worry that talking about family will deflect attention from more pressing social issues, such as poverty, the environment, immigration, and racism. Theologians who lean "conservative" are more likely to view family as socially important, but their interests often lie in historical theology, sexual ethics, or fundamental moral theology rather than CST. Wanting to talk about family *and* CST is unusual, especially when one's focus is on the daily lives of families, a topic that many academics view as "pastoral" and thus less worthy of serious theological attention. Ordinary Catholics, too, are often wary of what I call "family ethics," perhaps because it does not quite fit with either the social justice agenda or the agenda of those who care deeply about sex and marriage.

Despite these disconnects, official Catholic teaching has consistently attended to the significance of family, and this is why the topic of this symposium — *Catholic family life* — is so important. Because the ethical choices of families shape persons, communities, Church, and society (and vice versa), family practices should concern all of us — liberals and conservatives (and those who find those labels inadequate), scholars, pastoral ministers, and people in the pews. In CST, families are called the first cell of society, domestic churches, and schools of virtue where, ideally, children and adults learn how to be good people, faithful Catholics, and active citizens. Catholic teaching understands family as a crucial part of the social order and a key to the creation of a civilization of love. Yet the potential of this thinking remains unrealized due to insufficient attention to the practical questions of daily life and counterproductive ideological and cultural divides in the Church. I want to argue that by focusing on practices of ordinary family life, Catholics can find common ground and take up potentially transformative work. In this chapter, I will lay out the problem of insufficient attention to families; highlight the contributions of CST to family ethics; illustrate how this framework can be applied in concrete practices; and show how theologians across the ideological spectrum are doing innovative work that reveals the possibilities of focusing on families. Attending to family life could bring Catholics together, deepen Catholic identity, and contribute to the healing of a broken world.

INSUFFICIENT ATTENTION TO FAMILIES

Catholic theologians do not pay a whole lot of attention to family life. Consider the annual meetings of the major Catholic theological academic societies in the United States — the Catholic Theological Society of America, the College Theology Society, Catholic Theological Ethics in the World Church, and the Academy of Catholic Theology. Of these, only the CTS has a section dedicated to marriage and family, and this section was recently broadened in scope due to lack of interest. If information available online is accurate, no society has chosen family as a theme for its annual meeting, though the CTS will do so in 2020. (I worry about attendance.) In my own experience of twenty-five years of presenting at academic conferences, I have noticed a pattern. If my paper is about a controversial issue in sexual ethics, the room will be filled, but if I am talking about *family life*, the crowd will be small. Notice, too, that the most visible media commentators during the recent Synod on the family, as well as those who have written about it since, often did not have expertise in theology on the family, perhaps because so few theologians do. To be sure, the Pontifical John Paul II Institute for Studies on Marriage and Family at The Catholic University of America offers a strong counterpoint to my claim, but the need for a separate institute is perhaps more evidence of the problem I describe. Moreover, even when academics do engage in reflection on family, their writing tends to be more philosophical than practical, and I hope we all can agree on the need for more *practical theological reflection* on the family. This is why I use the term "family ethics," to encourage recognition of family life as a legitimate area of academic theological interest.[1]

Although I will argue below that CST has much more to say about families than most Catholics realize, we would not need to host a symposium (or launch a movement?) if we already had everything we needed. Unless the Catholic social tradition is read carefully with a trained eye, a modern reader might miss its focus on the family. Arguably, only *Familiaris Consortio* (1981) fully addresses the social mission of the family, even if *Casti Connubii* (1930) and *Amoris Laetitia* (2016) also consider social context in their otherwise mostly internal treatments of familial relations. Much Catholic attention has gone, understandably, to moral norms in sexual ethics and to canon law on marriage and divorce. Social issues such as poverty and immigration are most often treated apart from family. I see the ramifications of this lack of attention when I speak to diocesan priest convocations. While I am grateful to have several days to talk with priests about family ethics in relation to parish life, I

1. The relative lack of interest in family ethics in academic theology is particularly puzzling given the strong interest in family among scholars in sociology, psychology, and social work (e.g., Bradford Wilcox, Stephanie Coontz, Jessica Calarco, Andrew Cherlin, and Robert Putnam).

am always distressed to hear that previously, their formal education has rarely engaged these topics. Most priests, regardless of their ideological leanings, welcome the space to reflect on what they can do to support and empower families in their parish communities. Similarly, I have found both students and adult Catholics with whom I have the opportunity to interact in parishes and universities to be hungry for theological reflection on the ethical shape of their family lives. I am sure that others who share their research on the family have had similar experiences. The work we do at the Symposium is needed.

FAMILIES IN CST

Though family life has not been the subject of much Catholic theological analysis, connections between family and society have marked CST from its very beginnings. Elsewhere, I have summarized this tradition at length, but here allow me to highlight the contributions of Pope Leo XIII, who established the central place of family in Catholic thinking about the social order, and Saint John Paul II, who gave to families a socially transformative mission.[2]

Pope Leo XIII wrote *Rerum Novarum* in response to the growing social crisis brought about by industrialization, and yet his prescriptions for change were directed to governments, communities, *and* families. Most European movements for social change at this time advocated some government action, but they also hoped for a reconstruction of the social order through small groups organized around professions that brought workers and owners together.[3] These visionaries believed that society had lost its organic unity and had become impersonal.[4] Out of this concern came proposals for regulation of industry from government and smaller organizations with moral motivations. The goal was restoring humanity to society by reinvigorating local community with help from above (government) *and* below (community).

---

2. Material in this section is drawn from Julie Hanlon Rubio, *Family Ethics: Practices for Christians* (Washington, DC: Georgetown University Press, 2010), 37–65.
3. Marvin L. Krier Mich, *Catholic Social Teaching and Movements* (Mystic, CT: Twenty-Third Publications, 2001), 6–10.
4. Mich, 14.

Rerum Novarum follows this pattern in decrying the inhumanity of industrialization and calling for government efforts to secure a just wage, unions, and a safety net for the poor, but it also devotes a great deal of attention to family, community, and religion. Leo did not adopt a utopian model; he accepted that suffering would dominate life for the majority, but offered a social solution that relied on the work of intermediary associations.[5] Although these sections of the document are not always well remembered by contemporary Catholic scholars who tend to focus on *Rerum Novarum's* call for reform from above, they are nonetheless crucial to Leo XIII's social ethic.[6]

Leo XIII's vision of social transformation centered religion and families in ways that challenge assumptions of the political right and left then and now. Later Catholic social documents would correct for Leo's acceptance of social class structure by embracing the legitimate struggle on the part of the disenfranchised, but this development did not negate the import of Leo's essential insights. Progress is often slow in coming, and major political changes are not always possible. A belief in gradual social change from below grounds Leo's focus on the right of human beings gifted with reason to labor, provide for themselves, and plan for the future.[7] His defense of the person and the family as prior to the state leads him to disapprove of interference by the state with the right of workers to provide for their families. Even though he affirms a positive duty of the state to aid struggling families, his hope lies elsewhere.[8]

While modern readers rightly question Leo's confidence that social inequality is natural and his claim that "humanity must remain as it

---

5. Mich, 21.

6. For instance, Charles Curran says pre-Vatican II CST does "not give central importance to the change of heart," and cites as an example *Rerum Novarum*, which only mentions the significance of religion in the last paragraph. Curran, *Catholic Social Teaching 1891–Present: A Historical, Theological, and Ethical Analysis,* Moral Traditions (Washington, DC: Georgetown University Press, 2002), 46. In his summary of the central themes of *Rerum Novarum*, Marvin Krier Mich highlights the economic teachings and refers only briefly to the role of the Church in educating citizens, *Catholic Social Teachings and Movements*, 20–21. He labels Pope Leo XIII's claim that "disorder in society is at root a moral and religious issue," 23–24, "arrogant." David J. O'Brien and Thomas A. Shannon's summary of *Rerum Novarum* in their *Catholic Social Thought: The Documentary Heritage* (Maryknoll, NY: Orbis Books, 2003) does refer readers to the moral critique of Pope Leo XIII, but identifies advocacy of "human rights in the economic order" as his major contribution, 12–13.

7. *Rerum Novarum* (1891), in O'Brien and Shannon, eds., *Catholic Social Thought*, no. 5.

8. O'Brien and Shannon, nos. 6, 10, and 9.

is,"[9] his consistent return to religion and the home as fundamental to the amelioration of the social problem is worth attending to. Leo does not reject political solutions, but he insists that the meaning of this life is unclear without an understanding of the world to come. This is the foundation of his claim that Christian faith allows people to see that money and possessions have only relative worth, and virtue must be cultivated so that resources are used well and shared.[10] Though the pope does not name the family as the sole locus of these lessons in virtue, his quarrel with socialism is rooted in a concern for the family as the crucible within which Christian faith inspires a desire to live well.

Leo's treatment of the "private" moral life of families and communities is significant as well. Just as the employer is to recognize the human and religious needs of workers, workers are to labor well and live frugally, avoiding envy, so that their wages will meet their needs.[11] If Leo misjudges how much nonviolent coercion will be needed to motivate governments act justly, he does understand the need for families to "study economy" and virtue, for labor groups to form their members in faith and morals as well as advocate for common needs,[12] and for all persons to practice charity, whatever their station in life.[13]

The Church and smaller communities such as families are central to Leo's argument because, as he sees it, only they have the power to change hearts and encourage virtue. He believes that free persons who form families, labor to provide for themselves, join with others in local organizations and churches, and practice virtuous living will form more humane communities. Leo's social analysis of the impact of industrialization on families and his stress on the role of intermediary groups like families provide a social ethic that speaks to Christians of their obligations in public life, in local communities, and at home.[14]

---

9. *Ibid.*, no. 14.

10. *Ibid.*, no. 19.

11. *Ibid.*, no. 34.

12. *Ibid.*, nos. 42–43.

13. *Ibid.*, no. 45.

14. Pope Leo XIII can justly be criticized for trusting too much in the Church's ability to train the faithful in virtue. He does not offer a perfect solution, but his concern with the "private" realm in this document remembered as the founding statement of CST is notable.

It might seem that CST's emphasis on the significance of families and intermediary associations was lost after Vatican II, but the structure of *Gaudium et Spes* suggests continuity and development, rather than rupture. Not everyone sees it that way. In a commentary on *Gaudium et Spes*, social ethicist David Hollenbach highlights the document's strong claims about human dignity, the social responsibilities of persons, and the relationship between Church and world.[15] He then discusses the sections on justice, human rights, and war, while skipping over the sections on family and culture.[16] Hollenbach misses an opportunity to show how the council's understanding of human dignity and social responsibility is advanced through a systematic treatment of ever-larger social groupings, beginning with families.[17] The structure is not accidental, but rather brings together key pieces of the CST heritage, linking the meaning of human life revealed in Christ to the dignity of individuals marked by sin and grace, to family life that is a "school for deeper humanity," to culture, and only then to national economic policy and international politics. Reading this fundamentally important social document without attention to family and culture neglects the role of intermediary associations and exacerbates a problematic tendency in modern Christian social ethics to place all hope in politics. We need to pay attention to the consistent focus on families in CST.

The social teaching of Saint John Paul II further develops the role of the family in the transformation of the social order identified by his predecessors. He affirms the importance of lay responsibility for the world and suggests that bringing Christ to the world is not simply a matter of political activism, but rather something that should shape every aspect of one's life, including family life. Saint John Paul II's personalism marks all of his theological writing, especially his social teaching in *Laborem Exercens*, *Sollicitudo Rei Socialis*, *Centesimus Annus*, and *Familiaris Consortio*. All of these documents treat the responsibilities of Christians in

---

15. David Hollenbach, "Commentary on *Gaudium et Spes* (Pastoral Constitution on the Church in the Modern World)" in Kenneth Himes, ed., *Modern Catholic Social Teaching: Commentaries and Interpretations* (Washington, DC: Georgetown University Press, 2005), 271–79.

16. Hollenbach, 279–84.

17. My former colleague, philosopher Gregory Beabout, taught me a great deal about *Gaudium et Spes* when we taught it together in 2002 and 2003 at Saint Louis University.

the world. When read through a personalist lens, two key themes stand out: personal responsibility for social injustice and the social mission of the family.

In *Sollicitudo Rei Socialis*, the pope focuses directly on political and economic issues that undermine human dignity. He is particularly concerned with the inequities that divide the world and the failure to achieve authentic human development, but his personalist concerns ensure that this is not simply a political document. As theologian Richard Gaillardetz comments, "The emphasis in the writing of John Paul II was placed more on the cultivation of Christian personalism that speaks to the sinfulness of the human heart as the root cause of social injustice."[18] As the pope sees it, poor countries are hampered by their lack of resources, and rich countries are limited by materialistic desires, which ensure that "dissatisfaction reigns."[19] He calls all citizens to take individual responsibility for authentic human development, with a concern for the whole person. He speaks of the option for the poor not simply as a priority for political decision-making, but as something that "affects the life of each Christian inasmuch as he or she seeks to imitate the life of Christ, but it applies equally to our social responsibilities and hence to our manner of living, and to the logical decisions to be made concerning the ownership and use of goods."[20] The example that follows is one of his most prophetic statements: "Private property is in fact under a social mortgage," and it begins to show how solidarity could function as a norm for families. In John Paul II's personalist social teaching, meeting "social responsibilities" means examining daily life. Because what he offers is a moral rather than a political ideology, even when it sounds more political, it applies first of all to families as the smallest of intermediary associations of the polis.[21]

---

18. Richard Gaillardetz, "The Ecclesiological Foundations of Modern Catholic Social Teaching," in Himes, ed., *Modern Catholic Social Teaching*, 77

19. Saint John Paul II, *Sollicitudo Rei Socialis*, 28, http://www.vatican.va/content/john-paul-ii/en/encyclicals/documents/hf_jp-ii_enc_30121987_sollicitudo-rei-socialis.html.

20. *Sollicitudo Rei Socialis*, 42.

21. *Ibid.*, 41. The pope's insistence that his offering is primarily theological seems designed to return attention to neglected aspects of CST and check efforts to associate it with specific political programs. It does not deny all interest in political solutions.

The pope's personalist approach to social change continues in *Centesimus Annus*, his most significant social encyclical. In it, he puts forward a distinctive understanding of the importance of the middle realm between individual and government. Notably, he recalls that *Rerum Novarum* was a defense not only of governmental action but also of families and other intermediary groups.[22] He offers a distinctively personalist understanding of solidarity as moral empathy and commitment. Social ethicist Daniel Finn writes that self-gift is as relevant to this document as it is to Saint John Paul II's writings on sexuality; this is a call to individual conversion.[23] There is also a deep concern for the "subjectivity" or character of society that implicates communities and inspires a desire to "help entire peoples," not just one's nearest neighbors.[24] Social responsibility means examining everyday choices and joining together with others in order to work for social change.

Personal responsibility for social change translates into a social mission for the family in *Familiaris Consortio*. The family becomes not a private haven where one escapes from the world, but a community with a mission that goes beyond itself. In *Familiaris Consortio*, Saint John Paul II defines the family as "a community of life and love" that has four major tasks. Each of these tasks has public dimensions. The first is the most obviously familial and the least obviously social. The family must "guard, reveal, and communicate love."[25] Saint John Paul II distinguishes himself from earlier popes by the inspired way in which he describes married love and demands that it rise to the heights for which it is destined. His personalist language represents an attempt to take seriously the importance that modern men and women give to spousal relationships. However, he insists that the love among family members is not an end in itself; but rather, the foundation for the rest of what the family does.

Second to love comes the task of "serving life." Parents have a responsibility to serve life by nurturing their own children *and* by bringing

22. Saint John Paul II, *Centesimus Annus*, 12, http://www.vatican.va/content/john-paul-ii/en/encyclicals/documents/hf_jp-ii_enc_01051991_centesimus-annus.html.
23. *Centesimus Annus*, 44s
24. Daniel Finn, "Commentary on *Centesimus Annus*," in Himes, ed., *Modern Catholic Social Thought*, 451, 455.
25. Saint John Paul II, *Familiaris Consortio*, 17, http://www.vatican.va/content/john-paul-ii/en/apost_exhortations/documents/hf_jp-ii_exh_19811122_familiaris-consortio.html.

life to the world.[26] Serving life is not only having children but educating them, which includes instilling "the essential values of human life," especially the ideas that possessions do not make human beings what they are and the responsibility of adopting a simple lifestyle.[27] The pope also affirms that when parents teach their children about the Gospel, "they become fully parents, in that they are begetters not only of bodily life but also of the life that through the Spirit's renewal flows from the cross and resurrection of Christ."[28] This emphasis on the spiritual is extended when the pope uses the term "spiritual fecundity" to name the responsibility of families to share with others the self-giving love they nurture within.[29]

By the time we reach the third task, it is clear that families are not simply oriented toward their own good, for "far from being closed in on itself, the family is by its nature and vocation open to other families and to society and undertakes its social role."[30] Families "cannot," Saint John Paul II holds, "stop short at procreation and education;"[31] they have distinct social and political duties.[32] Specifically, the pope asks families to do three things: (1) practice hospitality, opening their table and their home to others, (2) become politically involved, assisting in the transformation of society, and (3) practice a preferential option for the poor, manifesting a "special concern for the hungry, the poor, the old, the sick, drug victims and those who have no family."[33] All of this is part of the social mission of the family, which is fundamental to a family's identity and calling.

Finally, the pope uses "domestic church" imagery to suggest that families have a responsibility to serve the church by being the church in their home.[34] As a "church in miniature," the family evangelizes its members, witnesses to the world, uses its home as a sanctuary (for rituals

---

26. *Familiaris Consortio*, 28.
27. *Ibid.*, 37.
28. *Ibid.*, 39.
29. *Ibid.*, 41.
30. *Ibid.*, 42
31. *Ibid.*, 44
32. *Ibid.*, 44 and 47.
33. *Ibid.*, 47.
34. *Ibid.*, 21.

of prayer and sacramentals), and serves the broader community — for like the Church, the family is a servant of humanity.[35] Here again, the emphasis is both on the social significance of practices in the home *and* on the sending forth of the family into the world. The pope's emphasis on the social responsibilities of the family implies that an internal focus is insufficient. Catholic teaching refuses to limit families by calling them just to care for their own.[36]

Some might worry that CST's distinctive view of family has been lost in recent years, but although Pope Francis does not contribute quite as much to a social ethic of the family as his predecessors, *Amoris Laetitia* continues the trajectory set in motion by Leo XIII and Saint John Paul II. Oppressive social forces acting upon families named in *Amoris Laetitia* include both problematic ways of thinking and harmful social structures. Pope Francis worries about "an extreme individualism which weakens family bonds" and encourages families to be "caught up with possessions and pleasures."[37] He connects the "throwaway culture," in which we buy things only to discard them when new things come along, to a temporary marriage culture in which partners are abandoned when they fail to satisfy.[38] These pervasive ways of thinking can limit individuals' capacities to choose marriage and fidelity to their families. Francis also identifies problematic social structures that hurt families, including: insufficient affordable housing; a failure to recognize family rights (including the just wage); a failure to adequately respond to violence against and sexual exploitation of women and children; economic situations

---

35. *Ibid.*, 49–64. Lisa Sowle Cahill also attests to this emphasis in recent Catholic teaching on the family; see her *Family: A Christian Social Perspective* (Minneapolis: Fortress Press, 2000) 89–91.

36. Cahill claims that, "[r]eactions [to *FC*] that minimize the socially radical mission of the Christian family are not numerous and do not seem to have been widely influential," in her "Commentary on *Familiaris Consortio*," in Himes, ed., *Modern Catholic Social Teaching*, 383. However, many theologians downplay the social dimension of *FC* and few Catholic lay people identify with it. The transformative potential of the document remains unrealized. See, for example, Janet E. Smith, "The Family: A Communion of Persons," in Gregory R. Beabout, ed., *A Celebration of the Thought of John Paul II* (St. Louis: St. Louis University Press, 1998): 85-104; Donald A. Miller, *Concepts of Familial Love in Magisterial Catholic Teaching: From Vatican II thru Christifideles Laici* (San Francisco: San Francisco Scholars Press, 1996); Christopher West, "A Basic Theology of Marriage, available at www.christopherwest.com); and, as Cahill notes, the *Catechism of the Catholic Church* (New York: Doubleday, 1995), 446-62.

37. Francis, *Amoris Laetitia* (2016), https://w2.vatican.va/content/,dam/francesco/pdf/apost_exhortations/documents/papa-francesco_esortazione-ap_20160319_amoris-laetitia_en.pdf, no. 33.

38. *Ibid.*, 39.

that drive migration and trafficking; and inadequate support for single parents living in poverty.[39] Like Leo XIII, Francis realizes that there are forces beyond families' control that make their life difficult, attends to sources of their brokenness, and lifts up the potential of all families to be "light in the darkness of the world."[40]

Pope Francis is somewhat less attentive than Saint John Paul II to the social mission of families. His focus, instead, especially in chapter four of *Amoris Laetitia*, is on providing a down-to-earth description of married love. Still, he follows Saint John Paul II in stressing the openness that should be an essential mark of family life. Married couples are called to "go forth from their homes in a spirit of solidarity with others," to become "more than just two."[41] Rather than servings as refuges from the world, families are to allow familiar biblical stories of the Last Judgement, the parable of the great banquet, and Paul's instructions about inclusivity in the practice of the Lord's Supper to shape their home, their feasts, and their way of being in the world.[42]

From Pope Leo XIII to Pope Francis, CST places families in their social contexts and gives them a crucial social role. Though occupying a small percentage of most social documents, the consistent focus on families suggests their fundamental importance as sites where identity is formed and society is shaped from the ground up. While others may take up social justice apart from family or embrace family apart from social justice, CST attends to families and calls them to live distinctively in love and justice. The Catholic social vision cannot be separated from family life.

FAMILY PRACTICES

If the vision for families in Catholic social thought is as powerful as I have suggested, why is it not more influential? In my view, this radical vision is limited by: (1) a lack of attention to the everyday life of families in theology and (2) polarization that divides Catholics. These two problems are connected. Focusing on practices has the potential to bring CST

---

39. *Ibid.*, 42–49.
40. *Ibid.*, 66.
41. *Ibid.*, 181.
42. *Ibid.*, 183–186. (Mt 25:40, Lk 14:12–14, and 1 Cor 11:17–34.)

into the daily lives of the majority of Catholics and bridge divides among Catholics that limit the impact of both Catholic teaching on family and CST. Intentional practices provide a concrete way for Christian families to live out their distinctive calling. Elsewhere, I describe five practices: sex, prayer, eating, tithing, and serving in depth.[43] Here, I focus on the latter three.

I draw on the language of practice with gratitude to philosopher Alasdair MacIntyre, whose seminal work *After Virtue* re-established the importance of actions that shape persons in the contexts of their traditions, and to Protestant theologian Stanley Hauerwas, who refocused Christian ethics on the church's work of forming "a people of virtue — not just any virtue, but the virtues necessary for remembering and re-telling the story of a crucified savior."[44] I also join Catholic moral theologians who, in the last few decades, have pivoted from a focus on norms to a emphasize character, virtues, and practices. I argue that family practices such as eating, serving, and tithing, can be faithful ways of living out a Catholic family's social mission as articulated by Pope Leo XIII and Saint John Paul II.

Eating, an ordinary practice that families engage in every day, can become an intentional practice oriented toward love and solidarity. By setting aside time to gather, leaving behind pressing household tasks, work obligations, and phones, family members express their commitment to being together. Their willingness to eat a common meal rather than the meal of each one's choosing signals their capacity to sacrifice for each other. Participation in conversation about each other's days enables reconnection as stories are shared, remembered, and woven together, solidifying a family's identity and binding them together. As prayers are offered day after day, the joys, burdens, and concerns of each person become the joys, burdens, and concerns of a family.

Viewing eating as a family practice through the lens of CST entails seeing the import of the ordinary and pushing beyond it. Inspired by

---

43. See Rubio, *Family Ethics*.
44. Stanley Hauerwas, *The Peaceable Kingdom: A Primer in Christian Ethics* (Notre Dame, IN: University of Notre Dame Press, 1983), 103.

emerging CST on environmental ethics, Catholic families might attend to their food choices. Concern about climate change, water access, pollution, and biodiversity might lead them to limit meat and dairy consumption and incorporate more plant-based foods; limit packaged food products; and to buy more organic, seasonal, and regional foods. Concern for labor justice might lead them to shop at markets that pay fair wages and to buy fair trade products. A commitment to subsidiarity might ground a priority on regional food sourcing to support local businesses and build up local communities. A desire to avoid the vice of luxury could mean trying to honor all of these commitments by eating a simpler diet and limiting non-necessities like snack foods, desserts, and alcohol, rather than shopping only at high-end grocery stores. A desire to imitate Jesus's inclusive meal practice and Saint John Paul II's call to hospitality might inspire a welcoming table practice for friends, neighbors, and others who would otherwise eat alone. Though each particular choice may be small, when added together over time, this kind of intentional practice would enable Catholic families to take up their role in bringing about a new social order from the ground up.

Tithing is another intentional family practice with transformative power, but it is difficult for most families to achieve. A market economy is oriented to growth and needs increasing consumption in order to thrive. Buying and having more are the default. In this kind of system, it becomes almost impossible to feel as though one has enough. When individuals are asked to give out of their excess, many find that they have little left over to give. Perhaps this explains why most US families end up giving away only two or three percent of their income. Without the framework of an intentional practice, efforts to encourage more giving are limited. Renewed attention to the Old Testament tradition of tithing, reformulated for a contemporary context, has the potential to address the roadblocks most families experience and encourage greater generosity. Tithing does not require a rejection of all unnecessary goods but, for most, giving ten percent or more would mean living more simply than those around them by trimming food bills, buying secondhand, reducing entertainment costs, doing themselves what others pay to have done for them, questioning cultural norms, and taking care of what they have so that it lasts. It might even call them to question their most significant choices: where to live and how much to spend on children's education.

The transformative power of tithing comes both from the sacrifice families must take on and from the impact of their increased ability to give. For most, a decision to tithe would mean shared discernment about budgeting and doing without that would, ideally, bind them more closely together — at least after the initial debates about what to count as luxuries! If families were then able to double their average contribution to their parish (from one percent to two percent), the average parish would see an increase of nearly half a million dollars. If a good portion of the rest of the tithe, in keeping with the biblical origins of the practice and contemporary CST's preferential option for the poor, went to organizations devoted to alleviating poverty such as Catholic Charities or Catholic Relief Services, the impact could be enormous. Unlike early and medieval Christians, who saw tithing primarily in relation to their own salvation, modern Christians, aware of progress that has been made already, believe with confidence that poverty can be significantly further reduced. In practicing resistance to overconsumption and living into the virtue of solidarity, Christian families can live distinctively and contribute to social transformation.

Serving, too, can be a powerful family practice, if reoriented by a vision of discipleship inspired by CST. Most families engage in multiple forms of service to school, workplace, parish, and community. Service requirements are increasingly common, and it can seem as though service obligations (e.g., to attend auctions and golf tournaments, contribute to parish festivals and food pantries, run for a good cause, collect baby supplies, buy Christmas gifts, fill Thanksgiving baskets, beatify a property, etc.) are overwhelming, especially when laid on top of already busy schedules. The sort of service I recommend would require both a pruning of other obligations and a commitment to take up more significant service that involves spending time and building relationships with people in need, walking with them as they strive to transform their lives and the communities they inhabit. We cannot fulfill Leo XIII's vision of families humanizing a cold social order or Saint John Paul II's calls to hospitality, political action, and the option for the poor by attending fundraising dinners or writing checks from a distance. Pope Francis's emphasis on accompaniment is exactly right. How might that vision re-shape our ideas about family service?

As with tithing and eating, service can be an important practice both because of the countercultural choices it would require and because of the impact it could have. Imagine the discussions at family dinner tables about what commitments might have to be let go by parents and children? Perhaps children need only do one sport or activity a season, or perhaps the parish or community team rather than a traveling or se-lect team would be sufficient. Perhaps parents can decide to forgo the elaborate craft or cake for the class party and focus instead on helping to connect families with development organizations embedded in local communities. Imagine what families of means might be able to do if they got to know poor families and those who work with them, and were able to place their resources, connections, and expertise in the service of transformative programs such as developing affordable housing, build-ing community health clinics, bringing grocery stores to food deserts, helping moms in crisis pregnancy centers find permanent housing, par-ticipating in job training, and contributing to successful schooling and child care? Redirecting energy from less crucial forms of service to most-ly relational, developmental, and empowering forms could allow families to embrace the lofty vision of Catholic social thought on the family in their everyday lives.

COMMON GROUND, IDENTITY, AND SOCIAL CHANGE

But what about my second contention? Is there any reason to think that focusing on practices could bridge polarizing divides among Catholics? My experience as a theologian suggests it might be possible. Although it is true, as I suggested at the beginning of my talk, that formal theologi-cal attention to families has not been robust in academic theology, some theologians today do reflect on issues facing families and on practices of daily life. This is especially true of younger theologians, who are less tied to the liberal/conservative divides that have marked older generations of scholars. Highlighting the interesting ways they engage key issues will suggest that family life does matter to a range of Catholic theologians. It will also show how focusing on family practices can bring people together when they might otherwise stand apart.

The New Wine, New Wineskins initiative founded by moral theologian Bill Mattison was begun to bring theologians together at Notre Dame each summer on the premise that the post-Vatican II generation could find the common ground that had eluded their elders. Often, they do so by bracketing controversies over norms, focusing on problematic cultural contexts rather than ecclesial controversies, and imagining distinctive ways of living out Christian discipleship. Their emphasis on practices allow them to focus in on Catholic identity and social transformation. This, I suggest, is a way forward.

What does this look like? Let me first focus on theologians on the "left," who tend to be more interested in social ethics. If these theologians focus on social issues they see as more pressing than family, this does not mean that their work in social ethics has no relevance for family life. For instance, racism is an issue that tends to attract liberal theologians with less interest in family ethics. Yet advances in the conversation make it impossible to separate racial justice from family ethics. Racism is defined by moral theologian Bryan Massingale as unconscious bias, "a cultural phenomenon … a way of interpreting human color differences that pervades the collective convictions, conventions, and practices of American life."[45] If this is so, racism must be shaped in families, and families must be shaped by it. Pastoral theologian C. Vanessa White notes that African-American families face unique challenges as a result. "Some of our families are in survival mode, struggling with under- and unemployment, divorce, and single parenthood. Families are simply trying to ensure that their children are not victims of the violence that plagues our city."[46]

Puerto Rican theological ethicist MT Davila names anti-immigrant laws and sentiment as another dimension of racism in the United States,

45. Bryan N. Massingale, *Racial Justice and the Catholic Church* (Maryknoll, NY: Orbis, 2010), 15.

46. C. Vanessa White, "*Amoris Laetitia* and the Black Catholic Community," in Grant Gallicho and James F. Keenan, SJ, eds., *Amoris Laetitia: A New Momentum for Moral Formation and Pastoral Practice* (New York: Paulist, 2018), 17. See also Ta-Nahisi Coates, "The Black Family in the Age of Mass Incarceration," *The Atlantic* (October 2015), https://www.theatlantic.com/magazine/archive/2015/10/the-black-family-in-the-age-of-mass-incarceration/403246/.

noting that she and her children are vulnerable to being stopped by law enforcement and asked for proof of citizenship, because they "belong to groups of racialized others."[47] Even though racism is a structural sin, because it "interrupts our relationships with God and our relationships with one another," it also pertains to family ethics. Davila claims that Christian ethics must "define what it is to live in Christian hope and love in a broken world. Traditionally, though, this has been done from a standpoint that lacks a proper appreciation of the stories and lived realities of those victimized and dehumanized because of the color of our skin."[48] Racism shapes the lives of the three percent of Catholics who are African American and the forty percent of Catholics who are Latino, and of the many more who "white." It is nurtured in the home and in our racially divided parishes.[49] If we are to "love in a broken world," it cannot be separated from family ethics, as all three of these theologians imply.

But it is not just liberal theologians who link social injustice to family life. Conservative scholars, too, makes these connections. The Catholic University of America moral theologian David Cloutier's recent work on luxury asks tough questions about spending that most families would like to avoid.[50] After clearing away economic arguments for stimulating the economy through buying, Cloutier recovers the Christian tradition's aversion to the vice of luxury and shows how it degrades us. While conscious of the need for structural change to address economic inequality, he also raises questions about how luxurious living harms both the poor (who suffer from our relatively thin charitable giving) and the rich (who are deformed by excessive buying and having). Lest the majority who think of themselves as middle class believe they are off the hook, Cloutier meticulously works through the economic data, claims that on average, a family can live decently on less than $60,000 a year, and devises categories for surplus that allow for "festival goods" (including things like symposia dinners that happen occasionally), while calling for much

---

47. M.T. Davila, "Racialization and Racism," in James F. Keenan, ed., *Catholic Theological Ethics Past, Present, and Future* (Maryknoll, NY: Orbis, 2011), 316.

48. *Ibid.*, 317.

49. Katie Walker Grimes, *Christ Divided: Antiblackness as Corporate Vice* (Minneapolis: Fortress, 2017), 123-45.

50. David Cloutier, *The Vice of Luxury: Economic Excess in a Consumer Age* (Washington, D.C.: Georgetown University Press, 2015), 253-71.

higher levels of giving for the sake of those with less *and* those with more. In raising questions about what it means for families of means to live ethically, Cloutier joins sociologists such as Robert Putnam and Jessica Calarco, who draw attention to the ways that middle class and wealthy families disadvantage poor families by their choices about where to live, where to send their kids to school, and how to parent.[51]

If we cannot separate family ethics from economic inequality, we also cannot fail to talk about family disruption. In *Singleness and the Church: A New Theology of the Single Life,* moral theologian Jana Marguerite Bennett focuses on the stories of well-known single Christians from whom married Catholics can learn.[52] She deftly argues that in its desire to affirm family life, the Church has sometimes neglected widows, the divorced, and single parents. While acknowledging the extra burdens born by families headed by lone parents, Bennett focuses on what those families might need *and* what they might be able to teach. Given that about one-third of children in the United States live with an unmarried parent, it would be difficult to attend to the reality of Catholic family life without taking account of single-parent families. Bennett suggests that Catholic theology should address those who, for a range of reasons, parent alone. Ten percent of Christians are widowed, which is more than the percentage of Christians who are cohabiting.[53] Bennett recalls ancient Christian duties to care for the widow and the orphan and suggests reviving the early church practice of supporting an Order of Widows, which seems to have "enabled widows in particular communities to reciprocate the care they received.[54] She suggests the possibility of seeing them as spiritual models of the dependence on God to which all Christian aspire.[55] She profiles single mother Servant of God Dorothy Day, and suggests that Day's "decidedly unsaintly parenting" might be a helpful

51. Robert Putnam, *Our Kids: The American Dream in Crisis* (New York: Simon & Schuster, 2015) and Jessica Calarco, *Negotiating Opportunities: How the Middle Class Secures Advantages in School* (Oxford: Oxford University Press, 2018. See also, Dawn Marie Dow, *Mothering While Black* (Berkeley: University of California Press, 2019).

52. Jana Marguerite Bennett, *Singleness and the Church: A New Theology of the Single Life* (New York: Oxford University Press, 2017).

53. *Ibid.,* 133.

54. *Ibid.,* 141.

55. *Ibid.,* 141.

counter-witness in a culture that prizes "supernatural parenting."[56] Perhaps if two-parent families saw themselves in Day and acknowledged their own imperfections and dependence on others, they might be better able to see all families as part of the Body of Christ, the most important community to which we all belong. Family ethics, according to these two conservative thinkers, cannot ignore the power of consumerism and its connection to luxury or the reality of the many lone parenting families among us.

Among conservative theologians, I would also love, if I had time, to introduce you to the work of Kent Lasnoski, who views family through the lens of religious orders and imagines family life marked by prayer, labor, liturgy, and meals.[57] I would also love to highlight the more liberal work of social ethicists Nichole Flores on Latino family life and Emily Reimer-Barry on families struggling with HIV-AIDS.[58] But I would also hold up scholars I simply cannot with confidence place in liberal or conservative camps — like David Matzko McCarthy, whose narration of an open home in a neighborhood of open doors never fails to inspire my students; Kathryn Getek Solis, whose writing on family practices in the context of incarceration raises profound questions about family rights; and other writing on parenting, technology, infertility, pregnancy loss, time, money, and the quest for holiness.[59] What all of these younger theologians have in common is a love of the Catholic tradition, worries about contemporary culture, and a desire to inspire intentional discipleship in the diverse contexts of real families' lives.

A new generation of Catholic theologians, across ideological boundaries, is doing work that those of us who focus on family cannot afford to ignore. They provide a thicker account of challenges shaping family life and broaden our sense of what families might be called to do

---

56. *Ibid.*, 205–206.

57. Kent J. Lasnoski, *Vocation to Virtue: Christian Marriage as Consecrated* Life (Washington, D.C.: The Catholic University Press of America).

58. Nichole Flores, "Latina/o Families: Solidarity and the Common Good," *Journal of the Society of Christian Ethics* 33.2 (2013): 57-72 and Emily Reimer-Barry, *Catholic Theology of Marriage in the Era of HIV and AIDS* (Lanham, MD: Lexington, 2013).

59. David Matzko McCarthy, *Sex and Love in the Home* (London: SCM Press, 2004) and Katherine Getek Soltis, "Families and Incarceration," forthcoming in Jason King and Julie Rubio, eds., *Sex, Love, and Families* (Collegeville, MN: Liturgical, 2020). Other essays in King and Rubio take on the issues referenced in the text.

in the Church and the world. Remarkably, unlike their theologian elders and unlike many Catholics today, they can eat dinner together without alienating each other, and they can see how their hopes and worries overlap. What might a movement be able to accomplish if it looked for people like this in the Church as a whole? My bet is that ordinary Catholics would be better at this work than theologians if they were given the right opportunities. What if we invited them to the table and named our common concerns? Then we would have a broader base from which to construct the movement we have just begun to imagine. The potential of families is immense. I suggest that this potential can only be realized if we harness the power of CST's linkage of family and the social order and focus on the everyday practices that make social theory concrete and enable conversations across lines of difference that unnecessarily keep us apart. Pope Francis says that "the family lives its spirituality precisely by being at one and the same time a domestic church and a vital cell for transforming the world."[60] If this sounds daunting, it is good to know that we are not alone. Walking together, we might arrive somewhere new.

DISCUSSION QUESTIONS

1. Why do you think that family life is such an overlooked subject of inquiry in theology? What, in your opinion, should be done to overcome the dismissive attitude theologians have toward exploring the spiritual life and social mission of the family?
2. How does viewing Catholic social teaching through the lens of family life change your perspective of both?
3. The author argues that simple family practices such as eating, tithing, and serving enable Christian families to participate in the salvific mission of the Church and powerful engines of positive social change. In your opinion, what other family practices empower domestic church life to facilitate social transformation?

------

60. *Amoris Laetitia*, 324.

Catholic Family Life and the Social Context: Who Are We? What Are We Up Against? How Must We Respond?

I n this section, we'll explore the various challenges Catholic families face in America, and what the research can teach us about the best ways we can respond to these challenges in a manner that reflects the power of the Catholic vision of family life to evangelize the culture.

In the opening chapter, Mark Gray, the director of the CARA Catholic Poll and a senior research associate at the Center for Applied Research in the Apostolate, offers an eye-opening, thirty-thousand-foot flyover view of the socioeconomic, educational, and religious condition of the average American Catholic family.

Next, Helen Alvaré, professor of law at Antonin Scalia Law School, George Mason University, and consultant to the Permanent Observer Mission of the Holy See to the United Nations, offers her insights on the centrality of the Catholic understanding of sexuality not only to a healthy understanding of family life, but also to the Church's ability to effectively engage the culture on every level.

Finally, Pat Fagan, founder and director of the Marriage and Religion

Research Institute at The Catholic University of America, picks up the theme of the central importance of a proper understanding of the Catholic vision of love and sex to engage the culture. He also addresses the research exploring the important role Christian fathers play in forming godly, sexually mature adults.

CHAPTER SIX

Early Twenty-First Century American Catholic Families

Mark M. Gray, Ph.D.

Center for Applied Research in the Apostolate, Georgetown University

---

FIVE QUICK TAKES

1. Overall, only 17 percent of Catholic families regularly pray together.
2. Only 42 percent of weekly Mass-attending parents pray with their children.
3. Sixty-eight percent of Catholic children are not enrolled in any type of Catholic education or formation.
4. Of all adults, parents are the least likely to attend Mass weekly.
5. Only 8 percent of Catholic parents discuss faith topics daily as a family.

Understanding the state of the Catholic family in the United States requires the examination of trends related to marriage and fertility. Marriage is generally in decline in the United States. This is also the case in the Catholic Church, according to the General Social Survey. In the 2010s, 53 percent of Catholic adults are married. By comparison, 71 percent of this population was married in the 1970s. The number of marriages celebrated in the Catholic Church in the US has gone from 426,309 in 1970 to 143,082 in 2018 (a decline of 66 percent). At the same time, the number of self-identified Catholics has grown from 54.1 million in 1970 to 76.3 million in 2018 (an increase of 41 percent). As shown in this graph, the number of Catholics who have never married and the number of those who are divorced or separated have grown since the 1970s.

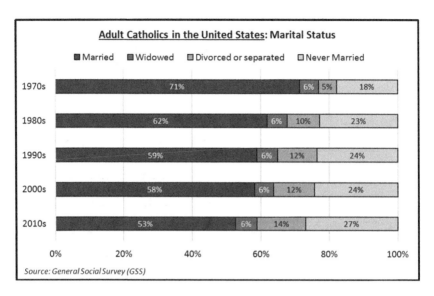

Although marriage is in decline, the number of children that Catholics have over the course of their lives is relatively unchanged. In recent decades, seven in ten or more adult Catholics indicate having at least one child. In the 2010s, 14 percent of adult Catholics have had one child, 25 percent have had two, 19 percent have had three, 9 percent have had four, and 8 percent have had five or more. One in four have not had children. The number of Catholics having five or more children has declined since the 1970s (14 percent to 8 percent), while the number having three has increased (20 percent to 25 percent).

These patterns of fertility are relatively independent of Catholic's beliefs about the "ideal number of children" that a family should have. In the 2010s, less than 1 percent believe having no children is ideal and only 2 percent believe one child is ideal. Most believe having either two or three children is ideal (42 percent and 32 percent, respectively). Eleven percent believe four children is ideal, and 13 percent believe five or more children is ideal. Beliefs among Catholics about these ideal numbers of children have been very similar in recent decades.

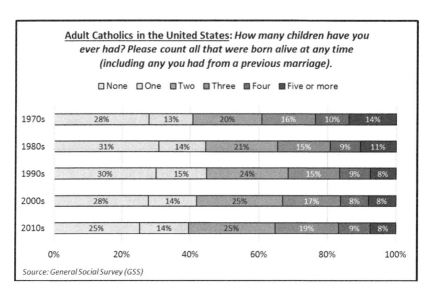

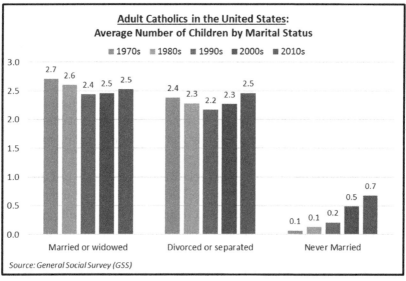

With fewer marriages and more stable fertility rates and beliefs about ideal family sizes, more never-married Catholics are having children. In the 1970s, never-married Catholics had an average of 0.1 children (i.e., one in ten having a child). In the 2010s, never-married Catholics have, on average, 0.7 children. By comparison, Catholics who have married typically have more than two children, on average.

Researchers at the National Center for Health Statistics note that "current low and late fertility and increased childlessness has been observed in all of Europe and in much of North America. This 'second demographic transition' is consistent with an observed increase in individual autonomy and a growth in gender equality. At the same time, there is the increase in socioeconomic activities competitive with childbearing."[1] They predict that "in the United States, childlessness may have plateaued or may continue to rise as this country adopts more of the demographic and social attributes recently seen in Europe." These researchers also note that "childbearing outside of marriage has increased significantly: the percentage of births occurring outside of marriage has increased from 33.2 percent in 2000 … to 41 percent in 2009."

On a national level, income is known to be related to decisions about family size. This has been especially evident since the Great Recession from 2007 to 2009 and the resulting slow economic recovery. Demographers at the Pew Research Center note that "a sharp decline in fertility rates in the United States that started in 2008 is closely linked to the souring of the economy that began about the same time."[2] According to the National Center for Health Statistics, "The 2017 TFR [Total Fertility Rate] for the United States of 1,765.5 was 16% below what is considered the level for a population to replace itself (2,100.0)."[3]

For the Church, another important dimension to consider is how children are being raised in the faith. Today, 4.7 million school-age children are enrolled in a Catholic school or parish-based religious education. By comparison, 9.9 million school-age children were enrolled in a Catholic school or parish-based religious education program in 1970.[4]

1. National Center for Health Statistics, "Transitions Between Childlessness and First Birth: Three Generations of U.S. Women," *Vital Health Statistics* 2, no. 153 (August 2011): 11.
2. Gretchen Livingston, "In a Down Economy, Fewer Births," *Pew Research Center Social and Demographic Trends,* October 12, 2011. https://www.pewsocialtrends.org/2011/10/12/in-a-down-economy-fewer-births/.
3. National Center for Health Statistics. "Births: Preliminary data for 2014" National Vital Statistics Reports; (1)68, 2019, pg. 4.
4. It is important to note that some of those enrolled in Catholic schools are not Catholic. According to the National Catholic Educational Association, 18.7 percent of students enrolled in the 2018–2019 school year were not Catholic.

One reality of the twenty-first century Catholic family that is immediately evident is that parents bear more of the responsibility of passing on the faith now than they did in the previous century.

CATHOLIC FAMILIES

In fall 2014, the Center for Applied Research in the Apostolate (CARA) at Georgetown University conducted a national poll of adult Catholics ages twenty-five to forty-five who were parents of a minor child to explore the twenty-first century Catholic family. This survey, completed in September and October 2014, included interviews with 1,014 self-identified Catholic parents, resulting in a sampling margin of error of ±3.1 percentage points. Using census and survey data, CARA estimated that there were approximately 15 million Catholic parents between the ages of twenty-five and forty-five in the United States in 2014.

Demographics

The median age of Catholic parents was thirty-seven (in other words, half were thirty-seven or younger, and half were thirty-seven or older). The Generation X respondents were between the ages of thirty-three and forty-five in 2014. Born between 1961 and 1981, this generation has no lived experience of the pre-Vatican II Church and came of age during a time of general peace and prosperity. The Millennial Generation respondents were between the ages of twenty-five and thirty-two in 2014. Born in 1982 or later, this generation has come of age primarily under the papacies of Benedict XVI and Francis and grew up using computers, the internet, and cellphones. As children and teenagers, they witnessed war after 9/11 and generally stagnant economic growth.

Generations Represented Among US Catholic Parents Ages 25 to 45 and All US Catholic Adults		
	Catholic Parents	**All Catholic Adults**
G.I. and Silent generations (born before 1943)	--%	10%
Baby Boomers (born 1943–1960)	--	34
Generation X (born 1961–1981)	77	35
Millennials (born 1982 or later)	<u>23</u>	<u>21</u>
	100	100

Eighteen percent of parents reside in households that earn less than $25,000 a year in income, likely placing them at or below the poverty line. About a third are in households earning $85,000 or more. These shares are similar to the percentages for the overall adult Catholic population.

Household Income Among US Catholic Parents Ages 25 to 45 and All US Catholic Adults		
	Catholic Parents	**All Catholic Adults**
Living at or below poverty (less than $25,000)	18%	17%
Below median income ($25,000 to $49,999)	25	24
Above median income ($50,000 to $84,999)	23	25
Upper income ($85,000 or more)	<u>34</u>	<u>34</u>
	100	100

Among individual Catholic families, family size is *inversely* related to income. Overall, 26 percent of parent respondents have three or more children under age eighteen in their home. However, this ranges from 40 percent among those living at or below the poverty level to 19 percent of those in homes earning $85,000 or more annually.

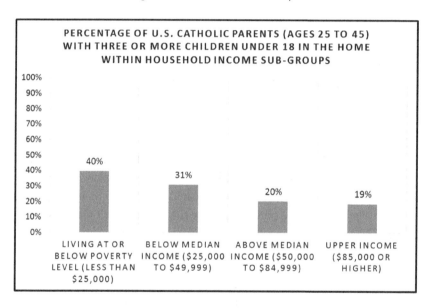

Nearly eight in ten parents are married (79 percent), and 13 percent are unmarried but living with a partner. Additionally, 4 percent are divorced, 3 percent are single and have never married, 1 percent are currently separated from their spouse, and less than 1 percent are widowed. Seventy-six percent of married parents indicate their spouse is Catholic. Among all Catholic adults, more report never marrying (16 percent compared with 3 percent of Catholic parents ages 25 to 45), being divorced (8 percent compared with 4 percent) or being widowed (5 percent compared with less than 1 percent). Catholic parents are more likely than all Catholic adults to be married (79 percent compared with 62 percent) or single living with a partner (13 percent compared with 8 percent). About the same small percentage of parents and all adults report currently being separated.

Parents who have separated or divorced or who are single and have never married are among the least likely to attend Mass weekly. Thirteen percent of separated or divorced Catholic parents are weekly Mass attenders. Fifteen percent of parents who have never married attend weekly. This becomes a bit more frequent if they are unmarried and living with a partner (20 percent). Weekly Mass attendance is most common among parents who are married, at 23 percent.

Nearly half of parents have a high school diploma or less. This is similar to the percentage of the overall adult Catholic population (44 percent). About a quarter of parents have had some college (24 percent), and 28 percent have a bachelor's degree or more. Overall, 8 percent of parents indicate having a master's degree, and 2 percent a professional or doctoral degree. Eight percent of parents indicate they have less than a ninth-grade education.

Education Among US Catholic Parents Ages 25 to 45 and All US Catholic Adults		
	Catholic Parents	**All Catholic Adults**
High school diploma or less	48%	44%
Some college	24	28
Bachelor's degree or more	28	28
	100	100

Among parents who self-identify as a "head of household," those who have attained higher levels of education are more likely to be in higher household income levels. Seventy-one percent of those with a bachelor's degree or more are in the upper income household bracket that collectively earns $85,000 or more per year. By comparison, only 4 percent of those who have not finished high school are in households earning this level of income. Nearly a third of head of household parents who have not finished high school (32 percent) resides in a home with income at or below the poverty level.

Although higher household incomes and education levels are associated with Catholic parents having fewer children than parents with less education living in lower income households, there is also a correlation between higher income and more education and parents being married.

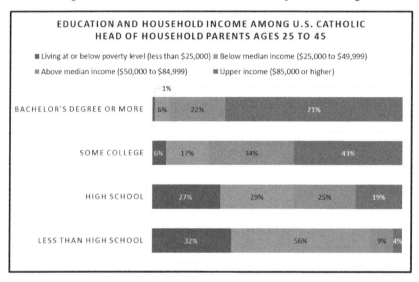

Only 55 percent of Catholic parents in households earning less than $25,000 a year are married. Eighteen percent of parents in this income bracket are single never-married, divorced, or separated and may be limited to one income.

Education, Income, and Marital Status Among US Catholic Parents Ages 25 to 45					
Education					
	Married	**Divorced or separated**	**Single, never married**	**Single, living with a partner**	
Less than high school	71%	5%	3%	20%	=100

High school diploma	72	6	5	16	=100
Some college	77	7	5	11	=100
Bachelor's degree or more	92	3	1	4	=100

Household Income					
	Married	**Divorced or separated**	**Single, never married**	**Single, living with a partner**	
Less than $25,000	55%	10%	8%	27%	=100
$25,000 to $49,999	77	6	6	11	=100
$50,000 to $84,999	84	6	1	9	=100
$85,000 or higher	89	2	1	8	=100

Note: There are too few widowed parents for inclusion as a sub-group. Thus, row totals do not sum to 100.

Nearly nine in ten parents (89 percent) in the highest income bracket, in homes earning $85,000 or more per year, are married. Only 3 percent of these parents are single never-married, divorced, or separated. More than nine in ten parents with a bachelor's degree or more are married (92 percent). Those with less education are more likely to be single and living with a partner.

A majority of parents self-identify their race and ethnicity as Hispanic or Latino (54 percent).[5] Only about a third of the overall adult self-identified Catholic population responds as such in recent CARA Catholic Polls. The disparity between these figures is attributable to the growing diversity of the Catholic population being more concentrated in its youngest generations.

Hispanic or Latino respondents are more likely than other parents to attend Mass at least once a month (56 percent compared with 48 percent) and to have three or more children (31 percent compared with 19 percent). At the same time, Hispanic or Latino parents are less likely than others to be married (73 percent compared with 85 percent) and more likely to be living with a partner (18 percent compared with 7 percent). However, among those parents who are married, Hispanics or Latinos are more likely than others to be married to a Catholic spouse (82 percent compared with 69 percent).

Race and Ethnicity Among US Catholic Parents Ages 25 to 45 and All US Catholic Adults		
	Catholic Parents	**All Catholic Adults**
White, non-Hispanic	40%	62%
Hispanic or Latino	54	32
Other race or ethnicity	<u>6</u>	<u>6</u>
	100	100

Sixty-five percent of parents in the South are Hispanic, as are 81 percent in the West, compared with 18 percent of parents in the Northeast and Midwest. Sixty-five percent of parents in homes earning $85,000 or more per year are non-Hispanic white. By comparison, 87 percent of those in homes earning less than $25,000 per year are Hispanic or Latino. Differ-

---

5. Overall, 31 percent of respondents chose to take the survey in Spanish (59 percent of Hispanic or Latino respondents). Forty percent of parents pray in Spanish and 59 percent in English. One percent pray in some other language (e.g., Polish, Portuguese).

ences by region or household income are thus strongly related to racial and ethnic differences among parents. Twenty-nine percent of Hispanic parents are in households with incomes at or below the poverty line. Only 4 percent of non-Hispanic white parents report this level of household income. Hispanic or Latino parents are also more likely than other parents to not have completed high school (37 percent compared with 3 percent).

Hispanic or Latino parents are also less likely than others to have their children enrolled in some formal religious education program. Seventy-three percent reported that none of their children were enrolled in Catholic schools or parish-based religious education. By comparison, 62 percent of non-Hispanic parents reported this in the survey. Differences are most evident for enrollment in Catholic elementary and middle schools. Here, only 5 percent of Hispanic or Latino parents indicate they have a child enrolled, compared with 12 percent of all other parents. Income differences may play a key role in limiting these parents from enrolling children in Catholic schools.

Geographic Region of Residence for US Catholic Parents Ages 25 to 45 and All US Catholic Adults		
	Catholic Parents	**All Catholic adults**
Northeast	18%	27%
Midwest	17	21
South	31	27
West	<u>34</u>	<u>25</u>
	100	100

Nearly two-thirds of parents reside in the South and West (65 percent). By comparison, 52 percent of the adult Catholic population resides in these regions. Parents are more likely than Catholic adults to be Hispanic or Latino and, as previously mentioned, this population is disproportionately concentrated geographically in the South and West. Only 17 percent of Catholic parents reside in the Midwest and 18 percent in the Northeast.

Fifty-eight percent of Catholic parents surveyed are female, compared with 51 percent of the overall Catholic adult population. The disparity between these figures is from single-parent households disproportionately being headed by mothers. Eighty-five percent of divorced or separated parents surveyed are mothers, and 69 percent of single, never-married parents surveyed are mothers.

The Average Catholic Family

The average Catholic family with minor children in the household today includes two Catholic married parents in their late 30s. They attend Mass two to three times a month. They live in a suburban area near a city in the American Southwest and are bilingual. They have two kids between the ages of six and twelve who are *not* currently enrolled in any formal religious education (i.e., Catholic school or parish-based religious education). At the same time, they say it is "very important" that their children celebrate their First Communion and Confirmation.

The parents have a high school diploma and may have been enrolled in a few college courses in their life. They reside in a detached single-family home that they either own or have a mortgage on. They are both working and have a combined household income of approximately $65,000 per year. They eat dinner together nearly every night as a family and spend at least one night a week gathered together for family time such as playing a game, watching a movie, or having a discussion. Few parents indicate that they pray together as a family, and instead consider prayer to be their personal conversation with God.

Sacramental Practice and Worship

Infant baptisms in the Catholic Church in the United States have been declining each year since 2002. Some of this is related to declining fertility rates. At the same time, the number of child baptisms has been increasing. *The Official Catholic Directory* began recording these in 2007, when 55,134 children were baptized at some point after their first birthday. In 2017, there were 58,832 children baptized.

There were 3,985,924 births registered in the United States in 2014.[6] Thus, infant baptisms in 2014 represent 17.4 percent of all these children born. With the Catholic affiliation percentage in national surveys ranging from 21 percent to 26 percent, depending on margin of error, there is an apparent shortfall. Some children born to Catholic parents in the United States are not being baptized as infants. Some of these children are later being baptized between the ages of one and seventeen; others, perhaps not at all or into another faith.[7]

After baptism, only two-thirds of parents say it is "very important" to them that their children receive their First Communion, and 61 percent place the same importance on their children being confirmed. Just under one in ten say this is "not important at all" to them.

How important is it to you that your child or children? *have celebrated each of the following sacraments?*		
	First Communion	**Confirmation**
Very important	66%	61%
Somewhat important	17	20
A little important	9	10
Not important at all	8	9
	100	100

As shown in the figure below, the more frequently parents attend Mass, the more likely they are to say that it is "very important" to them that their children receive their First Communion and are confirmed.

---

6. BE Hamilton, JA Martin, MJ Osterman, SC Curtin, "Births: Preliminary Data for 2014," *National Vital Statistics Reports* 64, no. 6 (June 2015).
7. Seventy-nine percent of parents are married, and 13 percent are unmarried but living with a partner. Additionally, 4 percent are divorced, 3 percent never married, 1 percent are currently separated from their spouse, and less than 1 percent are widowed. Seventy-six percent of married parents indicate their spouse is Catholic.

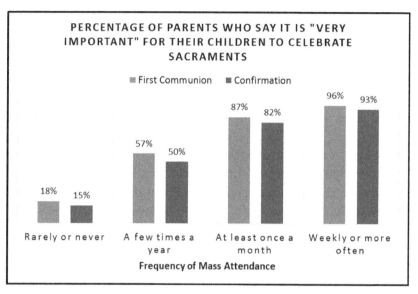

It is apparent that the strongest determinant of whether parents think it is important for their children to receive childhood sacraments is related to their connection to and participation in parish life. Just slightly more than one in five parents are in their parish every week attending Mass (22 percent). The same number say they never or rarely attend Mass (22 percent). One in four attends a few times a year — most likely on Ash Wednesday, Christmas, or Easter (25 percent). Three in ten attend at least once a month but less than weekly (31 percent). In total, a majority of Catholic parents, 53 percent, attends Mass at least monthly.

Aside from weddings and funerals, about how often do you attend Mass?		
	Parents	**All adults**
Rarely or never	22%	32%
A few times a year	25	25
Once or twice a month	16	9
Almost every week	15	10

Every week	20	21
More than once a week	2	3
	100	100

The frequency of weekly Mass attendance reported by parents is similar to the adult Catholic population overall, as measured in other recent national surveys conducted by CARA. However, parents are more likely than all adults to attend less than weekly, but at least once a month (31 percent compared with 19 percent) and less likely to say they attend rarely or never (22 percent compared with 32 percent).

Historically, in CARA's national surveys, women have reported attending Mass more frequently than men. The survey of parents indicates that Catholic fathers are significantly more likely than Catholic mothers to indicate that they rarely or never attend Mass (27 percent compared with 19 percent). About a quarter of mothers attend Mass weekly (24 percent) compared with 19 percent of fathers.

Aside from weddings and funerals, about how often do you attend Mass?				
	Number of Children			
	Fewer than 3 children	**Three or more children**	**Has an infant**	**Has a teen**
Rarely or never	24%	16%	26%	18%
A few times a year	28	18	21	24
At least once a month	30	33	35	32
Weekly or more often	18	33	18	26
	100	100	100	100

As table above shows, there are also some variations in frequency of Mass attendance by the number of children and age of children Catholic parents have. Two-thirds of parents with three or more children attend Mass at least once a month (66 percent). By comparison, a majority of those with two or fewer children attend only a few times a year or rarely/never (52 percent). Parents with at least one infant are more likely to attend Mass at least once a month than weekly (18 percent compared with 35 percent). A majority of parents with teens attend Mass monthly or more often (58 percent).

There are also differences in the frequency of Mass attendance by marital status. Fifty-six percent of married parents attend Mass at least once a month, compared with 44 percent of those who are separated or divorced, 30 percent of those who are single and never married, and 42 percent of those who are unmarried but living with a partner. Separated or divorced parents are most likely to say they rarely or never attend Mass followed by those living with a partner (28 percent and 27 percent, respectively).

Aside from weddings and funerals, about how often do you attend Mass?				
	Marital Status			
	Married	**Separated or divorced**	**Single, never married**	**Living with partner**
Rarely or never	21%	28%	21%	27%
A few times a year	23	28	50	31
At least once a month	33	29	15	22
Weekly or more often	23	15	15	20
	100	100	100	100

Religious Education

The family home may now be the most important place to study the transmission of faith because, unlike in past generations, most Catholic parents do not currently have their children enrolled in school- or parish-based religious education. More than two-thirds do not have any children enrolled in any formal religious education.

Do any of your children currently attend...? Percentage responding "Yes"	
A Catholic elementary or middle school	8%
A Catholic high school	3
A parish-based Catholic religious education program	21
A youth ministry program	5
None of the above	68

The figure above represents a snapshot in time for the 2014–15 school year. Some of the children not enrolled in a religious education program at that time may have been attending in the past or will be enrolled in the future.

Previous national polls of self-identified Catholic adults show that about half or more of those born in 1960 or earlier were enrolled in a Catholic elementary school at some point in their childhood. More than half also report being enrolled in a parish-based religious education as a youth. By comparison, only about a third of adult Millennial Catholics (born 1982 or later) report enrollment in a Catholic elementary school at some point, and fewer than half were ever enrolled in a parish-based religious education program.

It is likely that the Catholic children of today, members of yet to be named generation described by our survey (possibly Generation Z or iGen), will enter adulthood with less formal, Catholic Church-based religious education than their parents and grandparents.

As shown below, there are income-related differences for enrollment

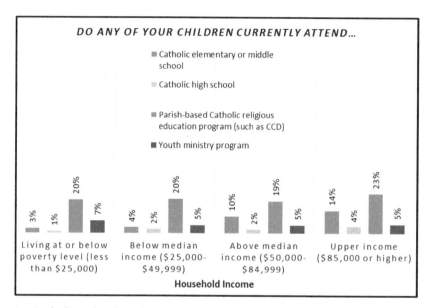

in Catholic schools. Those residing in households with higher annual incomes are more likely than those earning less to enroll a child in a Catholic primary school. However, there are no significant differences in the likelihood of enrolling children in other forms of religious education by income.

Faith at Home
About half of parents (49 percent) say that their Catholic faith is either the most important part of their life or among the most important parts of their life. Parents are slightly more likely than the Catholic population to respond as such (49 percent compared with 41 percent).

Mothers are more likely than fathers to consider their faith to be "among the most important parts" of their life or more (52 percent compared with 44 percent). Parents with three or more children are also more likely than those with fewer children to say that their faith is "among the most important parts" of their life or more (64 percent compared with 43 percent).

How important is your Catholic faith in your daily life? Is it...		
	Parents	**All adults**
The most important part of your life	15%	14%
Among the most important parts of your life	34	27
Important, but so are many other areas of your life	39	40
Not too important in your life	9	13
Not important in your life at all	3	6
	100	100

Eighty-four percent of those parents who attend Mass weekly or more often say their faith is "among the most important parts" of their life or more. By comparison, only 10 percent of those attending Mass rarely or never respond as such.

Fifty-nine percent of parents pray at least once a week (36 percent daily or more often) and only one in ten indicate that they rarely or never pray. Twenty-two percent pray at least once a year but less than monthly. One in ten pray more than once a month but less than weekly.

Aside from Mass, about how often do you pray?	
Rarely or never	9%
A few times a year	12
Once or twice a month	10
Almost every week	10
Once a week	3
More than once a week	20
Daily or more often	36
	100

Separated and divorced parents are more likely than others to report daily prayer. Forty-five percent do so compared with 37 percent of married parents, 32 percent of single, never-married parents, and 23 percent of those living with a partner. Those married to a Catholic spouse are much more likely to pray daily than those married to a non-Catholic (42 percent compared with 25 percent). Mothers are more likely than fathers to pray daily (40 percent compared with 31 percent). There are no statistically significant differences in daily prayer based on race or ethnicity. As one might expect, the best predictor of daily prayer is frequency of Mass attendance. Those who go to Mass at least once a month or more often are more likely to pray than those attending less frequently. Six in ten weekly Mass attenders (59 percent) indicate that they pray daily or more often. Just 12 percent of those who rarely or never attend Mass pray daily.

About three in four parents indicate that they more often pray individually than with family. Nearly a quarter report more prayer with their family, including 7 percent who pray more with their family than alone and 17 percent who pray about equally either with family or alone.

The likelihood that parents pray with their family (either more often or equal to the time they pray alone) increases with frequency of

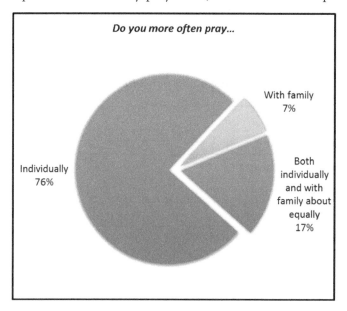

Mass attendance. Only 11 percent of parents who rarely or never attend Mass pray with family, compared with 42 percent of parents who attend Mass weekly or more often.

CATHOLIC WOMEN

In summer 2017, CARA conducted a national poll of adult Catholic women for *America Magazine*. A total of 1,508 women self-identifying as Catholic in the United States completed the survey (in English or Spanish). The margin of sampling error for the overall sample was ±2.5 percentage points. Using survey and census data, CARA estimated that there were 37.3 million Catholic females in the United States at the time of the survey. Of this population, 28.8 million were adults.

The poll indicated that 63 percent of Catholic women are married (46 percent are married to a Catholic spouse and 17 percent to a non-Catholic spouse). Six percent are widowed. One in ten are separated or divorced. Six percent live with a partner. Fifteen percent have never married.

Never-married Catholic women were asked whether it is important for them to marry a Catholic, and how important it is to them to be married in the Catholic Church.

Only 18 percent of never-married Catholic women say it is "very much" important to them to marry someone who is Catholic. Twelve percent said they don't plan to marry (2 percent of all adult Catholic women). About a third, 32 percent, of those who plan to marry in the future said it is "very much" important to them to marry in the Catholic Church. A majority of these respondents said it is at least "somewhat" important to them (56 percent).[8]

8. An additional 1 percent of the respondents for this second question said they did not plan to marry.

Marriage Questions for the Never Married

	"Very much" only	"Somewhat" or "very much" combined	Do not plan to marry
How important is it to you that you marry a Catholic?	18%	38%	12%
How important is it to you to be married in the Catholic Church?	32%	56%	1%

The typical Catholic woman in the United States has had two children, and both of those children are Catholic.[9] Most often, she grew up in a household where she had three brothers or sisters. Thus, her parents often had twice as many children as she has had.[10] For the typical Catholic woman, two of her three siblings remain Catholic as adults. Today, only one in ten Catholic women has four children (9 percent) and 20 percent have three. Twenty-eight percent have two children, 13 percent have one, and 25 percent have none.

The median number of children for married and for separated or divorced Catholics is two. The median number of children for widows is three. The median number for never-married Catholics is zero (80 percent have no children). For those living with a partner, the median number of children is one (47 percent have no children).

---

9. "Typical" refers to the median observation.
10. Among those with brothers and sisters, 59 percent indicate that all of their siblings are Catholic today. Fifteen percent indicate that none of their siblings is Catholic now. Twenty-six percent indicate some of their siblings are Catholic now and some are not.

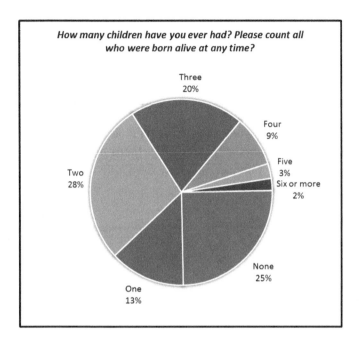

Respondents who had ever married or who are living with a partner were asked, "***Have you and a partner ever practiced Natural Family Planning, or NFP, which Catholic marriage preparation programs often teach as a method of postponing pregnancy without the use of artificial contraception?***" Overall, 22 percent said "yes" and 78 percent said "no."

About a third of ever-married Catholic women (including those living with a partner) who attend Mass weekly have used NFP compared with 12 percent of those attending Mass a few times a year or less often. Hispanic respondents are more likely than non-Hispanic respondents to say they have used NFP (27 percent compared with 19 percent). Generationally, the oldest and youngest generations of Catholic women are the most likely to indicate that they had used NFP. Thirty-six percent of those of the pre-Vatican II generation have used NFP, as have 26 percent of those of the Millennial generation. Vatican II Catholics, those born from 1943 to 1960, are the least likely to have used NFP (18 percent).

If respondents had used NFP, they were asked about their reasons for deciding to do so. The most common reasons cited were related to finances (38 percent "very important"), not wanting to have more children (34 percent), and their relationship with their husband (33 percent). Fewer indicated the following to be important: medical concerns (26 percent), time concerns (23 percent), or space concerns (20 percent).

How important to you, when using NFP, were the following in deciding whether to seek to postpone pregnancy? Of those who have used NFP	"Very"	"Somewhat" or "very" combined
Financial concerns	38%	66%
Not wanting to have more children	34%	54%
Relationship with husband	33%	54%
Medical concerns	26%	52%
Time concerns	23%	48%
Space concerns	20%	46%
Other	23%	32%

CATHOLIC TEENAGERS

CARA recently conducted a national poll of never-married Catholics regarding their consideration of a vocation. The survey included a total of 1,609 respondents interviewed (in English and Spanish) in May and June 2012. Of this sample, 683 respondents were ages 14 to 17.

Although all of the teens we interviewed had Catholic parents or a Catholic parent, and their parent believed their child self-identified as Catholic, we found some of the teens did not share their parents' faith. As the figure below shows, only three in four of all teens interviewed (75 percent) self-identified as Catholic. Twelve percent said they did not have a religious affiliation, 6 percent indicated that they were affiliated with a Protestant denomination, and 7 percent noted an affiliation with some other religion.

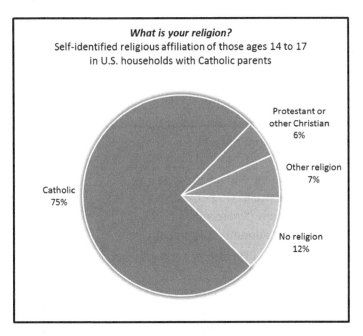

Ninety-two percent of the teens with two Catholic parents self-identified their faith as Catholic. Only 55 percent of those with one Catholic parent self-identified their faith as Catholic. Overall, 76 percent of the teens indicated they reside in a household with two Catholic parents.

Among only those teens who self-identify as Catholic, most report that they were baptized as infants (94 percent). Five percent indicate they entered the Church as a child, and 2 percent as a teen. Only 16 percent indicate that they have only celebrated the Sacrament of Baptism. Twenty-two percent indicate that they have also celebrated their First Communion. (Note: Some of the younger teens may not be of an age at which they could receive the Sacrament of Confirmation in their diocese.) Many, 62 percent, say they have celebrated Baptism, First Communion, and Confirmation.

Although many parents may express concerns about their teens not communicating enough with them in general, many Catholic teens say their parents rarely or never speak to them about religion. Eight percent report their parents talk to them about religion daily, and 20 percent say their parents do so at least once a week.

Two-thirds of Catholic teens (67 percent) say their faith is important to them. A third (33 percent) say it is either not important at all or not too important to them. The largest sub-group, 47 percent, say their faith is "important, but so are many other areas of my life."

The teens were also asked about the religious activities they take part in on a regular basis. They were most likely to indicate involvement in parish youth groups and retreats:

- Parish youth group (25 percent)
- Religious retreats (13 percent)
- Prayer groups (8 percent)
- Eucharistic adoration (7 percent)
- Bible study (7 percent)

Fifteen percent say they have been an altar server, and this percentage is the same for both males and females. Only 20 percent indicated that they read the Bible or pray with Scripture at least once a month. Six in ten say they "rarely or never" do this. Fourteen percent indicate they pray the Rosary at least monthly. At the same time, 71 percent say prayer is either "among the most important parts" of their lives (25 percent) or that it is "important, but so are many other areas of my life" (46 percent).

CONCLUSION

Changes in Catholic families in the United States are numerous, and the causes are complex. These causes are partially related to internal concerns within the Church but also represent broadly occurring cultural, demographic, and economic shifts in the country. Geographically, Catholic families are not well aligned with the brick and mortar of the Church, being more heavily concentrated in the South and West. Parents are also increasingly the primary religious educators of their children, with the Church playing no formal role here outside of Mass attendance. Despite the best efforts of parents, more children today than in the past are leaving the faith (and not telling their parents). The transmission of the faith across generations is at stake. Understanding the trends that are unfolding is an existential issue in the United States.

DISCUSSION QUESTIONS

1. What surprises you about the religious practices of American Catholic families?
2. How does your experience in your family-of-origin compare with the familes described in this chapter?
3. How do you think your current family and/or the families you know in your parish compare to the families described in this chapter?
4. Based on the data in this chapter, what do you think of the Church's efforts to help families live their faith? What do you think of Catholic parents' efforts to raise faithful children?

CHAPTER SEVEN

Sex, Marriage, and Parenting: Culture versus the Catholic Difference

HELEN M. ALVARÉ

Antonin Scalia Law School, George Mason University

FIVE QUICK TAKES

1. Catholic families can no longer trust that faith can be "caught" from participating in the culture. Faith must be taught at home in word and in action.

2. Catholic views on sex, marriage, and parenting are at the heart of the family and central to the mission of the Catholic family to evangelize the culture. The Church (both clergy and laity) must stop treating these issues as incidental.

3. In presenting the Catholic view of sex, marriage, and parenting, describing rules is not enough. We must teach parents and children to distinguish Christian and non-Christian ways of viewing these issues from first principles.

4. In presenting the Catholic view of sex, marriage, and parenting, we must engage reason. A great deal of data from the medical and social sciences support faithful views. We must become aware of these facts and teach them.

5. Catholic teaching on sex, marriage, and parenting must be understood as central to the ways Christians understand and order their lives as a community of believers.

INTRODUCTION

I "meet" the difficulties of transmitting Catholic family life in at least four arenas: in my own family, in the students I encounter ordinarily in their early to late twenties, in family law scholarship, and in media reports and encounters. To steal a line from, I believe, George Weigel, I have learned from these arenas that "osmosis is over" when it comes to transmitting Catholic beliefs in any of them.

This means that while it is always an excellent idea to display a fully lived Catholic family life, even this experience and witness of a community of love will not any longer be convincing enough for family members or other observers. Words narrating and explaining the family will be necessary.

Words are especially important today for several reasons. First, opponents of Catholic family principles have commandeered some of the most beautiful ones in service of their own ideas — words like equality, dignity, identity, and freedom. These need to be parsed and recovered. Second, these opponents are obsessed with sexual expression as the source and summit of each of these. This needs to be deconstructed with specificity. Third, the social media slipping into the minds and lives of children at every moment can out-talk all the live people in their lives. Counterbalancing discourse is required. Fourth, opponents are capitalizing upon — while also twisting — Catholic ideas and words, in order to build bridges that people raised Catholic can easily cross to the other side. Distinctions and objections need to be marshaled. And fifth, sexual expression obsessives have constructed a narrative tying sexual expression to the meaning of life, to individual destiny, in a way that holds the attention of the young and the searching, while Catholic religious education too often speaks "about religion," instead of engaging young people in the search for God as the answer to the question that they are asking.

I propose, therefore, that every Catholic family has to do a certain amount of "home schooling" regarding Catholic family teachings. This is true whether or not one's children are full time in Catholic school. With rare exceptions, even a Catholic school will not manage to devote the kind and amount of time necessary to respond to the contemporary obsession with sexual expression. They also usually will not manage to offer teaching that integrates a full Catholic vision of life with the best and truest senses of the beautiful values promoted popularly, and also with positivity, adequate reason, and in a manner engaging the fundamental questions that each individual harbors about ultimate meaning and destiny.

To this end, I propose that every family needs to be urged at this time to step up their response to the literally "disintegrating" contemporary messages about sex, marriage, and parenting. I recommend the following steps.

RECOGNIZE THAT OUR TIMES CALL ON THIS CHURCH

When the Smithsonian Museum and Disney parks are celebrating gay pride,[1] more than 70 percent of younger Americans are cohabiting before marriage,[2] and abortion and contraception are identified as the central elements of women's freedom, it can be concluded without overstatement that our ambient culture has roundly rejected Catholic sex, marriage, and parenting notions.

Furthermore, not only in public-square-rhetoric, but also in a seemingly endless stream of lawsuits demanding religious individuals' and institutions' cooperation with contemporary ideas about sexual expression, Christian beliefs and practices are fingered as the primary obstacles to a full realization of the new dispensation. They stand in stark contrast to a stream of legal opinions in which the U.S. Supreme Court has concluded that sex and marriage and children are no longer in any relationship to one another, as a matter of law. Marriage is described as "an association of two individuals each with a separate intellectual and emotional makeup."[3] Abortion is considered a fundamental constitutional right of women,[4] necessary for their liberty, identity, and social progress.[5] And as a result of the Court's same-sex marriage opinion, states are forbidden from favoring procreation over the inability to procreate, and forbidden from favoring children's *knowing* their parents versus their being *estranged* from one or both.[6] The state has only a minimal interest in the very poor and the very young avoiding childbirth, which interest the state promotes by massive contraception programs. As for everyone else, they can freely choose without any state interest to have children when they like — married or unmarried — so long as they can pay for them.[7]

Our situation appears serious, but is not wholly new; the movements for contraception, for no-fault divorce, abortion, and for same-sex mar-

1. Smithsonian, "Celebrate National Pride Month at the Smithsonian," news release, May 29, 2019, https://www.si.edu/newsdesk/releases/celebrate-national-pride-month-smithsonian; WDW Info, "Celebrate Gay Days at Walt Disney World, June 4 – June 8, 2020, https://www.wdwinfo.com/disney-gay-days.htm.
2. Scott Stanley, "Cohabitation Is Pervasive," *Institute for Family Studies*, June 20, 2018, https://ifstudies.org/blog/cohabitation-is-pervasive.
3. Eisenstadt v. Baird, 405 U.S. 436, 453 (1972).
4. Roe v. Wade, 410 U.S. 113 (1973).
5. Planned Parenthood v. Casey, 505 U.S. 833 (1992).
6. Obergefell v. Hodges, 135 S. Ct. 2584 (2015).
7. Helen M. Alvaré, "Curbing Its Enthusiasm: U.S. Federal Policy and the Unitary Family," *International Journal of the Jurisprudence of the Family* 2 (2011): 107.

riage have struggled against Christianity for nearly a century in some cases. What is new, however, is the lack of collateral support today by, or even the opposition of, secular authorities — the academy, the media, the entertainment industry, and the state (as noted immediately above) — of notions also supported by Christianity.

The reasons for the new level of conflict are numerous. Christian teachings haven't changed, but the obsession with sexual expression by the powers-that-be has ratcheted up to unprecedented levels. This is supported by important tectonic philosophical and cultural shifts as well. Each of these could (and does) occupy several volumes, but I will merely list them here in a way sufficient to identify them. They are treated at length in my book, *Putting Children's Interests First in U.S. Family Law and Policy: With Power Comes Responsibility.*[8] These include the turn toward the self, toward subjectivity, and away from a concern with objective truth, and with community. There is also a now half-century of feminism's latching onto freedom *from* reproduction as the centerpiece of female freedom. In other words, to achieve sex on men's bodily terms, there must be sex without pregnancy by all means available, including contraception and abortion. There is also the rise of materialism in the US; economic gain trumps personal relationships. Furthermore, some have argued (e.g., Charles Taylor) that the US has a particular fascination with/attraction to the achievement of personal "happiness"; sexual satisfaction has become today one of the leading — if not *the* leading — aspects of this.[9]

Thinking theologically about the contemporary obsession with sexual freedom, one could conclude that it is simply the latest version of the original sin: human pride. Today's version denies either that God created us, or that His creation is infused with His purposes and ideas. Instead, we deny or ignore the other-directedness of the male and female body, the significance of their union, of the link between sex and reproduction, and of children's desperate need for their parents' rather lengthy care and stability.

---

8. (Cambridge: Cambridge University Press, 2017), 50–57.

9. Charles Taylor, *A Secular Age* (Cambridge, MA: Belknap Press of Harvard University Press, 2007): 485–93, 618–20, 507–08.

One by one, the leading voices against the contemporary obsession with sex have fallen. Christianity stands nearly alone in its attempts to resist the ideas that sex, marriage, and parenting are unrelated to one another and are mostly vehicles for individual self-realization. It is not difficult to see, therefore, how this situation points to the existence of a particular Christian "vocation" on these subjects; i.e., there is a crying need, and few to no others to answer it. There is a victim lying on the road, and we are riding by. Like the Good Samaritan, we are often despised by onlookers, but our task is clear all the same.

In part, this analogy answers a frequent objection to Catholic activity in this sphere: the claim that we ourselves have become obsessed with the topic of sexual expression, although this is not the leading message of the New Testament. It is important to acknowledge the correctness of this latter observation here. In fact, the Good News is not primarily about sexual expression. It is instead easily argued that the New Testament speaks much more about the necessity of acknowledging Jesus as the Son of God and caring for the vulnerable and outcast. But it is also the case that the words of the New Testament and the lived experience even of the earliest Christian communities reveal the manner in which the Christian family is intended to live as one of the fruits of accepting Christ. And it is also the case that today, the goods of the family are being denied and undermined to a historic degree at this moment.

I add to this the observation that it has become clear the degree to which disordered family life is responsible for widespread human misery. When children are not procreated or reared within a stable (which almost always means marital) family setting, they suffer. The causal relationship is clear within contemporary research, even if other nested and interrelated factors play important roles, too. These include poverty (which exists within a vicious circle that includes divorce and nonmarital parenting), racial discrimination, and labor and educational policies. Nonmarital parenting and divorce are associated with long-run, diminished trajectories affecting the education, employment, and emotional stability of the children involved. There is even new and highly convincing evidence that the ascendant problems of boys — less education, more addiction and suicide, and less college than women — are closely associated with family structure deficits. These problems are then intergenerationally transmitted.[10]

At the same time, therefore, that Catholics affirm that our faith is not primarily focused on family life, *and* that sins and missteps in *this* arena are not more egregious than sins and missteps elsewhere (excessive materialism, violence, etc.), we should *also* acknowledge that our times are unusually obsessed with sexual license, that untold numbers of vulnerable people are suffering as a result, and that we are uniquely qualified to address it.

USE DISTINCTION, NOT MERELY DESCRIPTION AND/OR CONTRADICTION

When addressing family matters, the Catholic Church has a rich history and selection of pedagogies. We have Natural Law. We have Tradition, beginning with the earliest Christian communities. We have the *Theology of the Body,* respecting the deeper meaning of male-female bodies and relations. We have the social teachings especially of *Gaudium et Spes* and *Familiaris Consortio* regarding the roles of marriage and family in society.

These are powerful, but not sufficiently "comprehensible" today. Merely describing them will not be enough. Every concept within them is contested more or less: the good of marriage; the good of the link between sex and children; the goods of having two sexes and of their sexual union; the goods of fidelity and exclusivity; and the good of children.

This is true in part because social institutions other than Christianity no longer regularly support these goods in their own language. It is also true because the most valorized values in today's pantheon — equality, dignity, identity, freedom — are deployed in order to contradict, rather than not verify or amplify, Christian conclusions.

Today, therefore, Christians ought to take advantage of another pedagogical principle that is more effective than mere "description" of our values or our reasoning: distinction. Such a move acknowledges opposing principles, draws out their meanings and consequences more precisely,

---

10. Alvaré, *Putting Children's Interests First in US Law and Policy,* 58–65.

and unpacks our own in a manner that becomes more comprehensible.

There are many examples one might use — too many to cover in the space of this paper — but the following should convey the method. A Christian would point out, for example, the emphasis upon personal "choice" in current sexual expression arguments. We would counter with the notion that human beings are rather "chosen" to love one another, to take care of the "neighbor" strewn on our path of life. This is more in concert with contemporary values about care for the dispossessed (Black Lives Matter, care for immigrants we did not "choose" but who came to our shores, etc.).

A Christian would point out that the rejection of the importance of the "organic" family in favor of the "functional" family — the group of persons who take care of one another potentially even for a long time, but are not related by blood, marriage, or adoption — denies the importance of nature or creation. This is the same error implicit in the destruction of the environment: the notion that what God "sends" or creates has no intrinsic importance. What is important is human choice, human imposition upon nature, technological progress.

We might also point out that contemporary family mores stress *adult* fulfillment; thus the "soulmate" marriage, thus divorce following a couple's "growing apart," and thus conceiving babies via surrogacy, other ARTs, or as a single parent, in response to adult desires, despite the absence of the best family framework for children. Christians should distinguish the value of adult fulfillment from the value of service to persons in need. They might also discuss at length how service leads to true fulfillment, given that the human person is built for this. Scientific and personal accounts of human happiness confirm this too often to doubt. This ties well to contemporary suspicion of baked-in social privileges for the most privileged: today, for example, we hear a great deal about "white privilege," the privilege of the rich, and so forth. This is not to full-throatedly accede to all that these latter values imply, as I will note further below, but there is truth in them, and Christians need to tap into legitimate critiques of all value systems — including "powerful adults first" — that help "bake" disadvantages to others into the system.

Similarly, Christians should contrast the contemporary obsession with "rights" with the Christian case for "responsibility." This argument contains similar elements to those discussed above. It also applies to the contemporary valorizing of individualism versus the Christian affirmation of the priority of *community*. This Christian value should today have particular resonance given the link between so many emerging social crises — suicide, addiction, poverty, sexual identity crises — and the lack of community experienced by the victims of each.

Mere *description* of important Christian values, and mere *denunciation* of contemporary "family values," are methods insufficient to the times. The method of *distinction* is far more adequate.

ENGAGE REASON

It should come as no surprise that nearly three centuries following the Enlightenment, it remains wise for Catholics to engage reason as part of their discourse about the family. This should not veer into scientism (science as the only and final word on all matters), but it should both respect the very Catholic marriage of faith and reason, *and* the persuasiveness of overlapping empirical evidence.

Empirical evidence about the wisdom of Catholic family teachings — their association with individual, family, and social well-being — exists in profusion. Much of it is recent. It was not available during the height of the "contraception wars" of the 1960s and 1970s in the Church, nor at the height of the no-fault divorce tsunami that overlapped. But it is available today.

Interestingly, the evidence about the harms associated with same-sex parenting and same-sex unions and transgender identity is in its infancy today,[11] just as our society is making wholesale legal and cultural changes to recognize and even celebrate all of these. We will more than likely have to await its development before making better, empirically sourced arguments about these topics. But both logic and revelation — working together to illuminate one another — are available on these subjects, even before the "data is in." It seems, however, that Americans are

---

11. See, e.g., Katy Faust, "Study the Studies: What We Know About Same-Sex Parenting," *Them Before Us*, May 22, 2017, https://thembeforeus.com/study-studies-same-sex-parenting/.

unwilling to accept logic or revelation about any of these matters, but must rather pursue wrongheaded paths for quite a while until we can measure the wreckage and then — possibly — reassess.

The body of evidence that we do have about the harms of divorce or nonmarital parenting, and increasingly, cohabitation, is large and growing, but still is ignored or minimized. Some leading researchers and media will argue that the harmful results are more about selection effects than causation, even when causation has been demonstrated. They will pick apart even a good study design. They will claim author bias even in the case of a well-conducted study. They will claim that all family problems are really *economic* problems that new government programs can fix, despite sixty years of data indicating that nearly all government programs are ineffective or worse regarding family structure, even as they are pretty good at keeping food, clothing, and shelter coming.[12]

Empirical evidence will never be conclusive. It is also incapable of answering questions of meaning and values. But the fact that it so clearly affirms the wisdom of Catholic family teachings should be well-known to Catholic parents and institutions. It is additional evidence of the marriage of faith and reason, and of the intelligence of Catholicism in this area.

ENGAGE WHAT IS BEAUTIFUL IN CONTEMPORARY VALUES

So many contemporary values are intrinsically beautiful. These include the values — equality, dignity, identity, freedom — often used to beat Catholic family values over the head. No wonder so many Americans are attracted to them. But current descriptions of these values —and thus current colloquial understandings — are impoverished/incomplete. It is obviously not necessary or desirable to telescope all of Catholic teachings into these categories, but it is important to touch upon them when possible, not only in order to advance the appeal of Catholic teachings, but also to alleviate the harm done by sloppy, simplistic, contemporary understandings of these values.

For example, dignity needs to be grasped as more than self-esteem,

---

12. Alvaré, 66–85.

or mutual tolerance. It needs to be distinguished from a state of being devoid of constructive criticism or disagreement. Furthermore, colloquial uses of "dignity" suggest wrongly that dignity is given by one human being to another, versus being an intrinsic aspect of ourselves, as created by God. This rhetoric needs to suffuse our discussions of, for example, homosexuality.

The notion of identity, which has become synonymous with subjective belief usually about sexual desires and interests, needs to be transformed to incorporate objective reality, and to take the focus off sex. We are more than our sexual inclinations. And we are not merely what we believe. This is important in conversations about "gender identity" as well as any individual's vocation generally.

Freedom — today meaning license — has to be situated within ideas about the meanings and purposes of life, and of the lives of others. Choices contradicting these, and — in the context of sex — choices harming others as well as ourselves are, by definition, not freeing. This is particularly important to touch upon in conversations about nonmarital sex and parenting, and contraception and abortion.

Finally, the notion of equality is perhaps the nine-hundred-pound values gorilla dominating the conversations around sex, marriage, and parenting in the United States. It has become synonymous with freely available contraception and abortion (as "women's equality") and with same-sex marriage and transgenderism ("sexual orientation" or "gender" equality). Like dignity, however, a conversation about equality has to emphasize that human equality is intrinsic and God-given, not mutually accorded. It should also be emphasized that it is a value that applies to *persons*, not actions or situations or choices, even choices that are quite difficult to avoid. And finally, it should be emphasized that equality alongside diversity — diversity, e.g., of sex, culture, experiences, talents, needs — is the only form of equality true to the objective reality of the world as we encounter it.

Importantly and furthermore, we now have the results of a half-century of experimenting with the notion that equality is "grasped" by means of abortion and contraception. Due to the predictable workings of the "relationship marketplace," and the particular economic and social difficulties faced by the poor and minorities in the US, this experiment has brought us less and later marriage (against the interests of women in particular, but also men), more nonmarital births (harming children especially), more divorce (harming all parties), more abortions (harming women and children, but also men), more cohabitation (harming all parties, children in particular), and growing and hardening wealth, income, education, and family structure gaps between richer and poorer and especially between black and white and Hispanic persons.[13]   Equality, it turns out, is better served by recognizing that it is achieved *only* with deference to the structures of human sexuality, and with acknowledgement of differences between human beings.

AVOID MORALISM, BUT STRESS THE WAYS IN WHICH CATHOLIC PRACTICES FLOW FROM THE "WAY" OF THE CATHOLIC COMMUNITY

Currently, Catholic and other Christian institutions and individuals are responding to demands to cooperate with various legal demands regarding sexual expression (same-sex marriage, abortion, contraception, cohabitation, and transgender surgeries and recognition) with assertions of their rules against these. They state that they cannot cooperate with immoral acts. This is theologically true, but less than effective. As a result, some Catholics, and many media outlets and academics, are concluding that Catholicism hates women, homosexuals, and transgender persons. Even parishioners resort to signing letters or staging protests objecting institutions, while asserting that their behavior (e.g., firing the same-sex

---

13. See, e.g., George Akerlof, Janet Yellen, Michael Katz, "*An Analysis of Out-of-Wedlock Childbearing in the United States," The Quarterly Journal of Economics* 111, no. 2 (May 1996): 277–317 (finding that the sudden increase in the availability of both abortion and contraception in the late 1960s and early 1970s produced a "reproductive technology shock" that led to a dramatic increase in out-of-wedlock births, especially among poor women). See also Phillip Levine, *Sex and Consequences: Abortion, Public Policy, and the Economics of Fertility* (Princeton, NJ: Princeton University Press, 2007) (showing that when the "cost" of pregnancy is low due to easy access to abortion, sexual partners take more sexual risks); Raj Chetty et al., "Where Is the Land of Opportunity? The Geography of Intergenerational Mobility in the United States," *The Quarterly Journal of Economics* 129, no. 4 (November 2014): 1553–1623 (showing the relationship between single parenting and the fate of children).

married teacher) is not "loving."[14] As a result, religious freedom as a concept is taking a beating. But so are Catholic teachings on sex, marriage, and parenting, which are perceived to be separate and even different from overarching Catholic teachings (i.e., Love God … and your neighbor as yourself).

A better response would start with "we are a community that … " In such a response, the religious institution or person would articulate, positively and up front, the purpose of the teaching in the crosshairs. Regarding abortion, for example, it is superior to assert that "we are a community that values every life, and takes a special interest in the life of the most vulnerable. This is why we provide both for the protection of unborn humans, and for the care and protection of women facing crisis pregnancies." Regarding contraception, it would be superior to assert that "we are a community that takes sexual relationships seriously. Sex cut off from its intrinsic relationship to 'tomorrow' — to children, marriage, family, kin, love — inevitably harms the relationship of the couple, who are made for lasting love, and harms children, who are regularly conceived without the necessary stable, loving family every child needs." Regarding homosexual partnerships, it would be superior to say that "we are a community that takes the human body seriously, and knows that sex cut off from the structure and purposes of the human body and sex, and from the possibility of procreation, is readily exploitative, and harmful to the psychology and development of the human beings involved."

It is important to start with the *nature of the Christian community,* because this is where and how Catholic teachings on sex, marriage, and parenting originate. From the very earliest records of Christian communities, we know that Christians distinguished themselves by their practices in these areas. We know this from the Acts of the Apostles, from the letters of Saint Paul, from the Didache, and from historical records compiled by non-Christian historians of this early period. Through to the present day, while these teachings do not constitute a large fraction

14. See, e.g., Dick Uliano, "Catholic Girls' School in DC Adopts Policy Contrary to Church Teaching," *WTOP News,* May 13, 2019, https://wtop.com/dc/2019/05/catholic-girls-school-in-dc-adopts-policy-contrary-to-church-teaching/; Flo Martinez Addiego et al., "An Open Letter to Georgetown Visitation," *First Things,* May 23, 2019, https://www.firstthings.com/web-exclusives/2019/05/an-open-letter-to-georgetown-visitation.

of Christian history and writings, when they do appear, they support the following thesis: Christian practices in these areas grew out of *not only* specific prescriptions for Christian living (marital permanence, no homosexual relations), but also from our teachings about the necessity of care for the vulnerable (women and children, especially at that time) and "the neighbor," and from teachings about the implications of the Incarnation, bodily destiny, and the role of our sexual and marital choices in coming to know and live Christ.

In short, our teachings about sex, marriage, and parenting cannot be allowed to "stick out" as though they were unrelated to "the rest of" the Catholic project. If they do, they are not only incomprehensible to Catholics and outsiders alike, but also highly available for "target practice" by a world obsessed with freedom of sexual expression.

We might also note, at the same time, that we are expressing these teachings more integrally, that we fully realize that these are not the highest or most important or only Catholic teachings, but form rather part of the whole. We might also note that we do not single them out, therefore, for *special* condemnation, but have been put in the position again and again of being forced to defend them, or to be allowed to practice them ourselves and uphold them in our institutions, because of *society's* current obsession with promoting unmitigated sexual expression.

We should also note — and again simultaneously — that alongside these teachings, and our right to hold them as against invasive laws, we practice Christian accompaniment of all those who find themselves struggling to uphold these disciplines often with too little help from others. Thus, we accompany the homosexual, the pregnant woman, the individual suffering gender dysphoria. And when we don't, we are happy to be told to do better!

CONCLUSION

At different times during its historical unfolding, Christianity has been faced with particular challenges: earlier, identifying the relationships between the three persons of Christ; later, a lust for worldly power — war; today, the distortion of the meaning of sex, marriage, and parenting. Given the size of today's controversy, the appealing quality of our opposition, the ubiquity of communications reaching the young, and the near-absence of other institutions qualified to respond, it is important that Catholics become better qualified to speak. It will require a great deal of work — intellectual, communications, and pastoral work — and one can only hope that parents and other educators are sufficiently motivated by the stakes.

DISCUSSION QUESTIONS

1. The author of this chapter asserts that Catholic teachings on sex, marriage, and parenting are often presented as if they are incidental rules to be followed, rather than central principles that order the way we live in community as Christians. Does this ring true of your experience?

2. How would it change your view of Catholic teaching on sex, marriage, and parenting if you were to see these ideas not as rules to be followed but as the central principles that order the life of the Christian community?

3. How aware are you of the findings in medical and social sciences that are supportive of Church teaching on sex, marriage, and parenting? How might you become more aware of these findings?

4. How effective do you think you are in helping your children/students identify the distinctions between the way Christians and non-Christians think about personhood, the body, and community? What could you do to become more informed about these distinctions yourself?

CHAPTER EIGHT

Marriage: The Sacrament of the Fulfillment of the Sexual Nature of Man

PAT FAGAN

Marriage and Religion Research Institute, The Catholic University of America

FIVE QUICK TAKES

1. Christ revealed to man the fullness of man's sexual nature. All his followers are called to chastity even after marriage.

2. There is an organized, cultural movement to intentionally undermine the family by targeting fatherhood. This movement is succeeding by redefining the nature and focus of sexuality.

3. Every father now has the task of deliberately shaping the sexuality of his children — especially his sons — in successively refined ways as his boy grows from infancy to young adulthood.

4. For a father, his marriage is the greatest school of virtue; for his son, the marriage of his father and mother is the greatest influence in shaping his sexuality.

5. Evangelization of others outside the family takes second place to the pursuit of sanctity within the family, and centrally within the marriage.

In our times, both sacramental vocations, Matrimony and Holy Orders, are in crisis,[1] largely because too many within the Church have disregarded Christ's teaching about the sexual nature of man, which is at the heart of being male or female. This disregard of Christ's guidance on matters of fundamental human nature lets loose massive destructive forces within human nature. "Getting sex right" has always required vigilance, because everyone is fragile here, and a constant effort to reform and to repent are needed by all, whether followers of Christ or not. All suffer the same consequences, be they atheists, agnostics, Buddhists, Muslims, Marxists, Protestants, or Catholics, because the same human nature is in play and at risk.

---

1. Though the Mystical Body is never in crisis, ever, for Christ is never in crisis.

THE MODERN ASSAULT ON THE FAMILY THROUGH THE EXPLOITATION OF MALE SEXUALITY

The modern assault on the family began shortly before the French Revolution, in France. By the mid-1800s Marxism was gaining traction. Today, more than anything else, Marxists see the intact married family and weekly worship as their main obstacles. Hence, they have targeted monogamous marriage and religion. Parents' rejection of each other is a prized tool of deconstruction, and Lenin, shortly after gaining power in 1917, removed all legal protections of marriage. In the late 1960s, US Marxist feminists chose the "patriarch," the married father, as the keystone-to-be-removed to collapse the "bourgeois" (i.e., the Christian) family. The opening chant of the meetings leading up to the formation of the National Organization for Women illustrates the strategy of its feminist founders (brilliant, highly educated women) like nothing else:

> *"Why are we here today?"* / *"To make revolution,"* they answered.
> *"What kind of revolution?"* / *"The Cultural Revolution,"* they chanted.
> *"And how do we make Cultural Revolution?"* / *"By destroying the American family!"*
> *"How do we destroy the family?"* / *"By destroying the American Patriarch."*
> *"And how do we destroy the American Patriarch?"* / *"By taking away his power!"*
> *"How do we do that?"* / *"By destroying monogamy!"*
> *"How can we destroy monogamy?"* / *"By promoting promiscuity, eroticism, prostitution and homosexuality!"* [2]

Their tool of destruction was "sex gone wild": remove the monogamous husband, and society and its institutions gradually collapse — into the

2. Mallory Millett, "Marxist Feminism's Ruined Lives: The Horror I Witnessed Inside the Women's 'Liberation' Movement," *Frontpage*, September 1, 2014, https://www.frontpagemag.com/fpm/240037/marxist-feminisms-ruined-lives-mallory-millett.

open arms of the state. The Marxists already knew the chaos that would result, having seen the chaos that emerged in Russia from the 1917 decision.[3] Their social deconstruction insight was brilliant, and at the time not readily recognized by the opponents of Marxism, even by the Catholic Church, where the sacredness of family and lifelong marriage was universal doctrine.[4] The pivotal role of the father was not grasped until the effects of his absence became visible by the mid 1980s.[5] They have succeeded enormously. By 2014, there were 684 women's studies centers at universities and colleges in the United States, all devoted to this form of feminist Marxism, the first two at Cornell and Princeton, founded by women who likely participated in the chant above, being among the original founders of NOW. By 2014, only 46 percent of American seventeen-year-olds were still in an intact married family; the parents of the other 54 percent had already rejected each other. The Marxist feminists learned how to exploit nature so as to deconstruct society. They have succeeded more and faster than even they likely thought possible.

Biology makes the father the easier target. The mother's family situation is totally different from her husband's. Biology pulls and pushes her into an early and deep relationship with her child. For nine months, with increasing intensity, she gets to know her baby in her womb; the catharsis of giving birth yields its own bonding, while the breastfeeding that follows deepens the relationship. By contrast, the father gets little help from nature. His bonding is principally an act of his will, of virtue, of good habit. It can be very strong and has huge effects, but on virtually all levels the bond with mother is stronger.

Not because of an inherent male strength but because of an inherent male weakness, the father's relationship to his wife and to his children

---

3. Anonymous, "The Russian Effort to Abolish Marriage," *The Atlantic,* July 1926, https://www.theatlantic.com/magazine/archive/1926/07/the-russian-effort-to-abolish-marriage/306295/.

4. Though at this period, the hierarchy was acquiescing to the federal family planning (contraceptive) programs, even though all the powerful politicians were then afraid of provoking their opposition. See Donald Critchlow, *Intended Consequences: Birth Control, Abortion, and the Federal Government in Modern America* (New York: Oxford University Press, 2001).

5. Children stay with their mother 80 percent of the time when a family breaks up. Young soldiers, dying on the battlefields of Europe in World War I, cried out for their mothers, not their fathers. The mother-child bond, the first bond, is emotionally stronger than the father-child bond. See the significant literature on early infant attachment.

is the lynchpin on which the stability of the family and society lie.[6] His (virtuous) attachment is the treasured glue that makes the family whole, while simultaneously it is the most vulnerable family relationship and the one most often broken.

Furthermore, the attachment of son or daughter to his or her father is central to the formation of sexual identity. For instance, in the father-absent family, the rate of lesbianism in grown daughters is three times higher than in the intact family.[7] Ambivalence of father attachment to his son is one of the classic contributors to male homosexuality, even in the intact married family, especially when coupled with an over-involved mother.[8] The well-bonded married father is the foundation of the family, of the community, of the culture. Remove such males and community structures collapse, no matter how great the female. Without him we get increased poverty, violence, abuse, educational failure, gangs, crime, depression, and anxiety. These deficits compound when, generation after generation, the effects of fatherlessness compound. Strong marriages are thus the core strength of society.[9] There are clear indications for evangelization here.

The male's family vulnerability lies in the pull of sexual relations outside of marriage. The erotic is his weak spot. The Marxist feminists took it as their main tool and forged organizational alliances with all aspects of easy sex: contraception (Planned Parenthood), especially outside of marriage; abortion (Planned Parenthood); gay sex and marriage (LBGT); sex-ed groups (SIECUS and its affiliates).

The latest stage of the sexual revolution is gender plasticity. Though not part of the NOW founding group, Shulamith Firestone's work, *The Dialectic of Sex,* was the most influential book among feminist intellectuals. She is the most explicit of all: " … feminists have to question, not just all of *Western* culture, but the organization of culture itself, and fur-

---

6. This weakness is dramatically illustrated in the 1926 *Atlantic Monthly* article referenced above.

7. From the National Survey of Family Growth, 2002. Analysis by Paul Sullins, PhD. Data available on request.

8. Both types often match up.

9. I learned this lesson in my early years as a therapist. By my third year I would not work with children unless I could work with the whole family. Keeping the focus off the "identified patient," the child's symptoms disappeared for 90 percent once the marriage of the parents was healed and conflicts resolved — without any direct work with the child, yielding the lesson that the marital relationship shapes the family and each child.

ther, even the very organization of nature."[10]

That such is being taught in some schools and advocated across mass media indicates the total erosion of taboos, the cultural mechanisms that keep sexual expression within marriage. American culture today, defanged of taboos, instead is fast becoming an "anti-culture" that threatens marriage with divorce, serial cohabitation, out-of-wedlock births, abortion, hookups, pornography, polyamory, and polymorphous sexuality, all with debilitating consequences for the adults involved and particularly for the children who grow up in such families.[11] The implications for sexual formation within the family, and for evangelization on family, are enormous.

THE SEXUAL PARADIGM CHRIST GAVE US

The Blessed Trinity is "dependent on man" to give Them the very large family They want with Them for all eternity. This is the purpose of God's actions from the beginning with Adam and Eve. Virtually everyone in heaven will have come into existence through the sexual union of their parents. The sexual is at the core of human existence. Thus, widespread violations of the sexual, especially culturally normed violations, rip apart human nature, society, families, couples, and individuals. This culture has penetrated even the walls of the Church. The living out of sexual nature in its simple fullness is an extraordinary achievement of grace and a powerful means of evangelization.

To understand our modern crisis, it helps first to recognize how much Christ changed the sexual paradigm for all humanity, a change even the apostles thought "a bit much" (and moderns think "way too much"). He called Christians to live their sexual lives with a shocking simplicity.

First: Changing the norms of the Old Testament, He said there is no divorce (Mk 19:5–9), which so astounded the apostles that they retorted, "In that case it is better not to get married" (Mt 19:10). With time, Chris-

10. Shulamith Firestone, *The Dialectic of Sex: The Case for Feminist Revolution* (New York: William Morrow and Co., 1970), 4.
11. For overviews of the research on most of these issues, see www.Marripedia.org; and for more charts on the same, see http://marri.us/research/sexuality/.

tians have come to realize more fully the meaning of those words — that being children of the family of the Blessed Trinity, we marry in covenant with each other and with the Trinity and begin a life of unbreakable unity; unbreakable not because of perfected human nature, but because unity is of the essence of the Trinity, and covenanted family unity in Them is ontologically impossible to break.[12] Because marriage is a sacrament of the body, it ceases to be operative once a body dies and does not hold in the afterlife ... though personal relationships do in the communion of the saints.

Second: "If you look at a woman lustfully you have already committed adultery with her in your heart" (Mt 5:28). In New Testament lists of grave moral offenses, adultery often comes immediately after murder to drive home how grave it is. Christ wants this radical simplicity of heart, not just externally chaste behavior. This a game-changing, heart-changing "raising-of-the-bar" on matters sexual for all His disciples. He is more interested in the heart than the behavior (though the behavior tells much about the heart).

Third: "The few are called to be celibate for the Kingdom" (Mt 19:12). These are His elite disciples, His "special ops" units dedicated to an extreme love of all mankind.

There are radical implications from this teaching on matters sexual for all followers of Christ, including those called to marriage. Bottom line: All are called to celibacy — for most as a temporary stage in preparation for marriage — and for life for the leadership, for religious orders, and for those in special circumstances where they are not able to marry. The celibate man (priest, brother, monk, or layman) gives up all women for life; the married man gives up all but one. The early formation in purity of heart is the same for all Christians.

MARRIAGE: THE SACRAMENT AND PLACE OF THE SEXUAL

By natural law, in all cultures, but especially for Christians now that Christ has spoken, marriage is the only setting for sexual union. Thus,

---

12. There are many modern "martyrs" today: abandoned spouses of "civil law divorces" who stay faithful to their marriage vows. It would be great to have one canonized soon.

sex outside of marriage is taboo in most cultures, and became an even stronger norm in Christian countries.

In our own day the promotion of "sex outside of marriage" has affected the minds and hearts of even devout young adult Christians, as the work of Christian Smith of the University of Notre Dame has made clear: *unmarried*, weekly worshipping Christians (Catholic and non-Catholic) in their mid- to late twenties have had, on average, two sexual partners.[13]

The pursuit of sexual intimacy outside of marriage does not deliver the happiness most expect, as the data from a number of US national surveys make clear.[14] From all the measures taken, the enjoyment of the intact couple who worships weekly ranks highest, repeatedly.[15]

"Sex gone wrong" leads to weaker family structures, visible within the US federal data system. In all the data, for both adults and children, those in the intact married family always do best, on average. Only in the intact married family do children experience the stability of their parents belonging to each other. In all other family structures, rejection is present between the parents, with all its natural consequences for adults and children.

THE FUNDAMENTAL RESPONSE TO OUR CORRUPTED CULTURE: THE SEXUALLY WELL-FORMED MALE

For the first time since the early Church and pagan Greco-Roman times, modern parents are on their own, lacking support from the culture and even from formerly reliable institutions (school and sometimes even church pastors). They face an increasingly toxic sex education in the public schools.[16] Parents now have to undertake the sexual formation of their sons and daughters. Because this need is likely to remain acute for at least a few centuries, as old cultures unravel and before a new culture emerges, the Christian father has a duty that never had to be made an explicit part

---

13. Christian Smith and Patricia Snell, *Souls in Transition: The Religious and Spiritual Lives of Emerging Adults* (New York: Oxford University Press, 2009).

14. "Mapping America: Sexuality," Marriage and Religion Research Institute, http://marri.us/research/mapping-america/.

15. Though some couples have marriages that do not result in such enjoyment. Statistically this is expected to hold for the few at the tail end of the variance. The Cross is visible on the low end, ecstasy on the other.

16. As the perennial teaching of the popes makes clear, sexual education lies in the home, not the school.

of his family duties: the mentoring of his sons in matters sexual so that his son has the capacity for natural as well as sacramental marriage.

By the time the son leaves the family (around age eighteen), he needs not only to have developed the virtues needed for chaste living, but also that full understanding of matters sexual that all young adults desire. If not so educated, the son will be tempted to find a full understanding from a source hostile to Christ's teaching.

Because sex education in many public schools undermines Catholic morality (something no one will deny), it is a grave danger to the children exposed to it. As an increasingly emboldened enemy distorts the minds of younger and younger children, parents need to take the sexual formation of their children out of the school (if they can do so legally)[17] and into their homes. As the protectors of their children, husbands will need to take the lead and reassert parents' right to educate their child.

BUILDING A COMMUNITY OF FATHER-PROTECTED FAMILIES

This urgent need for fathers to take on the sexual formation of their sons is evangelically strategic on the human nature level — upon which grace builds. Because the sexual is so central to human relationships and, post puberty, is immediately in play between the sexes, Catholic parents need to have a network of families who agree with one another on the sexual norms and virtues they want for their children.

Because women form groups much easier than men do, they can build their own relational infrastructure that can bind families together and help them raise daughters who understand the need for holy purity. However, men tend to form fewer friendships. They don't form groups to discuss intimate issues, for they are not inclined to discuss intimate issues at all![18] Nor are they inclined to talk about these issues with their sons.

But, just as the armed forces have learned that men go into battle with much less anxiety when they have a buddy, so in this case a father

---

17. California may be the only state to prohibit totally opting out of sex ed. See http://www.ncregister.com/daily-news/does-california-law-deny-parents-right-to-opt-out-of-gender-education.
18. The difference between the sexes in rates of seeking counseling illustrates this.

who trusts another father can form an alliance to help each other in forming their sons. Also, men do form groups readily if there is an urgent task that is greater than any one of them can accomplish alone. The protection of their families and the sexuality of their children certainly qualifies. There is an urgent need to figure out how to do this so that all Catholic men take on this task.[19]

Imagine a father speaking along the following lines with authorities of a school where the sex-ed program undermines his family:

> *"This is my boy, not yours. My wife and I brought him into existence. This sexual domain is exclusively ours and belongs to no one else. One half of the DNA in every cell in his body comes from me, the other half from my wife. Nobody — and I mean nobody — has the right to come into this territory that is exclusively mine and my son's. I, the male who gave him life, am the one to teach him how to be a man so that he will be a great husband, so that he with his wife will bring another child into a loving family.*
>
> *[And, depending on the reaction, he might continue:] "For this my wife and I married. This is our life. It is not yours; stay out! Keep your hands off the sexuality of my son and my daughter!"*

Fathers thinking and talking this way among themselves and speaking this way to teachers, principals, and boards, is a form of re-evangelization, natural law re-evangelization. It is a universal moral issue, not solely a Catholic issue. The formation of sons, "the strategic spine" because of the strategic weakness, begins long before he begins to attend school.

STAGES OF THE SEXUAL FORMATION OF A SON BY HIS FATHER

The sexual formation of his son by a father begins at birth and continues through infancy, early and middle childhood, pre-adolescence and adolescence and finally into young manhood.

Infancy and Early Childhood Phases: The objective of these first two phases is a deep bond of affection with his son that blossoms into

---

19. There are a number of efforts under way, such as *The Dad Project* and *This Man Is You.*

the boy's trust in his father because of his father's delight in him. This achievement is critical for the boy's later acceptance of his father's tutoring on matters sexual. There are other benefits, including the formation of a good image of fatherhood, the psychological underpinnings of trust in God the Father.

Mid-childhood: This is a relatively quiet period in a boy's life, from about age three to around age eleven, when both he and his father can enjoy each other in games, outings, and shared interests. Though boys generally want to play with boys and not girls, it is a period of formation in matters sexual, such as modesty in dress and in relations with his sisters and kindness in the family, especially toward the women in his life: his mother and sisters. During this period his father deliberately tutors him in honoring females in a way different from honoring males. In times past it would have been toward the end of this period (timing it in consultation with his wife) that the father would have begun inoculation against pornography; but today, sadly, it is necessary to introduce the topic of pornography (briefly) much earlier because of the age of first exposure to pornography, which by 2018 has dropped to age eight.

During this stage, in consultation with his wife, the father times "the talk" in which he introduces his son explicitly to matters sexual: the nature of conception and intercourse. Later on (age eleven, twelve, or thirteen, depending on the boy), the father prepares him for the new biological experiences of impending puberty and its implications for the new habits of body, mind, and heart that he will be called on to develop: self-control and continence versus the temptation to masturbation and the long-term consequences of both. This catechesis in the nature of the body is the necessary foundation for any theology of the body and is the remote preparation for marriage that every man needs.

Adolescent Phase: The father tutors his son on the practicalities of honoring girls, of dealing with temptations (by teaching him how he deals with sexual temptations), guarding the eyes, and many other aspects of sexuality, all within a framework of God's great gift of sexuality and the intense human love that it makes possible between a man and a woman. Through the way his father talks, his son will pick up an attitude of holy purity that begins the packaging of the gift of an undivided heart for the woman who will be his spouse.

Late Adolescence and Young Adulthood: The father prepares his son for marriage, even though it may be a decade or more in the future: staying celibate until marriage, developing a devotion to his future wife's guardian angel and to Saint Joseph; frequent confession; how to date and what to look for in a spouse; how an unengaged couple can explore each other's understanding of marriage and having children, the great project they might undertake together; freedom and responsibility; preparing professionally to be a good provider so as to be able to support a large family should that happen. Myriad other issues will naturally arise and be the occasion of still deeper discussion and formation.

Should his son sense a vocation to one of the celibate vocations, all of the father's tutoring, by preparing his heart for generous self-giving in marriage, has also laid the solid foundation for this different call to total self-giving to God, his bishop, and his parishioners. The sexual preparations for both are the same.

THE CELIBATE STAGE PRIOR TO MARRIAGE

In both the married and celibate vocations, the nature of the sexual calling is central to the life one is called to — one in the generous giving and supporting of new human beings in cooperation with a lifelong spouse, the other in giving oneself unreservedly to many, many more. By embracing celibacy, the heart is made big "for the many." By contrast the married are called to intense love with all of one's heart for "the few."

But those called to the sexual vocation (marriage) are called to a celibate life prior to marriage, as the natural preparation of the heart so that it is undividedly given only to the other for life. This need is evident in the almost universal expectation of virginity prior to marriage for the female across all cultures and times prior to the age of "the pill."

The following data illustrate the need for this celibate stage even in the "age of the pill." It makes abundantly clear that the number of sexual partners prior to marriage has a destructive impact on the average marriage and, therefore, on the life of the average American child. Because of its multiple effects on all the institutions[20] (family, church, school, marketplace, and government), I deem this data the most important in all the social sciences. The chart shows the percentage divorced five years after getting married, given the number of sexual partners experienced before marriage. It depicts the impact of each additional sexual partner on the probability of the marriage breaking down. The data has been replicated two other times. Even one and especially two premarital sexual partners, especially by women, have big effects on divorce rates. Given the impact of premarital sex, expecting virginity in females prior to marriage is sound. The national average impact for women who have had sexual relations with one man other than their husbands is that one-third will divorce within the first five years, and if they have had two such partners, half of them will divorce. Many people need to be aware of this data: husbands-to-be; in-laws who will have much reduced access to their grandchildren; the bride's parents, who will have more damage to take care of; and, of course, the bride herself. My first thought on seeing this graph was: There was wisdom in the Mediterranean cultures' practice of chaperoning. It protected the woman, the man, the future children, and the community. And the male needs the same.

---

20. Patrick Fagan and Robert Rector, "The Effects of Divorce on America," *The Heritage Foundation*, June 5, 2000, https://www.heritage.org/marriage-and-family/report/the-effects-divorce-america.

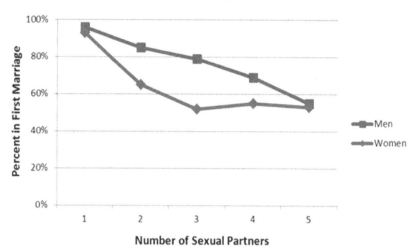

Other well-established findings reveal that the earlier the first un-married intercourse, the greater the number of sexual partners in a life-time, the more likely a woman will have an abortion, and have a child out of wedlock. Out-of-wedlock birth increases the likelihood of the mother's not completing her education, of a life in poverty, and of increased physical and sexual abuse.[21]

Given all this, Christ's call for celibacy for all his disciples makes sense, from a "human nature" and "natural law" point of view.[22] However, to live the virtue of purity implied, grace needs to abound, and that comes only with an operative faith, hope, and love, and an intense relationship with God.[23]

---

21. Fagan, "Rising Illegitimacy — America's Social Catastrophe," *The Heritage Foundation*, June 29, 1994, https://www.heritage.org/report/rising-illegitimacy-americas-social-catastrophe. Also, for multiple labeled charts, see http://marri.us/speeches_powerpoints/.

22. One good priest I know (with a doctorate in metaphysics) always uses the phrase "divine natural law."

23. There is no research on the impact of frequent confession on "life after sin" or even "life with repeated fall-ings into sin." I am sure that the data will be quite different on the impact of lack of purity on this sub-population that resorts to Confession.

THE EARLY CHRISTIAN FAMILY: HOPE OF THE FUTURE

Christ's transformative teaching on sexuality (quickly noticed by the pagans of the day)[24] had an enormous impact on culture, on nations, and on Western Civilization. As Christianity spread so, too, did its intact, married family.

With the retreat from marriage in recent decades, coupled with modern social science data that measures it, we grasp the massive positive impact stable family life had on societies in centuries past, the so-called Dark Ages and the early Renaissance. Now, by contrast, we see the opposite: "intergenerational compounding deficits" as more children are being raised without always-intact-married parents.[25]

At the heart of the early spread of Christianity was the community of families gathered weekly to worship in the Sacrifice of the Mass. Here we see the symbiotic relationship between the two sacramental vocations.[26] Together, these institutional forms of the two great loves (the love of God and the love of neighbor, the first neighbor being one's spouse) gave us the spiritual core of Western Civilization. We now know that these loves combined (weekly worship and intact marriage) give society the best outcomes possible on all the goods it desires and against all the evils it fears.[27]

It is within the healthy family that the well-formed young citizen learns the basic tasks of a well-functioning society. These basic tasks are marriage and family; the worship of God; education; working for a living (the economy); and government (safety, crime prevention, and taxation). The young citizen well formed in these tasks is the gift parents give to

---

24. Rodney Stark, *The Rise of Christianity: A Sociologist Reconsiders History*, (Princeton, NJ: Princeton University Press, 1996).

25. Especially in the inner-city black family.

26. The symbiosis was largely overlooked because of the emphasis on the "rejection of the world" aspect of religious life that came to dominate Church thinking for almost fifteen centuries, for roughly 1500 years, from the era of Saint Benedict to Saint Josemaria Escriva and Vatican II. In the process, the sacrament of marriage, the vocation of the many to "the sacrifice of self for the others" lost its proper standing in the Church's different vocational paths of union with God and instead was regarded as a ceding of that pursuit for more selfish, more worldly, pleasure-seeking ends (all of which are quite possible in the clerical and religious state, too, though this did not affect their "standing" as vocations). The hypnotic (deep suggestion/attitudinal) effect of this assumption led, over time to a massive distortion of the meaning of the sacrament of marriage, the correction of which is still in its infancy.

27. Mapping America, retrieved from http://marri.us/research/mapping-america/.

society, the gift that keeps on giving, generation after generation.

PRINCIPLES OF FAMILY SPIRITUALITY
The *a priori* Principle: Grace Builds on Nature

Catholic couples must first understand that grace builds on nature. Grace cannot perfect what is not there. Neo-Marxists inherently understand this, too; when they corrupt nature, grace has much less to work on. Therefore, parents have first to cultivate the human virtues necessary for their own happy marriage: kindness, forgiveness, honesty, order, industriousness, good budgeting, cheerfulness, sociability — virtues admired by all, no matter their religion. These virtues bring peace to all who practice them. They are universal. Assuming the human effort required, all who also pray have the help of God to perfect these virtues.

Secular situations — at work, in sports, and in politics — also demand virtues. The Catholic family will keenly cultivate these; not least because they provide a foundation for solid professional work, but also as the great bridge to friendship. Many who, having lost their happiness through materialism or sensuality, will be struck by their coworker's virtues, productivity, and especially their happiness. Having lost their way, they will be attracted to them.

Cultivating Human Virtues in Children

For children these virtues should be started during early childhood. The first virtue to teach is God's gift to mothers and fathers: the virtue of order. Two-year-olds can begin to live order by putting shoes under the bed, folding up clothes on the chair, and putting dirty socks in the laundry. Gradually expanding such habits benefits the child, the parent, and the whole family (see the chart below).

Cultivation of the Human Virtues --- Phases of Readiness				
	Up to Age 7	**From 8-12**	**From 13-15**	**From 16-18**
Predominant Cardinal Virtue	Justice	Fortitude	Temperance	Prudence
Principal Theological Virtue		Charity	Faith	Hope
Key Human Virtue	Obedience	Fortitude	Modesty	Prudence
	Sincerity	Perseverance	Moderation	Flexibility
	Orderliness	Industriousness	Sociaability	Understanding
		Patience	Friendship	Loyalty
		Responsibility	Respect for Others	Audacity
		Justice	Simplicity	Humility
		Generosity	Patriotism	Optimism
(With permission): David Isaacs, *Character Building*, Four Courts Press, Dublin, 1983 and 2001				

Though these insights have been around for decades, most American parents are unaware of them. In former times, living close to extended families, the younger generation learned much about marriage, family life, and child-raising. That pattern has vanished, though some mild compensations are emerging, such as the child virtue-development literature,[28] and organizations devoted to this work.[29]

Today most parents are unprepared to deal with the child-raising demands of their vocation because the culture and institutions that supported the character formation of children are absent or much diminished. The parish or lay associations in the Church are the natural places for developing such support and for young couples to seek it. The older, wiser couples are the natural ones to provide this service to younger couples, though they, too, have to figure out how to do it. But even more beckons the modern married couple.

Vocational Principle: United Spouses

The ascetical literature for religious devotes much space to poverty, chastity, and obedience. In marriage, their counterpart is unity. The ascetical literature is extraordinarily thin, if existent at all. The degree of unity between spouses is the degree of their happiness and also the degree of

---

28. James Stenson has multiple books for parents on forming character in their children. See his website, http://parentleadership.com.

29. For example: The International Federation for Family Development, http://iffd.org/; Parent Encouragement Program, http://pepparent.org/; or The Heights School podcasts for parents, https://heightsforum.org/podcasts/.

their children's inner strength.

The spouses have much to overcome if they are to achieve unity: their totally different styles, being male and female; the different ways their brains work; their different temperaments; their different attachment styles; their different talents; their different family backgrounds and expectations; sometimes their different cultural backgrounds; their different expectations of family life; and the care of their different weaknesses and wounds. Gradually learning to appreciate and accept these differences while learning to harness them, learning when to let one lead and the other follow and when to pull together, involves acquiring many virtues, especially perseverance. Here is a fertile field for faith, hope, and love, a unique program of virtue tailor-made for each couple.

For every couple, coming up with a family budget is a big step in forging unity, no matter their income level. Unity on a budget brings peace to the whole family and a spirit of poverty by the good use of money and property. For Catholic families seriously interested in being apostles, a well-oiled budget is a *sine qua non*.

Vocational Principle: Responsibility with Freedom

All the work of spouses toward each other and as parents guiding their children — especially during adolescence — needs to embody the entwined moral principles of "responsibility coupled with freedom." Our Lord wants both: "Let your yes mean yes and your no mean no" (Mt 5:37). This is *the sine qua non* of a healthy social life with friends and with God. With freedom and responsibility, nature can build, and grace (God) can perfect. Parents have a few years (those years before the child leaves home) to imbue their children with these intertwined principles. As each teenager gets older, he is increasingly treated as one free to choose (but reminded that there are natural consequences to every choice), and that he is responsible for becoming a mature adult; for becoming a child of God with his unique place in the universe; and, finally, that he is responsible for getting to heaven, the only thing that counts in the end (as well as the best way to live a full and happy life).

Vocational Principle: Sabbath, the Relationship Day

The data shows that man thrives on the two great loves — of neighbor and of God. These are most intensely displayed in family attendance at Mass. Sunday is the day of rest that is "made for man" (Mk 2:27), a day for rest and revival through the enjoyment of others — of God and of family and friends. Providing and partaking of this rest are key parts of family happiness and sanctity (grace perfecting nature). The Sabbath is part of the "rule of life" given us by Christ. Though keeping the Sabbath is clear matter for obedience (even if the culture clouds it); yet, done well, it is easy to obey because of the real enjoyment it brings.

The Sabbath day begins with the "grace" side, the worship of God by the family around the Eucharistic sacrifice with other families of the community. Then comes the "nature" side: a meal together — sometimes with extended family and friends. Throw into this mix those ways of having a good time: games, an outing, drinks, music, song, dance, story-telling, poem, limerick or joke-telling. Or "celebrities" can be invited: a former professor or teacher; the local pastor; a notable friend of a friend; a favorite uncle; or old friends of the parents who tell the children stories about their parents' growing up — a gift that will be treasured. Occasionally, a movie, if everyone is willing to discuss it afterward, turns a passive event into a shared activity. Some banish digital activity for the whole day, and intrusive sports.[30] The object of all this relational activity is re-creation by making the others happy or loving one's neighbor.

Sundays, lived this way, deepen relationships, first with God then among family and friends. Thus, parents develop the relational capacities of children, especially the capacity for friendships with other children who, over time, become their adolescent peer-group, the group that will play an important formative role in the teen years. It takes foresight for parents to develop this years in advance when it is very simple to foster friendships among children, an ability that vanishes as adolescence approaches.

---

30. For example, see Catholic News Service, "Detroit Catholic Schools and Parishes to Stop all Sports on Sunday," *America*, May 20, 2019, https://www.americamagazine.org/politics-society/2019/05/20/detroit-catholic-schools-and-parishes-stop-all-sports-sunday.

Sundays can prepare adolescents for when they leave their home. Wise parents will pull the children into planning and pulling off such Sundays, so that they are formed in receiving joy by giving enjoyment to their friends (and relief to their parents). There are multiple levels of virtue and love in such rituals for the Sabbath. Neighbors, starved of belonging, will be drawn to such families who display this "glory of God in man fully alive." Such families preach loudly without saying a word.

Fundamental Principle: I Am a Child of God

To know that he is a child of God is the core principal of so much of the spiritual life. It is the application of Saint Therese's and Saint Josemaria's insistence on a childlike trust in God, and it is Our Lord's constant attitude toward His Father: "How do I please my Father?"

Living life within the family of the Trinity becomes easier if parents work to form a constant attitude of seeing each of their children as a child of God entrusted to them for formation of their souls. Their vocation as a married couple is specially to serve the others in the family; first one's spouse, then in all the ways of creating affectionate family life. To do this always is to become a canonizable saint.

The paths to sanctity for both vocations (celibate and married) involve the same virtues and tools (doctrine, sacraments, prayer, mortification, and spiritual direction), but the settings and the modes of formation are worlds apart. The religious life involves a renunciation of the world. Married family life is an embrace of the world, yielding its own brand of spiritual life, embracing human nature to perfect it through grace and so as to aim to be, in Saint Irenaeus's phrase, "the glory of God, a man fully alive."

VOCATIONAL PRINCIPLE: THE CROSS IN MARRIAGE

Because of unforeseen difficulties and even disasters, married life, even in its sexual dimensions, may end up being a heavy cross, with little or no ecstatic union. Yet the end (total union with God) is the same for all and, across all vocations, often arrived at soonest by those with the heaviest burdens, their unique path to Calvary.

The literature of spiritual direction, marital therapeutics, and child development all witness the effects of parental marriage and parent-child relationships on the flourishing or blocking of the child's relational and intellectual capacities. No parent is perfect. No marriage is perfect. And the child is the unavoidable recipient of the weakness, dysfunctions, or wounds visited upon him by his parents. When the child marries in his turn, the "fallen human nature" cycle begins anew, *even if* he is blessed with intergenerational strengths from virtuous grandparents and parents. All couples, even the most romantically blissful, eventually realize the faults of the other and gradually realize the suffering their own faults cause their spouse. This phase (marked by mild or intense disappointment and anger) is the first stage of the mature marriage that adapts to reality and begins to flourish.[31] Given the extent of family brokenness today, many spouses are wounded in some way.

Identifying, forgiving, and overcoming these faults is the tailor-made curriculum of virtue for every married person, necessary for marital realism and tranquility, and the way by which individuals are likely to pass on fewer wounds to their own children.[32]

Dr. Richard Fitzgibbons lays out the multiple cycles of virtue acquisition entailed in growing a healthy marriage, while repairing the wounds inherited from parents.[33] He lists the five major weaknesses that wreck marriages: anger, selfishness, the urge to control, emotional distance,

---

31. Father Ron Gillis, of Washington, DC, spoke of a "revelation" he had as he looked at a young couple kneeling before him at the beginning of a Nuptial Mass: "I realized that someday (maybe within the week, or the next few months, or next year or three years from now) one of these love-birds is going to wake up one morning, look over at the other still asleep, and say *'How the hell did I get myself into this mess?'* That is when the real marriage begins. At that point I threw out the theological sermon I had prepared on the sacrament of marriage and spoke instead of the symbiotic relationship between the priesthood and marriage and how they support each other in carrying their two different versions of Christ's Cross." (personal communication)

32. The implications for the modern, non-intact black family are enormous. At age seventeen, only 17 percent of black Americans have parents who are in an always-intact marriage. The black child is likely the most wounded in the US ... most by "intergenerational-family-inflicted" wounds. There is a challenge in finding a way to say this without triggering the typical "politically correct" exploitation. In the early 1940s the black family was rather intact (see chart below for adults aged 35–39, by when most adults are "settled"). Note that the "widowed" and "always single" indicate that almost all black couple-parents were married. The 1930s and 1940s were the years of mass migration from southern to northern states, and mass migration and increase in family breakdown go together. It was in the late 1930s and early 1940s, too, that Planned Parenthood made its big inroads into the black community (through black pastors, with the best of intentions, no doubt). Out-of-wedlock births and marriage breakup universally follow the introduction of contraception, and frequently accompany mass migration. Ireland's changes in the 1970s to 1980s is the clearest illustration, internationally, of the effects of contraception.

33. Richard Fitzgibbons, MD, *Habits for a Healthy Marriage: A Handbook for Catholic Couples* (San Francisco: Ignatius Press, 2019).

and compulsions (which include addictions). Forgiveness, generosity, respect, responsibility, and temperance counteract these. This lifelong program of virtue[34] for married couples is clearly different from the way of the celibate Carthusian, but not necessarily any easier.

Vocational Principle: Evangelization through Friendship

We have just seen some of the ways in which the family takes care of the commandment of love, intensely loving "the few" entrusted to them. But the Church is always missionary, wanting for everyone the joy of a full life with God on earth and later in heaven for all eternity. There are many ways to be missionary; but given the level of family breakdown and the suffering that results, a main source of "repair" and rebuilding will be personal friendship: deliberately seeking to be friends with someone, doing them good for no ulterior motive than to serve them as they need to be served. Most frequently that will be just listening and understanding them. Once that happens, friendship goes where it will — for the good of both. To have friends one must be sociable with many to discover those with whom we have something important in common (the basis of friendship).

The capacity for real friendship begins only in the teen years, as adolescents become aware of their own inner life and seek to confide in others they trust. In turn, they have to have the capacity to listen and receive what others entrust to them by their self-revelation. The family dinner conversations are the natural way to tutor in sociability and friendship. Every Christian needs to learn how to be a friend, first by finding someone from whom he can receive friendship, then going on to spread the same among a few. The art of friendship needs much attention

---

34. Bob Enright, an award-winning professor of psychology at the University of Wisconsin, states: "Drawing on his experience of forty years as a psychiatrist, Dr. Richard Fitzgibbons presents twelve habits that can foster healing and growth in Catholic marriages. This book helps couples to identify and resolve the major emotional conflicts that weaken their relationships and hurt their marriages. *Habits for a Healthy Marriage* is unique because it draws on the field of positive psychology, which focuses on growth in virtues. Each chapter names a common marital problem along with a particular virtue that can help couples to overcome that problem. It shows that the road to healing is paved with forgiveness, not only between spouses but also within their families of origin. Along the way the author incorporates the luminous writing of Saint John Paul II on marriage and the timeless wisdom of the Catholic Church."

and rediscovery.[35] Many souls need friends, especially American souls, if Saint Teresa of Calcutta is to be believed: "The most terrible poverty is loneliness and the feeling of being unloved."

Vocational Principle: To Begin Again

The paths of a family spirituality are clear, but even when the spirit is willing (and it is not always willing), the flesh is weak. Repentance and asking forgiveness is so constant a need that it needs to be a discipline, hence the examination of conscience and acts of contrition at the end of the day, of which that proposed by evangelical pastor Emerson Eggerichs may be best adapted to married couples.[36] Frequent Confession is a "no-brainer," and foundational for children also. It is best learned by accompanying father to the sacrament.[37]

THE SOCIAL SCIENCES: ANOTHER FORM OF EVANGELIZATION

On many issues the social science data, well presented from good surveys, can be useful in discussions with children, extended family, friends, and work colleagues as a "natural law catechesis"; i.e., in discourse on human nature. Data illustrate, they do not prove; and therefore, are useful in opening up conversations and in getting people to think. Well done (repeatedly done), they illustrate human nature, or they help reveal man to himself. They lead naturally to conversations on the virtues required to achieve or avoid the outcomes under discussion. Many of the issues raised in this chapter have their beginnings in what the data say about human nature.[38]

For instance, at least eight US federal surveys track the frequency of religious attendance, permitting us to conclude that, for both adults and children, those who worship weekly do best.[39] These are national aver-

---

35. See Chapter 22, "Friendship," in David Isaacs, *Character Building: A Guide for Parents and Teachers* (Dublin: Four Courts Press
36. Emerson Eggerichs, *Love & Respect: The Love She Most Desires; The Respect He Desperately Needs* (Nashville: Thomas Nelson, 2004).
37. For a number of studies documenting the importance of the father's religious practice, see http://marri.us/wp-content/uploads/May-11.pdf.
38. Much more can be found at the MARRI website: https://marri.us.
39. Patrick Fagan, Mapping America Sampler Booklet, http://marri.us/wp-content/uploads/Mapping-America-Sampler.pdf.

ages, demographic maps of the average strengths and weaknesses of the American population.

Though these data are "only" correlations, they are robust descriptions of the American people and tell which group thrives most or least. The correlation is always strongest when both of the two great loves that Christ pinpointed are minimally present: love of God and love of neighbor.

When we combine both family structure and the rate of worship of God, **the intact married family that worships weekly does best on every outcome measured in the US federal data system**! By stark contrast, those from the non-intact family that never worships do worst on every measurement.

Man thrives on the two great loves: love of God — shown minimally in weekly worship, and love of neighbor — shown most powerfully in marriage and in the married family.

The data[40] lead to two conclusions about the social sciences:

1. The social sciences well done cannot but illustrate the way God made man, and
2. The social sciences, well done, reveal man to himself: how he thrives and how he wilts.

The implications of these data for the common good are enormous. The greatest "social policy program" on earth is the combination of marriage and worship. Nothing in the social sciences and nothing in the professional program evaluation literature begins to approach stable marriage and weekly worship — despite trillions of dollars spent on social policy programs since the beginning of "The Great Society" expansion of the welfare state in 1964–1965.[41] Social policy tends to miss the obvious,

---

40. See all the Mapping America charts at https://marri.us/research/mapping-america/.
41. As former Deputy Assistant Secretary of Social Policy at the Department of Health and Human Services, I testified before Congress (Senate) on this, drawing attention to all the extant evaluation literature procured by Congress. Nothing works in any of the federal programs in helping failing people thrive. Idiosyncratic programs at the local level often work, but they cannot be replicated with any steady predictability. Why? They too rely on love — the level of dedication on those doing the helping. That cannot be replicated by government program or funding.

that man's capacity to improve himself and his children lies mainly in the relational (the spiritual) dimension. The implications of this for the Catholic family's understanding of itself are enormous (as well as for all other intact married families who worship God weekly).[42] If only Catholics knew the human truthfulness of their faith (outside of Revelation, though aided by Revelation), so much, but not all, of the welfare state would not be necessary nor be leading us astray.

Greatly aided by this data when presented clearly, Catholics can educate their family, friends, and work colleagues on the two basic needs of human nature: faithful marriage and weekly worship of God. From these unvarying data we can draw two universal principles of human nature: the need of all for these two great loves.

A WRAP-UP FANTASY SERMON

The following fantasy sermon, which I would give if I were a parish priest, repackages the main issues:

Joe and Judy, this is my annual Family Mission Sunday Sermon. You know I want to make you both great evangelizers (and every other couple here), and I am not asking you to knock on strangers' doors.

Joe, I know you are saying to yourself "Father, I am up to my neck taking care of my family and my job. I might get a few hours' break a week — if I am lucky. And you know Judy is as stretched as I am!"

Don't worry, Joe, I am not asking you to do anything you are not already doing. But I am asking you to do it differently. I guarantee you will be happier and, in the process, become great missionaries. You both have something the world is looking for: you are married and have children. You are common-sense experts on marriage and family. With a bit of tweaking, you can become world-class experts on your marriage and your children. And this

---

42. Theological equivalence is not to be inferred, but the natural law impacts of weekly worship and intact marriage are.

will make you first-class missionaries.

Here are the steps, the few changes:

First, Joe, when you get home, I want you look Judy in the eye and ask her: "Judy, what is the single best thing I can do for you to make our marriage happier for you?" (I bet she already has the answer, but she may be afraid to ask.) The good news for you is she has to ask you the very same thing. Some men are afraid to ask that one thing of their wife. You can ask her for anything, for the best thing that would make being married to Judy much happier. Just one thing, one change.

The second step is more complex, but the first one is more important and makes the second step more possible. In this parish we all have to become "character forming" experts, and I have to help you all get there. You are going to put your heads together and think about each child and ask: "What is the one thing this child needs from us to make our relationship with him better?"

You are raising them to be great adults, great husbands and wives, and great friends.

The third step, the "missionary" step, is simple enough, as you only do it once a year: Throw a barbecue for your neighbors. That's it! Be friendly with them. Once a year at least!

By your third barbecue, you will receive a phone call from one of your neighbors: "Joe, I want your advice on a family issue. You and Judy seem to have your act together. Can we get together?" This is not the beginning of your missionary work, but the fruit of the work you have been doing all the time — by the power of your example. Just throw a barbecue and cultivate friendships with your neighbors in a normal way; no agenda, except to become friends with them (and with their guardian angels). If you have the faith, the fruit will come. So: a great marriage, one request at a time; great children, one gift of yourself to each one at a time; and a barbecue once a year. If every family here did this — what a parish we would become, because our neighbors would say, "See how they love one another." And my bishop will be asking me, "How do you do it?" And I would say "Barbecues, bishop. Barbecues!" And he would remind me of the fourth step.

You are already taking the fourth step — but you must do it better and better: worshipping God at Mass on Sunday. This is the center of our Catholic lives. Gradually, enter into the Mass more and more, better and better. Teach your children how to do it, so that they know what they are doing and will want to keep doing it when they leave home — soon enough! Their questions will be a great help to your going deeper into the Mass. Teach them that Christ comes right inside them at Communion and stays there until the appearance of bread breaks down into its biochemicals. Show them how to use these precious minutes each week and how to get the most out of Mass. With the Mass, the three other steps will be fruitful; without it, they won't. Every Sunday, you and I will enter into the Mass together and pray for each other that God helps us all through the next week. And do remember Him in the tabernacle when you pass by a church. Say hello at least. Sometimes drop in to visit with Him.

CONCLUSION

The most important dimension of family spirituality today may be our ability to give thanks to the Trinity for our capacity to be "man fully alive," living life in stark contrast to today's big heresy: the deliberate suppression of man's true sexual nature, a drowning of natural law in pursuit of things and pleasure and power, the neo-pagan culture of the West.

As ordinary Catholics begin to understand marriage as their way to God, and when they work, through grace, to bring family life to a high art, they will attract attention. If the world sees in them the happiness it seeks, it will come to learn their secret.

DISCUSSION QUESTIONS

1. What would be the effect on your children if, every day, you and your spouse asked each other, "Dear, what is the single best thing I can do for you today that would bring our relationship closer to what your heart desires?" ... and followed through on the answer?

2. Rank in order the importance of the major relationships in your life at present. What does each relationship require from you for it to move up to the next level?
3. How well are you and your spouse preparing your children to live that celibacy they are called to prior to marriage?
4. What would be the effect on your family and neighbors if at least once a month Father brought all the children under age thirteen with him to confession?

Parents Matter More Than They Think: What Does It Take to Pass on Catholic Faith and Values?

In this section, we explore some of the best research available on faith and moral transmission.

Vern Bengtson, a sociologist at the University of Southern California and author of the book *Families and Faith*, describes the results of his fifty-year-plus study of more than 350 families' efforts to pass on the faith to the next generation. He offers some surprisingly hopeful insights into just how much influence parents can have over their children's faith development and what factors increase the likelihood that parents can be effective in transmitting their faith to their children.

Justin Bartkus, lead researcher on the American Catholic Religious Parenting study sponsored by the McGrath Institute for Church Life, shares the equally hopeful and intriguing results of his major study into faith transmission.

Finally, Darcia Narvaez, developmental moral psychologist at the University of Notre Dame and winner of the APA's William James Prize for her book, *Neurobiology and the Development of Human Morality: Evolution, Culture and Wisdom,* explores the research on how parenting styles impact the development and function of the moral brain — the structures of the brain involved in empathy, self-control, moral reasoning, and other similar functions. She describes her evolved nest model as a parenting template that has been shown to help parents effectively raise moral children.

CHAPTER NINE

Millennials, Parents, Grandparents: Are Catholic Families Still Passing on Their Faith?[1]

VERN L. BENGTSON

University of Southern California

MERRIL SILVERSTEIN

Syracuse University

1. This paper is based on material from *Families and Faith: How Religion is Passed Down Across Generations* by Vern Bengtson, with Norella Putney and Susan Harris (Oxford: Oxford University Press, 2013). This research has been supported by grants from the John Templeton Foundation, the National Institute on Aging, and the National Institute of Mental Health. Data are from the Longitudinal Study of Generation's eight waves of surveys from 1970 to 2016. These have been archived with the University of Michigan's Inter-University Consortium for Political and Social Research and are available at no cost. We hope other researchers will feel free to conduct their own analyses of these data.

FIVE QUICK TAKES

1. Contrary to conventional wisdom, research shows that parents do still wield significant influence over whether children retain their faith as adults.
2. Contrary to conventional wisdom, research shows that the degree of parental influence over faith retention has not declined over the last several decades.
3. Parent-child closeness is the biggest factor in determining religious faith transmission.
4. Grandparents play a significant and under-appreciated role in faith transmission.
5. Catholics and mainline Protestants lag behind LDS, Jews, nonbelievers, and evangelical Protestants (in that order) in their ability to transmit their faith to the next generation.

Beverly Johnson, now sixty, is an African-American woman who was twenty-five when our thirty-five-year longitudinal study began in 1970. She was raised by her grandparents, Henry and Eleanor, and still attends the Catholic church that Henry converted to in the 1960s when they first moved to southern California. She says her grandfather and grandmother had the greatest influence on her life religiously. She adds that she raised her children as she was raised by her grandparents, with the Ten Commandments at the center of their instruction. Her daughter Erika (thirty-two) says, "My mother still maintains the attachment because my great-grandfather was so involved with the church." Erika is also a regular church attendee who says she is "very religious," though she stopped going to church between the ages of eighteen and twenty-seven. "I came back when I started having babies," she said.

The focus of our paper is on members of the Millennial generation, so-called because they were born about 1980 and thus came of age around the turn of the twenty-first century. As they have grown into young adulthood, much has been written about them. In many ways they appear to be quite different from their parents' generation, particularly in terms of religion. A highly publicized poll of religious affiliation in the United States found that almost one-third of Millennial generation members did not identify with any religious group, in comparison with 21 percent of Generation Xers, 15 percent of Baby Boomers, and less than 10 percent among older cohorts who identified that way (Pew Research Center, 2012).

However, public opinion polls such as this are often based on cross-sectional data about just one of many dimensions of religiosity — that of religious affiliation. In such surveys, questions are asked of individuals who are of different ages — young, middle-aged, and old — at one point in time, to people who respond to telephone calls asking them to take a survey. In the example of the Johnson family (above), we get a much more long-term perspective. Here we have data about not just one individual but about a family, with several generations of respondents. The information they provide spans several decades, from 1970 to 2005. The Johnsons have been participants in the thirty-five-year Longitudinal Study of Generations (LSOG), and they and the other 350-plus families in this study provide a broader perspective with which to view Millennials. We can compare their religious orientations with that of their parents and grandparents, and we can trace religious change over thirty-five years of historical time. By comparing these trends, we can make some predictions about what Millennials' religious practices and beliefs might be like in the future, as they themselves become parents and grandparents.

How different are the religious orientations of Millennials — Catholic or Protestant, Jewish or Mormon — from those of their parents? From those of their grandparents? How has familial religious influence changed over time — across the period of significant social religious changes that we have seen in U.S. culture since the 1960s? And how much should Catholic families be concerned about such trends, in the context of an increasingly secular society? These are some questions we examine in this paper.

GENERATIONAL AND CULTURAL CONTEXTS OF RELIGIOSITY TODAY

Millennials and Generational Differences

Many public opinion polls have focused on Millennials. They are the age cohort born between 1980 and 1995 (Pew Research Center, 2014), currently in their twenties and thirties. The defining characteristic of Millennials is that they were adolescents or emerging adults at the turn of the twenty-first century, during a time of significant technological, cultural, and religious change in US society.

Millennials made up more than one-fourth of the workforce in 2014 and appear different from their elders in many ways. In surveys, their responses often reveal a singularly individualistic outlook. Politically, they are more liberal: 29 percent say they are conservative, compared with 41 percent of Americans age thirty-five or older. Most of them (55 percent) believe that illegal immigrants should receive citizenship, compared with 44 percent of those thirty-five and older who believe that way. They are more ethnically diverse: 57 percent of Millennials are Caucasian white, compared with 72 percent of all the US population over age thirty-five. In some regions of the country, this generational contrast is even more striking; in California, which comprises almost one-sixth of the US population, over one-third of Millennials and those younger are non-Caucasian whites (Pew Research Center, 2014).

In religion, too, polls show differences between Millennials and their elders. Almost one in three are religious "nones" — that is, they say they are unaffiliated, describing their religion as atheist, agnostic, "spiritual but not religious," or "nothing" (Pew Research Center, 2012). Fewer than 19 percent of those over age thirty-five described themselves that way. One-third of Millennial respondents said they attended worship at least once a week, compared with 41 percent of adults thirty to sixty-five and 51 percent sixty-five and older. About half of Millennials said they pray every day (48 percent), compared with 56 percent of those thirty to forty-nine, 61 percent of those fifty to sixty-five, and 68 percent of those sixty-five and older.

We wanted to explore the significance of these differences in religion between Millennials and older age groups. To what extent is there a "generation gap" in religion? Are families failing to pass on their spiritual and religious values to their children? And how might the Millennials' own views and practices change as they become parents and grandparents?

Changing Cultural Contexts of Families and Religion

We began the Longitudinal Study of Generations (described more fully below) in the late 1960s, during a time of significant political and cultural change in American society. These changes were reflected in social institutions such as religion and the family. Thus, it is important to contextualize research on intergenerational transmission of religion by reviewing some relevant changes in American society and culture over the past half-century.

Changes in American Religiosity

There have been remarkable changes in American religious culture since the 1950s (especially recently), and often these have been linked to changes in intergenerational relationships. For most of its history, the United States has been a highly church-going nation. Affiliation and involvement with church activities increased in the years following World War II, hitting a peak in the mid-1950s (Chavez 2011; Wuthnow 1988, 2007). However, the economic prosperity and stability of the 1950s was followed by cultural changes in the 1960s; the first wave of Baby Boomer youth became involved in protests challenging the politics and values of their elders and created what seemed to be a "generation gap" of unprecedented magnitude in American history (Bengtson 1975). In the 1970s, researchers and social commentators described an increasing secularization of American society, prompting public discourse about the role of religion in education, politics, and mass communication (Bellah, Madsen, Sullivan, Swidler, and Tipton 1985; Wuthnow 1978).

More recently, there has been a remarkable increase in the numbers of "nones" in America — those who say they have no religious affiliation. By 2012, the unaffiliated represented more than 19 percent of the US adult population, a proportion that more than doubled from the decade before (Pew Research Center, 2012). One of the most sociologically interesting dimensions of this trend concerns its stratification by age. Younger people are much more likely than older ones to report that they have no religious affiliation or never attend services, creating a much greater age gap than observed in previous surveys (Pew Research Center, 2012). Thus, it would be plausible to expect that religious continuity between generations has declined over recent decades — that parent-youth simi-larity in religiosity would be less evident in the 2000s than it was in the 1970s.

Are Families Becoming Less Important?

American families also have changed over the past half-century, and this, too, may have led to a decline in religious influence by families. By 1990, one out of every two marriages in America ended in divorce, and by 2000, almost as many children lived in single-parent households as in dual-parent households. Of those children in two-parent households, one-fourth lived in "blended" families with stepparents and stepsiblings (Casper and Bianchi 2002; Cherlin 2010). In our 1970 survey, only 6 per-cent of the grandparents had divorced; in 2005, 26 percent had.

Trends such as these led to a growing chorus of public concern about the "decline of the American family." Within sociology, there was sup-port for this position by Popenoe (1993), who analyzed demographic data to conclude that divorce rates and dual-family employment had di-minished the influence of parents in the socialization of their children. Such perceptions of declining family influences continue as public and religious issues. In his 2012 presidential campaign, Texas Governor Rick Perry proclaimed a "Day of Prayer and Fasting" to focus on "the decline of our culture in the context of the demise of our families" (Sanders 2012). Catholic scholars have also voiced this view. In a review of the literature, Jesuit psychologist David Vitz (2005) concluded: "When one puts the big picture together, the decline of the family is obvious" (154).

Are Grandparents Becoming More Important?

On the other hand, another remarkable development over the past four decades has been the increasing importance of grandparents in American family life. Bengtson (2001) argued that grandparents have become more important to families than in any previous period of US history. More grandparents are involved in and contributing to their grandchildren's development than ever before, and this is resulting in intergenerational influence far beyond what most contemporary observers recognize. A recent review of research on intergenerational relationship (Swartz 2009) presents a variety of evidence concerning the importance of grandparents, and additional support is found in the AARP nationally representative surveys on grandparenting (Goyer 2012; Lampkin 2012). For example, 52 percent of older grandparents reported seeing a grandchild at least once a week; 26 percent said they communicated with a grandchild by e-mail, text, or Skype; 25 percent had spent more than $5,000 in providing support for grandchildren recently; and 59 percent felt they play a "very important role" in the lives of grandchildren (Lampkin 2012).

There are several reasons why grandparents may be more influential today and tomorrow than in the past. First is the growing availability of grandparents due the remarkable increase in life expectancy. Because grandparents are living longer than ever before, grandchildren today have the opportunity to spend a greater proportion of their lives with living grandparents. In 2005, 95 percent of American twenty-year-olds had at least one grandparent alive; at age thirty, almost 79 percent had a grandparent alive. A century ago, in 1900, the figures were 19 percent and 4 percent, respectively (Uhlenberg 2005, 2009). Second, because today's Baby Boomers have fewer children, they now have fewer sets of grandchildren; there are fewer grandchildren today to share more grandparents.

A third factor is that older people are healthier than in past generations, and as a group they have more resources to provide to grandchildren. In the AARP nationwide survey, 53 percent of grandparents reported providing help to grandchildren with educational expenses, 37 percent with everyday living expenses, and 25 percent with medical expenses. Fourth, a majority of grandparents have retired and thus have more opportunity to interact with and lend support to their grandchildren (AARP 2012). A fifth factor is technology: For grandchildren living far away, long-distance communication is much easier than in the past. Technologies such as cell phones, Skype, and Facebook offer more ways for cross-generational communication than ever before. Finally, with most mothers with young children in the labor force and with the growing number of single-parent households, more grandparents have been providing care for grandchildren than ever before (AARP 2012; US Bureau of the Census 2009).

For these reasons, grandparents today have greater opportunity to play a significant role in the lives of grandchildren than in previous decades. They provide tangible resources, offer both emotional support and useful information about the adult world, and can be transmitters of family and cultural history. Thus, it is not surprising that a majority of grandchildren report being emotionally close to their grandparents, as well as sharing similar views and values with grandparents (AARP 2012; Copen and Silverstein 2008; Silverstein, Giarrusso, and Bengtson 2003).

Nevertheless, empirical research on grandparents and their influence that goes beyond descriptive reporting is, as yet, underdeveloped. This is not surprising, since it has been only three decades or so since the first volume with empirical research on grandparenthood was published (Bengtson and Robertson 1985). Since then, an increasing number of studies have explored the complex roles of grandparents, grandchild perceptions of grandparents, grandparents who are raising grandchildren, and styles of grandparenting (Birditt, Tighe, Fingerman, and Zarit 2012; Michaleski and Shackleford 2005; Moserud 2008; Ruiz and Silverstein 2007; Szinovacz 1998; Swartz 2009). However, little research to date has focused on the *influence* of grandparents on grandchildren's outcomes, such as their religious orientations. This constitutes a significant gap in the research literature because youth today will have greater involvement with their grandparents — and for some, their great-grandparents — than any previous generation of grandchildren in American history (Bengtson 2001; Mueller and Elder 2003; Swartz 2009). Moreover, we know virtually nothing about patterns and processes of grandparent influences — and why some influence efforts are successful while others are not.

Theoretical Perspectives: Linked Lives, Cultural Change, and Religious Transmission

Despite the evidence for family influence reviewed above, some observers of American culture voice the opinion that religious inheritance across generations has declined over recent decades (Putnam and Campbell 2010; Wuthnow 2007). Thus, we wanted to explore two questions: To what extent do we see significant religious transmission by families in contemporary American society? And to what degree has this transmission changed over recent decades? We felt it was important to ground this inquiry in social science theory and determined the life-course perspective would be the most helpful theoretical orientation in understanding the intersections of families, religion, and time (both historical time and individual aging).

A central dimension of the life-course perspective is the concept of "linked lives": as individuals grow up and grow through the course of life, their development is tied to the changing lives of others, particularly parents and grandparents, siblings, then spouses, and eventually children and grandchildren (Bengtson, Elder, and Putney 2005). This is an important insight: an individual's religious identity develops in ways that are linked to other family members, particularly parents. Expanding on the concept of linked lives, we developed a theory to explain intergenerational continuity in values (Bengtson, Biblarz, and Roberts 2002). This theory posits conditions and socialization mechanisms by which older generations contribute to transmission of values and beliefs. A prominent mechanism of socialization concerns intergenerational solidarity, particularly emotional warmth. According to the model, intergenerational transmission of values is greater when the child perceives the parent or grandparent as warm and affirming, compared to cold and distant.

Research Methods and Procedures

Our analysis is based on data from the Longitudinal Study of Generations, which began in 1970–71 and has involved over 3,500 respondents from 357 three- and four-generation families for more than four decades. These multigenerational families were recruited in 1969 from among 840,000 members of a health maintenance organization located in southern California that had primarily served labor union members. The sample was generally representative of the southern California area, and results of the study matched those of nationally representative samples (for details, see Bengtson, Putney, and Harris 2013). There were 2,044 respondents at Wave-1 in 1970. Subsequent surveys took place in 1985, 1988, 1991, 1994, 1997, 2000, 2005, and 2016, with another survey in 2020. Response rates averaged 74 percent between waves. Beginning in

1991, the great-grandchildren (G4s) were recruited into the study when they reached age sixteen. In 2005, the Wave-8 survey, the number of respondents was 1,766, ranging in age from sixteen to 102.

Because the LSOG provides four-generation panel data collected over a long period of time, we have been able to utilize a "generational-sequential" analytic design by which matched cohorts of parents and children, grandparents and grandchildren, at roughly the same ages, can be compared at two different points in time, at roughly the same ages (Bengtson et al. 2002; Silverstein and Long 1998). Such a design allows evaluation of the effects of social change (historical or period effects such as religious trends) on socialization and family influence. We constructed family triads consisting of related grandparents, parents, and grandchildren; that is, if grandchildren had siblings, each grandchild was paired with the same parents and grandparents in the sample.

MEASURES
Aspects of Religiosity

We analyzed five dimensions of religiosity that were measured at every time wave of the survey. For *religious affiliation* we asked, "What religion are you?" or "How would you describe yourself in terms of religious affiliation?" Responses were coded in 102 separate categories and then condensed into six major American faith traditions (as depicted in figure 5). *Religious participation* was assessed with the question, "How often do you attend religious services these days?" (1 = *never* to 4 = *more than once a week*). For *religious intensity*, we asked: "Regardless of whether you attend religious services, do you consider yourself to be … (1 = *not at all religious* to 4 = *very religious*)." Two summed items assessed *conservative biblical reliefs*, reflecting a literal interpretation of the Bible: "All people alive today are descendants of Adam and Eve," and "God exists in the form described in the Bible" (1 = *strongly disagree* to 4 = *strongly agree*). *Conservative civic religiosity*, those beliefs about the place of religion in public life, was also measured by two items, summed: "This country would be better off if religion had a greater influence on daily life," and "Every child should have religious instruction" (1 = *strongly disagree* to 4 = *strongly agree*).

Parent-Child Relationship (Intergenerational Solidarity)

We conceptualize the strength of emotional closeness between generations, or *affectual solidarity* (Roberts, Richards, and Bengtson 1991; Silverstein and Bengtson 1997), as having an important mediating or moderating effect on grandchildren's (and adult children's) religiosity and other value outcomes. This is how the question was phrased to the youngest generation: "Taking everything together, how close do you feel is the relationship between you and your mother/father (grandmother/grandfather) these days?" (1 = *not at all close* to 6 = *extremely close*). This is the item that correlated most highly with the five-item affectual solidarity scale (Mangen, Bengtson, and Landry 1988).

Findings

We found several results in these data about families across generations that surprised us, many of which ran counter to conventional wisdom — or worries — about twenty-first century families and transmitting values across generations. We first summarize results from the entire sample, regardless of religious affiliation, looking at evidence for religious transmission effects. We used hierarchical regression to examine factors that predict variations in child and grandchild religiosity. In the figures presented below, numbers above the bars are standardized coefficients.

1. Parents do have significant religious influence.

Figure 1 shows that parents had relatively high influence on their Millennial children's religious orientations, higher than we had anticipated. The degree to which the young adults' religious behavior was related to their parents' was greatest in religious participation and second highest in biblical literalism. High parent-child similarity could come either from both generations reporting they attend church "at least once a week," or from both parent and child saying that they "never attend church."

2. Parental influence hasn't declined.

What about change over time, the contrast between intergenerational transmission in the 1970s and the 2000s? We had expected to see a decline in religious influence by parents over the thirty-five years of the study, given the significant cultural, religious, and familial changes over that time. However, the data did not support this expectation.

There was not a decline in the rate of religious transmission over time. The degree of intergenerational influence in 2005 was remarkably like that in 1970, at least in our sample. We caution that this is not a large, nationally representative sample, so generalization of these findings to the entire United States is unwarranted. However, these are the only data that exist with which to examine these issues.

3. Parent-child emotional closeness leads to religious transmission.
What are the factors associated with intergenerational influence? What do parents do that enhances their influence on children's religious values? We found several factors that are significant: for example, parents being role models in religious practice, bringing their children with them to church instead of just dropping them off at church. But the most interesting predictor was the quality of the relationship between parent and child. In figure 2 we see that there is greater intergenerational similarity where the child says her relationship with parent(s) is "close," compared with children who define their relationship as less close. Figure 3 depicts this in a different way, using a composite measure that combines all dimensions of religiosity. The relationship between high parental warmth and high religious transmission is clear.

Particularly important, it appears, is the father's warmth. In other analyses of these data we examined gender differences in transmission and the predictors of transmission (Bengtson et al. 2013). Fathers who were perceived as emotionally close were almost twice as likely to transmit faith to their children as fathers perceived as distant or authoritarian. The same did not apply to mothers, surprisingly; perceived closeness did not make much difference in the success of religious transmission. Fathers are more important than we often think.

4. Grandparents are important in value transmission.
How relevant are grandparents in religious socialization? The research evidence here is sparse; a recent search of the literature located only six journal articles published between 2000 and 2014 that contained anything about

grandparents and religion. As we noted earlier, however, grandparents are of increasing importance to families in the United States, and their influence on grandchildren should be examined. Figure 4 presents data from our study on religious similarity between grandparents and Millennials.

Our data show that grandparents are important, and their influence lasts well into their grandchildren's early- to-mid-adult years. The level of influence is not as high as that of parents (as shown in figure 1), and in statistical models, their effect is mediated through parental effects. However, the grandparent effects are still significant.

Furthermore, when we compare over time, the degree of grandparental influence on grandchildren's religiosity has not declined over recent decades. In figure 4, the magnitude of coefficients is not less in 2005 than in 1970; in biblical literalism, it is higher, though lower in religious participation.

5. Mainline Protestants and Catholics may be lagging behind in transmission.

Which faith communities are the most successful in passing their beliefs and practices down across generations? As can be seen from figure 5, the six religious groups in our sample varied considerably in the percentage of parents whose Millennial children shared the same religion as they did. Highest transmission in 2005 was seen among Mormons, where 85 percent of parents and young adults reported the same religion. Second were Jewish parents and children, 82 percent, though it should be noted that those who identified themselves as Jewish were often referring to cultural, not religious, factors. Next were parents and children who said they had no religious affiliation (63 percent) followed by Evangelical Protestants (62 percent).

Roman Catholics were second lowest of these groups, with 43 percent of parents and their Millennial children identifying themselves as Catholics. At the bottom were Mainline Protestants, 26 percent. Both groups showed large declines from the 1971 rates of parent-child similarity: Mainline Protestants declined by 27 percentage points, while Catholics dropped 41 points. These are also the two religious traditions that showed the greatest overall decreases in membership since 1970, just as they had been the ones whose membership showed a surge in the years following World War II. At the same time, the total number of Catholics in America has remained stable since 1970 because recent immigrants from Catholic countries have offset the large decline in native-born non-Hispanic Catholics (Pew Forum 2008).

For American Catholics, several reasons have been advanced to account for declining membership among non-Hispanic Millennials and their parents. Doctrinal and liturgical changes associated with Vatican II in 1972–73 influenced church-going; missing church or confession was no longer regarded as a serious moral lapse and, not surprising, church attendance declined. A second reason for declines in participation concerns disenchantment with conservative church doctrines on birth control, abortion, subordination of women in the church, and treatment of LGBTQ members. Third, clergy sex-abuse scandals and delays in acknowledging it within the Church have caused many to leave. These factors, some of which apply to the loss of members in Protestant churches as well, have relevance for rates of intergenerational transmission among those who remain. Disenchantment with overly rigid doctrines or hypocritical practice provides less motivation to socialize one's children in that faith.

6. But in taking a life-course perspective, we see they often return to the fold.

We pointed out earlier that surveys can give a somewhat misleading perspective on religiosity because they are cross-sectional, measuring individuals at one point of time and then comparing them by age categories. This does not allow us to see individual development and change over time, as people move through the life course experiencing challenges and new events that alter patterns of behavior. To capture such progression requires longitudinal data, measuring the same individuals over long periods of time.

Because we have such data in the LSOG, we can follow the religious trajectories of respondents. And what we see is that many people who drift away from religion in their teens and twenties come back in their thirties — or seventies (Bengtson, Putney, Harris, and Silverstein 2015). In our thirty-five-year data we also see evidence of a "return to religion" for Baby

Boomers as they move into retirement (Silverstein and Bengtson 2018).

In other words, Catholic families and clergy should take a life-course perspective when they see statistics such as that one in three Millennials say they are not religious or have dropped out of church. They often return to the fold.

DISCUSSION AND CONCLUSIONS

In this chapter, we have examined Millennials and their religiousness through a family perspective. Much has been written about the Millennial generation because they appear in many ways to be so different from their parents' generation. How much of a contrast is there between Millennials' religiosity and that of their parents? How much has family religious influence changed over time, across the period of social and religious changes we have seen in the United States since the 1960s? Are families still passing on their faith?

Data from the thirty-five-year Longitudinal Study of Generations, with information from grandparents, parents, and their grandchildren who are Millennials, have provided a means by which to examine these issues.

1) Is There a "Crisis" in Family Values Today?

No, despite what some politicians, pundits, and religious leaders say. From the data reviewed in this chapter and from other results of this study (Bengtson et al. 2013), we can conclude that family bonds and family influences are strong. In fact, multigenerational bonds may be stronger than ever before in America. The reason is found in "longer years of shared lives" between parents and adult children, grandparents and grandchildren, as people are living longer and maintaining better health.

2) Is There a "Generational Gap" in Values and Religion Today?

Not really. In religious values and beliefs, there is significant similarity in spiritual and religious life between parents and children. This is a result that has been repeatedly emphasized by Christian Smith and his colleagues (Smith and Denton 2005; Smith and Snell 2009) based on data from their National Study of Youth and Religion. The exception is religious affiliation, where there is less parent-child similarity.

Polls that show large numbers of religious "nones" among Millennials equate religion with belonging to a church. However, there is more to religion than belonging to church: "I'm spiritual but not religious" is what many young adults say. Many youths who reject churches are still religiously oriented, like their parents.

3) Are Parents Failing to Pass on Their Faith to Children?
Not true of families. In religious values and beliefs, a high percentage of young adults are quite similar to their parents. The quality (closeness) of the parent-child relationship is particularly important to passing on values. Parental religious influence does not appear to have declined over the past few decades; the degree of intergenerational similarity in the 2000s is relatively the same as in the 1970s.

4) Are Grandparents Relevant?
Very much so. It is important for us to look beyond the nuclear family. Grandparents are more relevant to family fortunes and functioning than ever before. Grandparents have significant influences on Millennials' religious orientations. Moreover, the extent of grandparents' influence has not diminished since the 1970s.

5) Are They Likely to Come Back?
If a child rejects the church in his or her college years, the chances are good that she or he will return later in life. A frequent point of return is when children come along or when they are confirmed. Another is the empty nest stage; a third is retirement.

LIMITATIONS
We must be careful not to overgeneralize from the data just reviewed. These findings are from one study and based on a Southern California sample. It may be that results would be different had the sample been nationwide and included families from Alabama and North Dakota, where religious attendance is higher than it is in California. But we are confi-

dent that, even with a larger and nationally representative sample, the three major findings of the study would hold. The first is that contemporary parents exert a strong and lasting influence on their children's religiosity. Second, the magnitude of such parental influence is robust, despite the significant social and cultural changes that have occurred since the 1970s. Third, a great many grandparents exert a significant influence on their grandchildren's religious lives.

Multigenerational bonds are strong in contemporary American society, stronger than often recognized, and what we have seen here is the strength of religious socialization, which spans multiple generations.

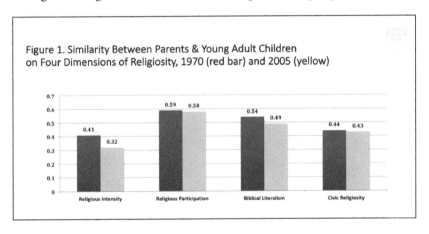

Figure 1. Similarity Between Parents & Young Adult Children on Four Dimensions of Religiosity, 1970 (red bar) and 2005 (yellow)

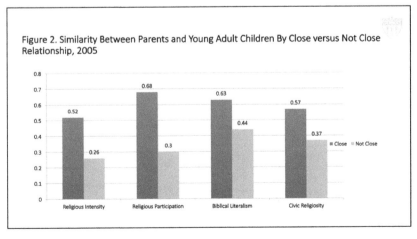

Figure 2. Similarity Between Parents and Young Adult Children By Close versus Not Close Relationship, 2005

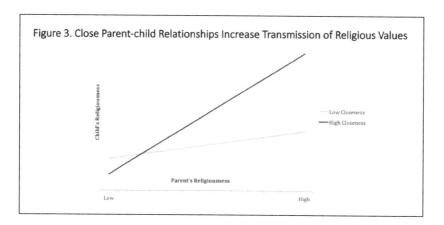

Figure 3. Close Parent-child Relationships Increase Transmission of Religious Values

CHAPTER TEN

Parents: The Decisive Agents in the Religious Outcomes of American Youth

JUSTIN BARTKUS

Institute of Design, Illinois Institute of Technology

FIVE QUICK TAKES

1. The main difference between the average child who retains the religious commitment of their parents and one that drifts from Catholicism is *not* the influence of peers, mass media figures, clergy, or youth ministers, but the quality of religious upbringing provided by their parents.

2. The key factor in successful religious transmission from parents to children is not simply how religiously committed a practicing Catholic parent is, but the degree to which he or she assumes complete and profound responsibility for the religious upbringing of their children.

3. Conventional Catholic frameworks for understanding the respective roles of clergy, educators, and professional ministers, on the one hand, and parents, on the other hand, can obscure the fact that parents are the chief protagonists in the task of religious transmission.

4. The parent who succeeds in religious replication has achieved a level of existential and intellectual synthesis of the Catholic faith; they have definite, articulable motives for Catholicism's intrinsic "rightness" or "goodness," as well as for the necessity of remaining committed to it and for giving it to one's children.

5. Institutional figures and networks in the Church — for example, the parish, parish programs, Catholic schools, Newman Centers, religious orders and clergy — can contribute significantly to the formation and retention of young Catholics, but the usual condition for the possibility of this outcome is the presence of strong parental witness in the home.

As everyone at this convention is aware, much evidence, both statistical and anecdotal, points to the troubling trend that young people are leaving the Church at an accelerating rate. A few numbers may suffice: the Pew Religious Landscape Study of 2015 found that 41% of adults who were raised Catholic no longer identify as such and that a full 12.9% of the American population was "ex-Catholic."[1] Sociologist Christian Smith of the University of Notre Dame observed among Catholic millennials a *fifty percent* attrition rate in one decade.[2] The dire nature of the situation is clear.

In the essay that follows, I propose that shifts in the sociological landscape have installed a "filter," a "middle man," between the Church and the younger generations: namely parents and the subculture that prevails under their respective roofs. Understandably, such a conclusion seems so obvious as to be banal; on the other hand, however, it seems that the full import and practical implications of this reality have not been sufficiently named or appreciated in the Catholic world.

1) A QUALITATIVE STUDY OF AMERICAN CATHOLIC RELIGIOUS PARENTING

We know from quantitative data that the religiosity of parents is the single most influential factor in predicting whether or not a young person will practice religion as an adult. A recent study takes a deeper look into what parents are doing about religion in the home.

What if, in addition to expending our energies to understand and prevail upon those already gone, we homed in on the cultural and relational machinery in the home that surrounded them in the very moments that the seeds of drift were planted? What if it were possible for us to examine the inner workings of the domestic *process* by which the outcome was generated?

This, essentially, is what the above-mentioned Dr. Christian Smith, a sociologist of religion, has attempted to do. Smith is well-known and well-regarded in religious circles for his previous work on the religiosity

---

1. "America's Changing Religious Landscape: Christians Decline Sharply as Share of Population; Unaffiliated and Other Faiths Continue to Grow," Pew Research Center, May 12, 2015, accessed May 30, 2019, https://www.pewforum.org/2015/05/12/americas-changing-religious-landscape/, 13.
2. Christian Smith, "The Situation with U.S. Catholic Youth Actually Is Grim," National Catholic Reporter, June 13, 2015, accessed May 30, 2019, https://www.ncronline.org/news/parish/situation-us-catholic-youth-actually-is-grim.

of millennial Americans, tracking their religious self-understanding as it developed from their teenage years to young adulthood. He did this in a project titled the National Study of Youth and Religion (NSYR). Out of that research emerged Smith's coinage of "moralistic therapeutic deism," a blanket term to describe the underwhelming, theologically vacuous, set of religious beliefs common to nearly all American teenagers, regardless of creed or denomination.

However, this was not all. Another crucial conclusion emerged from Smith's NSYR data. He discovered that the religious comportment and choices of parents were far and away the single most powerful predictive factor of the eventual religious outcomes of youth, that is, whether they maintained or discarded the religious commitment of their parents. Here's the proof: of the most religious 25% of Smith's NSYR subjects, 82% had parents who reported each of the following: that their family regularly discussed religious topics in the home, that faith was "very important" to them, and that they were regularly involved in religious activities themselves. By comparison, the least religious quartile of Smith's subjects had parents who reported that same combination at a rate of only 1%.[3] The main difference between the average child who stays and one who leaves is the quality of religious upbringing provided by their respective parents, not the influence of peers, mass media figures, clergy, or youth ministers.

Subsequently, from 2014 to 2016, Smith embarked upon a new project: an interview study of American parents, centering on the question of how this population understands and narrates the task of parenting in general and religion's specific place within it. Hundreds of parents gave in-depth interviews, lasting usually from two to three hours, in which they were invited to consider such questions as: "How would your life be different if you removed religion from it?" "How different could your children be from you religiously before it would bother you?" and "What

---

3. See the 25:19 mark of Christian Smith's and my lecture "Parents: the Real Pastors: On the Centrality of Parenting in Passing on Religious Faith and Practice to the Next Generation " at the 2016 Liturgy Symposium hosted by the Notre Dame Institute for Church Life, accessed May 30, 2019, https://www.youtube.com/watch?v=v0FzwlM5iLM&t=1787s&safesearch=1; cf. also Christian Smith. Soul-Searching: *The Religious and Spiritual Lives of American Teenagers* (New York: Oxford University Press, 2005), 109.

role does the church play in shaping your children religious, spiritually, or otherwise?" Of the 245 interviews that were done by Smith's team, 73 were of parents self-identifying as Catholic. I happened to perform two dozen of these latter interviews and spent a year analyzing all 73 of the transcripts.

2) THE SMITHS AND THE JONESES: WHAT WORKS AND WHAT DOESN'T IN RELIGIOUS PARENTING

Transcript data suggests that old paradigms of religious parenting might not be sufficient for the task of handing on religious commitments to children.

So what did we discover? In most cases, exactly what you would expect: general underperformance on the part of parents and reports of apathetic reception of religion on the part of children. Some parents experienced this result due to their own almost total religious apathy and others (though very few) due to their own strong ideological opposition to religion. There were still others who seemed to care about passing on their Catholicism, but registered feelings of unease at their own flawed efforts towards that end or towards the unfortunate results they were noticing. As much anecdotal experience and Smith's prior research would lead one to expect, many parents demonstrated a relatively low level of religious articulacy and some sounded just as committed to "moralistic therapeutic deism" as Smith's NSYR subjects. When asked whether their children "were interested in religious things or not," such parents couldn't really produce much in the way of a substantial answer. In all but a few cases, several hours of conversation yielded a fairly clear picture of whether the battle had been lost (or was destined for defeat), or whether parents' efforts at religious replication stood a very real chance of success.

However, as I was conducting these interviews and analyzing the transcripts, one truly unexpected storyline did emerge: the emerging profile of those parents who demonstrated the greatest success in religious transmission. One might expect that a simple assessment of a parent's level of religious commitment would be sufficient to predict whether their children would demonstrate a similar level of commitment, an apple-not-far-from-the-tree theory. However, it became abundantly clear that a high level of religious commitment on the part of parents was a necessary but entirely insufficient condition for successful replication of religious commitment in children; there was indeed no shortage of parents — in many cases recommended to our research team due to their unusually high level of participation in their parish communities — who demonstrated palpable feelings of loss and grief as they witnessed their children drifting away from the Church. They had been faithful, but not successful as it regarded religious transmission.

Take for example Camila, a middle-aged mother of several teenage daughters who was born in Mexico and now lives in the American Southwest. She was raised in a more traditional style of Catholicism, prays every day and entertains a special love for the Virgin. Camila mentioned to us that she and her husband consistently "discern" and inquire after their particular "vocation" as to how to contribute to the life of their parish — clearly, their vocabulary and self-awareness are saturated with religious language. They have nudged their children into becoming altar servers and attending parish retreats and youth group meetings. Slackers they are not.

And yet, it appeared to us that, beyond the family's habitual church-going and her children's own exposure to parish life, and despite Camila's own individual sense of religious devotion, there was a rather thin prevalence of substantial religious discussion or meaningful religious practices in the home. In our observation, it seemed that religious conversation tended to start and stop with moral prohibitions, when she would declare that something was "against God's law," "against the Bible," or "strange." It seemed that what Camila had intended to pass on was an exemplary model of her own attitude of spiritual "submission" (her term) to her children, while she counted on the Church — through the medium of the parish — to invest that attitude with theological, relational, and practical content. In no way can either Camila's own personal religious commitment or her desire for her children to remain Catholic be undersold, and yet she was not able to produce a single example of a meaningful religious experience in her daughters' lives and noted that they were unenthusiastic about going to Mass and more "liberal" in their ways. She was a classic example of a highly religiously committed parent who nonetheless was growing increasingly mystified by her children's drift from the Church.

By contrast, parents who succeeded in religious replication — and most without even realizing it — exhibited a profound grasp of their own personal (and nearly *exclusive*) responsibility for their children's religious formation. It was simply not the case that a parent's level of religious commitment, enthusiasm, devotion, regular practice, articulacy in theology, catechetics, or apologetics was ultimately what determined whether that parent would raise a child that remained Catholic. These things are clearly important, some even essential. However, what really mattered was not simply how *religiously committed* a practicing Catholic parent was, but more precisely the *degree to which he or she assumed complete and profound responsibility for the religious upbringing of their children, and had the resources of personal experience, articulacy, and dedication necessary to accomplish that formation.*

Perhaps we can clarify the stereotypical profile of the successful family by contrasting it with a "foil" stereotype emergent in the data. Let's imagine two different Catholic American families, the Smiths and the Joneses. The Smiths are happy to call themselves Catholic; they are members of a thriving parish, attend Mass most Sundays (though perhaps not all), send their children to Catholic school, and speak well of their local pastor. Though Mr. and Mrs. Smith are quick to assert that they themselves are technically responsible for their children's growth in faith, they are relieved that their kids receive catechesis in school, since they themselves feel rather less equipped to speak about religion in the home. Catholicism has always simply been "part of their DNA," a marginal, if ever-present, compartment of their lives.

From time to time, Mr. Smith decides to excuse himself from Mass, and at other times, he is visibly disengaged while at church. Mrs. Smith has, for her part, at times yielded to the ever-expanding demands of youth sports and absolved the family of the responsibility for going to Sunday Mass, though she expresses very definite regret about this. They both express that it can be difficult requiring their children to attend church every week, since the kids almost always seem bored to death during religious services. Despite all this, the couple genuinely means it when they say that they would very much like their children to remain Catholic and to marry a Catholic when they grow up.

The second family let's call the Joneses. Mr. and Mrs. Jones met in a Catholic volunteer cohort for recent college graduates. Shortly after this experience, they were engaged and married. They keep in close touch with many of their friends from those years, as well as with the chaplain priest of that community. Though their current parish may perhaps lack in dynamism, they nonetheless carry forward the spiritual values that they cultivated together when they first met — they volunteer frequently at the parish as lectors and make regular appearances at the diocesan soup kitchen. From time to time they invite the parish priest over for dinner, and in general they are not hesitant to expose their children to all kinds of religious figures from all phases of their life: from their childhood, their old volunteer community, and from their present parish. As far back as the Joneses' children can remember, their parents were invested in the kids' own religious growth and understanding, from teaching the sign of the cross to describing what was depicted in their church's stained-glass windows to requiring their children to say grace before every family dinner. The Jones enjoy bantering with their children about Sunday homilies, sharing news of what Pope Francis has tweeted, and at times get a little "preachy" with them about why faith matters so much to their family. It is an expectation that the kids are expected to attend Mass every Sunday, at least until they're 18. Though they understand well that they cannot force the religious choices of their children, the Jones are confident that they've left few stones unturned in the religious education of their children and find it hard to imagine that their kids could ever reject the faith that has long been so cherished by their family.

As you may have surmised, for all the Smiths' genuinely good intentions, for all their investment of time (spending most Sunday mornings in Church) and treasure (in writing decades' worth of checks to Catholic schools), we discovered that a family such as this can expect their children to drift from Catholicism when they become adults. Generally speaking, such an outcome is fated for parents whose ownership of their children's religious formation is only partial, and whose sense of religious rooting and identity runs somewhat shallow. When conversation with parents like the Smiths turned to the topics of their religious aspirations for their children and their concrete observations of how things were turning out, their tone would frequently communicate defeat, powerlessness, and guilt. These were parents whose efforts to transmit their faith to their children had taken on a defensive quality. Such parents frequently felt themselves to be at the mercy of inevitable, secularizing forces beyond their control — being irreligious was simply the "way of the world" among kids these days, and who were parents to think they could stop it? In this connection, we often heard parents communicate the sentiment that "religion can't be forced upon children," or that the final decision is ultimately "up to them." To us, it seemed that these were not the reflective, principled articulations of some profound parenting philosophy, but were retrospectively produced attempts to make sense of their children's drift or to salve the sense of loss or failure accompanying such an outcome.

By contrast, it is clear that the Joneses evince a deep commitment and authenticity in the faith they wish to give their children. The experience of talking to such parents was qualitatively different than speaking with the Smiths; the Joneses cut a principled, confident, and empowered profile, whereas the Smiths often communicated an ultimate sadness or regret regarding the religious dimension of their parenting. The Joneses' faith was existentially achieved and genuinely their own, though of course it was no less robustly Catholic for being so. Though perhaps their ethnic or childhood backgrounds had set the Joneses in the right direction, they did not cite these as their primary motives for transmitting their faith, but rather referred to the inherent correspondence of the Catholic faith with a good and existentially fulfilling life. Nor did they locate religion's utility simply in its furnishing of young people with a baseline moral decency that kept them out of trouble and fearful of consequences. Parents like the Joneses were true believers. Faith wasn't instrumental to anything; it was simply true and worthwhile and valuable in itself.

Though it is certainly possible that the Joneses' children might leave the Church one day, doing so would generate a tremendous amount of interfamilial friction and require, on the part of their children, a comprehensive discarding of childhood identity and a radical shift in worldview — religious assets that the Jones have deeded over to their children and the Smiths have not. For the Jones' children, rejection of faith would be tantamount to the rejection of a birthright, of an inheritance. Some emerging adults opt to dramatically exit in this way, but most do not. Accordingly, the Joneses are right to be content with the formation they've given their children. The transcripts demonstrate that even adolescents, for all their supposed angst and autonomy, tend not to maintain a sense of rebellion against received religious upbringing. When young people leave Catholicism, it is usually in the manner of drift, the process ending with a whimper rather than a defiant bang.

Ultimately, what the Joneses of the world hand on to their children — in contrast to the Smiths — is something genuinely synthesized, communicable, urgent, and available to their children. Children are given a worldview that is philosophically, culturally, and relationally to be reckoned with. When such children look at their parents, they witness a religious identity that is considered, serious, embodied, and most importantly, *communicated*. The Catholic faith in such cases is presented as something definite, with real shape and contour, not simply an ethnic or familial vestige that is granted some degree of due courtesy (perhaps even on a weekly basis!) but not serious consideration as a source of existential orientation or spiritual potency. Accordingly, in the vast majority of cases, the success or failure of religious replication in children depended upon two things: first, whether parents had made their faith "their own" and second, whether they made it a chief priority to communicate the fruits of this achieved religious worldview to their children in the day-to-day grind of family life. Those Catholic parents who were able to say "yes" to both were the ones most likely to witness the retention of their religious commitment by children.

3) DO PARENTS NEED THEOLOGY DEGREES?

We know that parents are the decisive agents in the religious outcomes of young people. What competencies does this require of them? And how does the Church play into it?

The present cultural moment is one in which the outward structures of local religious collectives persist — for example, the parish with the signature figure of its ordained pastor, its rituals, festal life and ministerial outreach; then there are lay associations and Catholic schools and universities. These outwardly persist, but unfortunately their inner sinews increasingly fail to entwine the hearts and minds of young people. Our research suggests that many young Catholics are exposed to a great deal of these things without thereby feeling any sort of existential urgency to commit their lives religiously. However, our research also indicates that this situation is not only crisis but opportunity. Parents can be powerful cultural synthesizers of faith, and by living and communicating their religious worldview, they bear potential to powerfully replicate Catholicism in those who are optimally positioned to receive their witness: their own children.

Parents need to know this. For reasons structurally endemic to Catholicism, parents have often understood themselves to fill a supporting role in the religious formation of children, enrolling them in the relevant institutions (the parish and its school, for example) while stepping back to model and morally support the substance of what children receive through those official channels. In this account, parents do the dirty work of putting bread on the table, offering day-to-day nurturance, and ensuring that children remain respectful and open towards their official religious guides, while at certain appointed times and places the Church then delivers the official, magisterial content. Much more than many other Christian denominations, initiation into the Catholic community requires conveyance of a relatively complex body of doctrine and ritual. As most parents simply don't have the time or expertise to channel this kind of specialized knowledge, it makes sense that they subconsciously assume that the canonical processes of initiation, catechesis, and formation will be handled by the clerical and ministerial class.

On the surface of it, this division of labor seems intrinsic to the Catholic Church, given its universal and centralized structure, one of whose primary functions is to safeguard and convey doctrine. Consequently, most parents we spoke with carried the implicit belief that they themselves were located somewhat "off-center" in the drama of the religious education of their children, and that the real work was being done by the local Church itself, its religious-ed teachers, youth ministers, parish priests, and local bishop. In one parish we encountered, several parents had absorbed the prescient mantra from their pastor that they were children's "first teachers," yet even these seemed to assume a level of efficacy to the supplementary efforts of parish personnel that simply did not exist. The line about being "first teachers" felt more parroted than absorbed, as was evident from these parents' lack of decisive initiative. The problem is that parents assume they're playing a supporting role when in fact they're the chief protagonists. Or, perhaps more accurately: they assume they have more support than they actually do.

Does this therefore mean that Catholic parents should flock to graduate theology programs on a mass scale? Notwithstanding the absurdity of the suggestion, the answer is still: not necessarily. In those households experiencing the greatest observed success of religious replication, parents were not conveying religious knowledge in the manner of a classroom instructor. Rather, the work was done more subtly, in myriad ways, often unspoken, frequently unintentional, though at other times explicitly verbal and intentional. This is because what parents were giving to children was not so much discrete knowledge ("Who are the three persons of the Trinity?"), as much as an entire worldview and an accompanying mode of existence, a way of life. The gradual but undeniably potent initiation to which such parents exposed their children was akin to a long-term apprenticeship, in which learning was done in the context of an ongoing relationship. Mastery of the "craft" was intuitively felt and practiced even more than it was intellectually understood. The faith formation parents gave to children only needed to be intellectual to the extent that it was existential.

Thus, it should be parents' objective to introduce, over many years, through long practice and relational intimacy, this sort of intuitive grasp of the Catholic *thing*, the Catholic "texture of life," to their children. In the language of theology, the parent must be a primary witness. Therefore, one of the most essential dimensions of our interviews with parents concerned their own religious views and upbringing. We needed to understand to what degree parents had achieved a level of existential and intellectual synthesis of the Catholic faith they had either inherited or chosen. By "synthesis," I refer to a consciously achieved, *personal* understanding of their faith through formative life experiences and regular practices that had noticeably led to the fermentation of very definite, articulable motives for Catholicism's intrinsic "rightness" or "goodness," as well as for the necessity of remaining committed to it and for giving it to one's children. The parent who succeeds in religious replication is a person who knows precisely what she is committed to and why, and whose certainty in such matters pervades every other moment of her daily witness, whether in its implicit or explicit moments. This synthesis hardly needed to be the fruit of book-learning or academic theology, though of course long exposure to the rich and varied Catholic lexicon of symbols, practices, and teachings provided such parents ample material to form and express their convictions.

To illustrate, I'll briefly introduce you to one of the most striking parents in the entire study. We'll call her Sherry. Sherry was 42 at the time we interviewed her, with a bouncy personality, red hair, and three children, ranging from 18 to 12. In many ways her life was difficult: she had lost her mother prematurely to cancer, had recently left her husband of 22 years, a gambling addict, despite lacking any pension or Social Security, and had recently re-entered the work force after a long absence, finding a blue-collar job that supported her and her children. Though she was not baptized until adulthood (as her father was not Catholic), she vividly and fondly remembered preparing holiday gift packages for the poor with her Catholic mother. There was a fundamental and deeply orienting significance to the religious experiences of her youth.

All her life, Sherry held the fundamental belief that life is simply better, fuller, and more joyous when God is involved. Adopting Pope Francis' phrase, she also lamented that without God, we become a "throwaway culture," not giving any consideration to the homeless, the poor, or the outcast. While her children were growing up, Sherry basically *lived* at her parish, teaching Vacation Bible School, doing setup and takedown for more events than she can remember ("the first person there and the last to leave"), and bringing her children along frequently, too. As she says, "For so many years, every day of my life we went there." For her, it was "very important" that her children attend Catholic school. At the school's weekday Mass, she would rotate among her three children, taking one of them each week to sit with one-on-one. Her most tender memories as a parent included teaching her children the Our Father, the rosary, and bedtime prayers. Her children's lives have, from a young age, been filled with lamb cakes, Christmas plays, and summers with their mom at VBS. She told us that she looks forward eagerly to the day her sons get married, so that she can gift their brides with handkerchiefs stitched together from her boys' christening bonnets.

In all this, there are many optimal signs of a vibrant interpersonal dynamic between Sherry and her children as it regards religion. There is a thread of continuity from the beliefs at her core, to the practices in which she engages her children, to the intimate conversation and affection they share daily. Her religious convictions animate the entirety of the family's common life together. Religion is neither compartmentalized nor is it a private holding of Sherry alone; though she draws deeply from her parish and has thoroughly exposed their children to the life of the local Catholic community, she does not expect or anticipate that it is someone else's responsibility to guide her children toward faith. And despite not having a lot in the way of money, Sherry's home is suffused with a simple happiness and buoyancy that is directly traceable to the faith given to her children and subsequently shared among them as a common inheritance.

It is important to note that Sherry is not an expert in catechism or apologetics, yet she does not thereby sense in herself any incapacity or lack of confidence in passing on her faith. In her case, it appears totally irrelevant that she is not a theological "specialist." It's likely that she may not even have a college degree. What matters is the personal texture of her witness, communicated consistently, intentionally, and profoundly in her talk and manner of life, in the relationships and practices she exposes her children to, and in the tenderness of her affection for them. It is all of a piece with her faith. It is no surprise, then, that her children demonstrated significant signs of a burgeoning, durable faith of their own.

Parents like Sherry lend credibility to the wider Catholic world and allow it to come to life, replete as it is with a rich diversity of practices, people, traditions, modes of intellectual reflection, and forms of public witness and political engagement. The Catholic world, across both space and time, is teeming indeed with convincing forms of witness that can genuinely speak to young people of the present day. We encountered families with a deep orientation towards social justice, who regularly practiced the works of mercy, followed the Pope on Twitter, and sent their children to Jesuit universities. We encountered other families where one or both parents were secular Franciscans, and whose children were altar servers, invested in apologetics and high school campus ministry, even considering the priesthood. Still other families, though not overtly committed to any ecclesial movement or form of public witness, exhibited a solid, "middle class" Catholicism: priests were frequent dinner guests of such households, parents were regularly to be seen volunteering at the parish or bantering about the Sunday homily, and rosaries were said in the car – not spectacular, perhaps, but effective. Some families were committed to the practice of international pilgrimage, others to practices of simplicity around the holidays, still others to devotion and research into the lives of the saints. The tapestry of vibrant and committed Catholic households was richly varied, and no matter the "type" of Catholicism evidenced therein, such homes stood out in excellent relief against the backdrop of a culture largely saturated by religious indifference, moralistic therapeutic deism, and incomprehension of religious commitments, discourses, and ways of life.

In all this, it should go without saying that, in emphasizing the indispensable role of parents in religious transmission, I do not at all wish to herald the irrelevance of traditional institutions or to impugn the class of clergy and religious professionals. Without the clergy, the parish, Catholic schools and the entire institutional universe of Catholicism, parents would possess scantly anything in the way of beliefs, practices, and relationships to give to their children in their Catholic formation. In such a scenario, Catholicism would cease to be itself. Parents are a bridge, a door, between children and the Church at large. When parents perform their task well, children are primed to experience the exponential expansion of their religious world as they grow older.

The Catholic world is populated with vast and overlapping global networks of people, ideas, institutions, media, communities, and practices. Think of Word on Fire, *America Magazine*, faith-motivated advocacy groups of both the left and right, urban young adult groups and practices such as theology on tap, the Catholic Worker, campus Newman Centers, and the variety of religious orders. The agents operating in such regions of the Church must be enthusiastic, ready and waiting when the opportunity comes for them to step on to the stage of a young person's life. When emerging adults meaningfully encounter any such network, the density and durability of their Catholic identity is bound to increase. However, the condition of the possibility for them to meaningfully encounter these fertile zones of the Catholic world is to have parents whose witness to and formation of their children rendered such experiences relevant to them in the years of adolescence and young adulthood. In the absence of strong parental witness, however, the world of Catholicism hardly registers as a blip on a young adult's radar.

4) WHAT DOES "DOMESTIC CHURCH" MEAN IN THE TWENTY-FIRST CENTURY?

The Church has long embraced the importance of the household in evangelization. What does this mean for the Church today?

At least since Vatican II, the magisterium of the Church has referred to the Catholic household as the *ecclesia domestica,* the "domestic Church." In the 1980s, the *Catechism of the Catholic Church*, following the mention of *ecclesia domestica* in Vatican II's *Lumen gentium*, observed with prescience that the household was becoming an increasingly important locus of evangelizing activity: "In our own time, in a world often alien and even hostile to faith, believing families are of primary importance as centers of living, radiant faith."[4] The *Catechism* additionally notes that the home is the "first school of Christian life and a school for human enrichment," wherein children receive instruction in many things: "en-

---

4. *Catechism of the Catholic Church*, 2nd ed. (Cittá del Vaticano: Libreria Editrice Vaticana, 2003), accessed online at http://www.vatican.va/archive/ENG0015/_P56.HTM, 1656.

durance and the joy of work, fraternal love, generous — even repeated — forgiveness, and above all divine worship in prayer and the offering of one's life."[5] What tradition hands us, then, is a strong affirmation of the *centrality* of the family in the Christian community and a substantial account of the pedagogical duties given to parents. As we have seen, the present sociological situation of the Church in the United States is pressing us to seek even further clarification of what this pedagogical duty looks like in the concrete, and how the ecclesiastical "center" that is the household relates to that other "center" of Christian community, the parish and the wider institutional Church.

Ultimately, what our interview transcripts point to is the *personal* nature of the evangelizing witness parents offer to children today. Parents' role is not limited to a list of duties or a moralistic obligation to remind their children that religion is good and necessary, an exhortation to eat your spiritual vegetables, as it were. It is essential to understand that, in the era of millennials and generation Z more so than before, the vessels which carry the faith from one generation to the next are neither institutions, nor disembodied teachings, doctrines, or documents, but flesh and blood *persons*. Traditional Catholic canopies of formation – entire vibrantly Catholic subcultures – have fragmented into household-sized "islands" in which parents are far and away the most authoritative influences, for better or for worse. One of our interview subjects, one of the most impressive in the study, related to us that he was a "force of nature" in the eyes of his kids. It was one of the most clear-sighted and sociologically accurate assertions we heard from a parent. Given the supreme and lasting influence that he knew he had, it was unthinkable that he would hesitate or lack confidence in conveying his deepest-held religious values to his children. In a sense, he knew that everything he wanted to be as a parent was at stake in that decision.

Parents are indeed cultural "forces of nature," able to steer their children in lasting and definite religious directions, even if such a lifestyle is growing increasingly inexplicable to and insufficiently understood by the culture at large. It is not too much to say that a parent renders the

---

5. *Ibid.*, 1657.

household a subcultural religious canopy unto itself. From the beginning, the parent is the sole and exclusive face of the Church in the eyes of children, the ignition switch which triggers the possibility of a child's own lifelong commitment to grappling with and practicing his faith. As we have mentioned, success in this regard depends not so much on what a parent *does,* but even more profoundly on who a parent demonstrably *is,* and what sort of conviction and clarity radiates from him or her over the many years in which the parent informs and shapes the values of the child.

So in light of this, what ought to be done? Here, at the close of this essay, we lay down a few principles and observations that might guide future responses to the present youth exodus from the Church.

First, parents must not only be made to understand the central role they play in the drama of intergenerational religious transmission — and our transcripts suggest that they are only faintly aware of this — but they also must be empowered to see what anchors there are in their own deepest values, experiences, and aspirations for their children. These can form the basis of a renewed effort to model, discuss, communicate and share their Catholicism with their children. Our study demonstrates nothing if not that an evangelizing impetus and energy must originate deep within the interior of parents themselves, and that no other actor or institution will be able to compensate for what they lack.

Moreover, we noticed that, between, on the one hand, those parents that were undeniably effective in their religious transmission and, on the other hand, those parents who were completely indifferent about passing on their faith, there was a middle group: parents who felt compelled to transmit their faith to some degree, and who had taken concrete steps in doing so, yet who ultimately were hesitant, lacking in confidence, or only halfway invested. Our transcripts suggest that these parents not only have something to lose on the emotional and existential level should their children drift from their faith, but also that they already bear at least the seeds of the conviction necessary to revive their efforts at religious transmission. It would seem to be an efficient use of time and energy to attend specifically to such parents as these.

Second, strategists of evangelization must apply creativity and resources in engaging newlyweds and young parents who retain a profound opportunity to provide a substantial and effective religious formation to their children. Additionally, when it comes to young adult outreach, it will prove useful for those who are invested in the effort of evangelization to understand how significantly childhood upbringing and parental influence play in a young person's own comprehension of religion and its inherent value. Those Catholics who are lapsed and yet may still return are not simply free-floating entities who are mysteriously "out there," lacking any kind of history, but persons who were raised in a Catholic household, and whose past in that regard must be engaged, empathized with, and connected to whatever new proposals or opportunities are offered by the parish or diocese.

Thirdly, many of the more successful parents we spoke to were immeasurably aided by local parishes that invited them to participate in an extensive and deeply collaborative manner in the life of the community. Such opportunities allowed parents to perceive themselves as protagonists in the community of faith rather than mere recipients or spectators; and naturally, whenever parents' energies were deeply engaged in their faith communities, their children were right there to witness and appreciate it, and in some cases were given opportunities of their own to contribute to the community's flourishing. These parishes gave whole families a stage and a set of roles to enact the drama of Christian witness and apprenticeship, processes which are essential to children's arriving at a definite apprehension of their parents' values, commitments, and worldview. Essentially, if the conditions are right, the parish can burgeon into a neighborhood grown through the common commitment and widespread participation of its members, rather than being a mere "heirloom" inherited by children, left to gather dust on the metaphorical shelf.

Lastly, for what it's worth, there was much evidence in the transcripts to suggest that the parish priest remains, in the minds of parents, a significant and potent figure. Parents, even those most on the fringe of their parishes, tended *always* to know exactly who the local pastor was, the sort of person he was, and had taken account of his preaching and the texture of his interpersonal style, with an especial preference for warmth and personality. For several parents whose connection to their parish was dangling by a thread, it was a positive relationship with the pastor that kept them attached at all. In these cases, the presence of a good pastor was itself an ongoing call to accountability and a perpetual occasion for the possibility that they might, given the right impetus, return to a deeper, regular practice of their faith. And naturally, a pastor who was involved in the lives of children, hearing their confessions, visiting their homes, and attending their sporting events, was an influential, supplementary point of religious reference beyond such children's parents. In the present social landscape, the preeminence of parents does not exclude clergy from exercising genuine modes of influence on the household. It seems that our current situation calls for clergy who are functionally, perhaps above all else, friends to and supporters of families.

$$\bullet \ \bullet \ \bullet$$

The statistical evidence regarding youth drift out of the Church is sobering. By now we should consider it the exception rather than the rule when a Catholic adolescent transitions to young adulthood while retaining the regular practice of his or her faith. We know that by the age of eighteen, most Catholics are already advancing along a vector that places them well outside the radio signal of the Church's ongoing invitation. However, there is also good news: during those *first* eighteen years, Catholic young people are consistently and attentively tuned in to the religious radio signal transmitted by their parents. Their ears and hearts are open; the question is what they'll hear.

DISCUSSION QUESTIONS

1. Do the planning and implementation of ministerial initiatives begin from the immediate concerns, constraints, and problem framing of the parish or ministry organization? Or from the concerns, constraints, and problem framing emerging from parents' lives and difficulties? What obstacles, internal or external, stand in the way of making our ministry friendly to and supportive of parents?
2. What obstacles stand in the way of parents and families being invit-

ed to take initiative and contribute to the wider faith community? Would you say that most parents in your community feel like it is "someone else's" role to take initiative in the Catholic community? Would you guess that parents in your community feel unprepared, unqualified, or unaccustomed to playing such a role? If so, how can that perception be changed or mitigated?

3. How are we informing parents of the central role that they play in the transmission of faith to their children? What opportunities are there to inform them of their role and prepare them for it? How are we challenging the idea that it is primarily *our* job as ministers to transmit the faith to children, while parents' function is mainly to support that effort? How can we create the inverse of this perception?

Raising Virtuous Children: Children's Basic Needs and the Evolved Nest

Mary S. Tarsha and Darcia Narvaez

University of Notre Dame

FIVE QUICK TAKES

1. The Evolved Nest is the system of care that matches up with the developing needs of the infant and child. This provides the child with a buffer of support, ensuring that the child receives appropriate care at the precise time in development that it is needed.

2. The Evolved Nest for infants and young children includes: soothing perinatal experiences, breastfeeding, responsive care, lots of positive touch (almost continual in the first year), positive home climate, alloparents (additional caregivers other than mother), social support (for both parents and children), and free play, in natural settings and with multi-age playmates.

3. The Evolved Nest provides the optimal environment for child flourishing, including mental and physical health and socio-moral capacities that form the foundation of virtue.

4. The Evolved Nest involves the entire community, giving both children and parents greater support, which results in better responsive, nurturing caregiving.

5. The Evolved Nest may seem contrary to modern, Western practices, but it is the ecological system of care that evolved over thirty million years ago because it made generations adapt and flourish.

All parents want to nurture good children. In ancestral contexts, the whole community — the village — helped foster virtue in the community's children. In modern societies, children have experiences that often go against virtue development, not only in the neighborhood but also in society and even within the family. We discuss how virtue develops and what needs to be provided by families and communities for virtue development.

THE NATURE OF VIRTUE

What is virtue? To help us make sense of what virtue is and why it is important, it is common to think back to the Greek philosophers, the writings of Aristotle and Thomas Aquinas. For example, Thomas Aquinas, after Aristotle, noted that all people desire the good in any given moment — and they act on that desire. He stated that "every creature is oriented toward its own goodness, that is, its fullness of being in accordance with the ideal of its species" (Porter 1990; Narvaez 2016a). This means that all creatures are geared toward their own optimization, and virtue is part of that aim. In fact, the whole of the cosmos is created in goodness and oriented toward goodness. Consequently, there is no difference between what is good for one and what one ought to do. In this way, virtue subsumes flourishing and involves living the life that is good for one to live. For humans, it involves cooperative attunement to others for good ends.

Living a good life, a life that involves flourishing, requires perceptive cooperation with one's ecological setting. To flourish does not mean that one's lifestyle hurts, harms, or diminishes the biodiverse world, but enhances. Human flourishing does not come at the expense of ecological health. To live a good life and to practice virtue means cooperation with all of life, including nonhumans.

While Aquinas sheds light on virtue and the goodness of creation, it is critical to understand how virtue is formed. Recent empirical evidence from neuroscience, developmental psychology, and ethnographic research helps illuminate how virtue is shaped by experience. Understanding the converging evidence about virtue development, we can add to Aquinas' view that when children are raised well, they become good human beings. That is, we are not born fully formed by any measure. This includes social and moral development. At birth, the human brain is very immature. Compared to other hominids, newborn humans are the most biologically immature, and human children have the longest maturational schedule of any animal (Trevathan 2017) — neuroimaging studies indicate that the brain does not fully mature until the third (sometimes fourth) decade of life (Westlye et al. 2009). As a result of the long maturational schedule of the human brain and other neurobiological systems, much of a person's development takes place through a dynamic interaction among physiological maturation, social experience, and quality of caregiving. Much of who we are and become is the result of the social ecology in which we are raised, the type of environment that surrounds us during these critical, sensitive years of development (Narvaez 2016a). Neuroscientist and epigeneticist Frances Champagne articulated this well when she said the "quality of the social environment becomes embedded at a biological level" (Champagne 2010, 299). Champagne was referring to the fact that experience has the power to act upon the genome, influence genetic expression, turning genes on or off (this is referred to as epigenetics). The influence of the environment on neurobiological architecture and genetic expression in early life often persists into adulthood (Gudsnuk and Champagne 2011; Bludau, Royer, Meister, Neumann, and Menon 2019). In other words, the type of care received during childhood and, most importantly, during the first years of life, shapes one's neurobiology. This, in turn, influences one's mental health, as well as social and moral capacities.

Infants and children are dependent on their caregivers to lay the foundations of sociality and morality. The socio-moral brain is co-constructed through the behavior of mothers and other caregivers. To put it a different way, infants are not born corrupt and selfish, needing strong coercion to force them toward goodness, sociality, and morality. There is no evil baby. In fact, the opposite is true. All creation is oriented toward goodness, including every infant and child, as Aquinas articulated. Children are hardwired for sociality and morality, but they need to learn the how's: how to be social and how to be moral in a life of relationships. The precise "how's" of sociality are co-constructed through caregiver interaction with infants and children, shaping the unconscious mind and laying the foundations for virtue (or vice). In this way, who the child becomes is biosocially constructed.

Understanding the importance of environment and the lifelong impact caregivers have upon shaping children's development leads us to wonder: What is the best environment for children to develop and flourish? Here are two less optimal strategies. A common reaction to learning about the importance of caregiving is to become child-centered. This means that parents/caregivers stop play or work and revolve family life around a set of engineered goals for the child with sports lessons, music lessons, and keeping them busy with achievement activities. Child-centered parenting can lead to smothering the child, becoming invasive and intrusive, a form of obsessive-compulsive behavior (tiger parenting). Here, the child is actually robbed of independence and autonomy, encouraged to be self-centered and focusing on winning. The child's unique spirit barely has a chance to grow.

The opposite parenting strategy is that of a parent-centered family. In this approach, parents are the center of the family, not the children. Parental work or other adult agendas take precedence over the child's needs, and this evokes a detached relational orientation (speaking in terms of attachment framework). In order to maintain the superiority of adult agendas, parents emotionally detach from their own emotions and their children's. Common phrases of detached mindsets include things such as "children should be seen and not heard," or reassurances like, "they won't remember." When parents practice emotional detachment, "tuning out" their children, known practices that are harmful for children are rationalized and made acceptable. These practices include cry-it-out sleep training (Middlemiss, Granger, Goldberg, and Nathans 2012; Callaghan and Tottenham 2016) and spanking (Gershoff et al. 2018).

The heart of the problem with both parenting approaches is that they assume the family is a competition, an either/or, zero-sum game. It is only the child's or the parent's needs that can be satiated. These approaches operate via a one-up or one-down operation so that one group or family member has more control and power. In the parent-centered family, parents' needs dominate, and children's are subordinate, whereas in child-centered parenting, children's presumed needs are higher than their parents'. The good news is that an alternative, healthier parenting approach is possible, one that incorporates the needs of all family members, fostering relational communion and psychological well-being: life-centered parenting.

In life-centered families, parents are sensitive to the needs of children while continuing to act as adults within a community. The children are treated as equals but with extra needs as they develop. Children are incorporated into adult life, coordinating the meeting of parent and child needs. For example, in life-centered parenting breastfeeding is understood to be normal and a natural necessity, and something that does not remove the mother and infant from society and community life. This means that on-request breastfeeding — the baby suckles and is nourished at will, without being rushed or denied or isolated — is understood to be fundamental to the infant's development. When the baby wants to breastfeed frequently, this is not seen as a demanding, selfish behavior, something that needs to be controlled or denied. Rather, the mother's continual free-flowing gift of responding to the infant's request to breastfeed is understood to build a healthy body and brain, as well as secure emotional attachment, a critical component of healthy psychological development. The mother and family function to meet the infant's needs and, simultaneously, remain integrated in community life.

THE EVOLVED NEST

For 99 percent of their genus history, humans lived in small-band hunter-gatherer (SBHG) communities around the world (Fry 2006; Lee and Daly 2005). SBHG adults are highly prosocial, compassionate, generous, caring, and egalitarian, with some scholars even recognizing their capacity for a higher consciousness (Fry and Souillac 2013; Ingold 2005; Martin 1999; Narvaez 2016b; Wolff 2001). The SBHG way of caring for their young — life-centered, companionship care — is described as the *evolved nest* (i.e., Evolved Developmental Niche or EDN; Narvaez and Gleason 2013). Every animal evolved a nest for its young, and humanity's is particularly intensive, providing deep companionship, responsivity, and nurturing. Humanity's evolved nest consists of many social mammalian adaptations, intensive parenting practices that evolved over thirty million years ago (Konner 2010). Among humans, nested care is a system that is provisioned by the community, not simply by mothers and/or fathers. The evolved nest includes: (1) affectionate touch: being held or kept near others constantly; (2) prompt and appropriate responses to fusses, cries, and needs, as to keep the young child in an optimal state of arousal; (3) breastfeeding on request (two to three times per hour initially) and on average for two to five years; (4) multiple allomothers, that is, frequent care by responsive individuals other than mothers (fathers and grandmothers, in particular) and social support; (5) multi-age, self-directed, social free-play in nature; (6) positive home climate; (7) soothing perinatal experiences; and (8) connection to nature (for reviews, see Narvaez, Panksepp, Schore, and Gleason 2013). When a community is sensitive and well-tuned to the needs of its youngest members by providing nested care to its young, then optimal development takes place, leading to a prosocial, virtuous, and peaceable personality (Narvaez 2018; 2019; Tarsha and Narvaez, in press).

Although nest characteristics may seem odd when compared with mainstream, Western culture, it is important to remember that nest characteristics make up the majority of the way in which our human species lived and thrived. In order to further understand the importance of the nest, we next briefly discuss empirical evidence for each component and how it relates to moral development. See figure 1 for the list of components.

Figure 1. The Evolved Nest for Young Children

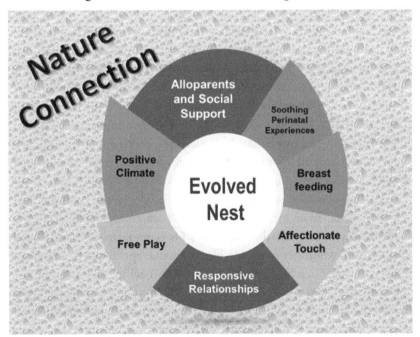

SOOTHING PERINATAL EXPERIENCES

Common obstetrical practices in the West include numerous painful, often developmentally disrupting procedures. Many of these practices began during an era in which infants were presumed to not feel pain (they do), but still continue in hospitals out of habit (Narvaez, Panksepp, Schore, and Gleason 2013). These painful procedures include but are not limited to: spanking, separating mother and child, circumcision, bright lights, noxious odors, gestational ultrasounds (which can influence neuronal migration and are correlated with autism), and sucrose solution to mitigate pain (which is not an effective analgesic) (Slater et al. 2010; Rosman et al. 2018; Ang, Gluncic, Duque, Schafer, and Rakic 2006). But most importantly, these intrusive perinatal experiences often disrupt the natural rhythms of development, including mother-child bonding and breastfeeding. Babies who experience natural births that provide immediate skin-to-skin contact and breastfeeding are more self-regulated and have more relational attunement with their mothers compared with those who are swaddled or separated (Van Sleuwen et al. 2007). A meta-analysis was conducted that consisted of thirty-eight randomized control trials totaling 3,472 mother-infant dyads to investigate the effects of skin-to-skin contact immediately after birth (Moore, Bergman, Anderson, and Medley 2012). Skin-to-skin contact improved breastfeeding duration, children's cardio-respiratory-metabolic stability, temperature, self-regulation, and reduced stress associated with birth, with benefits that persisted for ten years. Despite the overwhelming evidence for skin-to-skin contact and immediate breastfeeding, routine medical practices separate mother and infant worldwide, with fewer than half of newborns breastfed in the first hour (Cadwell, Brimdyr, and Phillips 2018).

Another common yet detrimental practice is selective (non-medically indicated) cesarean birth. In the United States, cesarean birth comprises nearly 32 percent of births (Hamilton, Osterman, Driscoll, and Rossen 2017), with the number of worldwide cesareans reported to be 21 percent (95 percent confidence interval, 19–22 percent), which is double the percentage since 2000 (Boerma et al. 2018). The long-term effects of cesarean births are still being investigated, but mounting evidence demonstrates that negative effects include: (1) for the infant, hormonal, physical, bacterial abnormalities that can subtly alter neonatal physiology, alternations to immune development leading to allergy, atopy, asthma, and reduced intestinal gut microdiversity, with some long-term effects such as obesity and asthma; (2) for the mother: increased risk of uterine rupture and complications for subsequent pregnancies that include, abnormal placentation, ectopic pregnancy, stillbirth, preterm birth, with these risks, for the mother, increasing in a dose-response manner (Sandall et al. 2018).

These birthing practices and invasive procedures (done to both the infant and mother) are far from traditional, evolved, and expected care (Trevathan 2013; 2017). Within nested care, parents follow the natural rhythms of the mother and child; in fact, this is true for all mammalian parents. What the nest provides for the mother and infant is the possibility to bond to each another immediately after birth; and this, in turn, promotes breastfeeding and many positive psychological outcomes. In fact, there is growing evidence that an infant's type of birth experience (cesarean or vaginal, stressful or not) effects epigenetic changes (Vaiserman 2015; Szyf 2009). This means that changes are made all the way down to the genetic level, not changing the sequence of the DNA but altering how these genes are expressed. In this way, we see that soothing perinatal experiences protect the infant and the mother against stress that can disrupt numerous neurobiological processes — including epigenetic alterations — that otherwise allow them to bond and the child to grow well.

Breastfeeding
While breastmilk is the most beneficial source of nutrition for an infant, breastfeeding involves much more than nutrition. It involves intimate mother-child contact and social bonding (Fouts, Hewlett, and Lamb 2012). This makes it a critical factor for humans to develop normally. Because it involves both nutrients and intimate social bonding, we examine each aspect separately, but it is important to remember that they are both interacting and dynamically changing, helping the baby to grow optimally.

Regarding composition, mammalian milk is both complex and

species-specific. More than four thousand different mammalian species produce milk, each unique to its own species (Beck et al. 2015). For humans, breast milk contains numerous macro and micronutrients and continually changes according to the needs of the infant. It is composed of sugars (oligosaccharides), fats (lipids), proteins, and numerous other bioactive agents, including compounds that reduce inflammation and enhance the immune system (Andreas, Kampmann, and Le-Doare 2015). When examining just the sugar component — which functions as prebiotics for the infant — we find diverse glycans (sugars) in each mother. This means that each mother produces a milk and prebiotic that is unique to her (Aako et al. 2017). It is also important to recognize that while human milk is packed with diverse, rich nutrients, it is also thin. Unlike other animals that have thick milk, human milk is very fluid, and this is related to the frequency of ingestion or suckling. Infants need to nurse more often than other mammals because of human milk's thin composition, nursing or sucking on average every twenty minutes (Hewlett and Lamb 2005).

When a mother begins nursing, the first milk produced is called colostrum, which is thicker than later milk. It is a fluid that is saturated with growth factors and immunoglobulins, health protective agents that support the infant's immune system (Ballard and Morrow 2013). Many of these vital elements that are ubiquitous in human milk are not found in infant formula. For example, breast milk contains diverse prebiotics (explained earlier), which are not found in infant formula (Martin, Ling, and Blackburn 2016). Formula also lacks adiponectin, which is a protein that helps the body process sugars and fatty substances. High levels of adiponectin are related to lower levels of obesity and disease (Martin et al. 2006). Another key compound that formula lacks and only recently was added as supplement is tryptophan, an important hormone for sleeping, waking, and maintaining emotional tone. Tryptophan and its impact on sleep-wake cycles and emotions are both related to depression (Salgado-Delgado, Tapia Osorio Saderi, and Escobar 2011).

When examining long-term benefits, there is a plethora of advantages to both the mother and child. For children, breastfeeding decreases the risk of numerous diseases and infections compared with formula-fed infants.[1] Breastfeeding significantly reduces the risk of diarrhea, meningitis, ear infections, diabetes and externalizing behaviors, including hyperactivity (Girard, Doyle and Tremblay 2018; Stuebe and Schwarz 2010). Put simply, feeding a baby formula is increasing the risk for the infant/child to get sick, in one way or another, either in the moment or long-term. For women, the benefits of breastfeeding for a long duration have been extensively studied and include reduced risk of breast cancer, ovarian cancer, endometrial cancer, metabolic syndrome, hypertension, myocardial infarction (heart attack), type II diabetes, and lastly, premature maternal death (Louis-Jacques and Stuebe 2018).

With regard to the nest, breastfeeding is on-request and goes on anywhere from two to five years or longer. In fact, the average age of weaning is around four years of age (Hrdy 2009). Unfortunately, in the United States, only around 25 percent of women exclusively breastfeed their infants at six months of age, and only 34 percent breastfeed at all at one year (Louis-Jacques and Stuebe 2018). Recent evidence demonstrates there exists a dose-response relationship between duration of breastfeeding and positive outcomes. This means that women and children who breastfeed for a longer period enjoy greater benefits and protection from adverse outcomes. In short, breastfeeding is a dyadic process that helps the infant grow well and protects him or her from numerous adverse health conditions, all while simultaneously promoting maternal health as well. Breastfeeding also comes with freedoms and financial benefits, liberating parents from the burden of preparing formula properly (~28 minutes/bottle according to our lab's calculations) and paying for formula. It is the best way to support every infant and mother.

Our lab empirically examines the relation of nest components, like breastfeeding, to child development and flourishing. For example, in a Chinese sample, breastfeeding length was related to young children's greater conscience development and inhibitory self-control (Narvaez, Gleason et al. 2016).

---

1. It should be noted that most studies comparing formula-fed and breastfed infants look at three months of feeding, not comparing children who receive several years of breastfeeding, which our species expects.

Positive Touch and Physical Closeness of Caregivers

The benefits of positive touch and the closeness of caregivers (or their absence) has been studied for many years (e.g., Harlow 1958). Continual contact and physical closeness with caregivers are critical for normal development (Barnett 2005). There is mounting evidence from animal as well as human studies that demonstrates the harmful effects of being separated from caregivers (Duhn 2010; Ardiel and Rankin 2010; Field 2014). Being separated from caregivers and being deprived of physical contact is stressful for any infant or child. This stress then ramps up the central nervous system's stress response (hypothalamic-pituitary-axis), and this can alter mental and physical health for a lifetime. But what exactly does closeness and physical touch mean?

In our ancestral context where the nest is provided, babies and young children are kept physically close, in contact with their mothers and others at all times. This included times during the night and during time of sleep (Narvaez, Panksepp, Schore, and Gleason 2013). Only 14 percent of infants in the United States regularly sleep in a bed near caregivers (National Institute of Child Health and Human Development 2013). We now know that physical touch influences brain development and secure emotional attachments, leading to the promotion of healthy social and cognitive functioning in adulthood, including prosociality and moral behavior (Cushing and Kramer 2005; Panksepp 2007).

Another important finding regarding the importance of touch is its relationship to anxiety. Numerous studies (both animal and human) show that deprivation of touch in early life or childhood leads to anxiety in later life (Cascio, Moore, and McGlone 2019; Fish et al. 2004; Franklin et al. 2014). The connection between lack of touch and anxiety is *not* correlational or an association. Scientists have begun to unravel the pathway and mechanisms by which lack of touch *causes* increased stress, which leads to the development of anxiety. In addition, research shows that increasing touch in childhood (before adolescence) with a simple gesture on the shoulder decreases anxiety for those children who need it most — the socially anxious child (Brummelman et al. 2019). If your child suffers from anxiety, it is not too late to begin implementing simple gestures of affection throughout the day. This easy, free intervention strategy can have many positive effects, benefiting your child for many years to come.

The modern, Western way of caring for infants and children promotes numerous devices for raising a child, things such as strollers, high chairs, cribs, and car seats. While these tools can be helpful from time to time, they can also stifle physical contact and closeness. It is important to remember that physical closeness does not mean a pat on the back once in a while, although that can be positive and reaffirming for older children. The nested way of providing for children's need for physical closeness and positive touch involves almost continual contact in the first year of life and plenty of carrying and closeness in the early years.

Our empirical examination of touch shows that greater affectionate touch in infancy is related to young children's empathy and inhibitory self-control in the US and China (Narvaez, Gleason et al. 2016). Among US adults reporting on their childhood experiences, greater affectionate touch and less corporal punishment was related to a more open-hearted moral orientation and less self-protectionist moral orientation, including greater perspective-taking and relational attunement (Narvaez et al., under revision).

Responsivity

Responsivity to infants and children means caring for their needs in the moment, not delaying or withholding care, and keeping baby in optimal arousal while the brain grows rapidly moment by moment. Unfortunately, several voices in popular Western culture suggest that responsivity is not important and possibly harmful to children. Some believe that meeting the needs of infants and children will exacerbate innate selfishness, vice, and dependency. Examples of such thinking include delaying food, sleep, or breastfeeding because otherwise providing them will make the baby "demanding," more "difficult," and "spoiled." The opposite is true.

Fortunately, we know there are decades of research that directly counter such claims. Evidence from numerous fields shows that rapid responsivity to infants — moving in when the baby shows discomfort — is the foundation of right-brain affect regulation (Schore 2015; 2003). Caregivers who respond to the needs of their babies (under age three) act as external emotional and psychological regulators and stabilizers so the many physiological systems under final development are established in healthy ways (Hofer 1994; Schore 2001). The bodies and brains of young children need the physical and emotional guidance of adult caregivers to learn to adjust their emotional and physiological responses to changes in the environment. It is only through the presence of these external helpers that children learn to calm down and return to a growth-inducing biochemistry instead of the panicked stress response that focuses on survival. Thus, when the adult caregiver is absent, hindered, or culturally prevented from providing responsive care, children establish dysregulated systems. When children are left unattended in distress, they eventually learn to shut down to stay alive, which looks to an insensitive adult like they are "self-soothing" (another myth). As one can see, nonresponsiveness builds dysregulation at the foundation of personality, rather than the mythical baby independence.

What, specifically, does responsive care promote? When warm, responsive care is provided, multiple positive effects take place. Children raised with abundant responsive care develop neurobiological systems that respond well to arousal and stress (e.g., via a well-developed oxytocinergic system), both on their own and with others (Liu et al. 1997; Schore 2003; Haley and Stansbury 2003). It helps shape a child's vagal tone, an important cranial nerve that helps calm, soothe, and restore both emotional and physiological stress (Porges 2011). It also provides an important foundation for developing prosociality, compassion, and openheartedness, all key ingredients of virtue development (Goetz, Keltner, and Simon-Thomas 2010; Carter, Harris, and Porges 2009).

Mutually responsive caregiving predicts better socialization; for example, stronger conscience development (Kochanska 2002; Kochanska, Boldt, and Goffin 2019). In our empirical work, responsiveness is always significantly related to positive child outcomes (well-being, happiness, low anxiety and depression, social attunement, empathy, conscience, self-regulation) and so we always use it as a control to see if other nest components matter, too.

Free Play

Play is an important part of mammalian childhoods and is shown to promote numerous positive outcomes in children. The kind of play discussed here is natural physical play — not play in organized sports or activities. While these structured events can and do have other benefits, the type of play that is known to facilitate important emotional and psychological benefits is self-directed free play — play that is unstructured, with other children of different ages, and as much as possible, in nature. This type of play promotes brain development in general, including affectively beneficial gene expression profiles, emotion regulation, and resilience to stress, and is an effective treatment for ADHD and promoting of prosocial behavior (Panskepp 2018; Burgdorf, Kroes, Beinfeld, Panksepp, and Moskal 2010; Burgdorf, Kroes, and Moskal 2017).

When play is missing from children's daily lives, as is happening in schools throughout the United States and elsewhere, children lose the chance to develop their right-brain hemisphere (Miller and Almon 2009). The right brain controls key aspects of prosocial behavior and self-regulation. Thus, it makes sense that play, especially rough-and-tumble play, is an effective intervention strategy for ADHD and other self-regulatory disorders. Those children who lack play in their early life have altered social, sexual, and conflict interactions with peers (van den Berg et al. 1999). Without play, children lack emotional and relational flexibility, the ability to shift and change actions when unexpected events take place (Spinka, Newberry, and Bekoff 2001). Play throughout childhood develops all of these important parts of the brain, giving the child the best chance to experience a healthy adult emotional life, which includes control over their body/mind/emotions and social flexibility — the ability to dynamically interact with others.

Our work on play shows that play facilitates healthy vagal tone in young children (Tarsha et al., in preparation), and correlates with young children's moral feelings and behavior in China (Narvaez, Wang et al. 2013) and with young children's empathy in the US (Narvaez, Gleason et al. 2016).

Alloparents and Social Support

Alloparents is a term that refers to caregivers other than the mother (aka, allomothers, Hrdy 2009). In order to provide intensive responsive, nurturing care to infants and children, multiple caregivers, or alloparents, are needed. These can include trusted family members such as grand-parents, aunts and uncles, or other members of the community who are capable of providing loving, kind care. When children are surrounded by a large network of caregivers, this increases the likelihood that they will be cared for in a kind, loving, and responsive manner, while also increasing mothers' experience of feeling socially supported; which, in turn, increases maternal responsiveness to her child (Hrdy, 2011).

Alloparents and high levels of social support do not refer simply to friends or homes where parents feel comfortable dropping off their children for a playdate. Having such friends is helpful, but alloparents typically refers to adults who are helping care for the children on a daily basis, best with the parents nearby. Ideally the adults and the children are together, living and functioning as a group. In this way, both the parents and the children feel supported. Alloparents provide a social network of care and concern, ensuring that children find at least one (best three) person who loves them unconditionally. In traditional societies, alloparents supported good rather than poor parenting, as the whole communi-ty would end up living with the shaped nature of the child.

In our empirical work using a longitudinal study, mothers reporting more social support when children were six months of age (staying the same at eighteen months) had children who were more prosocial at two and three years of age (Narvaez, Gleason et al. 2013). In an adult study, adults reporting more social support in childhood tend to be less socially withdrawn or emotionally detached; but, instead, communally engaged with others (Narvaez, Thiel et al. 2016).

Positive (Home) Climate

This nest component addresses the emotional climate in the home in which the child is immersed. The overarching feeling that is important for the child to have as they develop is a sense of being loved, cherished, and appreciated. This will enable a sense of security within the fami-ly, giving the child the experience of deep friendship both in the home (with other family members) and outside the familial unit. In turn, this promotes an openhearted orientation to life rather than a self-protection orientation.

In our measurement, positive home climate refers to a greater prevalence of positive rather than negative emotional atmosphere. Positive emotions include joy, serenity, and expansiveness, whereas detrimental (negative) emotions include sadness, fear, anger, and humiliation. Adults who report more positive emotions in childhood are more secure, mentally healthier, less distressed, and less likely to have a self-protective morality. A negative home climate in childhood predicts self-protectionism of various kinds in social situations (e.g., withdrawal, opposition, sense of superiority, viciousness) (Narvaez, Thiel et al. 2016).

Nature Connection

All components of the nest reflect a humble approach to nature, honoring humanity's social mammalian heritage, immaturity in early life, and the evolved system of care proper development requires. But with ecological crises affecting everyone's daily life, it is important to emphasize that honoring creation require emotional commitment to the well-being of the biocommunity. Several scholars have pointed to the lack of ecological attachment — emotional connection — to the natural world as the deeper source of our ecological crises (Berry 2013; Louv 2005). Connecting to the natural world — all created things — occurs naturally in childhood, as long as children are regularly immersed in complex natural environs with freedom to roam. Nature connection is promoted not only by experiences in nature alone or with family, but in family conversations about ecological systems, animal and plant life, and respectful practices to honor the lives of animals and plants and the more than human. In our ancestral context, human communities learned from nature as well. Deep observation of animals and plants fostered awareness of how to promote well-being in the biocommunity (Martin 1999).

Connectedness to nature is deeply rooted within the Catholic tradition, where the goodness of the natural world is recognized. Some specific examples include Saints Francis of Assisi (brother sun and sister moon), Aquinas, and Anthony of Egypt. Anthony made the famous remark that to learn about God and to relate to Him, he preferred the book of nature to the written word (Athanasius 1950). The idea is that connecting to nature is a basic human need, but it also is a way to connect with God. Connecting to nature means taking time to wonder at the created world, breathing in its complexities and beauty, all while wanting to respect and cultivate it, rather than dominate and control it.

The Evolved Nest (or Lack of It) Shapes Society

The nest components are part of our heritage and shape well-being and the foundations for morality. When the evolved nest is provided by the community to infants and children, their brains develop properly, building foundations for prosocial and moral capacities. When we asked mothers to report on a young child's experience of the nest in the past week (self-directed play, affection, no corporal punishment, family togetherness), it predicted children's moral socialization (e.g., empathy, self-control) and children's social thriving (relational attunement) (Narvaez, Woodbury et al. 2019).

In our ancestral context, the nest continued through life, prompting healthy functioning generally, with remedies for healing when, inevitably, a person failed in their virtuous treatment of others, including the other than human (Ross 2006). Well-cared-for, well-formed, nested individuals grow up to become adults who prosocially engage with their family and community. Nested adults are motivated to help others, exhibit concern for others around them, including the created world. Ultimately, they become wise elders. These wise grandparents and elders demonstrate wellness, openheartedness, compassion, and virtue. In this way, it is evident that a *cycle of cooperative companionship* develops (Narvaez 2014), where the wise and healthy elders help meet the basic needs of younger generations. It creates a cascade of benefits flowing from the older members of the community to the younger ones. Because healthy grandparents are capable of being present, both emotionally and physically, to participate in caring for the needs of the youngest members of the family and community, parents are not isolated in their caregiving activities. This means that infants, children, and parents are surrounded — *nested* — with care from many adults, not just the mother or father.

WHAT HAPPENS WHEN THE NEST IS NOT PROVIDED?

When aspects of the nest are not provided, this deprives infants and children of what they need to grow well, shifting a child from an optimal trajectory to one of dysregulation. As discussed above, physical and neurobiological processes are thwarted, along with the basic building blocks of socio-emotional intelligence, self-regulation, and morality (Schore 1997; 2002; Narvaez 2014). Children who experience less than optimal development are not given their uniqueness but learn to be on guard, bracing against the world. They age into adults and elders who are absorbed with their own needs, unable to care for the new generation. They are unable to fully engage with others or attend to the needs of the community and are unlikely to reach wisdom as a community leader. The deterioration of the nest means that the cascading benefits from generation to generation do not take place. Instead of a cycle of cooperative companionship, a *cycle of competitive detachment* takes hold (Narvaez 2014). This means that children are deprived of numerous alloparents, the much-needed broad network of adult caregivers. It also means that parents lack support themselves, which can lead to less responsive, warm parenting (Taraban et al. 2018). Basic needs are not met and impair development and outcomes across generations.

BASIC NEEDS

Abraham Maslow (1970) identified a set of basic needs that humans need fulfilled in order to reach their potential. He listed (in our words) physiological, security, social belonging, competency, and self-actualization needs. In our view, a baby needs all of these simultaneously to grow well (Narvaez 2018). Susan Fiske (2004) identified a BUCET list of basic needs: belonging, understanding, competence/control, self-enhancement, and trust. Erik Erikson (1950) identified sensitive periods in development for developing some of Fiske's BUCET list (or their opposite): trust in the first year of life; autonomy versus shame/self-doubt in toddlerhood; initiative versus guilt in the preschool years; industry versus inferiority in childhood; identity versus role confusion in adolescence; intimacy versus isolation in young adulthood; generativity versus stagnation in adulthood; and integrity versus despair in elderhood. Each of these components is seeded in early life, when psychosocial and neu-robiological structures are set on trajectories for the lifespan. In more traditional societies, community practices necessarily supported these phases across the lifespan. But it is rare to find such supports in anyone's life in industrialized, economically-focused societies.

WHERE TO GO FROM HERE?

For most of us, it is easy to identify with the cycle of competitive detach-ment and recognize that many communities lack most, if not all, com-ponents of the nest. It seems to be a cultural trend in which we are im-mersed (in the West), one that emphasizes production and materialisms, a "Sacred Money and Markets" orientation (Korten 2005). However, it is becoming more apparent that the price tag for emphasizing econom-ic wealth over all is social and ecological poverty (ibid). The wealthier societies become, the more detached they become from those in need, including nonhumans and their ecological surroundings.

When we adults consider the components of the nest in our own lives, it can stir up a sense of unmet needs in our childhoods. While this might be initially painful, it is important to remember that changing the societal cycle from competitive detachment to cooperative companion-ship begins within each adult, the leaders of the family. Trauma and un-der-care in our own childhoods can make providing responsive, nested care aversive. A child's needs may seem overly demanding, and rational-izations to ignore the intensive needs become attractive. Thus, parents need to understand how the parental brain can shut down in the face of child needs, leading to "blocked care" (Hughes and Baylin 2012). Parents can learn to recognize their own unmet needs and address their primal wounds with sensitivity, working through the painful realization and promoting self-healing (Narvaez 2014).

Many modern structural and cultural practices make it difficult for families to provide each component of the nest. These challenges include inflexible work schedules, short maternity/paternity leave, financial debt, lack of education, and missing social support. In this way, modern families are faced with the challenge of meeting their children's needs at a time in history with more obstacles than ever before. Trends within unnested cultures are to minimize the needs of the child, rather than to try to correct the unjust systems and structures that are in place. So, what are families to do?

One solution to these seemingly insurmountable obstacles is moral innovation. This is the idea that when one has a deep, rich understanding of oneself, other people, and the human existence, he or she is equipped with the ability to generate solutions to even the most difficult circumstances. Moral innovation is "the capacity to frame and to realize more comprehensive and inclusive ends that make it possible for us to live well together with others" (Johnson 1996; Narvaez 2010). We can create new ways of living and being within our unique family situations, ways that support the nest, life-centered parenting, and living well together. With their deep, intimate (hopefully) understanding of their children, parents and family members are capable of creating new ways of living well together in order to provide the nest components.

An example of implementing moral innovation in the family as an adult family member might be to consider asking, on a daily basis, if the children's needs are being met. This helps offset the sometimes consuming focus of work, finances, and other adult demands. Decide to ask yourself, or with your partner, this question every day at the same time (e.g., while brushing your teeth, driving home from work). As your children become older, you can include them in the questioning. For example, questions can be posed to toddlers or school-aged children: "Did you get enough hugs today? Did you get enough self-directed physical play (running around time) today? Did you get enough social bonding experiences today?" Questions like these can help foster reflective capacities, teaching children to recognize their own needs as they grow. Eventually, the child will learn to recognize the feeling of an unmet need, will be able to articulate his or her want to the loving caregiver, and figure out ways to have the appropriate experience. With older children, discussions about the nest (you can use the Child Nest as a guide, see figure 2) and basic needs are very constructive. These conversations can include questions about how their needs might be changing as they grow and develop.

Figure 2. The Child Nest

Another example of moral innovation includes trying to change behaviors that irritate the adults. Oftentimes, an adult reaction to annoying behavior is either passivity, ignoring, or control, exerting power and punishment. Rather than resorting to these extremes, ask the question: "What basic need is being expressed?" If the child is older, you can even ask them directly, talking through the nest components. Satiating the unmet need will ameliorate the troublesome behavior and catalyze prosocial behavior and child flourishing (Narvaez 2018).

In addition, it might be helpful to reflect upon the basic mechanics of the family, asking the question: Is there enough time built into the daily schedule for children to freely play (not organized activities or screen time)? If the answer to this question is no, that could indicate that more downtime is needed, creating space for the child to interact with nature, engage in pretend play, or take up a wrestling match (rough-and-tumble play). Recognizing that time to be free, create, and play are just as fundamental to familial health as good nutrition is an important step toward creating a countercultural home environment. This goes against the current trend in society that indicates weeknights and weekends are intended for busy schedules packed with carpools, organized sports, music lessons, and numerous other activities. Even seemingly good things like social or prayer groups could stretch family life to the point that children are deprived of the freedom to play and create. Safeguard time, every day if possible, to rest and play in the family.

Play, like the other components of the nest, consists of practices that are part of everyday life and could appear mundane, boring, and unsensational. There is strong focus within our current culture that utilizes exciting experiences, such as expensive birthday parties or luxury vacations, as the basic metric for evaluating optimal parenting. But the nest and meeting the basic needs of children is not about extraordinary experiences, but about providing responsive, nurturing care from moment to moment, day to day. Psychological and neurobiological research continue to underscore the importance of these seemingly "mundane" experiences (as described above) for healthy sociomoral development. When a child is on the floor playing, resting in his or her parents' arms, or taking in nature attentively or through play, such activities may appear uneventful and unimportant. However, these "uneventful" experiences are necessary nourishment for virtue development — learning to be empathic and responsive to one another and to the natural world. Practicing virtue requires attunement to the others (including other-than-humans) who are involved in the specific context and practicing responsiveness in changing moods and situations (Narvaez 2016).

THE NEST AS LIVED THEOLOGY

The nest promotes an authentic "domestic-church-based spirituality." The nest is about meeting the needs of all family members, most especially those of infants and children, so that their unique spirits can flourish. In this way, living and applying the nest in families and communities is a way of putting theology into action: living out justice, mercy, and love. Because justice is concerned with right relationship, the nest is a way to implement justice at a personal and familial level (Philpott 2012). Right relationship requires satiating of needs, for all family members, and the nest provides concrete ways to bring this into fruition. The nest also assumes the ecclesiological understanding of mercy, because it is focused on restoring human dignity and safeguarding against the feeling of humiliation (Saint John Paul II 1980). When unnested care is implemented in the family, the basic rights of all members are degraded, and this creates feelings of humiliation, distrust, and shame. The nest is concerned with prevention of these adverse outcomes and, in this way, is a form of agape love. It is important to recognize that love in action involves prevention, not just correction, of wrongdoing. Nested parenting contains many similarities to early Christian communities' way of living, where intensive nurturing was expected and supported by the community (Tarsha & Narvaez, in preparation).

CONCLUSION

The nest is an ecological system of care for infants and children that promotes human flourishing, including moral and virtue development. Humans are made to be cooperative, but it requires extensive, responsive care, as outlined in the nest. Each component of the nest has extensive empirical evidence from multiple areas of research, including developmental psychology, neuroscience, and anthropology, showing how critical it is for healthy development to unfold.

The nest is universal and applies to all children because it centers on upholding the dignity of the child, the dignity of the parents, and the dignity of the family, including extended family members. By promoting and implementing the nest, families meet the basic needs of their children so that their spirits can grow and flourish unimpeded by feelings of abandonment, anger, or fear. Nest provision promotes human flourishing and virtue — in both children and adult family members — generating communities of cooperative companionship.

DISCUSSION QUESTIONS

1. What components of the Evolved Nest are already implemented in your family/community? Which are missing?
2. Which component would you like you try to enhance in your family/

community?

3. How can you motivate others to adopt the component? How can you make it easy to do so? Remember, you can start changes slowly.
4. What obstacles do you anticipate, and how might you overcome them?

REFERENCES

Aakko, J., H. Kumar, S. Rautava, A. Wise, C. Autran, L. Bode, E. Isolauri, and S. Salminen. "Human Milk Oligosaccharide Categories Define the Microbiota Composition in Human Colostrum." *Beneficial Microbes* 8, no. 4 (August 24, 2017): 563–67.

Andreas, N. J., B. Kampmann, and K. M. Le-Doare, "Human Breast Milk: A Review on Its Composition and Bioactivity." *Early Human Development* 91, no. 11 (November 2015): 629–35.

Ang, E. S., V. Gluncic, A. Duque, M. E. Schafer, and P. Rakic. "Prenatal Exposure to Ultrasound Waves Impacts Neuronal Migration in Mice." *Proceedings of the National Academy of Sciences* 103, no. 34 (August 22, 2006): 12903–10.

Ardiel, Evan L., and Catharine H. Rankin. "The Importance of Touch in Development," *Paediatrics & Child Health* 15, no. 3 (March 2010): 153–56.

Athanasius, Saint. *The Life of Saint Antony*, Issue 10. Mahwah, NJ: Paulist Press, 1950.

Ballard, O., and A. L. Morrow. "Human Milk Composition: Nutrients and Bioactive Factors." *Pediatric Clinics* 60, no. 1 (February 2013): 49–74.

Barnett, Lynn. "Keep in Touch: The Importance of Touch in Infant Development." *Infant Observation* 8, no. 2 (August 2005): 115–23.

Beck, K. L., D. Weber, B. S. Phinney, J. T. Smilowitz, K. Hinde, B. Lönnerdal, I. Korf, and D. G. Lemay. "Comparative Proteomics of Human and Macaque Milk Reveals Species-Specific Nutrition During Postnatal Development." *Journal of Proteome Research* 14, no. 5 (May 2015): 2143–57.

Bergman, N. J., L. L. Linley, and S. R. Fawcus. "Randomized Controlled Trial of Skin-to-Skin Contact from Birth Versus Conventional

Incubator for Physiological Stabilization in 1200- to 2199-Gram Newborns." *Acta Paediatrica* 93, no. 6 (June 2004): 779–85.

Berry, Wendell. "It All Turns on Affection." 2012 Jefferson Lecture. Washington, DC: National Endowment for the Humanities.

Bird, Rebecca Bliege, and Eleanor A. Power. "Prosocial Signaling and Cooperation among Martu Hunters." *Evolution and Human Behavior* 36, no. 5 (September 2015): 389–97.

Bludau, A., M. Royer, G. Meister, I. D. Neumann, and R. Menon. "Epigenetic Regulation of the Social Brain." *Trends in Neurosciences* 42, no. 7 (July 2019): 471–84.

Boerma, Ties, Carine Ronsmans, Dessalegn Y. Melesse, Aluisio J. D. Barros, Fernando C. Barros, Liang Juan, Ann-Beth Moller, Lale Say, Ahmad Reza Hosseinpoor, Mu Yi, Dácio de Lyra Rabello Neto, and Marleen Temmerman. "Global Epidemiology of Use of and Disparities in Caesarean Sections." *The Lancet* 392, no. 10155 (October 13, 2018): 1341–48.

Brummelman, Eddie, David Terburg, Miranda Smit, Susan Bögels, and Peter A. Bos. "Parental Touch Reduces Social Vigilance in Children." *Developmental Cognitive Neuroscience* 35 (February 2019): 87–93.

Burgdorf, J., R. A. Kroes, and J. R. Moskal. "Rough-and-Tumble Play Induces Resilience to Stress in Rats." *NeuroReport* 28, no. 17 (December 2017): 1122–26.

Burgdorf, J., R. A. Kroes, M. C. Beinfeld, Jaak Panksepp, and J. R. Moskal. "Uncovering the Molecular Basis of Positive Affect Using Rough-and-Tumble Play in Rats: A Role for Insulin-Like Growth Factor I." *Neuroscience* 168, no. 3 (July 2010): 769–77.

Cadwell, K., K. Brimdyr, and R. Phillips. "Mapping, Measuring, and Analyzing the Process of Skin-to-Skin Contact and Early Breastfeeding in the First Hour After Birth." *Breastfeeding Medicine* 13, no. 7 (September 2018): 485–92.

Callaghan, B. L., and N. Tottenham. "The Neuro-Environmental Loop of Plasticity: A Cross-Species Analysis of Parental Effects on Emotion Circuitry Development Following Typical and Adverse Caregiving." *Neuropsychopharmacology* 41, no. 1 (January

2016): 163.

Carter, C. Sue, James Harris, and Stephen W. Porges. "Neural and Evolutionary Perspectives on Empathy." In *The Social Neuroscience of Empathy*, Jean Decety and William Ickes. Cambridge: MIT Press, 2009: 169–82.

Champagne, F. A. "Epigenetic Influence of Social Experiences across the Lifespan." *Developmental Psychobiology* 52, no. 4 (May 2010): 299–311.

Cascio, Carissa J., David Moore, and Francis McGlone. "Social Touch and Human Development." *Developmental Cognitive Neuroscience* 35 (February 2019): 5–11.

Cushing, B.S., and K. M. Kramer. "Mechanisms Underlying Epigenetic Effects of Early Social Experience: The Role of Neuropeptides and Steroids." *Neuroscience and Biobehavioral Reviews* 29, no. 7 (2005): 1089–1105.

Duhn, L. "The Importance of Touch in the Development of Attachment." *Advances in Neonatal Care* 10, no. 6 (December 2010): 294–300.

Erikson, Erik H. *Childhood and Society*. New York: W. W. Norton & Co., 1950.

Field, Tiffany M. *Touch in Early Development*. New Jersey: Psychology Press, 1995.

Fish, E. W., D. Shahrokh, R. Bagot, C. Caldji, T. Bredy, M. Szyf, and M. J. Meaney. "Epigenetic Programming of Stress Responses Through Variations in Maternal Care." *Annals of the New York Academy of Sciences* 1036, no. 1 (December 2004): 167–80.

Fiske, Susan T. *Social Beings: A Core Motives Approach to Social Psychology*. New York: Wiley, 2004.

Fouts, H. N., B. S. Hewlett, and M. E. Lamb. "A Biocultural Approach to Breastfeeding Interactions in Central Africa." *American Anthropologist* 114, no. 1 (2012): 123–36.

Franklin, T. B., H. Russig, I. C. Weiss, J. Gräff, N. Linder, A. Michalon, S. Vizi, and I. M. Mansuy. "Epigenetic Transmission of the Impact of Early Stress Across Generations." *Biological Psychiatry* 68, no. 5 (2010): 408–15.

Fry, Douglas P. *The Human Potential for Peace: An Anthropological Challenge to Assumptions About War and Violence.* New York: Oxford University Press, 2006.

Fry, D. P., and G. Souillac. "The Relevance of Nomadic Forager Studies to Moral Foundations Theory: Moral Education and Global Ethics in the Twenty-First Century." *Journal of Moral Education* 42, no. 3 (July 23, 2013): 346–59.

Gershoff, Elizabeth T., Gail S. Goodman, Cindy L. Miller-Perrin, George W. Holden, Yo Jackson, and Alan E. Kazdin. "No Longer Up for Debate: Physical Punishment Causes Negative Outcomes for Children." *PRC Research Brief* 3 no. 12 (September 2018). DOI:10.15781/T22R3PG2X.

Girard, L. C., O. Doyle, and R. E. Tremblay. "Breastfeeding and Externalizing Problems: A Quasi-Experimental Design with a National Cohort." *European Child & Adolescent Psychiatry* 27 no. 7 (July 2018): 877–84.

Goetz, J. L., D. Keltner, and E. Simon-Thomas. "Compassion: An Evolutionary Analysis and Empirical Review." *Psychological Bulletin* 136, vol. 3 (May 2010): 351.

Gudsnuk, K. M., and F. A. Champagne. "Epigenetic Effects of Early Developmental Experiences." *Clinics in Perinatology* 38, no. 4 (December 2011): 703–17.

Haley, D. W., and K. Stansbury. "Infant Stress and Parent Responsiveness: Regulation of Physiology and Behavior During Still-Face and Reunion." *Child Development* 74, no. 5 (September-October 2003): 1534–46.

Hamilton, Brady E., Joyce A. Martin, Michelle J. K. Osterman, Anne K. Driscoll, and Lauren M. Rossen. "Births: Provisional Data for 2016." *Vital Statistics Rapid Release,* Report No. 002, June 2017. http://www.cdc.gov/nchs/data/vsrr/report002.pdf.

Hewlett, Barry S., and Michael E. Lamb. "Emerging Issues in the Study of Hunter-Gatherer Children." *Hunter-Gatherer Childhoods: Evolutionary, Developmental, and Cultural Perspectives.* Piscataway, NJ: Aldine Transaction Publishers, 2005: 3–19.

Hofer, M. A. "Early Relationships as Regulators of Infant Physiology and

Behavior." *Acta Paediatrica* 83 (June 1994): 9–18.

Hrdy, Sarah Blaffer. *Mothers and Others: The Evolutionary Origins of Mutual Understanding*. Cambridge, MA: Harvard University Press, 2011.

Hughes, Daniel A., and Jonathan Baylin. *Brain-Based Parenting: The Neuroscience of Caregiving for Healthy Attachment*. New York: W. W. Norton & Co., 2012.

Ingold, Tim. "On the Social Relations of the Hunter-Gatherer Band." In *The Cambridge Encyclopedia of Hunters and Gatherers*, Richard B. Lee and Richard Daly, eds. New York: Cambridge University Press, 2000: 399–410.

Saint John Paul II. *Dives in Misericordia*, Encyclical Letter. November 30, 1980. http://w2.vatican.va/content/john-paul-ii/en/encyclicals/documents/hf_jp-ii_enc_30111980_dives-in-misericordia.html.

Kochanska, Grazyna. "Mutually Responsive Orientation Between Mothers and Their Young Children: A Context for the Early Development of Conscience." *Current Directions in Psychological Science* 11, no. 6 (December 1, 2002): 191–95.

Kochanska, G., L. J. Boldt, and K. C. Goffin. "Early Relational Experience: A Foundation for the Unfolding Dynamics of Parent–Child Socialization." *Child Development Perspectives* 13, no. 1 (March 13, 2019): 41–47.

Lee, Richard B. and Richard Daly, eds. *The Cambridge Encyclopedia of Hunters and Gatherers*. New York: Cambridge University Press, 2000.

Liu, D., J. Diorio, B. Tannenbaum, C. Caldji, D. Francis, A. Freedman, S. Sharma, D. Pearson, P. M. Plotsky, and M. J. Meaney. "Maternal Care, Hippocampal Glucocorticoid Receptors, and Hypothalamic-Pituitary-Adrenal Responses to Stress." *Science* 277, no. 5332 (September 1997): 1659–62.

Louis-Jacques, Adetola, and Alison Stuebe. "Long-Term Maternal Benefits of Breastfeeding." *Contemporary Ob/Gyn* 64, no. 7, July 11, 2018. https://www.contemporaryobgyn.net/breast-health/long-term-maternal-benefits-breastfeeding.

Louv, Richard. *Last Child in the Woods: Saving Our Children from Nature Deficit Disorder.* New York: Workman Publishing Co., 2005.

Martin, Camilla R., Pei-Ra Ling, and George L. Blackburn. "Review of Infant Feeding: Key Features of Breast Milk and Infant Formula." *Nutrients* 8, no. 5 (May 2016): 279.

Martin, Calvin Luther. *The Way of the Human Being.* New Haven, CT: Yale University Press, 1999.

Martin, L. J., J. G. Woo, S. R. Geraghty, M. Altaye, B. S. Davidson, W. Banach, L. M. Dolan, G. M. Ruiz-Palacios, and A. L. Morrow. "Adiponectin Is Present in Human Milk and Is Associated with Maternal Factors." *The American Journal of Clinical Nutrition* 83, no. 5 (May 2006): 1106–11.

Maslow, Abraham. *Motivation and Personality, Second Edition.* New York: Harper & Row, 1970.

Middlemiss, W., D. A. Granger, W. A. Goldberg, and L. Nathans. "Asynchrony of Mother–Infant Hypothalamic–Pituitary–Adrenal Axis Activity Following Extinction of Infant Crying Responses Induced During the Transition to Sleep." *Early Human Development* 88, no. 4 (April 2012): 227–32.

Miller, Edward, and Joan Almon. *Crisis in the Kindergarten: Why Children Need to Play in School.* College Park, MD: Alliance for Childhood, 2013.

Moore, Elizabeth R., Gene C. Anderson, Nils Bergman, and Therese Dowswell. "Early Skin-to-Skin Contact for Mothers and Their Healthy Newborn Infants." *The Cochrane Database of Systematic Reviews* 5, no. 5. CD003519. doi:10.1002/14651858.CD003519.pub3.

Narvaez, Darcia. "The 99 Percent — Development and Socialization within an Evolutionary Context: Growing Up to Become 'a Good and Useful Human Being.'" In *War, Peace, and Human Nature: The Convergence of Evolutionary and Cultural Views.* Douglas P. Fry, ed. New York: Oxford University Press, 2013: 643–72.

Narvaez, Darcia. *Neurobiology and the Development of Human Morality: Evolution, Culture and Wisdom.* New York: W. W. Norton & Co., 2014.

Narvaez, Darcia. "Baselines for Virtue." In *Developing the Virtues: Integrating Perspectives,* Julie Annas, Darcia Narvaez, and Nancy E. Snow, eds. New York: Oxford University Press, 2016: 14–33.

Narvaez, Darcia. "Revitalizing Human Virtue by Restoring Organic Morality." *Journal of Moral Education* 45, no. 3 (June 2016b): 223–38.

Narvaez, Darcia, ed. *Basic Needs, Wellbeing and Morality: Fulfilling Human Potential.* New York: Palgrave Pivot, 2018.

Narvaez, Darcia, Lijuan Wang, Alison Cheng, Tracy R. Gleason, Ryan Woodbury, Angela Kurth, and Jennifer Burke Lefever. "The Importance of Early Life Touch for Psychosocial and Moral Development." December 2019, under revision.

Narvaez, Darcia, T. Gleason, J. B. Lefever, L. Wang, and A. Cheng. "Early Experience and Ethical Orientation." In *Embodied Morality: Protectionism, Engagement and Imagination,* by Darcia Narvaez. New York: Palgrave Macmillan, 2016: 73–98.

Narvaez, Darcia, Jaak Panksepp, Allan N. Schore, and Tracy R. Gleason. "The Value of Using an Evolutionary Framework for Gauging Children's Well-Being." *Evolution, Early Experience and Human Development: From Research to Practice and Policy.* New York: Oxford University Press, 2013: 3–30.

Narvaez, Darcia, A. Thiel, A. Kurth, and K. Renfus. "Past Moral Action and Ethical Orientation." In Darcia Narvaez, *Embodied Morality: Protectionism, Engagement and Imagination.* New York: Palgrave Macmillan, 2016: 99–118.

Narvaez, Darcia, Ryan Woodbury, Tracy R. Gleason, Angela Kurth, Ying Cheng, Lijuan Wang, L. Deng, Eveline Gutzwiller-Helfenfinger, Markus Christen, and Catherine Näpflin. "Evolved Development Niche Provision Report: Moral Socialization, Social Maladaptation and Social Thriving in Three Countries." *Sage Open* 9, no. 2, April 2019. https://doi.org/10.1177/2158244019840123.

Panksepp, Jaak. "The Neuroevolutionary and Neuroaffective Psychobiology of the Prosocial Brain." *The Oxford Handbook of Evolutionary Psychology.* Oxford: Oxford University Press, 2007: 145–62.

Panksepp, Jaak. "PLAY and the Construction of Creativity, Cleverness, and Reversal of ADHD in our Social Brains." In *Play and Creativity in Psychotherapy*, Terry Marks-Tarlow, Marion Solomon, and Daniel J. Siegel, eds. New York: W. W. Norton & Co., 2018: 242–70.

Porges, S. W. *The Polyvagal Theory: Neurophysiological Foundations of Emotions, Attachment, Communication, and Self-Regulation.* New York: W. W. Norton & Co., 2011.

Rosman, N. Paul, Rachel Vassar, Gheorghe Doros, James DeRosa, Allison Froman, Audrey DiMauro, Sherry Santiago, and Jodi Abbott. "Association of Prenatal Ultrasonography and Autism Spectrum Disorder." *JAMA Pediatrics* 172, no. 4, (2018): 336–44.

Ross, Rupert. *Indigenous Healing: Exploring Traditional Paths.* Toronto: Penguin Canada, 2014.

Salgado-Delgado, Roberto, Araceli Tapia Osorio, Nadia Saderi, and Carolina Escobar. "Disruption of Circadian Rhythms: A Crucial Factor in the Etiology of Depression." *Depression Research and Treatment.* 2011:839743.

Sandall, Jane, Rachel M. Tribe, Lisa Avery, Glen Mola, Gerald H. A. Visser, Caroline S. E. Homer, Deena Gibbons, Niamh M. Kelly, Holly Powell Kennedy, Hussein Kidanto, Paul Taylor, and Marleen Temmerman. "Short-Term and Long-Term Effects of Caesarean Section on the Health of Women and Children." *The Lancet* 392:10155 (October 13, 2018): 1349–57.

Schore, Allen N. "Effects of a Secure Attachment Relationship on Right Brain Development, Affect Regulation, and Infant Mental Health." *Infant Mental Health Journal* 22, no. 1-2 (January 2001): 7–66.

Schore, Allen N. *Affect Regulation and the Repair of the Self.* New York: W. W. Norton & Co., 2003.

Schore, Allen N. *Affect Regulation and the Origin of the Self: The Neurobiology of Emotional Development.* Abingdon, United Kingdom: Routledge, 2015.

Slater, Rebecca, Laura Cornelissen, Lorenzo Fabrizi, Debbie Patten, Jan Yoxen, Alan Worley, Stewart Boyd, Judith Meek, and Maria Fitzgerald. "Oral Sucrose as an Analgesic Drug for Procedural Pain in Newborn Infants: A Randomized Controlled Trial." *The Lancet* 376:9748 (September 1, 2010): 1225–32.

Spinka, Marek, Ruth C. Newberry, and Marc Bekoff. "Mammalian Play: Training for the Unexpected." *The Quarterly Review of Biology* 76, no. 2 (June 2001): 141–68.

Stuebe, Alison M., and E. B. Schwarz. "The Risks and Benefits of Infant Feeding Practices for Women and Their Children." *Journal of Perinatology* 30, no. 3 (2010): 155.

Szyf, Moshe. "Early Life, the Epigenome and Human Health." *Acta Paediatrica* 98, no. 7 (2009): 1082–4.

Taraban, Lindsay, Daniel S. Shaw, Leslie D. Leve, Misaki N. Natsuaki, Jody M. Ganiban, David Reiss, and Jenae M. Neiderhiser. "Parental Depression, Overreactive Parenting, and Early Childhood Externalizing Problems: Moderation by Social Support." *Child Development.* February 20, 2018. https://doi.org/10.1111/cdev.13027.

Tarsha, Mary S., and Darcia Narvaez. "Early Experience and Aggression." *Peace Review.* In press.

Trevathan, Wenda R. "Birth and the First Postnatal Hour." In *Evolution, Early Experience and Human Development: From Research to Practice and Policy,* edited by Darcia Narvaez, Jaak Panksepp, Allen N. Schore, and Tracy R. Gleason, 221–240. New York: Oxford University Press, 2013.

Trevathan, Wenda R. *Human Birth: An Evolutionary Perspective.* New York: Routledge, 2017.

Vaiserman, Alexander M. "Epigenetic Programming by Early-Life Stress: Evidence from Human Populations." *Developmental Dynamics* 244, no. 3 (October 2014): 254–65.

Van den Berg, C. L., T. Hol, Malcolm James Ree, Berry M. Spruijt, H. Everts, and J. M. Koolhaas. "Play Is Indispensable for an Adequate Development of Coping With Social Challenges in the Rat." *Developmental Psychobiology* 34, no. 2 (March 1999): 129–38.

Van Sleuwen, Bregje E., Adele C. Engelberts, Magda M. Boere-Boonekamp, Wietse Kuis, Tom W. J. Schulpen, and Monique L'Hoir. "Swaddling: A Systematic Review." *Pediatrics* 120, no. 4:e1097-e1106 (November 2007).

Weaver, Ian C. G., Michael J. Meaney, and Moshe Szyf. "Maternal Care Effects on the Hippocampal Transcriptome and Anxiety-Mediated Behaviors in the Offspring that Are Reversible in Adulthood." *Proceedings of the National Academy of Sciences* 103, vol. 9 (February 2006): 3480–5.

Westlye, Lars T., Kristine Walhovd, Anders M. Dale, Atle Bjørnerud, Paulina Due-Tønnessen, Andreas Engvig, Hakon Grydeland, Christian K. Tamnes, Ylva Ostby, and Anders M. Fjell. "Life-Span Changes of the Human Brain White Matter: Diffusion Tensor Imaging (DTI) and Volumetry." *Cerebral Cortex* 20, no. 9 (September 2010): 2055–68.

Wolff, Robert. *Original Wisdom: Stories of an Ancient Way of Knowing.* New York: Simon and Schuster, 2001.

PART FOUR

Catholic Family Life and the Multicultural Context

In this section, we explore the multicultural context of family life.

Andrew and Terri Lyke, founders and directors of Arusi Network, a marriage ministry to African-American Catholics, and authors of *Marriage on a Lampstand,* explore the unique challenges affecting the family life of African-American Catholics. They also offer insights to help pastoral ministers more effectively support the family life of African-American Catholics.

Hosffman Ospino, a theologian at Boston College and director of the graduate program in Hispanic ministry, offers important insights into the Hispanic American Catholic experience of family life. He proposes several suggestions for ways pastoral ministers can more effectively support Hispanic Catholic families.

Finally, Jomon Kalladanthiyil, CSC, director of pastoral care at Saint Joseph's Oratory, one of the largest pilgrimage sites in North America (serving more than two million pilgrims each year), offers insights into the challenges of cultivating Catholic spirituality in an interfaith household.

CHAPTER TWELVE

Black Families Are Holy and Worthy!

ANDREW AND TERRI LYKE

Arusi Network

FIVE QUICK TAKES

1. Catholic family life ministry is systemically indisposed to effective catechesis and evangelization with African Americans. Current and longstanding trends in black family life statistically place these families outside the scope of ministerial outreach with families by the Church.

2. The historical, cultural, and spiritual narratives of the African Diaspora in the United States depict a prophetic story that illuminates God's compassion and mercy — a story that, as with the biblical narratives, reveals God's magnanimous love that carries us through the "Red Sea" and over to the "promised land." Though the narrative is *about* black people, it is a prophetic story *for* the whole Church — white, black, and brown — and enriches the Church's catechesis and evangelization.

3. Endemic among Americans of the African Diaspora is a worldview that individuals, couples, and families have symbiotic relationships with the broader community. We refer to it as defining the "I" in the "We." The Igbo and Yoruba proverb, "It takes a village to raise a child," underscores this. We further state that it takes a stakeholding community to sustain a healthy marriage. Strong families form strong communities and strong communities form, protect, and hold accountable strong families.

4. The local parish can be a catalyst in establishing intentional small faith groups to form couples in symbiotic relationships of mutual support. However, it is important that great care is given to ensure that these groups do not degenerate into social cliques that exclude or can be perceived as clubs. Careful design and discipline can greatly assist in maintaining healthy boundaries that are appropriately permeable to create "brave space" and effective adult faith formation for marriage.

5. The institution of marriage has virtually collapsed among African Americans, who have the lowest rate of marriage compared with all measured groups, while also having the highest divorce rate. The resources of the Church that teach, support, and encourage skills for healthy love relationships must be made available also to couples who are ambivalent about marriage but are raising children. Catechesis for the Sacrament of Marriage, to be effective, must begin long before traditional marriage preparation and must include anyone discerning a vocation in family life, whether or not marriage is in their sights.

"BLACK FAMILIES"

By Servant of God Thea Bowman, FSPA

large families, small families, nuclear families, extended families,
single-parent families, adopted families, foster families,
augmented families, makeshift families,
Southern, Northern, Eastern, Western families,
rural or urban families, suburban families, inner city, central city, ghetto families,
Fifth Avenue or mansion families, condominium families, apartment families,
project families, shotgun-house families, duplex families,
laboring families, farming families, business families, professional families,
academic families, artistic families, athletic families, fishing, swimming and relaxing families,
uptight families, together families, happy, healthy families, whole families,
patriarchal families, matriarchal families, anarchical families, syncretic families,
rich families, poor families, working families, jobless families,

middle-class, upper middle-class, upper-upper middle-class families,
old, established families, aristocratic families, nouveau riche families,
moving-on-up families,
educated, urbane, cultured families, opera-going families, poetry-reading
families,
finger-snapping, gospel-loving, shouting, testifying families,
shucking and jiving families, fussing and fighting families,
oppressed families, disadvantaged families, struggling families,
disenfranchised families,
separated families, broken families, mobile families,
stay-at-home, stick-in-the-mud families,
jet-setting, pace-setting, go-getting, keeping-up-with-the-Joneses families,
high-society families,
ebony families, sable, swarthy families, brown, chocolate, caramel and/or
tan families,
mahogany and cinnamon, nutmeg and brown sugar, bronze, red, tan,
magnolia or honeydew, coal black or passé blanche, mixed families,
mixed-up families,
multicolored, multitonal, curly headed, straight haired, Afroed families[1]

Our life experiences as black Catholics who are highly engaged in the Church's ministry to families leave traces — breadcrumbs, if you will — for families to forge intentional disciples among their members and become outposts for evangelization and social change. Because of the inexhaustible, unearned, magnanimous compassion, mercy, and love that God pours over us and is made tangible to us through faith, our fears and anxieties are put in check. We are free to respond with the same for each other, our families, our community, and even those who are blind to our God-given dignity because of racist ideologies. We have learned to battle chaos with order, dysfunction with skill, hate with love, sin with mercy and forgiveness, and cultural chauvinism with the richness of cultural diversity. Marriage and family have been our school

---

1. Thea Bowman, F.S.P.A., Servant of God, Families: Black and Catholic, Catholic and Black, (Washington, DC: USCCB, 1985).

for this learning, and our relationship has been our laboratory. The witnesses of other couples have given us models to study and examples of what is doable in this herculean mission to keep our promise to love. In those witnesses, God's promise shines through and is our most compelling motivator.

Our Catholic roots are in the Industrial North, where during the Great Migration of African Americans from the agricultural South to the North during the earlier half of the twentieth century, Catholic parishes in large urban cities such as Chicago and Detroit accommodated the needs for quality education for upwardly mobile black families seeking a better life in the North. Catholic education was a draw for those families and presented opportunities for Catholic evangelization. The Church met those families in their practical needs, and thus booming black Catholic populations evolved. Through the Sacraments — Baptism, Confirmation, Eucharist, Penance, Holy Orders, Anointing of the Sick, and Marriage — the Catholic Church strategically reached out to African Americans, despite the disaffection of most white Catholics, and the second-class status to which black Catholics were consigned in the Church.

Today those booming black Catholic populations have greatly diminished. Catholic parishes that once served black urban populations are fewer. And family life looks different, especially regarding marriage. African Americans have the lowest rate of marriage among all measured groups, while also having the highest divorce rate.[2]
Nonetheless, men and women mate; children are born; and families are formed. Yet, Catholic resources for forming and sustaining healthy, lifelong, loving relationships are reserved for those who are married or preparing for marriage. The Catholic Church, regarding its outreach to

2. Population Reference Bureau, analysis of data from the US Census Bureau, Census 2000 Supplementary Survey, 2001 Supplementary Survey, 2002 through 2014 American Community Survey. The data for this measure comes from the 2005 through 2014 American Community Survey (ACS). The ACS, fully implemented, is designed to provide annually updated social, economic, and housing data for states and communities. (Such local-area data have traditionally been collected once every ten years in the long form of the decennial census.) Race/ethnic groups represented in this table are not mutually exclusive. The category of white includes only non-Hispanic white. The categories Black or African American, American Indian, and Asian and Pacific Islander include both Hispanic and non-Hispanic. Those in the Hispanic or Latino category include those identified as being in one of the non-White race groups.

families, dismisses a significant population of African Americans and ripe opportunities for Catholic evangelization. Is the Catholic Church in the United States disposed to providing effective outreach to African-American families? Amid the political climate of 2019, the rise in white nationalism, and the Catholic Church's leaning to the right of the political spectrum, this is a valid rhetorical question.

Effective Catholic outreach to black families acknowledges the realities of white supremacism, the original sin of America. The horrors of the four-hundred-year holocaust greatly shaped the spirituality and cultures of the African Diaspora. To deny it or attempt to downplay it undermines the authenticity of the Black Experience. And it diminishes the prophetic role that the progeny of those who endured dehumanization through slavery, those who suffered Jim Crow, domestic terrorism, and today's Prison Industrial Complex and pervasive police brutality — the "injustice" system — play in the life of our country and our Church. This is our reality. A Church we call home cannot deny or downplay this reality. The Catholic Church cannot yield (or appear to yield) to the forces that want to sustain the privilege of White America and the continued subjugation of people of color.

The Catholic Church in America, to have an effective outreach to black families, must also claim a share in the prophetic voice of the black Protestant Church for the transformation of our society in the struggle for civil rights and the eradication of systemic and institutional racism.[3] This prophetic witness shouldn't be limited to the margins of the Catholic community, only among peoples of color or merely categorized under "Peace and Justice" special initiatives. The Catholic Church must be "all-in" regarding the important work of healing our nation from the ravages of historical and current racism, whether personal or systemic.

---

3. Racism is America's "original sin" and has greatly influenced American culture. For the sake of clarity, we define racism as overarching white supremacy that relegates persons who are not white to a lower status of humanity. While individual race prejudice and racism are associated with each other, they are not synonymous. Race prejudice is racial chauvinism of which whites, blacks, and other persons of color may express openly in words and actions, or harbor in their hearts. Racism, however, is race prejudice buttressed by systems and institutions to advance white privilege. Racism, as we define and understand it, is not necessarily the intent of its perpetrators, who may unknowingly participate in outcomes that do harm to people of color.

OUR BEGINNING

We married in 1975. We lived a mile apart on the same street in Chicago's Auburn Gresham community. Our wedding was in the living room of Terri's family home, ironically across the street from St. Kilian Catholic Church, where her family had been formed in the Catholic Faith. At the tender ages of twenty-three and twenty-one, we were perceived as veterans within our inner circle of family and friends at being a couple. For them, our getting married was looked upon as part of a natural sequence of events. Our courtship was affirmed by the people closest to us. We were two people who were well-embarked into adulthood, as we were both solidly employed and adeptly steering our love boat responsibly and smartly. It seemed to us that life had dealt us decent hands, and we had every expectation that the stroke of luck we were in would continue.

Where was God? Our hindsight reports that God's grace and mercy poured profusely over us in those budding years of our relationship. Though it was the nascent secularist culture that began in the 1960s that influenced us and led us to believe, as did many of our generation, that God was not a player, let alone a guiding force in our lives.

Our earliest years of marriage were stormy but transformative. We moved to a suburban community where black people were very few. We weathered those storms in our marriage with the help of a Marriage Encounter retreat we attended in 1978. It was truly a conversion experience that set us on a new path and brought us back home to our Catholic Faith. It was through a deeper consideration and understanding of *sacrament* that put us on a path that we came to recognize as our personal mission in marriage.

Marriage Encounter deeply touched us, gave us a renewed sense of personal worth, and a new sense of God's indwelling in our marriage. It gave us language to articulate our own story. The expression "I am good. God doesn't make junk" was on a banner that weekend in the summer of 1978 and was especially helpful for us to restart on a path of faith that debunked our then cynical perspectives. In the ensuing few years, themes from the weekend continued taking shape in us. *Open and Apostolic Couple*, the final theme of the weekend, rooted most deeply. It focused on marriage in a public context that was evangelizing. We learned that while God is the author of love, married people are ghost writers who make God's love visible and tangible. Through the prism of the unique personalities of a couple, God's love takes on characteristics that make God relatable. People learn about marriage from the marriages they see, the married people in their lives. Though we knew we had much growth to gain, we also felt the Holy Spirit pulling and pushing us into a movement of sorts in Catholic marriage ministry.

Returning to the Catholic Church was both enheartening and dismaying. Partaking of the Eucharist nourished us and reminded us that we are what we eat, always becoming what we truly are, the Body of Christ. Yet, we found plenty of reminders that the Catholic Church, as with the broader society, is wrought with the social sin of racism. Our newly energized commitment to each other and this sense of becoming in the Holy Eucharist directed us toward being agents for the needed change in the Church and society. As we were learning to embrace each other in our brokenness, we were learning to embrace a broken Church and determined to take part in some needed healing. We wouldn't argue against a charge that the Catholic Church is a white, racist institution. But we would contend that the Church is so much more than just that. We got aboard the nascent black Catholic movement that bridged our experiences that once made us cynical with our faith in God who is all-good and all-loving. Expressing our Catholic Faith within the historical narrative of African Americans, a culture of resilience, and a spirituality that got us through the holocaust of chattel servitude, domestic terrorism, second-class citizenship, systemic societal structures designed to diminish our inherent dignity as creations of God, was cathartic. All this was made palpable in the Sacred Liturgy that incorporated the drama of the Story of God and the passion of Black Spirituality.

The Eucharist stimulated in us "sacramental imagination" that sees the invisible God in ordinary substances and even ourselves. This sense of indwelling of God in us didn't completely remove our brokenness, but it freed us to see so much more in us. Our sacramental imagination wasn't just about our perceptions of God but also ourselves, our society, and the Church. The perennial vexes in our relationship didn't vanish, but were no longer disabling. We discovered that many, if not most, of our issues weren't things to get over but get through. The burdens of married life, instead of ridding, we learned to carry. It felt as though we had uncovered the secret to successful marriage: perennial reconciliation. Our goals in marriage became less about fixing each other and more about understanding and accepting each other.

Our growing love for God made us dynamically different than we were before. It transcended our love for each other and drew us closer in new ways. Particularly when we were stuck in disillusionment about any perennial vexation of our relationship, it seemed that the most expedient and effective path back to each other was through our crying out to God, drawing nearer and attuning our ears and hearts to God through prayer, worship, praise, and ritual.

We discovered that the best of what we the Church do to minister to marriages is illuminate a couple's life with God and draw them closer to God, who is the source and summit of their love. Their communion with God is one to which they may go for deeper intimacy with each other, and for one they may seek in each other. Consider marriage as a triad relationship with God at the top-center angle, and the spouses flanking the bottom left and right angles. Notice that as we bring the husband and wife closer to God, following the trajectory of the respective sides of the triangle, they become closer to each other. When they experience and honor this sacramentality of their marriage — God-in-them — they also come to revere the marriage as a holy relationship, a communion with God that is much bigger, more significant than the two of them.

God

Husband   **Wife**

Andrew and Terri Lyke, *Marriage on a Lampstand: Exploring a New Paradigm for Modern Christian Marriage* (Alpharetta, GA: Heavenly Light Press, 2019).

SACRAMENTAL MARRIAGE REFLECTS GOD IN ALL THREE PERSONS

The process of falling in love is a glimpse of God's abundant love that seems to never run out and fills us, comforts us, makes us feel safe in each other's arms. The love privileges us to be co-creators with God and bring new life into our world — new life in the self, new life in our coupleness, and new life in our children. God the Father, our Creator, shines through us.

The growing process of our relationship is God's ongoing invitation to love the way God loves, unconditionally and forever. We grow into that through the nudging of the Holy Spirit. From acquaintances to dating to engagement to marriage, the Holy Spirit prods us and forms us each step along the way. God the Spirit radiates through us.

As we traverse through life with its ups and downs, we bargain with each other; we compromise; we sacrifice; we suffer each other. In time we encounter the other, our spouse, in their sin, their wretchedness, and in their darkness. To continue the journey together, to stay the course to forever, we must reconcile our differences, forgive the other's brokenness, make room for their issues, and carry their load with them. There are times when the other, our spouse, may seem undeserving and unworthy of the love we give. The promise with which we began may seem to have faded, if not vanished. The promise we made can feel like a sacrifice. Yet, it shapes us. We find that, though the burden can be heavy, we can bear it. It makes us stronger, and it creates in us new resolve. The promise we made to each other when we married begins to make us into who we need to be for the sake of our marriage, and for the glory of God. The paschal mystery of Jesus, who died for undeserving people, is revealed in us, it shapes us, and we learn to love on a higher level.

CATHOLIC MARRIAGE MINISTRY AMONG AFRICAN AMERICANS

With the encouragement and support of our pastor at St. Sabina, Andrew's family's parish to which we had returned for regular Sunday worship, and pastors in other parishes that served in Chicago's black Catholic community, we hosted gatherings and visited other parishes for after-Mass presentations to promote Marriage Encounter. These assemblies attracted many couples, and we gave them what we felt competent to give, a "taste of the weekend" in our presentations. Yet, few couples chose to go on a Marriage Encounter weekend retreat, and the few who did were much less enthused with the experience than we had been.

In November of 1981 our pastor "voluntold" us to work with a new initiative of the Family Ministries Office in the Archdiocese of Chicago. PreCana for the Black Community was to be the first initiative of its kind in the United States, a diocesan Catholic marriage preparation program design by and for black Catholics. It was clear at the onset that Family Ministries wasn't simply looking for a way to make their current marriage preparation design available to black Catholics. Rather than giving us instructive training, an outline, and a schedule, they gave us resources for catechetics, tools and processes for presentations, and the freedom to design a culturally authentic program to serve the many parishes that served the predominantly black communities in the archdiocese. Assembled at the initial meeting were four couples, including us, the director of family ministries, and a priest who would be the chaplain for the program. It was well received and celebrated as a successful program and the first of its kind.

Soon after the launch of PreCana for the Black Community, we took on the role of volunteer coordinators of Marriage Ministry for the Black Community for Family Ministries, which included scheduling programs and maintaining two sites on Chicago's South Side and West Side. Our team expanded to include as many as eight couples, four priests (including a bishop), and one vowed religious sister. We extended the ministry beyond marriage preparation in a collaboration for a marriage enrichment program entitled The Best Is Yet to Come that was presented in black parishes in Chicago.

In 1984 Worldwide Marriage Encounter invited us to participate in an experimental gathering of black couples in Los Angeles for a "Black Expression" Marriage Encounter retreat. With the support of Family Ministries, we flew to Los Angeles for the innovative program. The structure and design of the retreat modeled a typical Marriage Encounter retreat, except for the social component that was infused into the process and the importance given to music. Both the Black Expression Marriage Encounter and The Best Is Yet to Come experiences revealed and confirmed what we had already sensed: Catholic marriage ministry is very different when its focus is on black couples. Different indeed! As we already knew so well in how black culture and spirituality intensifies the worship experience in the Sacred Liturgy of the Mass, it transformed the Marriage Encounter weekend retreat and further fueled our Catholic sacramental imaginations for authentic marriage ministry. The Black Expression Marriage Encounter retreat was short lived, as it was held only a few times, including when we took part in bringing it to Chicago at Imani House, the same facility as the PreCana for the Black Community's South Side site. The Black Expression Marriage Encounter retreat's short run was disappointing. But it gave us more practical expertise in program design and development, and it planted seeds for our future efforts in Catholic marriage ministry with black folk.

The Archdiocese of Chicago was among the many Catholic dioceses that established Offices for Black Ministries (OBM) in the 1980s. As Chicago's OBM assessed existing areas of ministry in the archdiocese in service to the black community, Marriage Ministry for the Black Community was considered and included as a focus of ministry in the community. Andrew was invited to serve on the advisory board and served as the ex-officio representative of the OBM on the Archdiocesan Pastoral Council. Our network for ministry leadership blossomed in those early days of our work.

In light of the virtual collapse of marriage among African Americans, who marry at the lowest rate among measured ethnic groups and divorce at the highest rate, we advocated for black Catholic leaders and pastoral leaders in black parishes to give priority to its support of marriage as a viable strategy to strengthen families. We must go beyond the usual messages about marriage that come from Church leadership. This new paradigm we advocate for marriage is not so new. Yet it is fresh and grounded in the spiritual life of community. It is very Catholic, and very African, in that it defines the "I" in the "we" and places the success of marriage also in the hands of the village and not just the hands of the couple.[4] Black families are holy. Of course, they are; all families are holy. However, for emphasis we aver that black families are holy as a rhetorical

---

4. Andrew and Terri Lyke, Marriage on a Lampstand: Exploring a New Paradigm for Modern Christian Marriage (Alpharetta, GA: Heavenly Light Press, 2019), 173.

expression like "Black Lives Matter" in the limited context of Catholic family faith formation, which is sorely lacking in black communities (Catholic Charities aside). We think of holiness as being innate in family life, whether members see themselves as such. God chooses us despite ourselves. In *Familiaris Consortio,* Saint John Paul II says, "Each family finds within itself a summons that cannot be ignored, and that specifies both its dignity and responsibility: family, become what you are."[5]

The Holy Father speaks of a summons, an ongoing invitation to families to live a mission to become, grow into what they are: "a living reflection of and a real sharing in God's love for humanity and the love of Christ the Lord for the Church, His bride."[6] Having that invitation from the Creator, families embody a sacred trust to become what God made them to be. For the Church, effective evangelizing is helping families come to recognize and follow that call, that summons from God.

Pope Francis, in his apostolic exhortation *Evangelii Gaudium,* says, "In a culture paradoxically suffering from anonymity and at the same time obsessed with the details of other people's lives, shamelessly given over to morbid curiosity, the Church must look more closely and sympathetically at others whenever necessary. In our world, ordained ministers and other pastoral workers can make present the fragrance of Christ's closeness and his personal gaze. The Church will have to initiate everyone — priests, religious, and laity — into this 'art of accompaniment' which teaches us to remove our sandals before the sacred ground of the other (cf. Ex 3:5). The pace of this accompaniment must be steady and reassuring, reflecting our closeness and our compassionate gaze, which also heals, liberates, and encourages growth in the Christian life."[7]

We assert that this is the right approach for the Church's outreach to families. We interpret the Holy Father's words, when addressing families, as speaking of their living spaces as sacred ground, sanctuaries and places of holiness. And the inhabitants of those sacred spaces are indeed

5. http://w2.vatican.va/content/john-paul-ii/en/apost_exhortations/documents/hf_jp-ii_exh_19811122_familiaris-consortio.html
6. *Ibid.*
7. http://w2.vatican.va/content/francesco/en/apost_exhortations/documents/papa-francesco_esortazione-ap_20131124_evangelii-gaudium.html

holy, even despite themselves. The urgency and priority given to such outreach to families, particularly black families, come from this understanding that they are holy and worthy. Black families are an appropriate focus for Catholic Family Life Ministry. The concept that families are holy was set as a foundational principle of Catholic Family Life Ministry in the 1980s. However, the lack of engagement and focus on the plight of modern black families by the Church warrants the challenge to recognize that marginalized communities must be placed at the center of the Church's outreach. Perhaps placing a silent "too" after the phrase would aid in understanding the message: Just as black lives matter (too), so are black families holy (too). The message isn't to suggest anything further. There is irony in the statement "Black Families Are Holy" that challenges the Church in the spaces where it serves black families, and it reminds us that the Church is a prophetic voice, leaven for society. It tells truth to power in the omission of the Church's Family Life outreach.

IT TAKES A VILLAGE

Pope Francis teaches that "when love is expressed before others in the marriage contract, with all its public commitments, it clearly indicates and protects the 'yes' which those persons speak freely and unreservedly to each other. This 'yes' tells them that they can always trust one another, and that they will never be abandoned when difficulties arise or new attractions or selfish interests present themselves."[8] Stemming the tide of the encroaching darkness on family life among all racial and ethnic groups requires new approaches by the Church. Speaking as a Catholic couple and as a black couple, we have inherited survival skills from our sacramental imagination that make God visible and present in ordinary substances, everyday situations, and even imperfect human relationships. In our darkest moments we hunger for God and look around us and within us to find God, who is always faithful and merciful. God is present to us in the promise we made at our wedding. God is present in the village that forms and instructs us as stakeholders

---

8. Pope Francis, *The Joy of Love* (*Amoris Laetitia*): Post-Synodal Apostolic Exhortation (Washington, DC: USC-CB Communications, 2016), 132.

in our marriage. As the progeny of souls who were forcibly taken from their homeland and held captive in chattel servitude, we have in our spiritual DNA an inherited "God-consciousness," an acute awareness of a faithful and merciful God who accompanies us through life's sufferings and keeps our hearts supple and open to new beginnings with renewed promise. We call on God who always "shows up and shows out." not always on our timetable but always on time. God meets us through the actions of stakeholders in our village, actions that give us a profound sense that forever-love is doable, promises are keep-able, and we are not limited to our sin and dysfunction. Our Black History and our Catholic Faith reveal for us a God who loves us beyond reason and challenges us to do the same for each other, our children and grandchildren, our neighbors, our friends, and our adversaries, through his grace and mercy of which we have plenty.

Through the sacraments of the Church, particularly marriage, we bear witness to this and have a testimony to bring others to God. As do countless other couples whose powerful testimonies of faith lay dormant and unutilized in the sacramental life of the Church. Faith formation with married folk must lead couples to this sense of themselves — this God-consciousness — living in accompaniment with God and the People of God. We can't do this alone. Our love for each other isn't enough. Nor is our fickle resolve to keep promises. We need the practical wisdom of faith that is transmitted to us through our associations with other couples who accompany us and we them. They are elders who model and teach us how it's done; they are peers who open themselves to us and we to them as we journey together in faith and give each other a sense that keeping the promise is doable; they are also those who look to us for evidence of what is possible, seekers of the risen Christ who see Jesus in the lives of the married couples in their lives. We call these couples "God-couples," as they participate with us in sharing the faith and making God real to each other. They are the immediate village that raises us, guides us, and sustains our resolve to living in God's promise. Identifying such God-couples in their lives is happenstance for most couples. The commonly used idiom "you can't be it if you don't see it" is painfully true regarding lasting healthy, happy marriages among African Americans. We suggest that these God-couple dynamics are critical to successful marriages and should not be left to chance alone. The parish, as the center of our public faith life, is the best place to facilitate the forming of God-couple relationships.

Forming a marriage support ministry can start with gathering couples together for faith sharing. However, great care must be taken to keep the ministry healthy. Having ground rules of conduct are necessary to establish and keep healthy boundaries. Here is an example of a set of rules we have used in our ministry for facilitating couple sharing groups:

Rules for Sharing[9]

- **Sharing is personal**. We share who we are as individuals and as a couple in our marriage relationship.
- **Sharing is specific to the topic**. We share our attitudes and feelings stimulated by the presentation or sharing question.
- **Sharing is brief**. Do not ramble on. State the situation and how you feel about it with as few words as possible.
- **Sharing requires mutual consent**. We do not share negative feelings and attitudes unless we have already shared it with our spouse, and we both agree to share it with the group.
- **Sharing is not discussion**, nor is it meant to solicit a response or initiate a debate.
- **Sharing is not done on a soapbox**. We do not share to get a point across. Avoid preaching.
- **Sharing is in the first person** (*I feel, I think*). Speak only for yourself. We should not speak for our spouse (*you feel, we think*, etc.).
- **Sharing is directed to your spouse**. The group is there only to witness your sharing.
- **Sharing is unqualified**. Please resist the temptation to judge another's sharing or to give unsolicited advice. Remember that just as feelings are neither right nor wrong, what we share is neither right nor wrong.

---

9. Andrew and Terri Lyke, 111–112.

- **Sharing is confidential.** Nothing shared in this setting is to be discussed outside the group. Also, nothing shared here should be discussed without permission of the person sharing.

Key to the success of a parish-based marriage ministry and avoiding common pitfalls is keeping such "rules of engagement" in the interactions of each gathering.

To aid in sustaining a sense of ministry in the gatherings, each meeting should have these three elements[10]:

1. **Spiritual**: There should be an element of prayer at every meeting. Couples should be creative in the form that prayer takes. Music, dance, poetry, incense, drums, singing, spontaneous incantations, or simple, traditional prayers are all valid. Whatever the form that prayer takes, it should be authentic to the culture(s) of the couples participating.
2. **Educational**: Each meeting should be informative and provide the participants with new insights into Christian marriage and family living. Topics of discussion may center on current issues. They may be philosophical. They may be very practical topics about childcare, sexuality, developing primacy in the marriage, conflict management, inlaws, fidelity, etc.
3. **Social**: If the group is not fun it won't last. Having time to relax and laugh will help to bond the group.

It is critical that all three elements are present, though the emphasis may weigh more heavily on one element from time to time, depending on the Liturgical Calendar, season, or appropriate special themes. Still, it is important to have all three elements present.

A pitfall to avoid is having groups too large. Keeping the size of

---

10. *Ibid.*, 159.

the group to what is manageable and practically open for rich conversation is important. Ten or fewer couples in a group allows for full participation of all within about two hours. Another limitation is the risk of the group becoming a social clique where outsiders are not welcomed. The group may become self-serving and isolate themselves from the natural support systems in their families, neighborhoods, parish, and friends. Having a limited number of times the group will meet gives the ministry the opportunity to evaluate, invite other couples into the group, or expand the ministry by creating an additional group. The Liturgical Calendar may suggest seasonal themes and the number of meetings organically. These suggestions will ward off the tendency for such groups to devolve into cliques. And it will be easier for participants to commit to a process that has an "expiration date."[11]

Pastors should encourage outreach beyond the group, such as sponsoring a parenting class that married and single parents are invited to participate in. The group can be an excellent resource for the parish marriage preparation ministry.

AN AFRICAN WORLDVIEW: SYMBIOSIS BETWEEN MARRIAGE AND COMMUNITY

From 2004 to 2009 we had the privilege of working closely with the Healthy Marriage Initiative (HMI), a federally funded program for marriage education that targeted low-income couples. The curriculum we used focused on low-skilled, low-income African-American mothers and their male partners. HMI was based on sociological studies that showed marriage as a key factor in the well-being of children. When children are raised in a family headed by a healthy marriage, their prospects for a good life educationally, economically, socially, and in other aspects of life greatly improves. Such children are less likely to be entrapped by the "schoolhouse to jailhouse" pipeline, and more likely to become productive contributors to the common good. Because the program was federally funded, we were required to exclude concepts of faith, religion, and spirituality in the presentations. At first this seemed a great challenge, as

---

11. *Ibid.*, 167–168

our experiences had focused on marriage solely in a faith context. As we shaped the curriculum for our team, we struggled with the idea of teaching skills as a means to a healthy marriage without the foundation of faith. We knew many couples without such skills who nonetheless have sustained lifelong, good marriages. We also knew couples who couldn't hold on through great trials despite their skillfulness in communicating, problem-solving, budgeting, etc. Our experiences in Catholic Marriage Ministry gave us firm resolve that faith is the key factor for keeping promises and getting through difficulties in marriage. Faith is the motivator for building skills for a happy, healthy marriage.

Being among the collaborators for the HMI, we reconciled in ourselves our concerns regarding the absence of faith as an important factor through the conference calls in which we participated with other service providers, personnel from the Administration for Children and Families and their technical advisors. While the exclusion of proselytizing on religion in any form was nonnegotiable, we found a way forward with integrity by making our purpose to invite the couples we were to serve into "Godly behavior" through the skills we would teach them, and to make the learning space feel more like a retreat than a classroom. Even still, we proceeded into the initiative tentatively "holding our noses."

By design, the program was eight weekly two-hour sessions preceded by a meal with the entire families. While the curriculum, which was culturally and generationally relevant and appropriate, was highly effective in teaching relationship skills, the process led the learning experience beyond skills building to community building. The couples bonded with the group and were generally eager for each of the sessions. We witnessed transformation in many of the couples. Some of them moved forward into marriage. Some decided that their best way forward was as unmarried parents committed to skillfully co-raising their children, but with a better sense of themselves as potential married partners. Some recognized that their current partner was not someone with whom they could sustain a committed relationship.

The program equipped the participants in an unexpected way. Having new skills for relationships and better awareness of resources at hand, they were free to dream again about committed love and view permanent, committed love as something to which they could aspire. Because so few had real examples of successful marriages, committed love in their lives, they were more susceptible to cynicism about marriage or unrealistic fantasies about love relationships. Unlike most other such HMI programs around the United States, all the facilitators were African American or Latino married couples who modeled successful marriage. At the end of each series we presented each couple with a Native American dreamcatcher as remembrance of the program and the group with which they bonded.

We learned something crucial through this work: The population of unmarried couples with children is the "new frontier" for Catholic family outreach. Given the current virtual collapse of the institution of marriage among African Americans, directing the Church's resources for supporting couple relationships to only those who are married or engaged misses a significant population that is hungry for the *Good News* of sacramental marriage.

Catholic ministry in the new frontier must recognize that couples who have children but are ambivalent about marriage are holy, too, and worthy of strategies to accompany them. We iterate here what we express in our book: "When accompanying someone in an 'irregular' family arrangement, we must be very careful to view them through a lens that reveals their holiness rather than one that sees first their irregular circumstances and their dysfunction. Pope Francis, in *Amoris Laetitia*, instructs that "families are not a problem; they are first and foremost an opportunity."[12] For example, encountering a couple cohabiting without marriage is an opportunity to encourage and empower rather than fix them. To suggest or infer that they are "living in sin" would work against the nurturing relationship that we must develop with them. As we walk alongside them, we must recognize that we also walk alongside God who is with them. As Pope Francis said, we must "remove our sandals before the sacred ground of the other"[13] to reverence their holiness as we accom-

---

12. Pope Francis, *The Joy of Love*, 7.
13. Pope Francis, *The Joy of the Gospel* (*Evangelii Gaudium*) (Washington, DC: USCCB Communications, 2013), 169.

pany families."[14]
Marriage has inherent duality in tension between aspiring toward God

Fulfillment Model	Commitment Model
• It's about me	• It's about God
• My vision	• Faith
• Promise of ease	• Promise of effort
• Happiness is the goal	• Relationship is the goal
• Limited to what we know	• Open to the unknown
• The integrity of the relationship is proven by how well things are going	• The integrity of the relationship is proven by keeping the promise
• Susceptible to being put under a bushel basket	• Puts Marriage On A Lampstand

Fulfillment vs. Commitment Models of Marriage

and fulfilling one's personal visions for self. However, the dichotomy isn't between God and self. For God is merciful and frees us to be humanly flawed and even broken, and still the focus of God's loving gaze.

There is a quid pro quo character to marriage that doesn't reflect God, but our own egos. In search of personal fulfillment, we discover promise beyond our personal aspirations. God meets us in our perceived needs for fulfillment and directs us to a better path to commitment, on which we reflect and transmit God's love. Growing in wisdom, age, and grace, we become more trusting in the new vision for ourselves through the model of commitment from God. Over time we find our goals shifting more toward God, who patiently accompanies us and delights in our growth.

BEING A DOMESTIC CHURCH

Our parenting years were the 1980s and 1990s. Lessons learned and principles followed during that phase of our family life now carry over

14. Andrew and Lyke, 139.

in fresh ways with our grandchildren. Our participation in the broader faith community began with our practices within our family setting. Going to church on Sundays, we valued the principle of bringing something to share, to bring our faith, our needs, our assistance, our longings, our generosity, our caring, our service, our praise, and our love. We didn't come to Mass to be with God. God was evident in our family life. We brought our family spirituality with us to share with other families, to connect with others and be a part of a larger collective of worshippers.

Andrew's late uncle, Archbishop James P. Lyke, in his pastoral letter on the African-American family, said:

> "The black family teaches black people values, a philosophy, a view of the world rooted in ancient tradition and theology learned on the other side of the Jordan, a theology with God's calling and coming 'for to carry us home.'
>
> "The black family teaches us the notion of sacrifice for kin, reverence for the aged and the child, and belief in the natural sequences of cause and effect.
>
> "The black family is the place of our life; the place in which we move; the mirror through which we discover our being. The black family is the '<u>domestic church</u>' in which we learn who we are and whose we are and how we are to live."[15]

Uncle Jim eloquently articulated the essence of black family life in his pastoral letter. However, his words are just as true for families in general. When raising our two children, we identified how we and other families are *domestic churches*. Our domestic church has five components:

- Teaching
- Witnessing and living the Gospel
- Service/ministry

---

15. Most Reverend James P. Lyke, OFM, PhD, "So Stood Those Who Have Come Down Through the Ages: A Pastoral Reflection On THE FAMILY IN THE BLACK COMMUNITY" (Addressed to the Black Catholics of the Diocese of Cleveland), 1986.

- Prayer
- Communion

We are a teaching domestic church in how we instructed our children on what is right and wrong. We saw ourselves as the primary purveyors of religious education to our children. We read the Bible as a family and discussed the Scriptures and homily after Sunday Mass. We shared family faith stories that were passed down through the oral tradition. We encouraged our parents and grandparents to tell our children stories from their earlier life. An important way that we are a teaching domestic church is through advocating social justice in our words and actions.

We gave witness to the Gospel through our selection of quality TV programming, books, and activities, for our children and ourselves. We tried to show respect for one another and did for one another in selfless ways. We tried to deal with family conflict in respectful ways. It was important that our children saw the power of forgiveness in us.

We lived the Gospel through our choices at work and school, adhering to the laws of the land, and to the higher laws of God. Following the laws of the land was not always a moral choice. Jesus Himself was a social dissident and countercultural. We accepted the possibility that making moral choices may bring us in direct conflict with the laws of the land. We believe that a part of our challenge to live the Gospel is to be prepared to defy unjust laws, to take actions against injustice, and to work for peace.

When it came to service and ministry, we knew that charity begins at home. Simple service to one another and demonstrating generosity among ourselves were paramount in our domestic church. Our marriage was a model of service for the kids. They observed the care and service we gave to each other. Our morning "coffee ritual," when Andrew prepares coffee for Terri; the preparation of meals; household chores; and doing things for the benefit of each other were on display for the kids to observe. And they were encouraged to do the same for each other and us. But we also identified as a family with service to the community. We took part in community service or ministry through the broader Church and social institutions. Our children shared in our ministry to marriage in as many ways as possible, setting up chairs, stuffing and stamping envelopes, and any other ways they could pitch in. And we looked for ways to serve as a family. When Andrew was a campus minister at DePaul, our family often took part in service initiatives during spring and winter breaks. Easter Sundays were spent preparing and serving meals at a local homeless shelter.

The old axiom is true: "The family that prays together stays together." We recognized God as the center of family life. All of our teaching, witnessing, and service was done with God's will in mind. Our family called on God to be in our midst, to strengthen the bonds between us, to guide us when we were in darkness, to dance with us when we were in joy, to comfort us when we were in sorrow, and to show us how to do all this for one another. We established a regular rhythm of prayer at home, before meals, bedtime, when dealing with family stress, celebrations, bereavement, and any moment when God's grace was apparent. Acknowledging God, calling on God, thanking God, and praising God were elements in the atmosphere of our dwelling, which is anywhere we are gathered as a family.

For our domestic church, Communion is the end result of our teaching, witnessing, service, and prayer. We think of our family table at home as an extension of the altar at church. It is making and taking the time to be one with each other by giving our marriage, the cornerstone of our family, priority over all human relationships, even our children. (Notre Dame's Father Hesburgh once said, "The greatest gift a father can give his children is to love their mother.") We held sacred our family meals as a time to not only nourish ourselves physically, but also to nourish our relationships. We valued recreational activities as a family, like our annual "Lykes on Bikes Cross-Country Bike Ride." Our domestic church is Communion by our giving ourselves in prayer to God, asking Him to bless, protect, and guide us, by feeding and being fed by each other.

With the gifts we received from the domestic church, we were compelled to seek communion with the larger church. We attended church to not only receive, but to bring our faith experience, our talents, and our gifts of service and dedication. We shared our total selves as expressed in our domestic church — our uniqueness, our special identity as a family, and the richness of our African-American culture. We were enriched by the other unique and special domestic churches that came together to form a larger community of believers.

Our domestic church is as intrinsic to us as the seeds planted in the wombs of our mothers, our grandmothers, and great-grandmothers. It is where we discover our true selves and encounter God. And it is from that experience that we are called forth to enrich the broader Catholic community.

CONCLUSION

This is the Good News that being black, Catholic, and married leaders of a family have taught us. Our encounters with God have been most profound in this setting. The historical narrative of Africans in America, the spiritual components of that narrative, and the incorporation of the narrative in the Christian walk yield much substance for organized Christianity. When the incorporation is within the Roman Catholic context and our Catholic sacramental imagination, the yield is even greater. Black families indeed are holy and worthy of the focused attention and resources of Catholic Family Life Ministry not just for what the Church can offer to black families, but also for the spiritual enrichment the narrative of Africans in America can bring to the Church. Is the Catholic Church in the United States disposed to providing effective outreach to African-American families? We pray that it is.

We are grateful for the timing of our life in which we have engaged the Church. We have received the best of Catholic outreach to marriage. Perhaps it was the timing of Vatican II, the Civil Rights Movement, and the National Black Catholic Movement that began in the late 1960s. For sure it was heightened expectations of the nephew and his wife of one of the pioneer black bishops that opened doors for our efforts in Catholic marriage ministry with black Catholics. Nonetheless, we were encouraged and supported by the black Catholic community and fully embraced by Catholic Family Life leadership. We are deeply grateful to have had the opportunity to serve.

We close this essay with a quote from the epilogue of our book, *Marriage on a Lampstand: Exploring a New Paradigm for Modern Christian*

Marriage[16]:

> The initiative of the couples is to put their marriage on a lamp-stand of public scrutiny where they spread the light of God's love on the community. The Amen spoken at the wedding and repeatedly throughout their lives is not limited to what they know, their experiences, and what they understand. It is undergirded by the knowledge, wisdom, strength, and faith of the village. Equipped with the resources of the village, the couple is better able to step out on faith. The village increases their faith and lessens their fears and makes their burdens light. In the Gospel according to Matthew, Jesus encourages us with comforting words to not fear but embrace life with faith. Jesus says, "Come to me, all you who labor and are burdened, and I will give you rest. Take my yoke upon you and learn from me, for I am meek and humble of heart; and you will find rest for yourselves. For my yoke is easy, and my burden light."[17] With faith, that of the couple and the village, the yoke of marriage, though it may not be easy, is bearable and even joyful. The burdens of marriage feel lighter because we are stronger in the symbiotic relationship between marriage and community.

This is our lifelong journey with God, growing closer to God through the bonds of love between spouses and their symbiosis with the people of God. This is the new paradigm that we want the Church and Church leaders to embrace and say "Amen" to. Every parish must be a resource center for families and a place of encouragement and support for those who lead families. We call on the Church, particularly in parishes serving in the margins of society, to fully engage in an effective outreach to support, encourage, and protect the bonds of love between men and women, mothers and fathers, and husbands and wives in the community.

---

16. Andrew and Terri Lyke, 174–175
17. Matthew 11:28–30, NABRE.

DISCUSSION QUESTIONS

1. Using your Catholic sacramental imagination, how do you see Catholic evangelization that strategically targets African Americans innovating Catholic Family Life Ministry?

2. In your experiences in family life, how do you see *all* families as holy and worthy of focused strategies to render the resources and attention of Catholic Family Life Ministry?

3. What adjustments would be necessary for the Church to include couples ambivalent about marriage as targets of Catholic Family Life Ministry?

4. How might highlighting the "new paradigm," the symbiotic relationship between marriage, family, and community, strengthen Catholic Family Life Ministry to be more effective in evangelizing and serving all families?

CHAPTER THIRTEEN

Hispanics and Family Life in Twenty-First Century America: A Catholic Call to Action

Hosffman Ospino, Ph.D.

Associate Professor of Theology and Religious Education at Boston College, School of Theology and Ministry. Director of Graduate Programs in Hispanic Ministry

FIVE QUICK TAKES

1. Hispanic Catholics constitute more than 40 percent of the entire U.S. Catholic population. About 60 percent of U.S. Catholics under eighteen are Hispanic.

2. The present and future of the conversation about Catholic family life in the rest of this century will depend largely on the vibrancy of Hispanic Catholic life.

3. Hispanic Catholics have a strong sense of family life, influenced in great part by centuries of Catholic influence throughout the continent. Such sense of family is always a starting point for family ministry with this community

4. The Hispanic Catholic experience is complex and shaped by significant socioeconomic dynamics that often affect family life; for instance, poverty, low educational levels, large numbers of undocumented adults, etc. Family ministry demands advocacy to overcome such challenges and thus form strong and stable families.

5. Pastoral efforts about Catholic family life with Hispanics must take into consideration a population that is mostly U.S. born (about 64 percent), yet highly influenced by immigrant practices and convictions.

T he Catholic experience in the United States in the twenty-first century is in the midst of a major transformation. To be more exact, it is in the midst of a major cultural, demographic, and socio-religious transformation. At the heart of such phenomenon is the fast-growing Hispanic[1] presence: Nearly 43 percent of all Catholics in the country self-identify as Hispanic. As Catholics in this country, we cannot speak of family life these days without paying attention to what it means to be

---

1. The term "Hispanic" is more widely used by the U.S. government and Catholic officials on documents and public communications. "Hispanic" is more common among academics, artists, and advocacy leaders. Though evoking distinct nuanced meanings, many people in the United States use the terms interchangeably. In this chapter I privilege the use of Hispanic.

a Hispanic family and the major dynamics that shape the experience of this population.

This chapter contributes to a very important conversation: What do we need to do as pastoral leaders, counselors, and scholars to best accompany Catholic families today in the United States? This is a very important question, mindful that the health of our Church, as a community of faith, and that of the larger society often reflect the health of family life. The more we invest in the family, especially addressing the dynamics associated with raising the next generation of Catholics, and the support of couples to live stable relationships so they can raise healthy children, the stronger we will be as Church and society. I answer this question through the lens of the Hispanic Catholic experience.

The chapter has three sections. First, I provide a substantial overview of who Hispanic Catholics are and how we practice our faith in the context of parish life. Why parish life? Because the parish is the space where most likely pastoral efforts of outreach to Hispanic families have a chance to flourish. Parishes are privileged spaces where Hispanic families interested in celebrating what they believe, passing on the faith to the younger generations, and growing in their relationship with Jesus Christ coincide. Granted, millions of Hispanic Catholics are not involved in parish life on a regular basis. Millions are "nominal Catholics" who come to parishes sporadically, often to receive a sacrament or to participate in a ritual (e.g., funeral, wedding, baptism). Yet, as a pastoral theologian, I pick my battles. If my work and reflections about how to best accompany Hispanic Catholic families are going to have any effect, I need to start somewhere. Parish life seems like a good place to do so. Second, I highlight three areas in the experience of Hispanic families that I believe demand pastoral attention and significant investment if we want to support Catholic family life in the United States in the rest of this century. I end the essay with a short conclusion that serves as a call to action.

HISPANICS, DEMOGRAPHICS, AND PARISH LIFE

The Hispanic presence is not new to the United States of America. In fact, after Native Americans, Hispanics have lived in the U.S. territory longer than any other group. Hispanic Catholics have been celebrating the faith in this territory for more than five centuries. The first Catholic families in this land were Hispanic. However, during the last seventy years, the number of Hispanics — immigrant and U.S. born — has increased significantly in our country, thus remapping the U.S. Catholic experience. Civil wars in Central American countries, economic hardship, political unrest, natural disasters, lack of jobs and opportunities, and the search for the so-called "American Dream" (*el sueño americano*) are among the top reasons that have thrust millions of immigrants from Latin America and the Caribbean to settle in the United States. Most have arrived legally, yet about nine million lack legal migratory status to live in the country. Immigrants from every Spanish-speaking country in the world live in the United States. It is estimated that about twenty million Hispanic immigrants — from Latin America and the Caribbean — currently live in the United States;[2] about 70 percent of these immigrants are Catholic.

When speaking of Hispanics in the United States, it is important not to assume that all U.S. Hispanics are immigrants. In fact, 64 percent of the Hispanic population — about thirty-five million — are U.S. born. About eighteen million in this group are under the age of eighteen,[3] though many are being raised in immigrant households. While in the second part of the twentieth century the U.S. Hispanic experience was significantly defined by immigrants from Latin America and the Caribbean, in the twenty-first century it will be mainly defined by their U.S. born descendants.

By the middle of the twentieth century, about 90 percent of Catholics in the United States were Euro-American white, largely English-speaking. At least half of them had transitioned into the middle class. In fifty years, however, new migratory patterns and birth rates among Catholic immigrants have practically transformed the face of Catholicism in the United States. More than 40 percent of the seventy-seven million U.S. Catholics today are Hispanic. Hispanics constitute about 60 percent of

---

2. See Renee Stepler and Anna Brown, "Hispanics in the United States Statistical Portrait," *Pew Research Center*, April 19, 2016, https://www.pewresearch.org/hispanic/2016/04/19/2014-statistical-information-on-hispanics-in-united-states/.

3. See Eileen Patten, "The Nation's Latino Population Is Defined by Its Youth: Nearly Half of US-Born Latinos Are Younger Than 18," *Pew Research Center*, April 20, 2016, http://www.pewhispanic.org/2016/04/20/the-nations-latino-population-is-defined-by-its-youth/.

the U.S. Catholic population under eighteen — certainly not a minority anymore.[4] By the year 2050, about two-thirds of Catholics in the United States will likely self-identify as Hispanic — assuming that U.S. born Hispanics will continue to retain this religious affiliation in large numbers.

The fast-growing presence of Hispanics is reshaping the entire U.S. Catholic experience, at least on four levels: culture, geographical location, socioeconomic status, and parish life. Catholicism in the United States is presently a multicultural experience with an increasingly Hispanic face. In those regions of the country where it is growing and thriving, Catholicism is a de facto bicultural and bilingual experience — English and Spanish. Most of the growth of Catholicism in the United States is happening in the South and the West regions of the country. These are the places where the majority of Hispanics live: 61 percent.[5] As Hispanic Catholic immigrants and their families continue to settle in the South and the West of the country, the Catholic Church will need to urgently develop a new infrastructure and pastoral programs in these regions to better serve this population.

The parish continues to be the center of spiritual and pastoral life for most practicing Catholics in the United States, immigrant and U.S. born. The first point of contact for Catholic immigrants with the Church in the country is usually a parish.[6] Despite the fact that more than four thousand Catholic parishes have closed during the last five decades, the remaining network of 17,300-plus Catholic parishes in the United States remains one of the largest and strongest in the world. U.S. Catholics frequently speak of Hispanic parishes. There are approximately 4,500 parishes with Hispanic ministry, or about 25 percent of all Catholic parishes in the United States.[7] These are not the "national parishes" of the past, or communities built by national groups to meet their own spiritual and pastoral needs isolated from other parochial and national communities.

---

4. Hosffman Ospino and Patricia Weitzel-O'Neill, *Catholic Schools in an Increasingly Hispanic Church* (Huntington, IN: Our Sunday Visitor, 2016), 55.
5. Hosffman Ospino, *Hispanic Ministry in Catholic Parishes* (Huntington, IN: Our Sunday Visitor, 2015), 13.
6. Hosffman Ospino, "Glimpses of Christian Hope along the Migrant Journey," in Richard Lennan and Nancy Pineda-Madrid, eds., *Hope: Promise, Possibility, and Fulfillment* (Mahwah, NJ: Paulist Press, 2013), 108.
7. Ospino, *Hispanic Ministry in Catholic Parishes*, 10.

These are regular territorial communities serving large bodies of Hispanic Catholics, mostly immigrants.

The first-ever National Study of Catholic Parishes with Hispanic Ministry, which I had the privilege to conduct as its principal investigator between 2011 and 2014, offers the best and most accurate analysis of life in Hispanic parishes in the United States. The study also identifies key dynamics that are transforming the entire U.S. Catholic experience.[8] Allow me to highlight a few of these dynamics, which provide a good framework for any form of pastoral outreach to Hispanic families:

- Hispanic parishes are defined by pastoral leaders mainly as faith communities that offer services in Spanish: 98 percent of them offer sacraments and other religious services in this language. Most Hispanic Catholics actively involved in these communities are immigrants.
- Hispanic parishes typically started celebrating Masses and baptisms in Spanish around 1995, which coincides with the peak years of immigration from Latin America and the Caribbean. Only 20 percent of Hispanic parishes began offering services in Spanish before 1975; about 36 percent did so after 1995. These numbers are a reminder of how recent and fast-moving has been the Hispanic migratory phenomenon that has been transforming U.S. Catholicism during the last five decades. Most parochial communities serving Hispanic immigrants are mainly responding to the initial impact of this presence, yet most have not experienced the deeper transformations that are coming as Hispanics settle for at least one full generation while their children embrace their socio-religious and cultural identity as American Catholics who are also Hispanic.
- Parishes serving Hispanics on average celebrate four weekend Masses (Sunday and Saturday Vigil) and six weekday Masses. Of these, one or two of the weekend Masses and

---

8. All data in this section comes from Ospino, *Hispanic Ministry in Catholic Parishes.*

one weekday Mass are likely to be celebrated in Spanish. On average, 1,419 parishioners attend weekend Masses in Hispanic parishes. This is about 22 percent higher than the average for all parishes nationally (1,110 parishioners). The median for Mass attendance on weekends in parishes with Hispanic ministry is 1,000 parishioners, compared with 750 in all parishes. The higher the number of Hispanic Catholics who attend Mass in a parish, the more likely they are to be Spanish-speaking.

- The spiritual and liturgical celebrations that attract the largest numbers of Hispanic Catholics to parishes are:

    * Lent, Ash Wednesday, Holy Week, Easter
      30 percent
    * Our Lady of Guadalupe
      25 percent
    * Sacraments, Masses, weddings, first Communions,
      19 percent
    * Advent, Christmas, Christmas Eve, Epiphany
      10 percent

- Finances play an important role in the life of the multicultural parish, particularly in terms of how much each group contributes to support the day-to-day operations and the mission of the community. On average, Hispanic parishes receive $7,744 in weekly parish offertory collections (median of $5,000). This is 15.7 percent lower than the average $9,191 collected in all parishes nationally. On average, $1,502 of the weekly offertory in Hispanic parishes comes from parishioners at Spanish language Masses (median of $840). These numbers reveal the struggle of parish communities serving Hispanics or transitioning into mostly Hispanic congregations. The socioeconomic situation of most Hispanics, especially that of the immigrants who are most likely to attend these communities, directly impacts conversations such as defining priorities, expanding ministries, hiring of staff, investing in pastoral initiatives, and even determining the viability of these parishes.

- Ecclesial movements play a very important role in parishes serving Hispanic Catholics. About 10 percent of all active Hispanic Catholics are somewhat associated with an apostolic movement in their parishes. About half of all parishes serving Hispanic Catholics have groups associated with the Catholic Charismatic Renewal. Other significantly active groups in these faith communities are the Knights of Columbus, Cursillo, the Legion of Mary, and the Christian Family Movement. More recently, groups associated with the Neocatechumenal Way, Schoenstatt, Communion and Liberation, and Marriage Encounter, among others, have made major inroads in these parishes. Two-thirds of parishes serving Hispanics report that at least one apostolic movement has prayer groups rooted in the movement's particular spirituality. In 53 percent of Hispanic parishes, apostolic movements form small faith communities. Apostolic movements are credited as an important source of vocations to the ordained priesthood and vowed religious life among Hispanic Catholics. Several of them focus their ministerial efforts to support families.

- Though two-thirds of Hispanics are U.S. born, the vast majority of Hispanic pastoral leaders serving in parishes are immigrants: 85 percent of Hispanic priests, more than 95 percent of Latina vowed religious, about 70 percent of Hispanic permanent deacons, and 70 percent of Hispanic lay ecclesial ministers. The overrepresentation of foreign-born Hispanics in positions of pastoral leadership mirrors the predominance of ministerial outreach to Hispanic immigrants in the Catholic Church in the United States. It is natural that Hispanic foreign-born pastoral leaders will focus on and find themselves more comfortable reaching out to the also-foreign-born Hispanic population. Yet, this reality uncovers the urgent need to identify, mentor, and invest in U.S. born Hispanic pastoral leaders to better serve the two-thirds of Hispanics who are U.S. born and the rest of Catholics in the country.

- Hispanics in general are very young. The average age of Hispanics is twenty-nine, compared with thirty-seven for the overall population in the United States. About a third of Hispanics in the country are under the age of eighteen. For Catholics this is very significant, because approximately 60 percent of the Catholic population eighteen and younger is Hispanic. Pastoral outreach to Hispanic Catholics at this historical point is to focus on youth ministry and support of young adults, especially those who are starting their families.

ACCOMPANYING HISPANIC CATHOLIC FAMILIES: THREE PRIORITIES

The above statistical overview of the Hispanic Catholic population, and what happens in Catholic parishes serving Hispanics, gives us a good sense of the challenges and opportunities that the Catholic community has in the United States as we journey with Hispanic families. In light of such numbers and realities, I propose that ministries aiming at supporting Hispanic Catholic families focus on the following three priorities:

1) Emphasis on Young Adult Families

There is no doubt that an approach to supporting family life in the Hispanic Catholic community must begin with serious attention to the young. Hispanic ministry is de facto young adult ministry and youth ministry. Many Catholic family ministries in our country focus on engaging grandparents and supporting families when the parents are in their midlife years. This often means helping adult Catholics to renew marital commitments, supporting them as they make financial decisions that will affect their retirement years, and dealing with the transitions that come when children leave home for college or professional life. There is a growing number of ministries focused on supporting the spiritual growth of couples (e.g., retreats, support groups), many of which require some level of socioeconomic stability and somehow having settled into a geographical region where such resources exist.

While all these are important, the majority of Hispanics in the United States are far from those ages and from the socioeconomic stability that many such ministries presuppose. We are confronted with a very young population for whom family life means being a U.S. born child or adolescent, often being raised by an immigrant parent — or being exposed to an immigrant adult at home. For many Hispanic Catholics, family life begins with the rocky dynamics of having children in the late teens and early twenties, usually out of wedlock. Socioeconomic stability for many of these young couples is rather a dream that few will ever achieve, considering the low levels of educational attainment among Hispanics (e.g., only 16 percent of Hispanic adults have a college degree) and the lack of access to good education for most (e.g., more than 70 percent of school-age Hispanic children attend underperforming Catholic schools; only 4 percent of school-age Catholic children attend Catholic schools).[9]

Considering how young Hispanics are, family ministries with this population must focus on the young adult population. This means that such ministries are to begin with assisting such families, and those who are about to start family life, to gain some form of social, economic, emotional, and religious stability. Ministry with this particular population places pastoral leaders before the situation of working with young people raising young people. Family ministries in the Hispanic community, therefore, must be planned in close conversation with catechetical initiatives and youth ministry programs. Finally, since the vast majority of Hispanics under the age of thirty are born and raised in the United States, family ministries with this population cannot be limited to replicating models of ministry used primarily with immigrants or models imported from Spanish-speaking countries. We need models of family ministry that respond to the needs and expectations of a population highly influenced in its values and societal upbringing by the larger U.S.

---

9. Ospino and Weitzel-O'Neill, *Catholic Schools in an Increasingly Hispanic Church*, 7.

culture, especially in urban settings where most Hispanics live, while retaining socio-religious and cultural elements of an immigrant generation that still exerts major influence upon them. Of course, doing this under the current models of Hispanic ministry, which focus primarily and sometimes exclusively upon the immigrant population, represents a major challenge.

2) Advocacy and Accompaniment

Family ministries that aim at serving Hispanic Catholics require an intentional understanding of the socioeconomic realities affecting this population. Pastoral leaders working with Hispanic families cannot pretend to want to bring the best of our Catholic spiritual resources about family life while ignoring the complex everyday realities that shape the lives of these couples and their children. The fact that about 23 percent of Hispanics live in deep poverty and another 50 percent are slightly above the poverty level should give us pause as pastoral leaders. Hispanics families are profoundly impacted by dynamics such as domestic violence, high levels of incarceration,[10] undocumented immigration, and the effects of family separation because of deportations. Because of the low levels of educational attainment affecting the majority of Hispanics, mobility into the middle class is a very slow process. Millions of Hispanic adults work in the agricultural and service industries, known for paying low wages.

These circumstances, among many others, make a vision of Catholic family ministry that promotes homeschooling, regular engagement in retreats, counseling sessions that require high-levels of sophistication, and even the idea of a parent to stay home full time to care for young children, practically unattainable for millions of Hispanic Catholics. This does not mean that pastoral leaders are to give up on such practices. They should remain a goal; yet we need pastoral approaches to family ministry that start where Hispanics are, in the contexts where they live, and address the socioeconomic realities that shape their lives. We need models of family ministry that build upon patient, caring, and merciful

---

10. Hispanics constitute the second largest prison population in the United States.

accompaniment:

> An evangelizing community gets involved by word and deed in people's daily lives; it bridges distances, it is willing to abase itself if necessary, and it embraces human life, touching the suffering flesh of Christ in others. Evangelizers thus take on the "smell of the sheep" and the sheep are willing to hear their voice. … Evangelization consists mostly of patience and disregard for constraints of time.[11]

Catholic pastoral outreach to Hispanic families demands a strong element of advocacy. If we want Hispanic Catholics to form strong families, then we need to advocate as a community of faith for conditions where such families can thrive. Let me mention at least five areas of advocacy that can be part of our Catholic family ministries: better wages and treatment of farmworkers (the majority are Hispanic), immigration policies that privilege family reunification, better education of Hispanic children and youth in public educational institutions, access to quality health care, and better support systems that lead to the reduction of poverty. Without improvement of these social dynamics, one cannot credibly expect that Hispanic Catholics can form stable and thriving families.

3) Adult Faith Formation that Leads to a Stronger Understanding of Family Life

At the heart of strong family ministries must be a strong catechesis that leads Catholics to understand well, embrace, and live the vision for the family that the Church communicates as part of its evangelizing mission. Catholic pastoral leaders may sometimes take for granted that because someone is baptized as a Catholic or belongs to a cultural tradition with strong Catholic roots, therefore there is a clear understanding of the Church's vision about family life. If that is the case, the assumption is naïve. While most Hispanics self-identify as Catholic, particularly the

---

11.. Pope Francis, *Evangelii Gaudium*, 24, http://www.vatican.va/content/francesco/en/apost_exhortations/documents/papa-francesco_esortazione-ap_20131124_evangelii-gaudium.html.

majority of the twenty million Hispanics living in the country, many struggle to understand the Church's vision about family life and marriage, and it is likely that many have never heard it articulated because of lack of appropriate faith formation. Studies on religious literacy often reveal that Hispanic Catholics have a strong sense of family life and a profound spirituality, yet at the time of naming or articulating their faith, they struggle.[12] While one may "get by" with some form of cultural Catholicism in a Latin American society where the majority of the population is Catholic, that is not necessarily the case in the United States.[13] The proof of this is the low number of sacramental marriages among Hispanic Catholics nationwide, the lack of family participation in Sunday Mass, and the struggle of many Hispanic adults to pass on the faith to their young, especially those born in the United States.

Parishes with Hispanic ministry should be the ideal place for Hispanics — especially for immigrants, since most Hispanic ministry there happens in Spanish — to access adult faith formation about family life and marriage. Yet, this is not happening in most of these parishes. Where it happens, the numbers are very small: less than twenty persons enrolled in adult faith formation programs.[14] This is why a good pastoral strategy for family ministry among Hispanic Catholics should be the strengthening of adult faith formation programs and initiatives with this particular focus.

But faith formation about family life should not wait until adult life. It is imperative that all Catholic programs of faith formation, starting with those engaging the youngest children, have strong components and units about family life. Every Catholic should reach adulthood with a clear understanding and appreciation of the Church's vision about family life.

12. See Luis Lugo, Alan Cooperman, Erin O'Connell, and Sandra Stencel, "US Religious Knowledge Survey," *Pew Research Center,* September 28, 2010, https://www.pewforum.org/2010/09/28/u-s-religious-knowledge-survey/.
13. See Hosffman Ospino, "Stop Marginalizing Popular Piety: The Case for Embracing Cultural Catholicism," *US Catholic* 84, no. 2 (February 2019): 20–21.
14. See Ospino, *Hispanic Ministry in Catholic Parishes*, 40.

CONCLUSION

The vibrancy of Catholic family life in the United States in the rest of this century will be closely linked to how Hispanic Catholics form, cultivate, and support families. We have a major task on our hands engaging this population, especially young Hispanics. To do this, we must embrace a language that challenges the so-called "two churches" paradigm; that is, language that speaks of Hispanic Catholics as if we were visitors or outliers, assuming that there is an established church — mostly white, Euro-American, middle-class and English-speaking — that out of benevolence "welcomes" or "serves" a body of Catholics that look, speak, and celebrate their faith in different ways. There is only one Catholic Church in the United States, and Hispanics as well as Catholics from various cultural communities are an integral part of it. If we care about Catholic family life, we must first see ourselves as one Church.

I conclude this reflection with a call to action: Let's support Catholic family life in the United States by making a preferential option for young and young adult Hispanic Catholics, advocating for and accompanying them as they form the families that will soon become the backbone of our Catholic faith communities, and offering them the best faith formation resources so they can grow in the Church's vision for family life.

DISCUSSION QUESTIONS

1. What is your faith community/office/ministry doing to support Hispanic Catholics to form strong and faithful families?
2. What can parishes do better to accompany Hispanic Catholic families amidst the complex realities that shape their lives?
3. What strengths do you see among Hispanic Catholics that need to be affirmed to support vibrant family ministries?
4. Do your catechetical program and youth ministry initiatives have a good component about the Church's vision for family life?

CHAPTER FOURTEEN

Challenges of Cultivating Catholic Family Spirituality in Interfaith Households

Jomon Kalladanthiyil, CSC

Director of Pastoral Ministry, Saint Joseph's Oratory, Montreal

FIVE QUICK TAKES

1. For the Christian, true inclusiveness is Christocentric.
2. All religious expressions of humanity are included, in one form or another, in God's plan in which Jesus Christ is at the center.
3. The declaration on the Relationship of the Church to Non-Christian Religions significantly opened the Church to all religious traditions, not only to Jewish customs.
4. There are many practical ways an interreligious family can build a shared spiritual life, but any successful attempt to accomplish this must be rooted in mutual respect, openness, flexibility, communication, and a willingness to share and learn from each other.
5. When the Catholics in interfaith households practice their faith with much devotion and fervor, others in the same family will naturally be inspired by their lives and discover Jesus Christ.

INTRODUCTION

I hail from India. During my life in Europe and North America, when I introduced myself as an Indian, many people asked me if I was a Hindu. Many people think that all Indians are Hindus and vegetarians. Some of them think that the Ganges is the holy river and immersion in the Ganges will forgive all sins. They also think that cows are sacred and worshipped across India. These elements might be true for some Hindus, but they're not true for all Indians, especially for some who belong to different religious traditions. I hail from a traditional Catholic family in Kerala. Catholic parents in Kerala households baptize their children when they are young. If a child is not baptized, some family members and relatives criticize the parents for not taking enough care of the child to introduce him to Jesus Christ. Therefore, in my native neighborhood, interfaith household is a rare phenomenon. Nevertheless, there are many Hindu households near my parents' house. As a child, I grew up with

Christians and Hindus in the neighborhood. We cherished peace, harmony, and friendship. However, this pattern of Catholic living is not observed in other parts of India. Interfaith households are common among those who converted to Christianity in the sixteenth century.

A few years ago, while living in the Maharashtra, I used to visit the houses of some of my Hindu friends. I observed that many of them keep statues and pictures of Jesus, Mary, and Joseph in their houses along with other Hindu gods' statues and images. Some of the Catholic saints are popular among Hindus, and they pray invoking their names. Hindus do not hesitate to visit Catholic shrines and churches for novenas and feasts.

During my doctoral studies in the University of Montreal, I interviewed Kavita, one of the Hindus who visits Saint Joseph's Oratory in Montreal, the biggest shrine dedicated to Saint Joseph in the world. I asked her about her activities at the Oratory. She had plenty to tell me; expressing a lot of gratitude for all the blessings she received from God. She said, "At the entrance, there is a statue of Saint Joseph. I go there and pray"; "I go to the Crypt Church and pray there"; and "I go to the cross, to the statue of Brother André. When I touch the cross, my hands tremble. I get a special power. I close my eyes, and I give everything to God. My nerves are touched when I touch the cross and feet of Jesus. I close my eyes and tell him everything. I thank him and request of him all that I want." Kavita was from a practicing Hindu family. She had a profound Hindu religious life as she performed Hindu *pūjās* and rituals with her family members at home and in the temple. She lived with her husband and two children. She went to Hindu temples along with her family. When she came to Saint Joseph's Oratory, she preferred coming alone and spending time in silent prayer. Her devotional activities at the Oratory helped her to regain spiritual energy that she considered to be important in her life.

Jews, Christians, Hindus, and Muslims have some similar religious practices. Jews were the first Semitic people who bowed in prayer. Christians and Muslims have borrowed the practice from them, but they bow in prayer in different ways. Jews, Christians, Buddhists, and Muslims use prayer beads. Catholic Ashrams in India have adopted some of the Hindu ways of prayers and chants with a Christian color. In some parts of the world, Jews, Hindus, Muslims, and Buddhists decorate their houses for Christmas with a Christmas tree and stars. When we put all the religious practices and cults of different religions together, we observe that many of them have similarities. In interfaith households, we observe that some members of the family are more inclined toward the "religious," whereas the others are more "spiritual."

The primitive Christians made a spiritual movement with Jesus of Nazareth, who was a Jew. Jesus was filled with the life of God and obedient to his father in heaven. This gave him a greater freedom to be what he was, and his connection to the father was much noticed. By doing so, he discovered his humanity and divinity in fullness. However, he was not well understood by the chief priests and religious elders of his time. He had to undergo certain tensions and hardships as he opposed the institutional religious structures and functioning of his time. In the end, he had to give his life as a prize for his spiritual movement. The spiritual movement initiated by Jesus did not come to an end with him. The disciples of Jesus continued to live in his spirituality, and they became instruments to spread his message. Communities were formed to live with the same spirituality and liberty that Jesus himself initiated. Through him, human beings were called to grow in spirituality by becoming sons and daughters of God. In the gradual process of time, as communities of believers took form and shape, they had to be institutionalized with certain norms and criteria. Christianity became the official religion in the Roman Empire. Then the world witnessed the role of Christianity in building up the society as well. Christians contributed to the new civilization of the entire human race.

Catholic families try to grow in the spirit of the teachings of Jesus Christ. Catholic family spirituality has been developed with traditions handed down from generation to generation. The spirituality in Catholic families can vary from place to place with the inculturation of faith, traditions, and practices. However, the interfaith households bring some new challenges to traditional faith practices and spirituality. In this paper, I would suggest a praxeological framework for looking at the challenges of cultivating a Catholic family spirituality in interfaith households. I would observe some of the faith practices in the Catholic Church from the early time. Then, I would analyze how the Catholic Church has opened up her views toward people belonging to other religious traditions following the Second Vatican Council. I would also interpret some of the challenges of interfaith households and suggest ways of intervening for a better future. The entire discussion, especially the section of interpretation and intervention, will help us see how the Catholics in interfaith households forge intentional discipleship and do a better job in bringing up the next generation of intentional disciples.

PRAXEOLOGICAL WAYS OF BUILDING A CATHOLIC FAMILY SPIRITUALITY IN INTERFAITH HOUSEHOLD

Praxeology is a science, and is also a methodology when applied in a scientific study. Jean-Guy Nadeau is one of the founders of praxeology. He noted that it's an empirical and reflective science of action. He underlined that praxeology is a reflective and critical discourse on the practice, the sensible action of which it aims improvement in terms of relevance, coherence, and efficiency. Pastoral praxeology is interested in the practices of human beings in their existence in connection with Jesus Christ (Nadeau, 70–100). Praxeology is concerned with the past, present, and future of a given pastoral situation.

OBSERVATION OF FAITH PRACTICES

Early Christians mixed Christianity with already existing practices. The Jewish Christians continued to pray in the temple (Acts 3:1). Jesus had warned his people not to use vain repetitions in their prayers as the heathens did (Mt 6:7), but to accept others who performed miracles in His name (Mk 9:38–39). Saint Paul told new Christians to be separate from the world and to show discretion when eating meat sacrificed to idols, but he also told them not to call anything unclean that God has made clean (2 Cor 6:14–18). And he told them that he had become all things to all people, that he might save some (1 Cor 9:22). Later, the Church Fathers worked with Christians from various backgrounds to keep their faith and their identity. When Islam was born in the 600s, Jews and Christians kept their identity. Later, as Christians and Muslims met with Eastern religions such as Hinduism, Buddhism, and Jainism, interfaith neighborhoods and families became a reality.

Some Asian people were praying at Taoist altars, Buddhist temples, and Christian churches without making much distinction. Sufi Muslims in Kashmir turned to the non-dualism of Hinduism and Buddhism. Aztec and Mayan people in Mexico and South America adopted the forms of Catholic worship, but continued their indigenous worship practices. In the United States and Canada, cultural Jews began practicing Buddhist mindfulness while continuing to worship in their synagogues. Some of the Catholic Mexicans also follow some Hindu ways and rituals (Bidwell, 29).

Over the years, the traditional religious practices have changed in European and American families. Multiplication of religious denominations and fast-growing immigration contributed to interfaith households in Europe and North America. Though some people may think that religious and spiritual identity are the same for all American Catholic families, it may not be the same anymore. Crossing the boundaries of one religious identity is observed in American Catholic families. Some people opt to belong to multiple religions, and others keep changing from one religion to the other. Some people do not hold on to religion as they give more importance to spirituality. Asian Americans seem to mix Christian, Hindu, Buddhist, and Confucian practices. African Americans might tend to mix their Christian practices with ancestral religious practices. Jewish-Christian intermarriages increase in the United States. As religious diversity has increased in America, so have interfaith marriages. According to a Pew Research study, four in ten Americans who married between 2010 and 2014 have a spouse who belongs to a different or no religious group: 15 percent between two Christians from different traditions, 18 percent between a Christian and an unaffiliated spouse, and 6 percent between spouses of other religions. An even higher percent (49 percent) of unmarried couples are living with someone of a different faith. Hindus (91 percent), Mormons (82 percent), and Muslims (79 percent) who are married or living with a partner are doing so with someone of the same religion. Jews (65 percent), mainline Protestants, and unaffiliated people (56 percent) are less likely to cross religious lines (Bidwell, 2018).

One-third of U.S. marriages seem to be interfaith. It is by default that these families and their children become part of more than one religious community. Many Christians, Jews, and Muslims integrate Hindu practices of yoga and Buddhist practices of meditation into their lives. Almost one-third of U.S. residents are inclined to practice more than one religious tradition for their own personal reasons and pleasure. Thirteen percent of U.S. residents seem to be influenced by Buddhist spirituality, even though less than one percent of the U.S. population identifies as Buddhist. Spiritually fluid people have become a norm in today's common living. Scholars want to study and write about "multiple religious belonging," "complex religious identities," "dual practitioners," and "multiple religious bonds" (Bidwell, 18). Interfaith households have multiplied in different parts of the world.

In 2015, the Center for Applied Research in the Apostolate (CARA) at Georgetown University in collaboration with Holy Cross Family Ministries in Easton conducted a study on Catholic families. The study was entitled "Faith in the Family: A Survey of U.S. Catholic Parents." The survey was completed by 1,014 self-identified qualified respondents. CARA estimated that there are around fifteen million Catholic parents between the ages of twenty-five and forty-five in the United States in 2014. The study underlined that the older post-Vatican II generation parents (born 1969 to 1981) are more likely to attend regular weekly Mass than the younger Millennial generation parents (born 1982 to 1989). It is 24 percent compared with 14 percent. Seventy-one percent of parents agreed that prayer is essential to their faith, and 36 percent of parents pray at least once a day. Seventy-six percent of parents prayed by themselves, while only 7 percent prayed with family members, and 17 percent prayed alone and with family. The study focused on Catholic families in the United States (CARA, 2015). The CARA study ultimately revealed that faith practices have changed over the years from some traditional ways of being together to nurture a Catholic family spirituality.

From another perspective, the rise of the so-called "nones" in today's Western world is alarming. Some people do not identify themselves with any religion. From 2007 to 2014, the percentage of American "nones" increased from 16 percent to 23 percent. The "nones" do not care for any religious belief. It seems that among the Millennials who are born between the 1980s and early 2000s, around 35 percent are religiously un-affiliated. However, many "nones" do not identify as atheist. They claim to be "spiritual" (Vogt, 32). It would be interesting to observe if there are a few "nones" and others Catholics in the same household trying to cul-tivate a Catholic spirituality.

The classification of exclusivism and inclusivism was common in the Catholic Church. Exclusivism was an *ecclesiocentric* perspective in the Church. The axiom *extra ecclesiam nulla salus,* or no salvation outside the Church, was well known in the early Church. Pope Pius XII condemned this attitude of the Church, and the Second Vatican Council opened up the Church to the entire world through *Lumen Gentium.* It is not the Church that is at the center of the mystery of salvation, but Christ himself. Jacques Dupuis described the viewpoint of the Second Vatican Council as a radical "decentralization" of the Church that helps to "refocus" on Jesus Christ (Dupuis, 153). Some theologians continue to affirm that the mystery of Christ is understood in the mystery of the Church (Comeau, 49). The ax-iom *extra ecclesiam nulla salus* is attributed to Saint Cyprian of Carthage. Saint Ignatius of Antioch was the first Father of the Church to have widely used this axiom. He emphasized the need for the unity of the Church and union among bishops as a condition for all people to be in union with God in Jesus Christ. Saint Irenaeus considered that those who separated them-selves from the Church were deprived of salvation. Origen of Alexandria was also explicit that salvation was only possible within the Church (Sul-livan, 24).

Inclusivism was the *Christocentric* perspective in the Church. It si-multaneously acknowledged both the universal salvific will of God and the necessary mediation of Christ. All religious expressions of human-ity are included, in one form or another, in God's plan, in which Jesus Christ is at the center. All humanity is included in Christ, especially in his human nature of Word made flesh. There are many opinions about inclusivism, especially after the Second Vatican Council. Some theolo-gians attribute Bible passages that promote inclusivism. Jesus said, "for whoever is not against us is for us" (Mk 9:40). The Apostle Peter wrote of God: "He is patient with you, not wanting anyone to perish, but everyone to come to repentance" (2 Pt 3:9). Cornelius believed in God before Peter preached to him the Word of God (Acts 10:1–48). "Then Peter opened his mouth and said: 'in truth I perceive that God shows no partiality, but in every nation whoever fears Him and works righteousness is accepted by Him' (Acts 10:34–35). In the Gospel of John, while speaking to the Samaritan woman, Jesus said, "You worship what you do not know; we worship what we know, for salvation is from the Jews" (Jn 4:22). This indicates an inclusivist belief that it is possible to worship the true God without explicitly knowing him.

Later, when Jesus was asked about what to do to inherit eternal life, he narrated the story of the Samaritan and said: "Go and do likewise" (Lk 10:25–37). During the Second Vatican Council, among other theologians, Karl Rahner also stood for inclusivism. He was concerned about the salvation of all people who never had the opportunity to listen to the Gospel of Jesus Christ. He argued that it is God in Jesus Christ who reaches out to the individual to save him in his journey of faith. He used the term "anonymous" to refer to people of other religious traditions who experienced the grace of God through Jesus Christ.

ANALYSIS OF INTERFAITH DIALOGUES FROM SECOND VATICAN COUNCIL

The Second Vatican Council had participants from the entire world. The so-called "mission countries" had their native representatives to share their experiences of living in multi-religious, multicultural and interfaith household backgrounds. The Council members reflected on the needs of the time. Fraternal dialogue with separated Christians and people belonging to other religious traditions was one of the major concerns of the Council. Interfaith dialogues and inculturation of Catholic faith had an important place in the Council (Ratzinger, 26–27). Interfaith households can gain a lot from the reflections of the Council. The participants in the Council searched for ways in which they could help people keep their faith alive through various religious practices. The Council looked for a new understanding of the structure of the Church and how she related to the modern world. A broader understanding of the diversity and pluralism was one of the major concerns in various discussions. The Council emphasized that faith remained alive in those who were simple at heart and who passed on the torch of hope to future generations (Ratzinger, 262). The decree *Unitatis Redintegratio* on ecumenism helped the Catholic Church into the modern ecumenical movement in a lasting way. The concept of a "universal brotherhood" of Christians became a firm ecumenical conviction rooted in the recognition of the oneness of baptism (Cassidy, 104–107).

In his encyclical letter *Redemptoris Missio,* Saint John Paul II stressed the role of the Catholic Church in today's situation where people search for meaning in life amidst religious pluralism. He said that the "phenomenon — the so-called 'religious revival' — is not without ambiguity, but it also represents an opportunity. The Church has an immense spiritual patrimony to offer humankind, a heritage in Christ, who called himself 'the way, and the truth, and the life' (Jn 14:6): it is the Christian path to meeting God, to prayer, to asceticism, and to the search for life's meaning." (Saint John Paul II, 38).

The Jews were considered to be the chosen people of God. They awaited the promised Messiah. Some Jews accepted Jesus Christ as the Messiah and Savior, and others refused. Those who accepted Jesus Christ as their Savior formed the new people of God, and they are now called Christians. For many years, Christians believed that salvation for people belonging to other religious traditions, including the Jewish people, was only possible through their conversion to Christianity. The Second Vatican Council gave much importance to the relationship between Christians and Jews. At this point, Christian scholars, including the reformed theologian Karl Barth, Catholic philosopher Jacques Maritain, and the Jesuit biblical scholar Cardinal Augustin Bea, contributed to a renewed understanding of God's covenant with the Jews (Gaillardetz and Clifford, 182–183). Their work on a schema entitled "Relationship of the Church to Non-Christian Religions" was mainly intended to progress the relationship between Christians and Jews. But when the declaration *Nostra Aetate* was approved by the Council, many Council fathers observed that people are "being drawn closer together, and the ties between different peoples are becoming stronger" (*NA,* 1). The Church teaches "one is the community of all peoples, one their origin … one also is their final goal" (*NA*, 1). The declaration on the "Relationship of the Church to Non-Christian Religions" significantly opened up the Church to all religious traditions, not only to Jewish customs (Cassidy, 125–128).

The Second Vatican Council acknowledged that "from ancient times down to the present, there is found among various peoples a certain perception of that hidden power which hovers over the course of things" (*NA*, 2). There is a certain religious sense in people belonging to other religious traditions, as some of them recognize a Supreme Divinity and even a Supreme Father. A special reference was given to Hinduism and Buddhism where people have profound spiritual insights. Other religious traditions aspire to encounter the restlessness of the human heart by proposing "ways" and giving rules of life, teachings, and sacred rites (*NA*, 2). *Nostra Aetete* called Catholics to enter into dialogue with people of other religious traditions. It is "through dialogue and collaboration with the followers of other religions, carried out with prudence and love and in witness to the Christian faith and life, they recognize, preserve and promote the good things, spiritual and moral, as well as the sociocultural values found among these men" (*NA*, 2). The Council noted that Catholics "cannot truly call on God, the Father of all, if we refuse to treat in a brotherly way any man, created as he is in the image of God" (*NA*, 5). This perception of the Council invited the Catholic Church to open wider to the practical realities of various religious traditions. There could not have any more condemnation of other religious traditions but an effort to understand how they bring hope as well. Interfaith households can search for meaning in such teachings of the Church.

One of the dogmatic constitutions of the Council, *Lumen Gentium,* affirmed that all people of faith belong or are related to the people of God in different ways. These people are the members of the Catholic Church (*LG*, 14); other baptized Christians (*LG*, 15); and finally, "all men are called by the grace of God to salvation" (*LG*, 13, 16). *Lumen Gentium* makes a particular connection between the three Abrahamic religions, in recognition of their common foundation of faith in one Creator God, without overlooking the fact that all people belonging to various religious traditions are in search of meaning in their lives (Gaillardetz and Clifford, 183–185).

The Dogmatic Constitution on the Church *Lumen Gentium* declared that people who did not yet receive the Gospel are also connected to the people of God (16). The Divine Providence does not deny the help necessary for salvation to all people who do not have an explicit knowledge of God, but, with His grace, strive to live a good life. The Pastoral Constitution on the Church in the Modern World, *Gaudium et Spes*, underlines that the Holy Spirit guides every person in the direction of being associated with the paschal mystery (22). *Ad Gentes,* the Decree on the Mission Activity of the Church, underlines that the mission of the Church is fulfilled by her missionary activity that is influenced by the grace and love of the Holy Spirit (5). The Spirit is fully present to all peoples in every nation. The Church, by the example of her life and preaching and the sacraments, may lead people to the faith. In this way, they might have an open door before them to experience the mystery of Christ.

Nostra Aetate enlightened and encouraged Christians to receive non-Christians into their milieu in an esteemed manner (2). The Church recognizes that human beings are drawn closer together, and that the ties between different peoples are becoming stronger in the modern world. The Church promotes unity and love among all peoples and nations, and she admits the fact that some people come to the recognition of a Supreme Being, or even of a Father. This perception and recognition penetrates their lives with a profound religious perception. Other religions try to encounter the restlessness of the human heart by proposing "ways," comprising teachings, rules of life, and sacred rites. The Church appreciates anything that is pure and holy in other religions. She regards with sincere reverence those ways of conduct and life. The Church opens her door to help all people belonging to other religious traditions to discover the beauty of God, who is Truth.

In 1964, Paul VI instituted a particular department of the Roman Curia for promoting relations with the people of other religions. It was called the Secretariat for non-Christians and, in 1988, it was renamed the Pontifical Council for Interreligious Dialogue (PCID) in accordance with the spirit of the Second Vatican Council, especially the declaration *Nostra Aetate.* The PCID tries to promote mutual understanding, respect, and collaboration between Christians and the followers of other religious traditions; it encourages the study of religions and promotes the formation of persons dedicated to dialogue. The two official documents of PCID reaffirm the spirit of the Second Vatican Council and create a conducive atmosphere for further collaboration among Christians and non-Christians. In the same perspective, Saint John Paul II, in his encyclical letter on the permanent validity of the Church's missionary mandate, *Redemptoris Missio,* explains that salvation in Christ is offered to all (*RM*, 10). The dialogue is supported by speaking and listening, and giving and taking.

The Post-Synodal Apostolic Exhortation *Ecclesia in America* reformulated for the American continent the criteria to evaluate non-Christian religions as per the Vatican II declaration *Nostra Aetate*. According to this criterion, the Catholic Church, while affirming the specific originality of Christianity, does not reject anything that is true and holy in non-Christian religions. This document affirms that the Church in America takes steps to do her ecumenical and interreligious activities keeping in mind the pastoral guidelines laid down by the Second Vatican Council and subsequent Magisterium. *Ecclesia in America* highlights the good relations that exist with other Christian denominations and non-Christians. With regard to indigenous religions that existed before Christianity's arrival, the document states that the Church seeks to discover elements that are in connection with the Gospel so as to purify and integrate them into the life of the local church. It is a genuine challenge to the Church in the process of new evangelization because, through energetic proselytization, new groups and sects spread rapidly in big cities and wherever the Church's presence is weak.

All the above elements contribute to building a Catholic family spirituality in interfaith households. The openness of the Catholic Church to recognize the good elements in other religious traditions will encourage interfaith household members to listen to each other and cherish a unique spirituality.

INTERPRETATING THE CHALLENGES OF INTERFAITH CATHOLIC HOUSEHOLDS

There are many challenges to cultivating a Catholic family spirituality in interfaith households. Catholic families have traditional ways of doing things together. Here are some common practices that Catholic families would typically engage in to nurture their spirituality and deal with real challenge for interfaith households.

Daily prayer: Prayer is an essential part of a Catholic family. All the members of the family gather in common prayer at home. They engage in devotional prayers, recitation of the Holy Rosary, novenas, Bible reading, etc. Daily prayer is a time of uniting oneself with others and God. In interfaith households, this coming together may not easy.

Eucharist: Catholics go for Mass and receive special grace from God as they believe that they receive the Body and Blood of Jesus Christ. The Holy Eucharist is the source and summit of every Catholic life. This practice of going to Mass may not be agreeable to people who belong to other faith practices in the same household. They may not even believe in the real presence of Jesus Christ in the Holy Eucharist.

Adoration: Catholics believe that Jesus is really present in the Blessed Sacrament. Adoration is a time of blessing and spending time with the Lord in contemplation. People of other faith background do not commit to this faith.

Bible study: Many Christian denominations gather for Bible study. However, it's not necessary that they do the Bible study in the same way as Catholics do. Catholics have a holistic way of studying the Bible as they give importance to the Scripture, Tradition, and Dogmas.

Faith formation of children: In interfaith households, it's not easy to hold faith formation of children. Parents might struggle to bring their children to traditional Catechism classes, as parents might have different opinions on faith formation.

Reception of sacraments: The seven sacraments have a primordial place in the Catholic Church. In interfaith households, it may not be easy to receive the sacraments. For instance, in mixed marriages, one party may not agree that Marriage as a sacrament be received in the Catholic Church. In interreligious marriages, one party may not even want to get baptized. In some cases, the party who is not Catholic might want to please her partner by getting baptized; but later on, may not continue to practice that baptismal engagement.

Confusion of accompanying the children: In interfaith households, it's always a challenge to accompany the children. Parents may not know in which faith the children should be guided. If parents belong to different religious traditions, they might even tell their children about both traditions, but the children might get very confused as to which one to follow. In some cases, they end up following no religion.

Food habits: Food habits vary for people belonging to different religious traditions. Some are vegetarians, and others are non-vegetarians. Some people in interfaith households may not even tolerate cooking non-vegetarian food in the house. This can create tension in daily living, and members of the household may fight with one another and split their family.

INTERVENTION TO DEVELOPING AN INTERFAITH FAMILY SPIRITUALITY

Intervention is done to improve the existing religious practices in interfaith households. I would like to give some practical suggestions that would help to cultivate a Catholic family spirituality in interfaith households.

God image: In interfaith households, it's important to have a bigger God image where the members of the household will feel comfortable to share their God experience. Imposing the God image of one person will not help in dialogue and growth. Catholics in the interfaith household should communicate to others that our God is fully divine, human, and alive. God in Jesus Christ is a friend, a brother, and, above all, the Savior.

Respect for the other: Listening to every member of the house will build up an atmosphere of respect and communion. Rejecting the religious practices of the others in the household would not help in sharpening a good spirituality.

Communication: Marriages become successful when there is good communication and understanding between husband and wife. Interfaith households need to have more communication than single-faith households. For instance, husband and wife will have to discuss in detail how they would bring up their children and what kind of faith and religious practices they want to transmit to their children. They have to decide what religious celebrations they would honor in their household.

Openness in sharing: Cultivating a Catholic family spirituality in interfaith households would mean to be open in sharing with other members of the household the values and practices that Catholics cherish. Everything may not look positive in the Catholic Church with the historical review and present situations. However, it is important to share with others the core values that go beyond the errors that are committed by a few people in the Catholic Church.

Flexibility: Imposing the religious tradition of one party would not work in interfaith households. Sometimes, it is important to let go of the rituals and practices to give more space for relationship building. When the relationships are solid in interfaith households, it's easier to build up a Catholic spirituality.

Grandparents: They could play big role in interfaith households to nurture a Catholic family spirituality. A few years back, I officiated a Christian-Hindu wedding. The bride was a Catholic, and the bridegroom was a Hindu. The parents of both parties were much involved in the life of this newly married couple. Now the couple had a child. The Catholic grandparents took great interest in nurturing the child in faith as they always accompanied the new family in their prayer. Through the initiative and invitation of the grandparents, this interfaith couple decided to baptize the child. The involvement of the bigger family is helpful in cherishing a Catholic spirituality in interfaith households.

Discovering the faith of the partner: For cherishing a Catholic family spirituality in an interfaith household, it's critical to know the faith of the partner. It's by discovering and respecting the religious practices of the other that one could propose a spirituality that is Catholic-oriented.

Cherishing the relationship: Building a relationship is key to the success of any marriage. In an interfaith household, it's essential for the couple to enjoy relationship without any prejudgment of and bias about the religious practices of the other party.

Family prayer life: Family prayer is essential in cultivating a family spirituality. In an interfaith household, Catholic members of the family can take the lead in organizing family prayer. Music and spirituality could take more space in family prayer. All members of the household would appreciate music. Taize chants, *bhajans*, and meditational songs could give more meaning in interfaith family prayer life. Father Patrick Peyton's slogan for families might help in such a gathering: "The family that prays together stays together." Praying together will help families stay together. It will also help families to emerge with a spirituality. Through prayer, even interfaith families can cultivate a Catholic family spirituality while respecting other members of the family.

Learning from the disciples of Jesus: Jesus called his apostles and gathered his disciples from all walks of life. All of them were not traditional Jews who had a unique spirituality. After joining Jesus, they learned from him about how to go ahead in life and form a community. They learned to come together in prayer with their differences. They developed a spirituality based on the life and teachings of Jesus. The challenges in interfaith households with all the differences of its members could take this model of the disciples of Jesus who developed a new way of life with Jesus. Intentional discipleship is all about learning from the disciples of Jesus, who had the same struggles as we do in our time.

Our Father — common prayer for families: The prayer Our Father is for all people. As the disciples of Jesus did not know how to pray, he gave them this prayer. The first part of the prayer is all about acknowledging God our Father in heaven and praying for his Will to be done on earth. The second part of the prayer is all about presenting our needs and asking for forgiveness to keep us united as one with God and people. Though Christians widely use this prayer in all gatherings, this prayer could be recited by anyone who turns his heart to God. A greater spirituality can emerge from the recitation of Jesus' prayer.

PROSPECTIVE OF CATHOLIC FAMILY SPIRITUALITY IN INTERFAITH HOUSEHOLDS

The prospective is oriented toward the future to foresee what the familial situation will be in a few years from now. It could highlight the hopes and limits of developing a Catholic family spirituality in interfaith households.

Interfaith households: There will be more interfaith households in the future as many young people do not hold on to their own faith tradition when it comes to marriage and family life.

Catholic identity: It is going to be a challenge to develop Catholic identity in interfaith households as faith formation has a lesser place in families.

Catholic family spirituality: Some interfaith households will want to nurture Catholic family spirituality as they discover and recognize the good values of Catholic life. Catholic members in interfaith households will take an interest in helping others learn more about Catholic ways of living.

Prayer life in families: Prayer will be the key element in any interfaith household to sustain a Catholic spirituality. Catholic prayers will help members of other faith traditions to discover the beauty of the person of Jesus Christ.

Spirituality and retreat centers: Spirituality and retreat centers could play a vital role in accompanying people who search to develop a Catholic family spirituality in interfaith households.

Shrines and pilgrimage places: Catholic shrines and pilgrimage places would attract many interfaith households for their spiritual journey.

Anonymous city churches: Interfaith households may not want to identify themselves with any local parish church. They might seek to visit anonymous city churches where their identity is not revealed.

Family spirituality museums: Developing Catholic family spirituality museums could attract more interfaith families to discover the faith and nourish it. Digital and interactive spaces for children in the museums will help them learn more about the Bible and stories of saints. When children are occupied in the museums, parents also will take time to learn more about educational items. A creative way of faith formation can take place in Catholic family spirituality museums.

Religious tourism: Religious tourism might help some interfaith households who visit religious sites such as notable churches and family spirituality museums. The families will get inspired by the richness of religious traditions and will reflect much upon their need to develop a Catholic spirituality in their households.

CONCLUSION

Discipleship is a choice that people make to follow someone in whom they are convinced. The organized religions had a tremendous influence in the lives of people in both individual and collective spheres. They aspired to protect human beings by bringing them salvation. Religions played a great role in education and social change. In every undertaking and accomplishment, religions made a connection to the Sacred. The institutional framework of religions tried to establish a historical link that enveloped a theological summing-up justification. Interpretations and clarifications of various practices helped to frame a doctrinal setup for religions. All these were done in order to reach the ultimate goal of building up relationship with God.

From my childhood, I have been engaging in Catholic religious practices. Coming from a traditional Catholic family, I have always seen my parents, grandparents, and siblings involved in Church activities. As family relationships are strong in India, one cannot easily dissociate from what is happening in a family. Religious practices are not limited to the church, as my family members gather to pray together every day. I have experienced my family as a domestic church. I became a disciple of Jesus in my family, and parents have played a big role in accompanying me. Grandparents and relatives helped me to become a strong disciple of Jesus. My bigger family taught me how to be strong in faith even in times of struggles and hardships in life. My friends from other religious traditions were not obstacles for me to be an intentional disciple of Jesus. My conviction that Jesus is my Savior is a learned one over the years. As I became an adult, my faith also grew in Jesus Christ. Just as the apostles of Jesus, I also had moments of doubts in my faith journey. Experiences of life and prayer life helped me grow in intimacy with Jesus Christ, who constantly nourished and guided me by the Holy Spirit.

Traditional Catholics might find it hard to nurture Catholic family spirituality in interfaith households. However, if Catholics open themselves in line with the teachings of the Second Vatican Council, they would invite others who belong to different faiths to be part of them and understand the good elements in them to foster a spirituality that is not simply bound to religious rules and rituals. Catholic members of interfaith households can take leadership in sharing their Divine experience and Jesus experience with others in the family. There is no harm in listening to others who belong to different traditions. Like the first disciples of Jesus, who came from different backgrounds and shared their commonness, today's interfaith households should take inspiration from them. Like the first disciples of Jesus who made an intentional decision to be disciples of Jesus despite many fears and hardships, today the Catholics in interfaith households should not be afraid to follow Jesus by being authentic disciples. When the Catholics in interfaith households practice their faith with much devotion and fervor, others in the same family will naturally be inspired by their lives and discover Jesus Christ.

DISCUSSION QUESTIONS

1. What role does respect play in navigating interreligious differences in a household?
2. What are some ways families can find points of spiritual agreement in an interreligious household.
3. How can the Catholic members of an interreligious household maintain their religious integrity while simultaneously being open to what is true, good, and beautiful about their non-Catholic partner's faith?

BIBLIOGRAPHY

Bidwell, Duane R. *When One Religion Isn't Enough: The Lives of Spirituality Fluid People*. Boston: Beacon Press, 2018.

Cassidy, Edward Idris Cardinal. *Ecumenism and Interreligious Dialogue: Unitatis Redintegratio, Nostra Aetate (Rediscovering Vatican II)*. Mahwah, NJ: Paulist Press, 2005.

Comeau, Genevieve. *Grâce à l'autre – Le Pluralisme Religieux, Une Chance Pour la Foi*. Paris: Editions de l'Atelier/Ouvrieres, 2004.

Dupuis, Jacques. *Vers une théologie chrétienne du pluralisme religieux*. Paris: Cerf, 1999.

Gaillardetz, Richard R. and Catherine Clifford. *Keys to the Council: Unlocking the Teaching of Vatican II*. Collegeville, MN: Liturgical Press, 2012.

Gray, Mark M. and Thomas P. Gaunt. *Faith in the Family: A Survey of U.S. Catholic Parents.* Washington, DC: Center for Applied Research in the Apostolate, 2015.

Saint John Paul II. *Ecclesia in America.* http://www.vatican.va/content/john-paul-ii/en/apost_exhortations/documents/hf_jp-ii_exh_22011999_ecclesia-in-america.html.

Saint John Paul II. *Redemptoris Missio.* http://www.vatican.va/content/john-paul-ii/en/encyclicals/documents/hf_jp-ii_enc_07121990_redemptoris-missio.html.

Knitter, Paul F. *Without Buddha I Could Not Be Christian.* London: One-World Academic, 2013.

Nadeau, Jean-Guy. "La praxéologie pastorale: faire théologie selon un paradigme praxéologique." *Théologique* 1, no. 1 (March 1993).

Pope Paul VI. *Nostra Aetate.* http://www.vatican.va/archive/hist_councils/ii_vatican_council/documents/vat-ii_decl_19651028_nostra-aetate_en.html

Pope Benedict XVI. *Theological Highlights of Vatican II.* Mahwah, NJ: Paulist Press, 2009.

Ruokanen, Miikka. *The Catholic Doctrine of Non-Christian Religions According to the Second Vatican Council.* Leiden: Brill Academic Publishers, 1992.

Sullivan, Francis A. *Salvation Outside the Church? Tracing the History of the Catholic Response.* Eugene, OR: Wipf and Stock, 2002.

Secretariat for Non-Christians. "The Attitude of the Church Towards Followers of Other Religions." *The Furrow* 36, no. 7 (July 1985).

Vogt, Brandon. *Why I Am Catholic (And You Should Be Too).* Notre Dame, IN: Ave Maria Press, 2017.

PART FIVE

The Building Blocks for a New Vision of Catholic Family Life and Spirituality

I n this section, we explore the building blocks for a new approach to understanding Catholic family life and spirituality.

In his chapter, Dominic Lombardi, executive director of the USCCB Secretariat of Laity, Marriage, Family, and Youth, explores the active dimensions of the term "domestic church" and how this term orders life within the home, the community, and the Church as a whole.

Next, Joseph White, family psychologist and director of catechetical resources for OSV, reflects on the divine pedagogy of family life. The divine pedagogy is a term from the field of catechetics. It explores the methods God uses to teach his children about himself and the truths of the faith. Dr. White reflects on how parents can use the principles of divine pedagogy to foster a relationship with God and a love of the Catholic faith.

Following this, Tim Muldoon, a pastoral theologian at Boston College, and his wife, Sue Muldoon, a licensed counselor and pastoral minister, offer principles to consider in constructing a spirituality of the home. They also speak to ways parishes can more effectively accompany families on their pilgrimage journey. Together, the Muldoons are the authors of several books on family spirituality.

Next, Bill Keimig, assistant director of the Catechetical Institute at Franciscan University, offers a model of pastoral accompaniment for parents and parishes and provides a case study of how his ministry promotes this vision of family accompaniment.

Finally, Damon Owens, the founder of JoyTOB.org, a ministry promoting applications of Saint John Paul II's *Theology of the Body* to family life, and his wife, Melanie, a licensed clinical social worker who, with her husband, is a prominent NFP speaker and family life minister, share the witness of their conversion and the role the *Theology of the Body* played in their ability to dynamically live and celebrate the Catholic vision of marriage and family life.

CHAPTER FIFTEEN

The Domestic Church and the Pilgrimage to the Father's House

DOMINIC LOMBARDI, STL

Executive Director, USCCB Secretariat of Laity, Marriage, Family Life, and Youth

---

FIVE QUICK TAKES

1. The family is a true church founded upon the unitive and fruitful Love of God. Families need to be encouraged to explicitly think of their identity in this context.
2. God's grace is **always** at work in the relationships and expressions of love, generosity, and forgiveness of the family.
3. Families need spiritual practices, and parents need to be intentional about establishing rituals of prayer and thanksgiving.
4. The family is a fundamental agent of the Church's mission and foundation for establishing a Christian culture.
5. Families need the support of the Church and other families.

The term "domestic church" might appear as a passive, comforting image; but in fact, it is a revolutionary one encompassing the radical identity and vocation of the Christian family, who has at its core the transforming encounter with Jesus Christ through whom it becomes an icon of Trinitarian love and sacrament of Christ's union with the Church. It is a sacrament of vocation rooted in Baptism and nourished by the Eucharist. It is of profound significance that Jesus Christ was sent by the Father through the power of the Holy Spirit to enter the world through the family. In this the family is confirmed as the principle "way" of humanity, and Jesus continues to come to the world today through the family.

Respecting the spiritual and evangelical dynamism of the Christian family, this reflection will view and develop its identity as an essential agent of the Church's mission and protagonist of the very form of ecclesial communion in the following areas:[1]

- Participation in the nuptial mystery in the "yes" to life
- Witness to the paschal mystery in the sincere gift of self
- The family's mode of being as "liturgy"
- The evangelization of culture through everyday witness

THE DOMESTIC CHURCH AS PARTICIPATION IN THE NUPTIAL MYSTERY

"The couple that loves and begets life is a true, living icon — not an idol like those of stone or gold prohibited by the Decalogue — capable of revealing God the Creator and Savior. For this reason, fruitful love becomes a symbol of God's inner life (cf. Gn 1:28; 9:7; 17:2–5, 16; 28:3; 35:11; 48:3–4)."[2]

"This" flesh and blood union of the spouses in their freedom, yet totally upon God's grace and in their imperfection, is a proclamation of God who is Love. A theology of grace, and specifically a Eucharistic theology, underpins the fruitfulness of the divine and human reality that is the domestic church. An event from the Gospels that offers an image of this fruitfulness is the miracle of multiplication of the loaves and fishes (Mt 14:13–21). Jesus takes the two fishes and five loaves, which is all his disciples have to offer, and transforms them to feed the multitude. Christian spouses likewise are called to give all they have to offer, including their imperfection, to God who in His goodness will bring about a superabundant fruitfulness in their family. This does not mean they will be spared suffering and loss, but that their love will endure and direct them and their family to the Love that is everlasting.

As an icon of the Unitive and Fruitful love of the Trinity, and of Christ's redeeming love for the Church, at the heart of spousal love is the reciprocal and total gift of self in their conjugal union. Like God's love,

---

1. In these themes, the Holy Family will be a significant source as it prefigures the domestic church of the family. Regarding Church documents, two sources will be most prominent: Pope Francis' Apostolic Exhortation *Amoris Laetitia* (AL), and Saint John Paul II's *Letter to Families* (LF).
2. Pope Francis, *Amoris Laetitia*, 11, https://w2.vatican.va/content/,dam/francesco/pdf/apost_exhortations /documents/papa-francesco_esortazione-ap_20160319_amoris-laetitia_en.pdf.

true spousal love is always unitive and fruitful, faithful and enduring. Spouses' love for each other is a "yes" to love as God loves. From this love emerges the "yes" to life.

At the outset of their marriage, Mary and Joseph were called in a radical way to witness to the fruitfulness of this "yes," which required that they give themselves and their destiny completely to God. Their "yes" witnessed to their radical openness and union with God, which prepared them for this moment. Couples today may not be aware, but they express a similar "yes" in their vows of fidelity, fruitfulness, and permanence. To support the "yes" of these vows, there is the necessity of an interior life, an ongoing conversion and readiness to give themselves completely to the Lord, and in the Lord to each other.

Whereas Marriage is part of the natural law, and the fruit of children part of God's creative plan for humanity, particularly in Western society today this is challenged by the denial that the desire for and openness to the gift of children is essential to marriage, or the assertion that the procreation of children can be pursued outside of marriage, or can be pursued outside of the conjugal act through the reproductive technologies. In this context, sexual union can be reduced to the ethics of use, and the body a means to an end.[3] In response to this emerging mentality now well established in the culture, Pope Paul VI prophetically affirmed the inseparable connection between the unitive and procreative dimensions of the conjugal act:

> The reason is that the fundamental nature of the marriage act, while uniting husband and wife in the closest intimacy, also renders them capable of generating new life — and this as a result of laws written into the actual nature of man and of woman. And if each of these essential qualities, the unitive and the procreative, is preserved, the use of marriage fully retains its sense of true

---

3. In this context, Pope Francis' warning about the throwaway culture is relevant: "We treat affective relationships the way we treat material objects and the environment: everything is disposable; everyone uses and throws away, takes and breaks, exploits and squeezes to the last drop. Then, goodbye. Narcissism makes people incapable of looking beyond themselves, beyond their own desires and needs. Yet sooner or later, those who use others end up being used themselves, manipulated and discarded by that same mindset" (*Amoris Laetitia*, 39).

mutual love and its ordination to the supreme responsibility of parenthood to which man is called. We believe that our contemporaries are particularly capable of seeing that this teaching is in harmony with human reason.[4]

Instead of the contraceptive mentality, Pope Paul VI proposed the teaching of responsible parenthood, which is a catechesis in the "yes" to life, and the dignity of the body in its unitive and procreative dimensions.[5] A focal point of responsible parenthood is the spouses' "yes," which echoes Mary's Fiat (and Joseph's consent), which is a yes to God's plan for their lives. Responsible parenthood is a discernment about fruitfulness. Proceeding from this stance and respecting the dignity, integrity, and structure of the conjugal act, couples can utilize medical knowledge and interventions to assist in conceiving a child (or postponing conception) with the intention of serving the fullness of life while respecting the nuptial meaning of the body, and hence neither attacking fruitfulness (fertility) or undermining union.[6]

Unfortunately, many couples (most?) are not aware of this catechesis on responsible parenthood or the *Theology of the Body*.[7] Hence, this is an ongoing pastoral and evangelical priority for the Church today.[8]

This formation in the yes to life has two dimensions. The first dimension has been addressed in the yes to a new human being. The second yes to life that spouses pledge in their marriage vows is to proclaim the Gospel to their children, each other, and ultimately to the world.

---

4. Pope Paul VI, *Humanae Vitae*, 12, http://www.vatican.va/content/paul-vi/en/encyclicals/documents/hf_p-vi_enc_25071968_humanae-vitae.html.

5. See *Humanae Vitae*, 10.

6. In this area the Catholic Church has become the leader in programs of Natural Family Planning and medical research and technology that respect the dignity of marriage and the right of children to be the fruit of the conjugal union of their parents.

7. "It is also through the body that man and woman are predisposed to form a "communion of persons" in marriage. When they are united by the conjugal covenant in such a way as to become "one flesh" (Gn 2:24), their union ought to take place "in truth and love," and thus express the maturity proper to persons created in the image and likeness of God." Saint John Paul II, *Letter to Families*, 8, http://www.vatican.va/content/john-paul-ii/en/letters/1994/documents/hf_jp-ii_let_02021994_families.html.

8. Times and places where formation in the *Theology of the Body* are essential are: from parents in dialogue with their children; guidance to young people regarding dating; marriage preparation for couples; and adult faith formation programs for married couples.

THE DOMESTIC CHURCH AND THE PASCHAL MYSTERY[9]

A primary characteristic and connection between Marriage, family life, and the paschal mystery is the structure of mutual self-giving and receiving love. Just as Christ's mission proceeded through the sincere gift of Himself to His Heavenly Father and receiving everything he had from the Father, so the spouses' sincere and mutual gift of themselves is their core identity and witness to the sacrament of Marriage making present the love of Christ. The form of their life mirrors Christ's life, death, and resurrection, a dying to self to give life.[10] In a real sense the vows the couple proclaim in matrimony give witness to Christ's words: "I came that they may have life, and have it abundantly" (Jn 10:10), and "No one has greater love than this, to lay down one's life for one's friends" (Jn 15:13). The wedding vows speak of this complete and irrevocable self-giving love, promising in good times and in bad, in sickness and in health, to love and honor all the days of their lives (and I would add transcending death). Looking to the witness of the holy family, we see this witness to the paschal mystery at the outset of their marriage: Mary's embrace of what would lead to shame and perhaps death, Joseph's acceptance of a different path of spousal union than he ever could have perceived. They gave completely and unconditionally in response to God's call in their vocation, which bore fruit in the inestimable gift of their son, Jesus. Their path of parenthood entailed the ongoing discernment of the Lord's will, revealed in such sublime moments as the finding of their child in the Temple: "Did you not know that I must be in my Father's house?" (Lk 2:49) The drama of Christian parents continues today, with both the joys and anxieties for their children but giving all for the pearl of great price, which is the family.[11]

The formation of the family in Christ's paschal mystery establishes

---

9. "For the sacrament of marriage flows from the incarnation and the paschal mystery, whereby God showed the fullness of his love for humanity by becoming one with us. Neither of the spouses will be alone in facing whatever challenges may come their way. Both are called to respond to God's gift with commitment, creativity, perseverance and daily effort. They can always invoke the assistance of the Holy Spirit who consecrated their union, so that his grace may be felt in every new situation that they encounter" (*Amoris Laetitia*, 74).

10. "Let this cup pass from me by thy will be done, not mine" (Mt 26:39).

11. Family life is dramatic, calling the members outside of themselves, stretching them whether they like it or not.

an ethic of generosity within the family, which overflows and reaches out to those in need in the world. Mary gives witness to this when, immediately following upon her "yes" to God, she goes to care for her kinswoman Elizabeth, who is with child and in need (Lk 1:39–45). We see this dynamism prominently in Jesus' teaching: "By this everyone will know that you are my disciples, if you love one another" (Jn 13:35), and "Amen, I say to you, whatever you did for one of these least brothers of mine, you did for me" (Mt 25:40). The point here is that the form that love takes within the family determines its relationship to the world. Hence, the more it is drawn into Christ's love, the greater its outreach to the world. From the very beginning the public witness of this self-giving love was a hallmark of the Church and the domestic church of the family, which cared not only for its own members, but also those beyond the family, giving witness to the universal family of humanity redeemed by Christ.[12] Today's domestic church has the same mission, and its witness in response to the needs of the community bears witness to the world of Christ's redemptive love.

THE DOMESTIC CHURCH AS LITURGY[13]

At the heart of the life of the Church is the celebration of the divine mysteries in the liturgy. This dimension of worship grounds family life as well, and it can be profoundly viewed through this lens. The *Catechism of the Catholic Church* states that "the Liturgy of the Church is a public work on behalf of the people."[14] The public dimension of Christian family life is a significant witness to the Gospel in the everyday lives and activities of its members: prayers together at the beginning and end of the day, the family meal, celebrations of birthdays and feasts, reception of the sacraments, in a word, within the *communio* of the family. The most mundane aspects of family life have the power to proclaim the Gospel when lived out in the spirit of discipleship. In such ways the family trans-

---

12. The mission of charity in the early Church became the foundation for hospices/hospitals, care for those imprisoned, the care of widows, etc. This was unique in the ancient world.

13. "The procreative meaning of sexuality, the language of the body, and the signs of love shown throughout married life, all become an 'uninterrupted continuity of liturgical language' and 'conjugal life becomes in a certain sense liturgical'" (*Amoris Laetitia*, 215).

14. *Catechism of the Catholic Church, Second Edition* 1069, U.S. Conference of Catholic Bishops,

forms the structures of society through the ordinary witness of daily life.

A path for this everyday witness is the Church's liturgical year. This begins with the central importance of the Third Commandment, keeping holy the Lord's day in the Sunday liturgy of the Mass. Here the family participates with and is joined by other families and members of the parish (described as a family of families) where the people of God encounter the Lord in Word and Sacrament and are sent forth to love and serve Him. The Sunday Mass identifies the deepest core and identity of the family as a Eucharistic community:

> The family's communal journey of prayer culminates by sharing together in the Eucharist, especially in the context of the Sunday rest. Jesus knocks on the door of families, to share with them the Eucharistic supper (cf. Rv 3:20). There, spouses can always seal anew the paschal covenant which united them and which ought to reflect the covenant which God sealed with mankind in the cross. The Eucharist is the sacrament of the new covenant, where Christ's redemptive work is carried out (cf. Lk 22:20). The close bond between married life and the Eucharist thus becomes all the more clear. For the food of the Eucharist offers the spouses the strength and incentive needed to live the marriage covenant each day as a "domestic church."[15]

The rhythm of family life is tuned to that of the liturgical year, which is a recapitulation of the life, death, and resurrection of Jesus Christ. Here the family encounters the meaning of time and history, beginning with Jesus' incarnation and reaching its climax in His death and resurrection. The family envisions for its own members this soteriological structure who, through Baptism, have been united with Christ, in this earthly life are accompanied by Christ especially in the Eucharist, and in their death are commended to the eternal love of God.

---

15. *Amoris Laetitia,* 318. See also *Amoris Laetitia, 15:* "Here too, we can see another aspect of the family. We know that the New Testament speaks of "churches that meet in homes" (cf. 1 Cor 16:19; Rom 16:5; Col 4:15; Philem 2). A family's living space could turn into a domestic church, a setting for the Eucharist, the presence of Christ seated at its table."

Another deeply rooted liturgical dimension of family life is the sacrament of Reconciliation. The Christian family is that place of encounter with the Father's love akin to the Parable of the Prodigal Son (cf. Lk 15). Family life is a school of mercy and reconciliation where the members are molded by the kenotic love of Christ, which exorcizes selfishness, and where the answer to how many times am I to forgive my neighbor is given concrete response (cf. Mt 18:21–22). Additionally, the sacrament of Reconciliation is an aid to the family, a constant source of grace for the healing of human brokenness:

> Do not be afraid of the risks! God's strength is always far more powerful than your difficulties! Immeasurably greater than the evil at work in the world is the power of the Sacrament of Reconciliation, which the Fathers of the Church rightly called a "second Baptism." Much more influential than the corruption present in the world is the divine power of the Sacrament of Confirmation, which brings Baptism to its maturity. And incomparably greater than all is the power of the Eucharist.[16]

The *Catechism of the Catholic Church* says that through the Liturgy, Christ the High Priest continues the work of redemption in, with, and through the Church.[17] Isn't this precisely the vocation and identity of the family who, in communion with Christ, continue His mission of redemption to the conclusion of time? The family cannot be this community absent prayer. The paradigmatic prayer for the family, as it is for all of Jesus' disciples, is the Our Father. The seven petitions of the Our Father encapsulate family life, its needs and hopes. In prayer together, the members of the family meet Chris and discover who they are, their identity in Christ, loved by their Heavenly Father, and guided by the power of the Holy Spirit. The lifelong dialogue with God, which

---

16. *Letter to Families,* 18.
17. CCC 1069.

is prayer, begins in the family.[18]

THE DOMESTIC CHURCH AND THE EVANGELIZATION OF CULTURE (AND CULTURE OF EVANGELIZATION) [19]

The family is where each of us receives life, love, and the life of faith.[20] Pondering this inestimable gift, theologian Hans Urs von Balthasar reflected upon the mother's smile as the first image to the newly opened eyes of an infant.[21] And speaking from experience, there comes the wonderful moment when the infant smiles back! In this moment life is revealed in its very gratuitousness and beauty through this relational radiance. The experience of the wonder of being and the radiance of relationality is ongoing throughout the whole of family life, communicating the radiance and beauty of God's relationship with us.

In all its dimensions, intentional and unintentional, the actions of family life, what is said, read, seen, done, listened to individually and collectively molds its members, and evangelizes them (or does not). In this context the Christian family offers formation for authentic freedom, a freedom to seek and share the splendor of the truth of our relationship with God, need for God, and that God comes to us through one another. This stands in contradiction to the destructive illusion proposed by contemporary culture:

---

18. "It is significant that precisely in and through prayer, man comes to discover in a very simple and yet profound way his own unique subjectivity: in prayer the human 'I' more easily perceives the depth of what it means to be a person. This is also true of the family, which is not only the basic 'cell' of society, but also possesses a particular subjectivity of its own. This subjectivity finds its first and fundamental confirmation, and is strengthened, precisely when the members of the family meet in the common invocation: 'Our Father.' Prayer increases the strength and spiritual unity of the family, helping the family to partake of God's own 'strength' (*Letter to Families*, 4).

19. "Today it is difficult to imagine a statement by the Church, or about the Church, which does not mention the civilization of love. The phrase is linked to the tradition of the 'domestic church' in early Christianity, but it has a particular significance for the present time. Etymologically the word 'civilization' is derived from 'civis' — 'citizen,' and it emphasizes the civic or political dimension of the life of every individual. But the most profound meaning of the term 'civilization' is not merely political, but rather pertains to human culture. Civilization belongs to human history because it answers man's spiritual and moral needs. Created in the image and likeness of God, man has received the world from the hands of the Creator, together with the task of shaping it in his own image and likeness. The fulfillment of this task gives rise to civilization, which in the final analysis is nothing else than the 'humanization of the world'" (*Letter to Families*, 13).

20. Cf. *Amoris Laetitia*, 16.

21. Hans Urs von Balthasar, "Movement Toward God," in *Explorations in Theology, III: Creator Spirit* (San Francisco: Ignatius Press, 1993), 15–55.

On the other hand, "equal consideration needs to be given to the growing danger represented by an extreme individualism which weakens family bonds and ends up considering each member of the family as an isolated unit, leading in some cases to the idea that one's personality is shaped by his or her desires, which are considered absolute." "The tensions created by an overly individualistic culture, caught up with possessions and pleasures, leads to intolerance and hostility in families." Here I would also include today's fast pace of life, stress and the organization of society and labor, since all these are cultural factors which militate against permanent decisions.[22]

Christian family life is the antidote to this growing danger, in its inefficient and messy approach to life, lavishing time on relationships, where we discover the meaning of our existence, to give and receive love. Contrary to the ethos of self, possession, and efficiency, one encounters in the Christian family the ethos of community, generosity, hospitality, and leisure.

When one enters a Christian home, he or she experiences that family's culture: their hospitality, values, priorities. This includes things like the books that are read, music listened to, how much and what is viewed on television, the use of the internet and smartphones (does one's son or daughter not look up from the smartphone when a visitor arrives?). The family culture is established in time spent together: through the rhythm of meals, walks or hikes together, sports and games, discussing books and ideas, etc. Of all these things, the family meal has a central place:

> It is for you, dear husbands and wives, parents and families! Did Jesus not institute the Eucharist in a family-like setting during the Last Supper? When you meet for meals and are together in harmony, Christ is close to you. And he is Emmanuel, God with us, in an even greater way whenever you approach

---

22. *Amoris Laetitia*, 33.

the table of the Eucharist.[23]

All these things create a family culture that bears fruit in a spirit of the gratuitousness of being the response to which is joy and thanksgiving, which can be expressed in many ways, but the words "thank you" are most appropriate.

When Jesus Christ is at the heart of the relationships of the members of the family, their culture is one of evangelization. For in their conversations the topic of God naturally arises (including questions about God's existence, or the meaning of suffering), the significance of the life of virtue, truth, and freedom. In the enjoyment of music both secular and religious, the beautiful is encountered and its immanence and transcendence are shared. It's the profundity and wonder of this shared experience that radiates in the joy the family, which shines forth to the neighborhoods and communities where these domestic churches live.

Another area of the culture of the Christian family is the art and images in the home. Perhaps they include a picture of Mary and the Child Jesus, or the Holy Family, the crucifix, a holy water font at the door, beautiful scenes of nature, pictures of one's family members, etc. Amongst other things these images remind the family of the larger Christian community they belong to: the Holy Family, the communion of saints, and the family of the Church spread throughout the world. A particular image to note is the Sacred Heart of Jesus. Placed in a prominent position in the home, perhaps across from a comfortable chair where one can sit and meditate upon the loving gaze of Jesus, one can place before Him the hopes and trials of and give thanks for the blessing of family life. This reminds the members of the family of Jesus' personal love for each of them and their family, that He died and has risen from the dead for them. As for Thomas, this image invites reflection upon Jesus' wounds, where we are called to see, believe, and find healing for our woundedness in Him.

THE FAMILY AS "MONASTERY"

The reflexive thought when one hears the term "monastery" is the notion

---

23. *Letter to Families,* 18.

of leaving the world behind for a life of prayer and contemplation. There is more to monastic life than this, including work that sustains the monastic community, community life and prayer, and study, but the overall sense remains the same. Such a perspective, though, misses the fundamental truth that monastic life is really for the world. It offers continual praise to the Triune God, and its members individually and collectively pray for the world and in their lives give witness to the world to that which is of highest priority, a life given completely to God. Furthermore, it offers a program of formation for its members who, in a true sense, are a family of prayer supporting one another in response to the call to holiness. In this context the monastery can serve as an image or paradigm for the family as the domestic church.

While the family is "in the world," it is called to be not of the world. It points beyond the world to the Kingdom of God, which is the destiny of the human family. The home, like the monastery, is that place where the members support one another through prayer, listening, acts of charity, witness, and other forms of communion and accompaniment. From this *communio personarum* the members of the family go out into the world (a distinguishing characteristic from the monastic vocation) to serve the Lord in response to the universal call to holiness. In their going out into the world to labor in the Lord's vineyard, the family as a community evangelizes in direct and concrete ways such as offering hospitality, friendship, and even shelter and care in times of need.

The challenge today is that the "world" in its fallen, unredeemed character has entered many homes, replacing relationship with Jesus and one another with consumerism and autonomy, and the fallout from this is evidenced in the wave of anxiety and depression for many people, especially the young. This has been a powerful force within American culture, permeating the home with the new barbarism of materialism. Perhaps more virulent than the old barbarianism, which did not know Christ, the new barbarism begins from the place of forgetting Him (or explicitly rejecting Him).

Responding to the call of the Holy Spirit, there are new movements afoot reaching out to reclaim and reestablish the domestic church: family-based lay movements, homeschool communities, and missionary families bearing witness to Christ in neighborhoods and at the peripheries of society, sowing the seeds of the Gospel in the world.

When Benedict established his rule in the fifth century, against the backdrop of the Barbarians overtaking the old and tired Roman Empire in the West, he did not know these same monasteries would become spiritual, cultural, and economic anchors for a new Christian civilization. Might a movement of families now serve the Church's mission, addressing the new barbarism of today?

HONOR AND THE FAMILY'S PILGRIMAGE TO THE FATHER'S HOUSE

In Luke 2:39–52 we encounter the story of Mary and Joseph seeking their son, Jesus, who had become separated from them during their annual Passover pilgrimage to Jerusalem. Finding him in the Temple, Mary reprimands Jesus with a sentiment borne by parents through time immemorial:

> "Son, why have you treated us like this? Your father and I have been anxiously searching for you." (v. 48)

Jesus's response to his parents is amazing, transcending their understanding:

> "Why were you searching for me?" he asked. "Didn't you know I had to be in my Father's house?" But they did not understand what he was saying to them. (vv 49–50)

This takes us to the heart of the domestic church of the family, to be in the Father's house, which is to be filled with the love of our Heavenly Father. Jesus' mission revealed this love and brought it to fulfillment. In Christ this is the mission of the family, to bring it to fulfillment in its members and to pass it on from generation to generation until the end of history, which has already been brought to completion in Christ, who is the first fruits (cf. 1 Cor 15:20–24). The Christian family instantiates this love, and hence it is sacred, hallowed, a place where members have honor for each other. In this honoring they see each other as God sees them, sons and daughters in the Son, and seek to be a "way" to the One who is the "Way" to the Father's house. This is the mission and pilgrimage of the Christian family.

DISCUSSION QUESTIONS

1. How can families make space for and protect their time together?
2. How can the family's formational needs be a priority for and addressed by the parish, which is a "family of families"?
3. How can families be both monastic and missionary — a place set aside from the world but also open to and for the world?

CHAPTER SIXTEEN

The Divine Pedagogy and the Family

———————

JOSEPH D. WHITE, PHD

Family Psychologist, Director of Catechetical Resources, OSV

FIVE QUICK TAKES

1. The term *divine pedagogy* is used to describe God's own way of teaching us.

2. Because parents are the first and most important teachers of their children, they are called to reflect the pedagogy of God.

3. Parents reflect God's pedagogy as they invite and welcome, bring the faith to life, build communion among family members, provide structure, and form family members for mission.

4. In order to faithfully reflect the pedagogy of God, families are in urgent need of evangelization and formation in Catholic teachings about the family.

5. Pastoral ministers can play a key role in educating families about, modeling, and coaching specific practices that strengthen the family.

In his great humility and mercy, God desires to share his divine life and truth with humanity. The term *divine pedagogy* is used to describe God's own way of teaching us. The *General Directory for Catechesis* (*GDC*) states, "Catechesis as communication of divine Revelation, is radically inspired by the pedagogy of God, as displayed in Christ and in the Church" (143). We are called to hand on the truths of the faith not merely by doing our best according to human standards of theology and educational methodology, but rather by echoing God's own way of teaching us his truths and respecting that, even as we teach others, God remains active in the heart of the human person, bringing growth to the seeds of faith that are planted there.

The family has a prominent role within our Catholic Faith. God himself is revealed as a "family" — Father, Son, and Holy Spirit. God creates us, male and female, in his image and likeness (Gn 1:26–27; CCC 2205). We are created to be in communion with one another, just as God is a communion of persons. Jesus reveals God as a Father who loves and cares for his children. The Church is revealed to us as a family into which we are adopted by God and become brothers and sisters to one another (Gal 4:4–5). Jesus' relationship with the Church is presented in Scripture as a marriage, with Jesus as the groom and the Church his Bride.

Saint John Paul II famously said, "As the family goes, so goes the nation, and so goes the whole world in which we live" ("Homily of John Paul II," November 30, 1986). We could just as easily say, "As the family goes, so goes the parish, and so goes the Church in which we live" — for our parishes are made up of families, and every child with a vocation to the priesthood and religious life is born within a family. For this reason, Pope Benedict has said, "The family ... is the cradle of life and of every vocation" (Angelus, February 4, 2007).

For all of these reasons, the family has a privileged place in handing on the faith. The *Catechism* states that "parents receive the responsibility of evangelizing their children" and calls them the "first heralds" of the faith (2225). The family is called "domestic church" — the church of the home (2224).

Here, we will explore five aspects of the divine pedagogy and how they relate to the family. The implications of these five aspects of divine pedagogy for parent-child relationships will be discussed, and particularly the role of parents as teachers. Practical recommendations will be offered for those involved in family life education and ministry.

FIVE ASPECTS OF THE DIVINE PEDAGOGY
God's Pedagogy Is Invitational and Welcoming

"For man would not exist were he not created by God's love and constantly preserved by it; and he cannot live fully according to truth unless he freely acknowledges that love and devotes himself to His Creator" (*Gaudium et Spes*, 19). These words from the Second Vatican Council speak to the truth that only God fully knows each of us, because he is our Creator. Because of his intimate knowledge of humanity in general and each person in particular, God reaches out to us in a manner that fully reflects our human experience, our current situation, our ability, and our need.

Use of Human Experience

The field of cognitive psychology postulates that each person interprets the world in light of his or her own schemata — sets of assumptions and beliefs, largely based on his or her own experience, that assist individuals in incorporating and classifying new information (Neisser 1967). Designed by God to receive his self-revelation, we are created such that our natural human experiences provide both opportunities to learn about God and bases for reflection on principles of faith. In this way, personal experience assists us in growing in knowledge of, and relationship with, our Creator. The *General Directory for Catechesis* states, "experience, assumed by faith, becomes in a certain manner, a *locus* for the manifestation and realization of salvation" (152).

Adaptation to Culture and Situation

The *General Directory for Catechesis* states that God, "assumes the character of the person, the individual and the community according to the conditions in which they are found" (139). Quoting Saint John Chrysostom, the Second Vatican Council speaks of the "marvelous 'condescension' of eternal wisdom … 'that we may learn the gentle kindness of God, which words cannot express, and how far He has gone in adapting His language with thoughtful concern for our weak human nature.' For the words of God, expressed in human language, have been made like human discourse, just as the word of the eternal Father, when He took to Himself the flesh of human weakness, was in every way made like men" (*Dei Verbum*, 13). In revealing himself to humankind, God speaks in a language that humans can understand. This is seen most clearly in the Incarnation, as mentioned above, but additional examples include Jesus' teaching in parables, which were generally stories about ordinary persons and situations within the context of the culture and time. Adaptation to culture is seen in a striking way on the feast of Pentecost, in which the Holy Spirit enables the Gospel message to be heard by each person in his or her own tongue (Acts 2:7–9, NAB). A further example is seen in the teaching of Saint Paul in the Areopagus, as he uses the Athenians' altar to "an unknown god" as a point of entry to preach the Gospel (Acts 17:22–31).

God's adaptation of his Word to culture and situation has important implications not only for our catechesis of others, but also for our proper understanding of Sacred Scripture. This is discussed in *Dei Verbum*:

> " ... since God speaks in Sacred Scripture through men in human fashion, the interpreter of Sacred Scripture, in order to see clearly what God wanted to communicate to us, should carefully investigate what meaning the sacred writers really intended, and what God wanted to manifest by means of their words." (12)

Accommodation for Particular Needs

In our attempt to comprehend God, we are limited by our humanity. God, however, enters into solidarity with us, coming to us in the person of Jesus Christ, who accepted the limitations of humanity so that we might enter into relationship with him.

> God, wishing to speak to men as friends, manifests in a special way his pedagogy by adapting what he has to say by solicitous providence for our earthly condition. (*GDC*, 146)

We can observe several examples in Scripture of God himself, as well men and women who are led by God, accommodating not only for the deficiencies of the human condition in general, but for various particular needs of individuals. For example, one might say that Saint Peter was impulsive. He was inattentive to Jesus at times, and likely to speak or act without thinking things through. Yet his gifts of leadership, his boldness, his ability to get others' attention, led Jesus to choose Peter as our first pope, and he remains one of the greatest saints in our history.

In Mark 2:1–12, we read the story of a person with physical disabilities whose friends want him to meet Jesus. Jesus is speaking in a house, and the crowds are so great that the men cannot even get their friend, whom they are carrying on a mat, in the door. They take him to the roof, cut a hole in the roof and lower him through.

In the book of Acts, Saint Philip encounters an Ethiopian who is traveling through the desert. He is reading passages of prophecy that related to the Messiah, but lacking both the context of Jewish tradition and the knowledge of recent events concerning Jesus, he is unable to make sense of what he reads. Philip offers to help, and after some study and discussion, the Ethiopian responds to the Gospel message by being baptized.

God reaches out beyond the limits of human persons and finds a way to draw us to himself. In the Father's relationship with his people Israel, Christ's willingness to accept the limitations of becoming a human being, and the Holy Spirit's work in the apostles of Jesus, we can see God's desire to meet our particular needs and challenges, for his "power is made perfect in weakness" (2 Cor 12:9).

The Family Mirrors the Invitational and Welcoming Pedagogy of God

A married couple mirrors God's invitational and welcoming pedagogy, first when they invite one another into this unique relationship (i.e., through the courtship and marriage proposal), and then when they are open to the new life that could come as the fruit of their physical union. And when pregnancy has been achieved, the mother and father prepare for this new life in multiple ways; for example, by creating a space for the new child in the home, buying baby supplies, and celebrating the coming child with family and friends. Similarly, a couple that chooses to adopt mirrors God's invitational and welcoming action toward us. Indeed, in his letter to the Romans, Saint Paul writes that we receive "a spirit of adoption, through which we cry, 'Abba,' Father!'" (Rom 8:15, NAB). God receives us with open arms and calls us sons and daughters. Young children, especially, are fully dependent on their parents, not yet having learned the skills they need for basic survival. They are not able to reciprocate the nurturance they receive from their mothers and fathers, but they are nevertheless "invited" into this "lopsided" relationship by mothers and fathers who have embraced the self-giving nature of parenthood. This mirrors the way in which God, who does not need anything from us, invites us into relationship with himself.

Children's experience of their parents helps them to understand what love is. Through the parents' gift of self as they meet the child's needs for food and drink, security and affection, the child grows in capacity for attachment and relationship and learns how to show love to others. Just as God accommodates for our particular needs, parents do for their children what they cannot yet do for themselves. They even adapt their style of speech for children at various ages, often talking in a different, high-pitched tone to younger children (a practice which child development experts have called "Motherese").

GOD'S PEDAGOGY IS INCARNATIONAL

Unity of Words and Deeds: *Dei Verbum* points out the "inner unity" of deeds and words in God's plan of revelation: "the deeds wrought by God in the history of salvation manifest and confirm the teaching and realities signified by the words, while the words proclaim the deeds and clarify the mystery contained in them" (2). From speaking the universe into existence, to his promise to Noah and his covenants with Abraham and Moses, to the Word made flesh in Jesus Christ, it is evident that God's word becomes action.

God wills that the same unity of words and deeds be expressed in the lives of each Christian. Through our baptism, we have put on Christ. We have been baptized into his death and raised with him to new life. Yet, as Saint Paul says, this new life is Christ living in us. Therefore, while we are no longer bound by the old Mosaic Law, which was fulfilled in Christ, we still have responsibility as disciples of Christ. It is God's grace, received through faith, that saves us. Yet, this is not "cheap grace," as the German theologian Dietrich Bonhoeffer (1963) called it, in which we understand God's grace to mean simply his unconditional mercy and forgiveness, and we assume that we have no responsibility whatsoever. Rather, Scripture tells us, "faith of itself, if it does not have works, is dead" (Jas 2:17, NAB). The Christian community is called to continue Christ's unity of words and deeds by providing a "living catechesis" (*GDC*, 141). We have especially recognized the great example that is given to us in the saints, who allowed God's Word to take root in their lives and produce heroic Christian virtue. We are called to cooperate with the grace God gives us, a grace that enables us to follow Christ and live the lives for which God created us. This theology of discipleship is especially important in the lives of catechists, who are called not only to be disciples, but to "make disciples" (Mt 28:19, NAB).

With respect to the Eucharist, Saint Augustine admonished his followers, "Receive what you are. Become what you receive." As Christians, we are all parts of the Body of Christ, and as we receive the Body of Christ in the Eucharist, we are called to form ourselves more and more to the image of Christ in our everyday action. God forms us by allowing us to grow in holy action through his gift of sanctifying grace, "a stable and supernatural disposition that perfects the soul itself to enable it to live with God, to act by his love" (*CCC*, 2000). The response of authentic faith to the grace of God causes good works to increase in the lives of the faithful. The Book of James states:

> So also faith of itself, if it does not have works, is dead.
> Indeed someone might say, "You have faith and I have works." Demonstrate your faith to me without works, and I will demonstrate my faith to you from my works. (2:17–18, NAB)

God's Holy Spirit, dwelling within the hearts of the faithful, serves as pedagogue, instructing the Christian in the ways of God, and the gifts of the Spirit bear visible fruits: charity, joy, peace, patience, kindness, goodness, generosity, gentleness, faithfulness, modesty, self-control, and chastity (see CCC 1832; Gal 5:22–23).

A Pedagogy of the Senses: From the very beginning of time, God, who desires to enter into relationship with humanity, has revealed himself to men and women in a variety of ways. *Dei Verbum* states that God "gives men an enduring witness to Himself in created realities" (3). Saint Paul points out that God reveals himself in creation itself: "Ever since the creation of the world, his invisible attributes of eternal power and divinity have been able to be understood and perceived in what he has made" (Rom 1:20, NAB). Jesus himself taught not only through words, but also through his healings and other miracles and his compassionate example as he cared for the poor and marginalized. As he taught about God's kingdom, Jesus frequently cited visible illustrations of what he was teaching. For example, on one occasion when he was teaching his disciples about humility (Mt 18:1–6), he brought a small child for them to see as an example of what God wants us, spiritually, to be. Jesus was a keen observer of his environment, and he watched for concrete examples of the principles he wanted his disciples to live. "Jesus perfected revelation by fulfilling it through his whole work making himself present and manifesting Himself: through His words and deeds, His signs and wonders, but especially through his death and glorious resurrection from the dead and final sending of the Spirit of truth" (*Dei Verbum*, 4).

Early Christian teachers followed Christ's example of multisensory methodology. Saint Paul, for example, taught both by preaching and the written word. He also used visual aids at times to engage his listeners; for example, the previously mentioned altar to an "unknown God" (Acts 17:22–34, NAB). The Church continued this tradition of multisensory methodology, further developing the signs of sacramental rites as well as using music and the visual arts to tell the Gospel story. The Church has enjoyed a rich history of painting, sculpture, music, and dramatic arts. Masterpieces like the works of Michelangelo testify to the importance that has been placed on this multisensory tradition. In recent decades, Catholic films and television programs have been produced to teach others about the Faith. In Mass today (particularly on important feast days), we might have the opportunity to smell incense, hear music, view beautiful icons and stained-glass windows, move into various prayer postures (e.g., kneeling and standing), and even taste Jesus under the signs of consecrated bread and wine.

Christocentric: The unity of God's words and deeds, the Incarnation of his revelation, is seen most fully in the person of Jesus Christ. "In these last days, he spoke to us through a son, whom he made heir of all things and through whom he created the universe, who is the refulgence of his glory, the very imprint of his being, and who sustains all things by his mighty word" (Heb 1:2–3, NAB). As Willey (2009) points out, Christ himself, on the road to Emmaus, explains "how all of the Scriptures have reference to Christ and find their fulfillment in him."

THE FAMILY MIRRORS THE INCARNATIONAL PEDAGOGY OF GOD

God's incarnational pedagogy is mirrored in parenthood from the very beginning. In God's plan for Marriage, the husband and wife, having been joined in the bonds of sacramental Marriage, share in the life and love of God himself. The fruit of the free, total, and faithful love between husband and wife may quite literally produce a third person — a child. The *Catechism of the Catholic Church* states, "The Christian family is a communion of persons, a sign and image of the communion of the Father and the Son in the Holy Spirit" (2205).

The love of God is enfleshed in the family as family members not only say "I love you," but show that they love one another through their actions. Parents serve as living witnesses of our faith in the examples they set for their children. As children see their parents pray, worship God, practice works of mercy, resolve disagreements, and use their talents in meaningful work both within and outside the home, children learn what it means to be disciples of Jesus Christ.

Mirroring God's multisensory methodology, parents tell, show, and engage their children in practicing the things they need to learn about life and faith. They provide experiences for their children in the various places they take them and the toys, books, and other learning tools that enrich the child's environment. Just as God's pedagogy finds its apex in the person of Jesus Christ, so the family, fully expressed in God's plan, is formed as the domestic church, the Body of Christ in the home.

GOD'S PEDAGOGY IS COMMUNAL

God is love (1 Jn 4:8), and he has created us to love and serve him and one another. It is through relationship with him and with others that he teaches us these truths. God initiates this relationship with us through the desire for God that is written into the human heart (*CCC* 27). God seeks and welcomes us as friends, desiring to enter into intimate relationship with each of us:

Through this revelation, therefore, the invisible God (see Col 1:15; 1 Tm 1:17), out of the abundance of his love, speaks to men as friends (see Ex 33:11; Jn 15:14–15) and lives among them (see Bar 3:38), so that he may invite and take them into fellowship with himself (*Dei Verbum*, 2).

A Communion of Persons: God's nature is one of love and communion, for the Holy Trinity is a communion of persons, three, yet mysteriously one. It is God's plan to teach us about his communal nature from the very beginning of our lives, for he has designed the family as a communion of persons as well (*CCC* 2205).

The Ministry of Jesus: Jesus spent a great deal of his ministry forming and nurturing relationships. This frequently happened around meals — from the wedding feast and Cana to the Last Supper, to the post-Resurrection meals such as the breakfast on the seashore with his disciples and the meal on the road to Emmaus in which "he was made known to them in the breaking of the bread" (Lk 24:13–35, NAB). Jesus sends his disciples to teach in groups of two (Mk 6:7). At the Last Supper, he clearly expresses his will that his followers continue to grow in communion with one another, stating "I give you a new commandment: love one another. As I have loved you, so you also should love one another" (Jn 13:34). The command to love one's neighbor was not a new commandment, as Jesus had previously spoken at length on this (see Lk 10:25–37). Therefore, this "new commandment" to love one another implies something more than merely showing love or mercy to another. Rather, one may argue that Jesus intended to call his disciples to a *relationship* of mutual self-gift.

Christ and the Church: God also chose the family, and marriage in particular, to reveal to us the mystery of his relationship with humankind; specifically, the relationship between Christ and his Church (Eph 5:21–33). Husband and wife are called to offer themselves to one another in self-giving love; and in doing so, they both model and experience the relationship between God and his people.

The Ecclesial Community as Family: The larger Church is also designed by God as a family, with God as Father (Eph 4:6). By virtue of our baptism, we are adopted as sons and daughters of God (Rom 8:14–17) and live as brothers and sisters in Christ. This familial character of the people of God is important in two ways. First, God chooses to reveal himself to us as Father, using the human experiences of parenthood and childhood to help us understand God and our relationship with him. (One may even go so far as to assume that God created marriage and parenthood to reveal these truths.) Second, God establishes the community of faith as a family, a communion of persons, showing us that we need one another to make this journey.

THE FAMILY MIRRORS THE COMMUNAL PEDAGOGY OF GOD

The family is, for most of us, the first place in which we experience relationship, beginning with the process of infant-parent attachment. When the parent responds to the cries of a baby for food and drink, security, attention, and affection, the infant learns that people can be trusted, and the capacity for relationship grows in the developing brain. From this initial primary attachment flow secondary attachments, including other family members and caregivers — and, as the child grows, peers and other significant persons. This process of attachment reflects the reality that we are created by God to be in communion with one another. This truth is first experienced in the family.

In addition to the previously stated ways in which the family images the communal pedagogy of God (i.e., the family as image of the communion of the Trinity and of Christ's relationship with the Church), we see this communal pedagogy reflected in other ways in everyday family life. One way in which families do this is through shared rituals. In their book, *Discovering God Together*, Dr. Greg and Lisa Popcak discuss the research on family rituals and routines. Citing research in the social sciences, they state:

> More than sixty years of research shows that, almost more than any other factor, the presence of regular rituals and routines that govern how and how often the family works, plays, talks, and prays together (e.g., family meals, game nights, prayer time, family days, holidays and celebrations, chores, bedtime routines, et cetera) dictates both how stable and how happy that family will be together over time. (Fiese 2006) (Popcak 22)

Just as shared meals were so central to the ministry of Jesus, they are an essential aspect of the way in which the family mirrors God's communal pedagogy. In a 2012 study, the National Center on Addiction and Substance Abuse at Columbia University found that children and teens who regularly eat with their families (five to seven times per week, as opposed to two or fewer times a week) have lower levels of tension and stress at home, are happier and have better peer relationships, get better grades in school, are more likely to confide in their parents, have healthier eating habits, have a lower risk of suicide, and have a much lower risk of substance abuse.

GOD'S PEDAGOGY IS STRUCTURED, SYSTEMATIC, AND COMPREHENSIVE

Systematic and Comprehensive: The *General Directory for Catechesis* says, "God, in his greatness, uses a pedagogy to reveal himself to the human person: he uses human events and words to communicate his plan; he does so progressively and in stages, so as to draw even closer to man. God, in fact, operates in such a manner that man comes to knowledge of his salvific plan by means of the events of salvation history and the inspired words which accompany and explain them" (38). The *Catechism of the Catholic Church* discusses several "stages of revelation" in which God made himself gradually known to his people (54–65). God revealed himself to Adam and Eve, our first parents. He made a covenant with Noah expressing the "principle of the divine economy towards the "nations" (56). God later made a covenant with Abraham, whose descendants became God's chosen people. God freed his people from slavery in Egypt and established a covenant with them, giving them his law (see *CCC* 62; Ex 19:1—20:17). God continued to form his people Israel; and, through the prophets, prepared them for the coming of his Son. "Through the prophets, God forms his people in the hope of salvation, in the expectation of a new and everlasting Covenant intended for all, to be written on their hearts" (*CCC* 64; cf. Is 2:2–4; Jer 31:31–34; Heb 10:16). *Dei Verbum* states, "When God himself spoke to them through the mouths of the prophets, Israel daily gained a deeper and clearer understanding of His ways and made them more widely known among the nations" (14).

Jesus comes as the last and definitive revelation of God, for he is the incarnation of the complete Word of God, and the Covenant established through him is everlasting (*CCC* 65–66). Therefore, it can be seen that God's pedagogy toward humanity is both systematic (God reveals himself over time, as his people are ready and able to understand and accept) and comprehensive (through Jesus, God has made his revelation of himself complete). As the Church continues to interpret this complete revelation of God, she goes forth with Christ's promise that the Holy Spirit will guide her "to all truth" (Jn 16:13).

What God does with all humankind, he also does with the individual person. The *General Directory for Catechesis* states that God "causes the person to grow progressively and patiently towards the maturity of a free son, faithful and obedient to his word" (139).

Structured and Disciplined: In addition, God's message is at once structured and imposes structure. It demands discipline of the student, and it imposes both limits and consequences. Scripture states that God disciplines those he loves (Heb 12:6). Rules and guidelines are sometimes associated with restrictions on freedom, but God's commandments are designed to give us the freedom to be the people he made us to be. The *Catechism* says, "Called to beatitude but wounded by sin, man stands in need of salvation from God. Divine help comes to him in Christ through the law that guides him and the grace that sustains him" (1949).

Gradual and Adaptive, But Not Relativistic: It is useful to make one additional point here regarding the truths taught by God to humankind. While God reveals himself gradually and adapts his message to various times, cultures, and situations, God does not contradict himself. Contemporary thinkers often echo the words of Pontius Pilate, who said not "What is *the* truth?" but "What *is* truth?" (Jn 18:38, italics added), implying that there may be no absolute truth at all. In an era when relativism, or even nihilism, is seen as the ultimate "truth," the Christian message is distinct: There is a truth, and it can be found.

THE FAMILY MIRRORS THE STRUCTURED, SYSTEMATIC AND COMPREHENSIVE PEDAGOGY OF GOD

Parents who are attuned to their child's abilities and needs understand that children acquire knowledge and skills gradually in ways commensurate with their growth. They understand that life lessons must be presented gradually and systematically. Competent parents do not try to teach infants to tie their shoes or encourage preschoolers to balance a checkbook. Rather, they present these life lessons as their children are ready and able to receive them.

At these various stages throughout the life of a child and teen, parents provide structure — guidelines and rules for their children. These rules provide a sense of security for the child and help the child to develop the self-discipline necessary to become a responsible adult. This is most effective when parents are aware of the balance necessary between providing enough structure for children to gain new skills, such as self-regulation, but enough flexibility within the limits to allow children and teens to practice the skills they are learning while they are still in the supportive environment of the family.

The structure parents provide should be gradual and adaptive, but this is not relativistic. There are truths about life that can and must be handed down. Rather than stifling the child, holding fast to principles gives children the freedom that can only be found in self-discipline and self-mastery.

GOD'S PEDAGOGY IS PERPETUAL

God has always existed, and since the beginning of time has invited humanity to learn of him. God's truth, wherever it is proclaimed, perpetuates itself until it accomplishes his will. Isaiah 55:11 states, "So shall my word be that goes forth from my mouth; It shall not return to me void, but shall do my will, achieving the end for which I sent it."

God's truths are handed on through the generations in the forms of Scripture and Sacred Tradition, which is the living memory of the Church. God's covenants do not end, but they come to greater fulfillment and realization.

In baptism, each follower of Christ is sent forth as missionary. In his encyclical letter *Redemptoris Missio*, Saint John Paul II wrote, "The mission *ad gentes* is incumbent upon the entire People of God. Whereas the foundation of a new church requires the Eucharist and hence the priestly ministry, missionary activity, which is carried out in a wide variety of ways, is the task of all the Christian faithful" (71). We are called to share Christ in word and action, first in the home, but also in the parish, the larger community, and in a particular way with the poor and marginalized.

THE FAMILY MIRRORS THE PERPETUAL PEDAGOGY OF GOD

God calls us outside ourselves and our home. Just as God himself is a communion of persons that does not stay closed in on itself, a family, as a communion of persons and a sign of God's love, is called to send forth its unique gifts in order to accomplish God's will in our world. When family members go out in daily life, and when children become adults and leave the home, they carry the family, and the family's mission, with them.

Families mirror the perpetual pedagogy of God when they use their gifts not only to serve one another, but also to serve the Church, the community, and those in need. Families begin this service outside the home when parents model it for their children and involve their children in activities of service in which families can participate together. As children and teens get older, parents help them to identify their God-given talents and nurture the gifts they have been given, encouraging their daughters and sons to use their gifts for the good of others. Finally, parents carry a hope that their children will carry forward the lessons they have learned in the family, practicing them in their adult lives and eventually handing them on to future generations.

IMPLICATIONS AND RECOMMENDATIONS FOR THOSE INVOLVED IN FAMILY LIFE EDUCATION AND MINISTRY

In order to assist families in responding to God's call to image the divine pedagogy, a few things are necessary. One urgent task is to help families know him whom they are called to image. Families cannot be effective in mirroring the pedagogy of God unless they know God. In a post-Christian culture, renewed efforts at evangelization are essential — first for helping families find eternal salvation, but also for helping families find harmony and joy by living their lives according to God's plan.

This brings us to a second urgent task. Not only do families today need to know God and his Church, they also need a clear, meaningful, and practical understanding of the Church's teachings on the family. Faithfully mirroring the divine pedagogy in family life requires the willingness to give ourselves freely, totally, faithfully, and fruitfully in marriage. It means being open to life and drawing upon God's grace to seek the best for our spouses and children. In a generation in which even the definition of marriage and family is ambiguous, the Church must present a clear and positive proclamation of the beauty of the family according to God's design.

Finally, we must educate families about, model, and coach specific practices that strengthen the family. Research in the social sciences, such as the study on family meals cited above, can assist us in helping families realize the importance of shared experiences and intentional practices that will help families become what they are called to be. Helping parents learn about child and adolescent cognitive, socioemotional, and spiritual development can give them the tools they need to respond more effectively to their child's needs. Finally, supporting families through struggles will provide encouragement that families need to persevere in faith and to grow in holiness.

DISCUSSION QUESTIONS

1. Do parents in our community recognize their primary role as educators in the faith? How might this be imparted in a positive way to parents (i.e., as a joy and privilege)?
2. How might we better evangelize families — that is, help them encounter Jesus Christ in a meaningful way and commit to a life of discipleship?
3. How might we implement mechanisms for modeling and coaching specific practices that strengthen the family?

INDEX OF CHURCH DOCUMENTS REFERENCED IN THE TEXT

Congregation for the Clergy. *General Directory for Catechesis.* http://
www.vatican.va/roman_curia/congregations/cclergy
/documents/rc_con_ccatheduc_doc_17041998_directory
-for-catechesis_en.html.

Congregation for the Evangelization of Peoples. *Guide for Catechists:
Document of Vocational, Formative and Promotional Orientation of Catechists in the Territories Dependent on the Congregation for the Evangelization of Peoples.* http://www.vatican.va
/roman_curia/congregations/cevang/documents/rc_con
_cevang_doc_19971203_cath_en.html.

"Interdicasterial Commission for the Catechism of the Catholic
Church." *Catechism of the Catholic Church.*

Saint John Paul II. *Catechesi Tradendae.* http://www.vatican.va
/content/john-paul-ii/en/apost_exhortations/documents/hf
_jp-ii_exh_16101979_catechesi-tradendae.html.

Saint John Paul II. *Familiaris Consortio.* http://www.vatican.va
/content/john-paul-ii/en/apost_exhortations/documents
/hf_jp-ii_exh_19811122_familiaris-consortio.html.

Saint John Paul II. *Redemptoris Missio.* http://www.vatican.va/content
/john-paul-ii/en/encyclicals/documents/hf_jp-ii
_enc_07121990_redemptoris-missio.html.

Pontifical Council for the Family. *The Truth and Meaning of Human
Sexuality: Guidelines for Education Within the Family.* http://
www.vatican.va/roman_curia/pontifical_councils/family
/documents/rc_pc_family_doc_08121995_human-sexuality
_en.html.

Sacred Congregation for the Clergy. *General Catechetical Directory.*
http://www.vatican.va/roman_curia/congregations/cclergy
/documents/rc_con_cclergy_doc_11041971_gcat_en.html.

Second Vatican Council. *Lumen Gentium.* https://www.vatican.va
/archive/hist_councils/ii_vatican_council/documents
/vat-ii_const_19641121_lumen-gentium_en.html.

Second Vatican Council. *Dei Verbum.* http://www.vatican.va
/archive/hist_councils/ii_vatican_council/documents

/vat-ii_const_19651118_dei-verbum_en.html.

Second Vatican Council. *Gaudium et Spes*. http://www.vatican.va
/archive/hist_councils/ii_vatican_council/documents
/vat-ii_const_19651207_gaudium-et-spes_en.html.

United States Catholic Conference. *Sharing the Light of Faith: National
Catechetical Directory for Catholics of the United States*. Washington, DC: United States Catholic Conference, 1979.

United States Catholic Conference. *Human Sexuality: A Catholic Perspective for Education and Lifelong Learning*. Washington, DC:
United States Catholic Conference, 1991.

United States Catholic Conference. *Welcome and Justice for Persons
with Disabilities: A Framework of Access and Inclusion*. Washington, DC: United States Catholic Conference, 1998.

United States Conference of Catholic Bishops. *National Directory for
Catechesis*. Washington, DC: USCCB Publishing, 2005.

ADDITIONAL REFERENCES

Augustine of Hippo. "Sermo 227." In *Sermons, Volume III/6 184–299*.
Hyde Park, NY: New City Press, 1993.

Bonhoeffer, Dietrich. *The Cost of Discipleship*. New York: Macmillan
Publishing Corp., 1963.

DiIorio, Colleen, Maureen Kelley, and Marilyn Hockenberry-Eaton.
"Communications About Sexual Issues: Mothers, Fathers, and
Friends." *Journal of Adolescent Health* 24, no. 3 (1999): 181–189.

Fiese, Barbara. *Family Routines and Rituals*. New Haven, CT: Yale University Press, 2006.

Gardner, Howard. *Frames of Mind: The Theory of Multiple Intelligences*.
New York: Basic Books, 1983.

Jaccard, James, Patricia J. Dittus, and Vivian V. Gordon. (2000). "Parent-Teen Communication About Premarital Sex: Factors Associated with the Extent of Communication." *Journal of Adolescent Research* 15, no. 2 (March 1, 2000): 187–208.

Karofsky, Peter S., Lan Zeng, and Michael R. Kosorok. Relationship
Between Adolescent-Parental Communication and Initiation of
First Intercourse by Adolescents. *Journal of Adolescent Health*

28, no. 1 (2001): 41–45.

Lederman, Regina P., Wenyaw Chan, and Cynthia Roberts-Gray. "Sexual Risk Attitudes and Intentions of Youth Aged 12–14 Years: Survey Comparisons of Parent-Teen Prevention and Control Groups." *Behavioral Medicine* 29, no. 4 (August 7, 2010): 155–163.

National Center on Addiction and Substance Abuse. *The Importance of Family Dinners VIII: A CASAColumbia White Paper.* New York, NY: Columbia University, 2012.

Neisser, Ulric. *Cognitive Psychology.* New York: Appleton-Century-Crofts, 1967.

Popcak, Dr. Greg A. and Lisa. *Discovering God Together: The Catholic Guide to Raising Faithful Kids.* Bedford, NH: Sophia Institute Press, 2015.

Resnick, Michael, Peter S. Bearman, Robert Wm. Blum, et al. "Protecting Adolescents from Harm: Findings from the National Longitudinal Study on Adolescent Health." *Journal of the American Medical Association* 278, no. 10 (September 10, 1997): 823–832.

Whitaker, Daniel, and Kim Miller. "Parent-Adolescent Discussions About Sex and Condoms: Impact on Peer Influences of Sexual Risk Behavior." *Journal of Adolescent Research* 15, no. 2 (March 2000): 251–273.

Willey, Petroc. *Introductory Paper, Catechetical Conference on the Pedagogy of God.* Rome.

CHAPTER SEVENTEEN

A Spirituality of the Home

———————

TIM AND SUE MULDOON

Authors of Six Sacred Rules for Families, The Discerning Parent, *and* Reclaiming Family Time, *and frequent speakers on the spirituality of family life.*

FIVE QUICK TAKES

1. A fruitful metaphor for considering a spirituality of the home is that of the shared journey or pilgrimage, with lessons learned along the way.

2. It is important to develop shared language and practices in a deliberate way, mindful of the changes that happen at different life stages.

3. A spirituality of the home is *perichoretic* (Greek: "making room all around") and mirrors the dynamic love of the triune God.

4. Ignatian practices are apt for this kind of spirituality, including practices of discernment and indifference.

5. The parish can be the place that journeys along with families, a community of fellow pilgrims.

Family life is a shared journey. It is characterized by the willingness of adults to walk with children toward an often unclear future. Clambering toward both specific goods as well as more distant hopes, it is a journey rooted in faith and practiced in love. Yet it can be a difficult journey for many, involving hardships of every sort. Not all who embark on this journey are able to continue; and some even find themselves severely injured along the way. Still, those who take it allow themselves to be fundamentally changed by their fellow travelers.

A spirituality appropriate to such a journey must, then, take into account the twists and turns, strategies and ad hoc tactics, misdirections and side routes that characterize wayfaring. In this essay, we will explore the theological and practical foundations for a spirituality rooted in Catholic faith, paying particular attention to the Ignatian tradition for reasons that will become clear below. Our aim is to provide some contours for a spirituality of the home that echoes the spiritual traditions of other forms of Christian vocation: monastic, mendicant, missionary, and others that involve formation in a "rule of life." While it is not possible to articulate a single rule for family life, given the vast array of circumstances facing different families, we believe that it is still possible to root a spirituality of the home in the metaphor of a shared journey, and suggest some appropriate practices.

A SHARED JOURNEY

Stories of shared journeys pervade the Bible. The central story of ancient Israel, and indeed of contemporary Judaism, is that of the Exodus: Moses leading the people of Israel to a promised land, enduring the grumbling of his people all along the way. In the New Testament, we see Jesus' meanderings around Israel with the disciples, culminating in his journey to Jerusalem and crucifixion. After the Resurrection, the story of the Road to Emmaus — itself a kind of parable — unfolds as a journey with Jesus. Paul's missionary travels, and indeed much of Paul's language about the life of faith, show faith as a journey toward God.

In suggesting that family life is a shared journey, then, we propose that by paying attention to these stories, we can discover clues about what constitutes a spirituality of the home.

EXODUS

Every year during Passover, Jews around the world celebrate the Seder to reflect on the Israelite exodus from Egypt. This practice, embedded for generations in family traditions, is more than an act of memory. It is a participation in the Exodus itself, a re-enactment of the journey from slavery to freedom in the promised land. The fact that children have roles in this drama is important: They too become participants in the Israelite story, and not merely passive recipients of someone else's story. They learn the significance of all the elements in the story: eating the karpas that recall the backbreaking labor of their ancestors; breaking the matzah to remember God's leading the people through the sea; leaving a glass of wine for Elijah, the harbinger of the Messiah.

The Seder — which gained new meaning for early Christians recalling the Last Supper — provides a template for considering several elements of a spirituality of the home today. We'll focus on three points: the shared story; the importance of shared practices; and the importance of ritual.

THE SHARED STORY

Fundamental to a spirituality of the home — as distinct from a spirituality of an individual in the home — is a shared story, celebrated in ways that are clear to all who are part of the family. The story will be different for each family, but the key point is that all members are actors in the story and not merely observers. Elements of the story might include the families of origin of each parent; how they met; marriage; birth or adoption days; key early childhood memories; stories of where the family lived or moved; important family milestones; sports, music, or other important activities; and so on.

Ordinary family life commonly involves celebrations of the shared story, in events such as anniversary celebrations, birthday or name days, and rites of passage like anniversaries, baptisms, first Communions, confirmations, weddings, and funerals. We note here, especially, the fact that the sacraments of initiation can be important milestones in a family story, and are opportunities to reflect and build on the story. To the extent that parishes can offer opportunities for families to reflect on their story, they will enhance the experience.[1]

The practical implication of seeing the family story as a cornerstone of the spirituality of a home is that it is important to take advantage of every opportunity to celebrate the story, and each family member's role within it. Many families, of course, already do this — and this point is important to acknowledge, because what we are proposing is fundamentally an approach to spirituality that follows the basic contours of attentiveness to God's "already-thereness" in the life of a family. Unlike the major spiritual movements that have emerged over the course of the Church's history, many of which have drawn individuals into communities distinct from families of origin, the spirituality of the home invites parents and children to live out their baptismal vocation within the

---

1. Note, to use one example, that the practice of baptism in many parishes is rather *pro forma*. It can be an opportunity for profound evangelization, especially in light of the fact that many young families (Millennials and later) are showing increasing disaffiliation from the Church. See Robert J. McCarty and John M. Vitek, *Going Going Gone: The Dynamics of Disaffiliation in Young Catholics* (Winona, MN: Saint Mary's Press, 2018).

context of everyday life.[2] Thus the shared story, and opportunities for reflecting and building upon it, are cornerstones of this spirituality — the prerequisites for rooting the spirituality in each member's growing identity as a participant in a domestic church.

THE IMPORTANCE OF SHARED PRACTICES

Shared practices are what build and deepen each member's participation in the life journey that is a family. Especially with children, who learn through tactile and emotional behavior, concrete practices are formative.

We have argued that the celebration of the Mass is the Catholic practice par excellence, and that it is important to invite children at all stages of life to deepen their faith as they grow more and more aware of the meaning of this practice.[3] Yet even as the "source and summit" of Christian life,[4] the Eucharist is itself not the most fundamental of practice of a spirituality of the home. Much more fundamental are those shared practices that emerge over the course of everyday life: preparing and eating meals; cleaning the home; going to school; playing games; going on vacation; and many others. The first emphasis is that these practices are shared: They are rooted in a basic faith that a life lived for others carries richness. Pastoral ministers are in a position to remind parents that holiness in the family arises first from these shared practices. Whether at baptismal preparation, conversations around religious education, or simply daily encounters, those who are in positions of influence can help parents to understand that just about any practice shared with children — doing dishes or homework, going to the park, cleaning around the house — is an opportunity for growth.

We might observe here that an orientation of the self toward the other is rooted in a theological conviction that human life mirrors the divine life. A spirituality of the home might thus be described theologi-

---

2. Note the Synoptic Gospels' strong emphasis on discipleship as a movement away from the home, as in Mt 10:35–37 ("I have come to set a man against his father"); 12:46–50 ("whoever does the will of my Father in heaven is my brother, and sister and mother"); Lk 14:26 ("If anyone comes to me and does not hate his own father and mother … he cannot be my disciple").
3. See our book *Reclaiming Family Time: A Guide to Slowing Down and Savoring the Gift of One Another* (Frederick, MD: The Word Among Us Press, 2017), 48–50.
4. *Catechism of the Catholic Church*, 1324–1327; cf. *Lumen Gentium*, 11.

cally as fundamentally perichoretic (Greek: *peri-choreo*, "making room all around"),[55] meaning that it is about making room for all members of the family to thrive. Church Fathers such as John Damascene[66] applied the term perichoresis to the relations within the Trinity, emphasizing the shared essence of the Father, Son, and Holy Spirit. It is noteworthy that Jesus' own use of family terms, such as "Father" and "Son," suggest that familial relationships provide the closest analogue to the perichoretic love within the godhead. We defer this theological exploration for another time, but wish only to suggest here that shared life within a family reflects a fundamental orientation of free persons living in love for one another, making room for one another, and that this orientation can be understood to be rooted in God's creation of persons capable of reflecting the divine image and likeness.

The development of shared practices at all stages of a family life cycle leads to a host of goods. Not only will they reap the benefits of the practice itself, whether guitar playing, cooking, soccer, reading, or anything else, but they also will also benefit from the formation in sociality — that cluster of "soft skills" that enable people to thrive in the context of other people. Today, parents must approach these goods with greater intentionality than might have prevailed in earlier generations, in large part (we are finding) because of the fragmenting effect of technology. For the sake of brevity, we will simply point to the studies that raise important questions about screen use, and the concerns that screens and other forms of technology impinge on the formation of shared practices.[7]

Emphasizing shared practices as a cornerstone of the spirituality of the home means always discerning how to invite toddlers, adolescents, teens, and young adults throughout the family life cycle. Some practices will remain much the same: We address these rituals below. Others — and indeed, the vast majority — will change as a family grows. What may be a delightful practice with small children will seem hopelessly

---

5. For an extended reflection on the rhythms of family life exemplifying "making room" (*choreo*), see *Reclaiming Family Time*, 92–95.

6. John Damascene, *Of the Orthodox Faith* I.8.

7. For an overview of many concerns, and a bibliography of studies that address them, see Jean Twenge, *iGen: Why Today's Super-Connected Kids Are Growing Up Less Rebellious, More Tolerant, Less Happy — and Completely Unprepared for Adulthood — and What That Means for the Rest of Us* (New York: Atria Books, 2017).

outdated with teenagers. Parents must embrace communication, flexibility, and willingness to adapt.

THE IMPORTANCE OF RITUAL

Rituals are repeated practices invested with meaning over time. Family rituals emerge for different reasons, either as inheritances from older traditions (like putting up a Christmas tree) or as practices that emerge from a particular family story. In our family, for example, celebrations of both birthdays and adoption days are yearly rituals. The focal point of ritual is the value it expresses: In our example, that focal point is the celebration of the adoption that has made the child a part of the family.

Religions function in large part through rituals, which focus a community's attention on a central mystery of faith. The example of the Seder meal above is suggestive of how important ritual is to a spirituality of the home. In this example, it explicitly connects the sociality of the family meal with the long story of Israel. While it is tempting to suggest that the Eucharist functions similarly within Catholic tradition, an important difference is that usually the Eucharist does not take place within the context of the home. What, then, might be some ways that Catholic families might similarly connect sociality and religious practice?

For our family, one ritual over the course of nearly twenty years of parenting has been the grace before meals. The words have changed with our children's capacity to understand, but the basic practice of giving thanks remains the same. This daily ritual draws attention to the focal point of practicing gratitude before God with the sociality and practices proper to an evening meal. In recent months, we have found ourselves making this ritual — and, more fundamentally, the practice of a shared meal — more deliberate. We have observed how easy it is to allow different commitments to get in the way of this ritual, and have tried to reestablish its importance in our family life.

Another ritual we have used in different ways over the years, in age-relevant ways, is various forms of reflection on the day, a ritual rooted in the Ignatian prayer of Examen. We invite our children to give thanks for the events of the day, and review them in order that they may attend to the feelings they evoke. Part of the point is to develop the habit of gratitude, but also to see the ways that God has been present in the highs and lows of life.

Other families we know have used a number of Catholic rituals to good effect: a family Rosary; regular confession; reading the Bible together; and many others. Yearly rituals around major celebrations (Christmas, Easter, and others) similarly help chart the course of a family's life and create lasting memories.

The family celebration of the Mass is certainly important at every stage of life. But children's participation in this ritual changes over time, and so we have found that it is important to have a certain flexibility in our expectations of the ways they participate in it. To be sure, we have made it a central part of our family life, but we are also aware of the pushes and pulls in many families' lives that make regular Mass-going difficult. For some, it is because one spouse is not Catholic; for others, it may be because of various difficulties with the Church; while for others, it may be rooted in spiritual, psychological, or practical difficulties. In any case, pastoral ministers must invite families to Mass with the strong message that it is a place where the whole community of faith celebrates its participation in the mission given us by Christ. The point is not to convey any note of judgment toward those families whose participation is irregular, but rather to gently invite them to understand and embrace its importance in the community of faith.

THE JOURNEY OF DISCIPLESHIP

The Gospels are fundamentally journey stories: the Father sending his Son into the world on a mission of reconciliation, drawing disciples into his mission, going to his death, rising as the one who defeats death, and returning to his Father in order to then send the Holy Spirit to continue the mission.

The theology of the family that has emerged over the past century, and in earnest since the Second Vatican Council, provides a framework within which to consider the spirituality of discipleship proper to the home. If the family is indeed "the domestic church," as *Lumen Gentium* avers,[8] then it is the fundamental unit of society wherein the Kingdom of God unfolds. The home is where heaven begins.

Here some obvious caveats are in order. First: Making this theological claim is (often!) far from a descriptive statement. Few parents we know, ourselves included, are likely on a daily basis to describe their homes as heaven. More often, they are likely — even in the best of circumstances — to describe them as messy places, sometimes physically but often metaphorically.

Second, we recognize that among the millions of homes where families live and grow, there are many where one finds the opposite of heaven: abuse, neglect, addiction, and many other forms of suffering and pain.

The claim that home is the beginning of heaven is a theological and eschatological statement, in the same vein that *Lumen Gentium* makes about the Church, broadly speaking. It reflects a vocational thrust: a call to be what God has created it for. This point becomes clear when considering the journey of discipleship to which Jesus invites his disciples throughout the Gospels. His use of the phrase "the Kingdom of God" and its cognates invites his disciples to discern the kind of world that the Father calls them to build: a world rooted in the divine mercy, called to reconcile those whose lives are marred by sin and the consequences of evil. In the Beatitudes, to use one example, Jesus points to a world that often seems far from reality, where the poor are happy and peacemakers inherit the earth. Underneath what Jesus does and says is an insistent undertone: If you follow me, you will know God and God's justice.

To say that the home is where heaven begins is to echo Jesus' invitation to come along on his journey toward the Father. Taking that journey need not mean leaving home, even though some of the disciples did that. Perhaps it means being more like the disciples Mary, Martha, and Lazarus, whose familial love extended outward toward Jesus so that he too might feel at home in their midst.[9] Perhaps it means that home might be the place where vocations are nurtured, as we see in the Holy Fam-

---

8. Second Vatican Council, *Lumen Gentium,* https://www.vatican.va/archive/hist_councils/ii_vatican_council /documents/vat-ii_const_19641121_lumen-gentium_en.html, par. 11.

9. Jn 11:5 (Jesus loved the siblings Mary, Martha, and Lazarus).

ily of Nazareth.[10] Perhaps it means welcoming children, recalling Jesus' words about how they reveal to us the Kingdom.[11] Perhaps it means recalling God's blessing of marriage in the beginning, and vigilantly nurturing that relationship as a foretaste of the heavenly banquet.[12]

All these Gospel stories point in the direction of the eschaton: What God has already begun through the work of the Holy Spirit reaches its fruition in the fullness of time. Yes, family life is messy. Yes, its protagonists are sinners in constant need of forgiveness. Yes, parents can be very aware of their own shortcomings and poor judgment. And yet the home is still the beginning of heaven, the place where the Holy Spirit transforms ordinary men, women, and children into disciples who, like Jesus' original disciples, stumble toward holiness.

What this theology means practically is that families are all over the map when it comes to the journey of faith. Families seeking holiness might be wrestling with sickness, grief, addiction, mental illness, or the consequences of any number of destructive behaviors. Christian families are not perfect families. They are like the Christian community as a whole: sinners redeemed by the love of Christ, on pilgrimage toward the Father. Their members may sometimes wound one another; they may make poor choices; they may stumble on their pilgrimage. The Church, mindful of these realities, must be the place of reconciliation, of hope, and of beauty. Its ministers — which include both clergy and lay men and women — must practice loving outreach to families that reminds them of the direction in which they are traveling, in a merciful way. Families will be drawn to the Church when they perceive it as the place that nourishes them for the journey of faith, offering forgiveness and consolation in the face of life's difficulties. It will take creativity to consider how to do this, but one thing today is clear: It will have to unfold in many cases outside the walls of the church building.

---

10. Mt 1:24–25 (Joseph took Mary into his home and she gave birth); 13:55 ("Is not this the carpenter's son?").
11. Mt 18:3; Mk 10:14; Lk 18:16 (Let the children come to me).
12. Mt 22:1–4, the parable of the wedding feast.

THE ROAD TO EMMAUS

The story of the disciples on the road to Emmaus is instructive for our deeper understanding of how the ordinary, everyday reality of family life is the beginning of heaven. It is a story of conversion: two disciples walking along a road and having a new insight after they realize Jesus has been walking with them.

They recognize him in the breaking of the bread; and, as a result, they recall how their hearts were burning within them. Luke's description of the story is rather sparse: We don't know what they were talking about, or how exactly Jesus commented on the various Scriptures that referred to him. What Luke focuses on instead is Jesus' very presence with them. He walks with them for a long while without their knowing who it is. On the face of it, this fact is rather surprising: Why did not the Risen Christ spend his precious time more efficiently, perhaps speaking to large crowds and proclaiming his divinity? Luke does not elaborate. Instead, he shows a Jesus who patiently allows the disciples to continue as they are, reflecting on their experiences and the news around Jerusalem.

The breaking of the bread is a moment of insight that transforms understanding of all that has previously happened. That moment is possible only because Jesus has walked with the disciples. In theological language, Jesus has provoked an encounter: He has allowed his companions to share their experiences; and they, in turn, have allowed him to help them understand those experiences.

The insight is the fruit of encounter: They now understand everything through the lens of that agapic love made sacramentally present in the Eucharistic sharing. They are reminded of the profound love that God has shown his people in the sacrifice of his Son, and their world is transformed. What was once confusing is now clear; what was a source of consternation is now a source of consolation.

The story of Emmaus is fundamentally a story about the transformation of memory: anamnesis. From this story we can draw perspective on the unfolding of a family's life story, by paying attention to the ways that ordinary people living ordinary lives can similarly experience the kind of transformation of memory that moves in an eschatological direction.

In some ways, what we are describing here is natural to the life cycle:

Children grow up and develop sophistication in the ways they remember things. The perpetual "now" of early childhood slowly grows into the existential angst of the teen years. The anxious cravings of young adulthood eventually simmer into more sober longings of adulthood. In the process of growing up, memories take on different meaning. Tooth-and-nail fights among childhood siblings might become sources of jokes when they are adults. Painful memories of breakups with boyfriends and girlfriends lose their sting as new relationships emerge and grow. The process of remembering can be a process of healing.

Of course, the reverse is also sadly true. Careless comments from childhood can become lasting sources of pain for teens. Early wounds can fester and grow; anxieties can become crippling; relationships can become irreparably damaged. The process of remembering can also be a source of hurting.

A spirituality of the home builds upon the natural dynamics of memory, in a manner reflecting Aquinas's observation that grace perfects nature.[13] To understand family life through the lens of agapic love, and to practice contemplative reflection on experience, is to walk, as it were, with Christ on the road to Emmaus. It is to see experience through Christ's eyes, and to allow the healing of memory and the emergence of new insight. For this reason, among others, we have found Ignatian spirituality particularly helpful. For the Ignatian tradition is one of carefully discerning one's life as a companion of Jesus (the name Ignatius gave to his nascent order), on a mission in the world.

FAMILY SPIRITUALITY IN AN IGNATIAN KEY

The spiritual practices that shaped the post-conversion life of Ignatius of Loyola, and which constitute his *Spiritual Exercises*, are thoroughly secular, in contrast to the practices proper to monastic traditions. One of the early Jesuits who worked closely with Ignatius in the early years of the Society of Jesus, Jerónimo Nadal, contrasted Jesuit spirituality with monastic spirituality, rooted as it was in the cloistered life of those who seek to create an alternate world, a home for those seeking Christian

---

13. Cf. Thomas Aquinas, *Summa Theologiae*, I.1, q.8, a.2.

perfection. Nadal's famous line was that "the world is our home" — the world, that is, of all those people created by God to live ordinary lives and thereby seek their happiness. Ignatius wrote his *Spiritual Exercises* as a lay person, and early in his public ministry gave them to other lay people seeking to live holy lives in the secular world.

We will focus on two themes in Ignatian spirituality that have struck us as particularly apt for a spirituality of the home: the focus on cultivating discernment and practicing Ignatian indifference.[14]

DISCERNMENT

It is not too broad a claim to suggest that Ignatius wrote his *Spiritual Exercises* as a guide to discernment. He prefaces the text with the epigraph that the *Exercises* are to help a person come to a rightly ordered decision; and, indeed, the thrust of the *Exercises* is to move a person through self-reflection to contemplation of Christ's life, in order that the person may discern the great desires that lead to a life mission of service of the divine will.[15] While Ignatius had in mind primarily the kind of life-shaping decision that a person might make in young adulthood, and secondarily the kind of vocation-affirming decisions that a person might return to in later adulthood, still the practices that he suggests are applicable to young people and even children. Most important, we have written, is the language that Ignatius uses in his First Principle and Foundation: namely, that God creates all people for a purpose, and that we find meaning in discerning which desires move us toward realizing that great purpose.[16]

A spirituality of the home takes seriously this fundamental orientation of discernment: that adults and children alike are created by God for a purpose, and that family life is the place where profound discernment unfolds in all the highs and lows of daily life. The task of parenting involves a constant attention to discernment, both of the specific daily choices the parents must make and of the ways they might cultivate

---

14. We expand on some of these points in *Six Sacred Rules for Families* (Notre Dame, IN: Ave Maria Press, 2013), which are drawn from theses within Ignatius's Principle and Foundation in his *Spiritual Exercises*.

15. References to the *Spiritual Exercises* are the version in George E. Ganss, SJ, ed., *Ignatius of Loyola: The Spiritual Exercises and Selected Works* (Mahwah, NJ: Paulist Press, 1991), shortened to *Spiritual Exercises* followed by the section number in the volume. Here, *Spiritual Exercises*, 21.

16. *Spiritual Exercises*, 23.

an attitude of discernment in their children. We have written about the kinds of opportunities and challenges parents face when their children are teens in our book *The Discerning Parent* (Notre Dame, IN: Ave Maria Press, 2017). An orientation to discernment is ultimately an orientation to live fully and freely in God's grace, and to invite children to realize their freedom through discernment of their desires. Our hope is that this orientation helps to make habitual the question "which desires lead most in the direction of freedom, of hope, of happiness, for myself and those around me?"

The Church is in the position of helping to form parents and children in discernment by helping them develop an imagination of the way that Christ walks with them in their daily lives. The first message of the Church to families, we suggest, is this: "Christ walks with you, and the Church walks with you." Perhaps the best image for this message is that of Matthew 11:28–30:

> Come to me, all you who labor and are burdened, and I will give you rest. Take my yoke upon you and learn from me, for I am meek and humble of heart; and you will find rest for yourselves. For my yoke is easy, and my burden light.

It is good to invite parents and children, again and again, in all life circumstances, to encounter Christ as the one who wishes to lighten our burdens. It is good to invite people to the practice of discernment, and to invite those who have already begun to deepen their practice of it. Practically, this might mean using homilies, children's liturgies of the word, and other non-liturgical opportunities to connect family life to the way of Jesus. It might mean pairing young families with more experienced ones, perhaps in baptismal preparation or sacramental preparation. It might mean offering books or online resources. It might mean doing a parish mission during Lent geared toward children.[17]

---

17. A favorite example is of the Frances Xavier Warde School in Chicago, which for many years has invited children to raise money to benefit children living in mission dioceses of the United States. See https://www.catholicextension.org/stories/growing-generosity-chicago.

IGNATIAN INDIFFERENCE

A corollary to this orientation to discernment is the practice of Ignatian indifference: the freedom to let go of those desires that, while attractive, do not lead in the direction of happiness, freedom, and ultimately holiness.[18] Regular encounter with people on the margins of society can help to foster this kind of indifference, for such encounters can help remind people that Jesus saw through the usual markers of social status.

Every family ought to have opportunities to serve others on the margins. In our parish, there is a monthly opportunity to work directly with the homeless population in Boston, and all our children have participated. Parishes have a particular opportunity to leverage opportunities for service. In our view, parishes or parish collaboratives might consider a staff person dedicated to coordinating service opportunities, vital as they are for the spiritual formation of people of all ages. Rightly practiced, they are opportunities to enter into service with the heart of Christ, and can leave lasting impressions. In an age of religious disaffiliation — which is usually measured by regular participation in liturgy — parish-guided service might well be the critical ember that may later enkindle active faith as young people mature.

CONCLUSION

We have suggested throughout this essay that the spirituality of the home is fundamentally about a shared journey. We have drawn from some of the journey stories in the Old and New Testaments to illustrate some of the characteristics of this journey, and paid particular attention to elements of the Ignatian spiritual tradition of discernment to describe how to proceed on the journey.

We will close by pointing to the particular opportunity presented to parishes in this view of the spirituality of the home. Let us note as a preface that the very word "parish" has an etymology that speaks very well to this opportunity. "Parish" comes from a Latin transliteration of an ancient Greek word, *paroikia*, meaning "sojourning." That word, in turn, is formed from the words *para-oikos,* "next to the home." The parish is

---

18. *Spiritual Exercises*, 23.

the place besides the home where we undertake our journey toward God.

This image, of course, is an ideal, but we wish to suggest it as an opportunity. Parishes have historically been the places where most Catholics live out their faith in the context of family life. There are, of course, many spiritual traditions in the Church that have emphasized different charisms, as we noted earlier. But the charism of family life is a distinctly parochial one, in the sense we are suggesting here: the parish as the place where families journey together toward God.

Today, we cannot be naive as to what the challenges and opportunities are. Many families are fractured; many do not prioritize the religious formation of their children; many find church to be an activity that is far less important than their child's hockey or soccer game. Our sense is that much of the Church's energy in recent decades is a kind of residual inertia from prior generations. What might it look like if parishes were robustly committed to the spiritual accompaniment of families?

The answers, we suggest, will arise with great creativity and spontaneity if moms and dads, grandmothers and grandfathers and children are invited to respond. What might a parish look like if it asked where difficulties in a life's journey happen? A parish's activities need not be exclusively liturgical. Parishes can be places where people share childcare or eldercare; meals; or job-seeking help. They can be places where people get together to do each other's home projects, or rebuild a house in a poor neighborhood. They can be homes to reading groups, cooking or crocheting circles, or any number of other forms of sociality in an increasingly fragmented world. And yes, they can be places where this sociality gives rise to the realization that it is Christ who has pitched his tent among us, inviting us to a heavenly banquet.

DISCUSSION QUESTIONS

1. What images come to mind when you consider the image of family life as a shared journey or pilgrimage? Do you consider your family members as fellow pilgrims? What sustains you on your journey?

2. What are some of the concrete practices by which you celebrate family life? Are there practices you wish to recover from your family of

origin?

3.   What might it mean to you that family life mirrors the divine life? Does this lofty vision offer any perspective on the day-to-day challenges, struggles, or joys of family life?

CHAPTER EIGHTEEN

The Gospel Still Works, Right? So What Have We Been Missing in American Families and Parishes?

DR. WILLIAM KEIMIG

Catechetical Institute, Franciscan University

FIVE QUICK TAKES

1. Personal discipleship to Christ is based on a persuasive, long-term witness of sacrificial accompaniment — others leading the way by immanent example.

2. Most parents can't drive their spiritual life by "high" theological knowledge and proofs only. Most people instead grow by a gentle leading to trust in God — by means of trusting a persuasive witness to Christ's inner life, particularly a witness who is easily accessible to them in their local community or normal life routines.

3. Formation must aim to grow *trust* as the first priority — it is the elemental hinge in all healthy and fruitful relationships between parents and their children and between God the Father and His children.

4. To do this, parents must be engaged at the parish level in an ongoing manner, in a life-fitting manner, and in a witness-based manner — seeking to provide structures of *relationship* and *gentle accountability* as much as materials and faithful, inspiring teachings.

5. A model is suggested here that *both* helps those in parish-level ministry grow as figures capable of authentic accompaniment and provides a structure to engage parents in ways that fit busy lives and attends to the need for long-term engagement.

This essay seeks to aim at one target — how to *reach* parents for the purpose of growing their own spiritual lives and deepening the spirituality of their family life. What are effective access points, in regular parishes, for *ongoing pragmatic engagement* of parents currently raising children?

There are abundant writings and products in every form of media that are faithful, artfully executed, and beautifully helpful. Parishes, however, struggle to connect them to parents in a formative, rather than incidental or occasional manner — to win the busyness battles enough times to not merely have a good contact or two, but to have *consistent formative engagement* that actually results in parents moving to places of new decisions, Gospel habits, countercultural boldness, and Catholic-inspired creativity. It's a plug-in problem — both to get the plug in the socket so the electricity can *begin* to flow, and for it to *stay* in the socket long enough to power great changes in the family.

PART I: PEOPLE IN VARIOUS FORMS OF PARISH MINISTRY BEING AIDES TO OPERATE DIFFERENTLY ...

Let's consider how adult formation can be viewed in a particularly person-to-person direction, in relation to *intimacy* or *immanence* in ministry. Any relationship a person has that draws him into a closer union with Christ is fundamentally a ministry relationship. If the point is *intimacy with Christ* (see *Catechesi Tradendae*, 5, 20), then it could be considered that those who impact the choice of and deepening in that intimacy are those *most* in ministry. If ministry is fundamentally the work of passing on a relationship (with Christ), then those *most* in relationship (with a person to be introduced to or deepened in Christ) or who should be, are prime in consideration as ministers. Instead of ranks or offices having sole priority in defining ministry, this method instead suggests an outcomes-based definition — whoever is best able to foster this kind of intimacy in a given situation should receive the most focused effort of ministry formation in a parish's life.

This concept is founded in Saint Paul's expressions of his closeness to those he sought to grow in the Lord: "Like a mother feeding and looking after her own children, we felt so devoted and protective towards you, and had come to love you so much, that we were eager to hand over to you not only the Good News but our whole lives as well" (1 Thes 2:7–8). To the Corinthians he wrote:

> We put no obstacle in any one's way, so that no fault may be found with our ministry, but as servants of God we commend ourselves in every way: through great endurance, in afflictions, hardships, calamities, beatings, imprisonments, tumults, labors,

watching, hunger; by purity, knowledge, forbearance, kindness, the Holy Spirit, genuine love, truthful speech, and the power of God; with the weapons of righteousness for the right hand and for the left; in honor and dishonor, in ill repute and good repute. We are treated as impostors, and yet are true; as unknown, and yet well known; as dying, and behold we live; as punished, and yet not killed; as sorrowful, yet always rejoicing; as poor, yet making many rich; as having nothing, and yet possessing everything. Our mouth is open to you, Corinthians; our heart is wide. (2 Corinthians 6:3–11)

This unmistakable tone of sacrificial intimacy is echoed in the way the *General Directory for Catechesis* (GDC) expresses the role of catechists:

[The exercise of catechesis] will cause [the catechist] to grow in respect and in love for catechumens and those being catechized: "What is this love? It is the love, not so much of a teacher as of a father, or rather of a mother. It is the Lord's wish that every preacher of the Gospel, every builder up of the Church should have this love" (*CT* 23; cf. *SC* 35). ... The formation, above all, nourishes the *spirituality* of the catechist, so that his activity springs in truth from his own witness of life. (239)

This deeply challenging call has been more recently communicated by Pope Francis, preferring to make use of a term analogous to intimacy and immanence — *accompaniment*:

The Church will have to initiate everyone — priests, religious and laity — into this "art of accompaniment" which teaches us to remove our sandals before the sacred ground of the other (cf. Ex 3:5). The pace of this accompaniment must be steady and reassuring, reflecting our closeness and our compassionate gaze which also heals, liberates and encourages growth in the Christian life. To accompany them would be counterproductive if it became a sort of therapy supporting their self-absorption and ceased to be a pilgrimage with Christ to the Father ... One who accompanies others has to realize that each person's situation before God and their life in grace are mysteries which no one can fully know from without. ... Someone good at such accompaniment does not give in to frustrations or fears. He or she invites others to let themselves be healed, to take up their mat, embrace the cross, leave all behind and go forth ever anew to proclaim the Gospel. Our personal experience of being accompanied and assisted, and of openness to those who accompany us, will teach us to be patient and compassionate with others, and to find the right way to gain their trust, their openness and their readiness to grow. ... Genuine spiritual accompaniment always begins and flourishes in the context of service to the mission of evangelization. Paul's relationship with Timothy and Titus provides an example of this accompaniment and formation which takes place in the midst of apostolic activity. Entrusting them with the mission of remaining in each city to "put in order what remains to be done" (Ti 1:5; cf. 1 Tm 1:3–5), Paul also gives them rules for their personal lives and their pastoral activity. This is clearly distinct from every kind of intrusive accompaniment or isolated self-realization. Missionary disciples accompany missionary disciples. (*Evangelii Gaudium*, 169–170, 172–173)

The way of parsing the concept of ministry is varied: One way is to divide "ministries" along *temporal* grounds (full time/part time). More accepted perhaps is to divide along lines of *authority* (for example, it could be argued that the concept of "extraordinary" ministry is relative to something other than "intimacy" — it is relative to hierarchy). A ministry can also be defined by who has *rights* (in the Church and in the natural law) in an official form (for example, a canonically-installed pastor) or relational form (for example, parents have inalienable rights to form their children due to relationship).

If a sense of being in ministry were also based on levels of *intimacy* or *immanence*, the definition of minister might instead be as follows: *those who, with intention, discern their vocational and life circumstances in light of the baptismal call to foster intimacy with Christ, in and through the Church, primarily by means of personal accompaniment, sacrifice, and witness (by works and words).* Initial discernment of whether to enter a given ministry might take the form of three questions: (1) What are my vocational duties? (2) Whom has God given me to love within those duties? (3) What gifts do I have (natural and supernatural), and how do I need to grow (formation sought within the context of vocational needs)?

CALLED TO HONOR THAT WHICH IS NEAREST

There are other applications of "sense of ministry" being derived from levels of intimacy or immanence. For example, this chiefly explains the primacy of parents in ministry to their children. But it is important to remember that the primary form of catechesis will always be adult to adult (*GDC*, 258). Because of this, it is necessary to ensure that catechesis is delivered to all adults, those newly reached as well as those who have already received the sacraments of initiation — implying a constant accompaniment. Adult accompaniment within a robust ministry of the Word is intended to bear significant fruit. Out of all Christians, "adults have the greatest responsibilities and the capacity to live the Christian message in its fully developed form" (*GDC*, 38) The mature lay Christian is primarily responsible for assisting in the accomplishment of the work of the greater mission of the Church as a whole.

To support the vital need for accompaniment in adult formation, it's useful to express a catechetical form of the principle of *subsidiarity*. For a definition of subsidiarity, the *Catechism of the Catholic Church* states:

> The teaching of the Church has elaborated the principle of *subsidiarity*, according to which "a community of a higher order should not interfere in the internal life of a community of a lower order, depriving the latter of its functions, but rather should support it in case of need and help to coordinate its activity with the activities of the rest of society, always with a view to the common good." (1883)

The principle of subsidiarity stems from the Church's social teaching and is rooted in the fundamental understanding that the human person is the principle subject of every social organization. Because society is founded and centered on the person, the principle of subsidiarity holds that human affairs ought to be dealt with on the lowest possible level — that closest to those affected. Subsidiarity promotes the dignity of the individual person by showing concern for the diverse areas of life and communities in which they are involved, a concern extended to "the family, groups, associations, local territorial realities; in short, for that aggregate of economic, social, cultural, sports-oriented, recreational, professional and political expressions to which people spontaneously give life and which make it possible for them to achieve effective social growth" (Pontifical Council for Justice and Peace, *Compendium of the Social Doctrine of the Church*, 185). The principle of subsidiarity allows for consideration of the whole of society while focusing on the people by whom society is made up. Subsidiarity considers the realm of civil society, which can be understood as "the sum of the relationships between individuals and intermediate social groupings ... [that] strengthens the social fabric and constitutes the basis of a true community of persons" (*CSDC*, 185).

Subsidiarity gives priority to *individual* relationships, the more local the better, allowing such relations to effect positive change within a community. In his landmark social encyclical, *Quadragesimo Anno*, Pope Pius XI gave the classic definition of subsidiarity:

> Just as it is gravely wrong to take from individuals what they can accomplish by their own initiative and industry and give it to the community, so also it is an injustice and at the same time a grave evil and disturbance of right order to assign to a greater and higher association what lesser and subordinate organizations can do. For every social activity ought of its very nature to furnish help to the members of the body social, and never destroy and absorb them. (79)

Making accompaniment a priority in ministry amounts to recognizing that passing on the faith is a *social* activity. All conversion is local, which is why faith formation must remain a robustly supported *local* activity.

From this principle arises the importance of mentorship, and for that guidance to be proximal and personal: a mentoring accompaniment. Failure to honor this principle risks disempowering the local community in favor of a cult of distance experts, and making instruction less able to address individual experiences and learning needs. As the *General Directory for Catechesis* explains:

> Catechetical pedagogy will be effective to the extent that the Christian community becomes a point of concrete reference for the faith journey of individuals. This happens when the community is proposed as a source, locus, and means of catechesis. Concretely, the community becomes a visible place of faith-witness. It provides for the formation of its members. It receives them as the family of God. It constitutes itself as the living and permanent environment for growth in the faith. Besides public and collective proclamation of the Gospel, person-to-person contact, after the example of Jesus and the Apostles, remains indispensable. In this way, personal conscience is more easily committed. The gift of the Holy Spirit comes to the subject from one living person to another. Thus, the power of persuasion becomes more effective. (158)

A NEW SKILL SET TO FORM DISCIPLERS, NOT JUST TEACHERS OF THE FAITH

Any oversight or higher-level formation should be designed to support and complement the formation being undertaken locally and personally, in parishes accompanied by those committed to personally coming to know participants over an extended time. Never forgetting that formation in the faith is always first and foremost God's attentive presence to the *individual*, adult formation should aim at that which best fosters actual *competency* in *those* individuals, rather than solely a generic approach to certifying. This includes encouraging personal accountability to excellence and creating formation structures that train toward effective soul-to-soul persuasion, dialogue, genuine openness to others, and empathic listening — the skill set of personal attentiveness.

This skill set helps those who minister to honor the movements of grace within each person, building people to serve people, encouraging relational ministry, with the goal of helping people discover by experience the value of making the effort to be more personally available to people.

Following this divine pedagogy, the work of forming souls must be attentive to the words of Pope Paul VI in *Evangelii Nuntiandi*:

> [I]n the long run, is there any other way of handing on the Gospel than by transmitting to another person one's personal experience of faith? It must not happen that the pressing need to proclaim the Good News to the multitudes should cause us to forget this form of proclamation whereby an individual's personal conscience is reached and touched by an entirely unique word that he receives from someone else. (46)

This recognizes that the work of forming souls is entrusted to other souls, rather than just the parish catechetical leader, *because* witness has the power to convict. "The one thing most likely to induce the faithful to lead a really Christian life is precisely the virtue of the one charged with teaching it" (Dom Jean-Baptiste Chautard, OCSO, *The Soul of the Apostolate* [Charlotte, NC: TAN Books, 1946] 135). The faith that is passed on is 'of necessity' profoundly personal — from human being to human being. The mature Christian adult has the ability to see himself or herself as a minister of God's own divine providence, called to be his hands, voice, and listening ear in the world.

The importance of individual attentiveness cannot be swallowed in the larger context of forming large numbers of people for the work of catechesis, for "every person, family, and intermediate group has something original to offer the community" (*CSDC*, 187). Faith is nurtured most naturally in a community of individuals centered on shared faith. The community of faith builds itself up as a body and finds individuals — accompanying figures — who can commit to the demanding task of building up the individuals within it, empowering them to strengthen and give back to that community themselves.

AN OLD WAY TO RENEWAL

In Acts 2:41–42, Luke describes the first local Christian community:

> So those who received his word were baptized, and there were
> added that day about three thousand souls. And they devoted
> themselves to the apostles' teaching and fellowship, to the break-
> ing of bread, and the prayers.

As noted in this passage and echoed in the structure of the *Catechism of
the Catholic Church*, four pillars marked this early community's way of
being together: (1) the apostles' teaching (Creed); (2) fellowship (life in
Christ); (3) The breaking of the bread (liturgy, centered on the Eucharist); and (4) the prayers (Christian prayer). Non-local efforts can aid or
enrich these four pillars, but their essence is fundamentally local. Fellowship is profoundly proximal. The Mass, and all sacramental celebrations, exist only when clergy and laity share a sacred space and a personal
moment of offering and reception. And prayers, always stemming from
Jesus' own emphasis, draw the faithful together in community: "If we
pray the Our Father sincerely, we leave individualism behind, because
the love that we receive frees us from it" (*CCC* 2792).

The first pillar, however, the one that encompasses catechesis and
formation in Catholic teaching, is less often recognized as a work self-ev-
idently local. In current times, guest speakers from afar and high-qual-
ity audio and video teachings threaten to replace local catechists. For all
their talent and all they have to offer, guest speakers — whether in person
or via media — are not, by their very nature, connected to those hearing
their presentations. They will never be involved with the ongoing work
of forming and loving any given parish group in any given place. They
are unable to participate in the struggles and graces involved with forming those people.

An over-reliance on distant experts can also undercut a diocese's
commitment to form people locally — a commitment that takes far
greater effort, time, and resources, but which also is able to more fruitfully address the particular needs of a parish, region, or diocese. Pope

Paul VI cut to the heart of this issue in *Evangelii Nuntiandi*: "Modern man listens more willingly to witnesses than teachers, and if he listens to teachers it is because they are witnesses" (41). Although a guest speaker or teacher may have impactful things to say, no teaching cuts to the heart more than that of an authentic witness. It is imperative that catechists give *personal witness* to those they teach.

In keeping with the principle of subsidiarity, this harder way is the Church's way: "The most precious gift that the Church can offer to the bewildered and restless world of our time is to form within it Christians who are confirmed in what is essential and who are humbly joyful in their faith" (Guide for Catechists, 8). To reemphasize, non-local helps and training can aid this first pillar (formation in creedal truths), but its essence remains fundamentally local. The long-term goal should be forming a confident parent in that place, a competent catechist in that place, a capable lay leader in that place, and, most important of all, a clearly empowered chief catechist in that place — a priest whose vocation can become the locus of teaching, community fellowship, liturgy, and prayers, allowing the immanent hospitality of Christ to enliven catechesis with a spirit of human warmth and welcome around that particular altar.

Accompanying figures are absolutely essential to accomplish this kind of formation for evangelization and catechesis to remain appropriately situated with those who can be in authentic ministerial relationships in the field. Accompaniment brings a necessary measure of intimacy, of closeness to those being formed, of sacrificial presence. Saint John Bosco reminds us: "It's not enough to love. People have to feel that they are loved."

An online formation program by Franciscan University of Steubenville's Catechetical Institute has recently been created that is very inexpensive (free to most) and designed for group or individual use. It's called www.FranciscanAtHome.com and includes a set of formation workshops called the Pastoral Accompaniment Track. The primary audience is those working in any ministry setting — clergy or laity — whose interactions with others require mentoring skills, evangelical hospitality, ongoing pastoral interactions in the course of catechetical work, small-group facilitation, parenting, nurturing, and intercessory prayer outreach. Anyone who has some degree of work in the care of souls can benefit significantly from these workshops.

The Pastoral Accompaniment Track is divided into three areas of emphasis in pastoral accompaniment: (1) mentoring; (2) spiritual guidance; and (3) counseling. Workshops in each of these areas are not designed for professional counselors, spiritual directors, or similar niche roles, but instead for those in more general catechetical or ministerial roles. I wish I had these online resources twenty years ago when I was a young DRE, trying to figure out effective and affordable ways to grow volunteers into a stronger ability to disciple others.

As background for discussing this approach to ministry and its potential impact on Catholic family life, the Catechetical Institute is a non-degree-granting outreach operated by the Franciscan University of Steubenville, for the purpose of offering catechetical formation in different ministry areas (tracks) utilizing a mentor-based distance-learning platform that can be customized by any diocese.

The Catechetical Institute doesn't replace diocesan services with distant experts. Rather, it works with dioceses to establish local, on-the-ground mentoring programs that connect participants to veteran catechists living and working in their dioceses. These mentors provide feedback and personal encouragement to participants.

Each workshop is designed to take the following integral approach: (1) spiritual formation of the catechist is prioritized; (2) a collaborative partnership model is employed and the step-by-step skills development pedagogical model for adult learning is used; and (3) the Franciscan charisms of generosity and preferential option for the poor drive the approach (for most of those using the system, it is free).

The workshops follow a model for online formation that is genuinely consistent with a Catholic anthropology — *serving and enhancing personal interaction rather than diminishing it.* The Catechetical Institute's whole system ensures this point and thus provides an important contribution to the Church, showing how online formation can be carefully designed so that it is used at the service of developing real communities and settings in which God's abundant grace is at work. This model of online formation reflects the fact that the faith must be transmitted by persons to persons, and formation can take place *only* in embodied ways in real communities — in the family, the parish, the school, the religious community, and so on.

The vision toward which the Catechetical Institute is working is that of supporting *families — the domestic family, the family of the parish, and other groups of "families" of believers — of lifelong and whole-life learners,* encouraging the development of mentoring and apprenticing bonds between them, and with the bonds developed in these "families of learners" following the most natural, *local* lines of community, so that they are both culturally and ecclesially appropriate. The methodology that the Catechetical Institute employs has the ability to do this — both the personal growth of the "mentee" and the guidance and assistance to help the "mentor" feel comfortable and confident in his role. Our goal is to help communities grow *themselves*.

The basic conviction is that all forms of Christian education should follow God's own pedagogy of salvation, so that proclamation, conversion, education, and sanctification flow together. The Second Vatican Council expressed it thus: "God ... does not make men holy and save them merely as individuals, without bond or link between one another. Rather has it pleased Him to bring men together as one people, a people which acknowledges Him in truth and serves Him in holiness" (*Lumen Gentium*, 9). In short, God saves us in bunches. Because this is how God saves, it is also how he acts as pedagogue and teacher, and this provides the model for our formative work.

The formation offered in these workshops seeks to accommodate and support the realities of local life and culture so that the education enhances rather than places tensions into that life, and at the same time accepts that responsibilities for learning *must* come from the learners themselves.

The Catechetical Institute's model — forming those who form others — might be compared to the old adage of teaching a man to fish, rather than simply feeding him. While a guest speaker may provide a really delicious "fish," our model instead seeks to teach the local teachers to fish well, robustly, and joyfully. They, in turn, are then prepared for a lifetime of investment in the lives of those around them in whatever, and however many, families they are a part of in their community.

This approach also provides the strongest access point for actually reaching large numbers of parents: most parish catechists, teachers, leaders, volunteers *are* parents. Developing these individuals to help other parents in a like-to-like manner, aims at fostering *long-term*, locally driven structures of *accountability* and *accompaniment* — mentoring and peers. Rather than generic program advertising and impersonal efforts to attract parents, these kinds of *relationships* are what most often attract others to begin new things in parish life, and it is what most holds them. The workshops themselves serve as a facilitator of such relationships and are designed for gentle but unequivocally ongoing *spiritual challenge* and a *kerygmatic call* to rise to daily vocational graces.

PART II: PARENTS BEING ENGAGED DIFFERENTLY, MORE THOROUGHLY, AND AS A CLEAR PARISH PRIORITY ...

Saint John Paul II, in his apostolic exhortation *Familiaris Consortio*, indicates the profound and blessed nature of the ministry of parenting when he notes that:

> The sacrament of marriage gives to the educational role the dignity and vocation of being really and truly a "ministry" of the Church at the service of building up her members. So great and splendid is the educational ministry of Christian parents that Saint Thomas has no hesitation in comparing it with the ministry of priests: "Some only propagate and guard spiritual life by a spiritual ministry; this is the role of the sacrament of Orders; others do this for both corporal and spiritual life, and this is brought about by the sacrament of marriage, by which a man and a woman join in order to beget offspring and bring them up to worship God." (38; citing Thomas Aquinas, *Summa Contra Gentiles*, IV, 58)

In terms expressive of its essential character in the overarching mission of the Church, *Familiaris Consortio* does not hesitate to use the term 'ministry' in the strongest manner. The ministerial role of parents is described as "irreplaceable and inalienable" (36), "incapable of being entirely delegated to others or usurped by others" (36), "original and irreplaceable" (53), "fundamental and irreplaceable" (60), "the primary and most excellent seed-bed of vocations" (53), and possessing "a special mission as apostles" (71). Complimenting this last quotation is the statement that, "It should not be forgotten that the service rendered by Christian spouses and parents to the Gospel is essentially an ecclesial service" (53). Saint John Paul II goes onto to describe matrimony as "a kind of consecration in the duties and dignity of their state" (56), marking this sacrament as a form of entry into a state of ministry:

> The Synod too, taking up and developing the indications of the Council, presented the educational mission of the Christian family as a true ministry through which the Gospel is transmitted and radiated, so that family life itself becomes an itinerary of faith and in some way a Christian initiation and a school of following Christ (*FC*, 39).

The theological position that seems reasonable to adopt at this point is that the parenting role is an authentic *ministry*, entered as an *act of hope* at the "consecration" of matrimony, and bestowed as an *intrinsic right* upon the "consecration" of the couple to their role at the Baptism of their first child.

Simply using the term "ministry" or the phrase "the ministry of parents" would, I think, have a helpful impact on developing evangelizing families. Many parish workers would agree that parents can often feel unempowered when encountering a strong parish program for children, and can get the impression or assume that the parish wants them to cede the duties of religious formation entirely to parish catechists or schoolteachers. Additionally, many parents, poorly catechized themselves, would not, however good-intentioned, know what to do with the notion that the Church wants them to be the primary evangelizers of their children in the Faith. Armed and encouraged by a clearer view of parenting as a critical ministry, many parents will begin to enter a new mindset — perhaps in a similar fashion to how laity, in general, felt increasingly empowered as lay ecclesial ministry began to be more encouraged in the life of Church. A certain positive feeling of ownership of the lay apostolate has clearly developed since the Second Vatican Council — but, as far as I can see, this is not largely the case in the parental role among those who have their children in day school and parish religious education programs (outside of the phenomenon of the explosive growth of homeschooling).

Such a change in emphasis and focus of the parish's formation efforts and "style" should be robustly supported from the pulpit and clear in the minds of the religious education catechists, and especially in the day school faculty. Too many view parents as an addendum in the process of faith formation of children, rather than the other way around. This can result, to coin a term, in a sort of "parishism" that can allow a parish and its accompanying school to commit sins (or nearly so) against family life, such as: overwhelming homework that destroys home life; significant and ever-present weekend homework assignments; significant parish events regularly held on Sunday evenings, which pull families in many directions for the sake of trying to "participate"; meetings scheduled too frequently or that do not consider family schedules; allowing a parish sports program or scouting program to hold games and activities at any time (especially on Sundays) or at any distance; no serious accommodation of homeschoolers or special-needs students; and lack of effort to incorporate parents in the planning of sacramental preparation programs and retreats, especially those related to chastity education.

These and other weaknesses evidence ways that a parish and school can bring harm to the needs of the domestic church by assuming an undue centrality in the life of the parish's children — thus "parishism." To conclude, the concept of *parenting as a ministry* seems to have a clear theological footing — explicitly in recent magisterial documents, and at least implicitly in the tradition at large. The *paradigm of intimacy* as the determinant of ministerial roles is not only consistent with the received tradition and the central mission of the Church, but also provides a potential path for a parish to reallocate its resources to suit the formation of adults as a *normative mission*, and parents as a *specific focus*. The clear witness from the tradition and from practical experience indicates the "irreplaceable" role of parents in their ministry of evangelical witness and sacrifice, leading their children forward to choose personal holiness. Their children will then be empowered to choose to generously follow the Lord's vocational leading in their lives and benefit society at large, as a result.

Do parents and parish staff understand what a Catholic home looks like? This is an open-ended question, along with those below — feeders for discussion.

How does a Catholic family pray? What does a Catholic family do in its morning gathering? In their time before they scatter in the busyness? What does a Catholic family do when the sun is going down and the children's eyes will soon close? How does a father or mother lay their child's heart and soul to bed as well as their bodies? How does the Catholic family go about that? How does a Catholic family help their children deal with illnesses? How does a Catholic family live on Sunday? Is it a day of rest or just another day of chores? How does the *day* get given to the Lord and the family life, not just at the hour of worship?

How is the family generous to other families and open to life genuinely? How does it relate to people who are older, perhaps older parents or grandparents or other relatives? How does the family enter into heroic calls relative to other people who are needy around them? How does the family model that to the children? How does the family model an openness of the home, which equals an openness to life? To mentor other families, to mentor other children; to share with them a space that is safe. To share with them a place where they can come and where they won't be present to the teasing that is common in their schools, and the teasing that is common in the neighborhood as a whole. With the pressures and the materialistic sort of peer influences that hit them, is the home an oasis from that? Is the neighborhood able to come in and be present to that oasis, other children, other parents who need mentoring?

What does the Catholic home look like in terms of beauty? How is the home made beautiful for God, not just beautiful in terms of the floor being swept and things kept somewhat orderly? What about meals, in terms of how they honor the need to keep the body healthy and the family gathered with some degree of regularity? What about in terms of how the home honors the need to have Godly discipline evidenced?

For a parish, these are various different sorts of touch points to discuss as a staff. What does a Catholic home look like if we're aiming to support it and to honor what is uniquely within a family's abilities?

What forms of outreach really reach families in light of a discussion on these kinds of questions? What are their real needs, their real worries, and their real hopes, listed out? Is the parish tuning into that in a very intentional way, or are parish adult offerings just happy to fill the chairs with whatever adults happen to come for more generic parish events?

The whole idea is to help families discern the shape of their family life according to the goal of being a "school of love." What's the point? To be happy, to have authentic joy, and to discover the most intimate human lessons within the life of the home, guided by the Church's wisdom in this regard, and especially the way God the Father parents us. Families are so often activity driven, rather than goal driven, and the chosen activities (whether it be sports or meal times or school clubs or weekend time or evening TV) are not determined by what serves a greater goal for family life, but instead by a rougher, more nebulous following of individual interests.

This secularized state of affairs often seems to be a given among parents who are already feeling overwhelmed by life, parenting challenges, or spousal relations. Often, in my experience, this is a form of denial on the part of parents, rather than an actual state of satisfaction with life as it is.

Since the broad solution already exists from the Church's wisdom, the questions relative to this issue would aim at an assessment of what would be the best first steps for a given family. The key is helping families implement things *incrementally*, in a way that will prevent unnecessary backsliding due to biting off too much or not moving forward deliberately enough. Whatever that mix is for a given family — that would be the "best" solution. The parish's role would therefore not only be a work of creative persuasion, but also provide a context in which parents can make well-considered and prudently incremental plans to move their family lives closer to God's plan for the domestic church. There is always going to be "something" that any family wishes were different. This provides a "hook" that the parish catechetical leader can use to help that particular family move toward greater holiness and mission.

To foster this, as I noted in Part I in discussing formation for pastoral accompaniment, Franciscan University has created a way forward to approach parents in a manner that allows them to be invited into gentle types of accountability, while engaging at their own pace and in their own place with the Church's magnificent vision for family life.

The Catechetical Institute's *Ministry of Parenting Track* has dozens of workshops developed from design through filming by experts in marriage and family life, catechetical formation, and youth and young adult cultural needs. These workshops are offered to parents, parishes, schools, and dioceses to provide ongoing catechetical learning, support, and training to parents, field ministry leaders, catechists, and non-experts alike.

Key to the development of these workshops is framing them in light of these questions:

- How to actually communicate and assist families in adopting a Catholic home culture?
- How to meet the needs of the newly married and new parents, with attention to those marriages and families in crisis?
- How can parents of Catholic families see themselves not simply as recipients of the dominant cultural trends but as living centers of hope for the new evangelization?

The Catechetical Institute emphasizes and focuses on the pragmatic realities in parish life and how those working in this setting are to address these realities.

Some of the ministerial formation and training issues and needs that this collection of workshops addresses include:

- Helping parishes have a *more explicit focus on adult formation*, and move beyond only offering on-site evening endeavors that parents find difficult to consistently attend.

- Helping families in pragmatic, persuasive ways to *plug in to the Church at large,* and the many resources that exist but remain unexplored due to lack of awareness.
- Challenging the language of "vocation" as focused only on clergy and religious life, to the detriment of *marriage being understood as a vocation.*
- Aiding parish ministers who often feel they lack of tools, training, and support to reach out and *assist* the hurting families in their community.
- Providing explicit formational guidance to foster a transition into *mature adult faith for Millennials* and others struggling to make the choice to seek God's call to a vocation.
- Encouraging parishes toward a *more ethnically respectful approach* to passing on the faith, impacting ministers' understanding and support of unique structures and practices within the home life of certain cultures that have been critical in fostering faith transmission in every era of the Church.
- Discouraging some prevalent attitudes in catechetical leadership circles that too often hobble a formation that aims for a *confident proclamation of the Gospel by parents* in the home, or favor forfeiting of the parental catechetical role, placing parents at the periphery.
- Assisting existing ministry positions (youth ministers, DREs, principals, etc.) in re-envisioning their jobs as needing to be *family focused,* thereby addressing the often uncoordinated, silo-plagued, atomized approach to formation of a parish's population.

Since the broad solution already exists from the Church's wisdom, the questions we asked to guide us in creating this large collection of workshops serve to help families in their *current* situation, not some imagined ideal.

In the midst of present-day challenging realities, in a homily for the Mass for the Family Day on the Occasion of the Year of Faith on October

27, 2013, Pope Francis emphasized how the family must focus on God's presence within their home — for only the presence of God can fulfill the family and bring them joy:

> Dear families, you know very well that the true joy which we experience in the family is not superficial; it does not come from material objects, from the fact that everything seems to be going well ... True joy comes from a profound harmony between persons, something which we all feel in our hearts and which makes us experience the beauty of togetherness, of mutual support along life's journey. But the basis of this feeling of deep joy is the presence of God, the presence of God in the family and his love, which is welcoming, merciful, and respectful towards all. And above all, a love which is patient: patience is a virtue of God and he teaches us how to cultivate it in family life, how to be patient, and lovingly so, with each other. To be patient among ourselves. A patient love. God alone knows how to create harmony from differences. But if God's love is lacking, the family loses its harmony, self-centeredness prevails and joy fades. But the family which experiences the joy of faith communicates it naturally. That family is the salt of the earth and the light of the world, it is the leaven of society as a whole. Dear families, always live in faith and simplicity, like the Holy Family of Nazareth! The joy and peace of the Lord be always with you!

We know that marriage and family life are keenly challenged. The family in the United States has faced unprecedented challenges that threaten its identity and even its existence. Too often ministries to families and youth operate in an antiquated manner, not taking into consideration the target age of Millennials and their special needs as they transition from youth to young adult; allowing this group to largely fall through the cracks. The formation offered through the Ministry of Parenting workshops is intended to inform, sustain, and encourage participants in the *modern* context. Likewise, it is intended to equip parents to envision family life in the fullest sense and to understand how to develop the *for-*

gotten vision of a Catholic culture within the home, which is the foundation of any community's ability to thrive.

The purpose of the Ministry of Parenting Track is to establish stronger formation structures, closer communion with parish priests and healthier models of family life for parents, whose present challenges may seem impossible to overcome. A prominent aspect of these workshops is helping families to understand the ways in which family life plays a central role in supporting *all* vocations in the Church: to priesthood, married, and consecrated life.

This Ministry of Parenting Track is designed for *sustained, long-term impact at the local level.* Providing workshops that are designed as a context for *local mentoring and pastoral accompaniment* (either one-to-one, two-to-two, or in groups) gives parishes a solid way forward to assist young people in appreciating their basic personal Baptismal vocations for the sake of the service of the Church, and of her mission of evangelization in the world.

This model of formation fits the parenting and family culture: busy parents needing a flexible and accessible learning platform, attuned to modern technology, affordable, and offering connection to helpful mentoring examples and relations. The Catechetical Institute is a natural collaborative environment within Franciscan University and outside with many other apostolates. We work in a strongly interdisciplinary manner, with experts and presenters from many disciplines, such as counseling, bioethics, humanities, political science, etc. The wide variety of backgrounds and skill sets our presenters bring to their respective workshops will serve to repair gaps in the formation of today's families and prepare the adult Catholics in the Church to be effective witnesses in their daily lives.

As I noted in Part I, these workshops depend on local parish ministers to become better trained in the skill set of pastoral accompaniment. Men and women who embrace this dynamic and interpersonal ministry formation model will be strengthened in this area of ecclesial life and see their confidence in the ministry of accompaniment increase. With this strengthened capacity, they will bring what they have learned back into their own homes, transforming not only their parishes, but their own family life as well.

Beyond this, our other ministry tracks form people for ecclesial work with a centralized vision of family ministry. Almost all the other Catechetical Institute tracks have intentionally listed Ministry of Parenting workshops among their electives. This was a *critical* design decision — it has the effect of making the Ministry of Parenting content ubiquitously present in *all* our planned offerings. This arises from our vision that *all* ministry formation must see family life and ministry to families as *central* to any success hoped for in the Church's new evangelization efforts.

MATURE EVALUATION AND ANALYSIS

One of the great struggles we all face in discovering what *actually* works (and to stop putting resources and time into things that don't) is the frequent lack of robust evaluation of ideas, programs, and initiatives that are tried at various levels of the Church in the United States to improve evangelization and catechesis. For example, an evaluation form used at the end of a formation event may more be focused on assessing whether the event was "pleasing or inspiring," rather than what is really needed — did the formation have impact, cause growth, or improve the skills of those attending, both now and on into the future? In other words, are the attendees any better at their ministry work one, two, five years later? If so, in what way can that be connected to the training effort? Could elements in the training be changed to cause greater impact over time?

All Catechetical Institute workshops function within an online learning management system that has strong evaluative capacities built in, focusing on *long-term* assessment tools and exercises for participants. Our vision is to establish the presence of a well-formed, *locally led* marriage and family ministry, as well as other myriad catechetical leaders in service to the parish community, who can sensitively respond to challenges facing married couples and families in in a *sustainable* manner.

In closing, the Catechetical Institute has been engaged in finding an *effective access point* that actually reaches parents in *substantial numbers* — a form of access that results in them *staying plugged in to long-term formation* that suits their day-to-day needs and *honors* their potential and place in the Lord's plan.

_____

DISCUSSION QUESTIONS

1. Do you know how to disciple another adult through the gift of presence, gentle listening, and encouragement, focused on the growth of his or her spiritual life?
2. What is a mature disciple (a mature Catholic parent)?
3. What is unique about the family, and what is done best by it?
4. What vocational companions do parents have, and what forms of fellowship do families need?
5. How can parish leaders encourage the domestic church as a sacred space?

CHAPTER NINETEEN

They Will Know We Are Christians by Our Joy

DAMON AND MELANIE OWENS

JoyTOB.org

FIVE QUICK TAKES

1. They will know we are Christian by our joy: The family was designed by God from the beginning to be that place where we experience the joy of being irreplaceably loved for who we are and certain that others are willing and capable of fulfilling our needs.

2. They will know we are Christian by our love: *"The family, this is the place where the theology of the body and the theology of love are interwoven."*

3. They will know we are Christian by our story: the story of who we were before we met Christ, how we met him, and how Christ transformed our life. Knowing and sharing our witness is a profound gift, cutting to the heart of who Christ is and why he is the answer to the deepest longings of our heart. Sharing our own story invites others to recognize Christ in their own life.

4. They will know we are Christian by our communion: We need a new marriage and family life *movement* that draws from the joy and zeal of rediscovering the God-ordained *munus* of matrimony and patrimony wherein the family discovers both what it *is* (a "community of life and love") and what it should *do* (*become* this "community of life and love").

5. They will know we are Christian by our stewardship: In what might rightly be described as the heart of what makes Catholic families dynamically different from other families is living our sexuality as a joyful, reverent *stewardship*.

INTRODUCTION

When did we first experience love and the joy that it brings? A look, a touch, a soothing voice — these are the first lessons in the school of love, the family. The family was designed from the beginning to be that place where we experience the joy of being loved, not for what we can do, but for who we are. Here we come to know that we are worthy to be loved and that others are willing and capable of fulfilling our needs. Sensual experiences of sights, smells, sounds, tastes, and touches, even as a newborn, transcend ideas, concepts, and abstractions of identity, love, belonging, and worth. Later in life, of course, the ideas, concepts, and abstractions are crucial to our search for understanding the meaning of love, but the *knowing* of love is sensual, sensible, and personal.

I want that kind of love, don't you? We all do. It is an immutable and inalienable truth of our humanity — *the law of the person*. So, if this is part of the "natural law" of the person, why is it so difficult for us to live family life as this "school of love" God has designed? What keeps so many families from living their mission to love and call to joy? How do we help every family live this noble calling of a school of love? What does it even look like today? What difference should the Catholic vision of family life make in the lived experience of Catholic homes?

We need a new intention for our families. And not just a new intention, but also a plan. And not just a plan, but also a passion for the purpose of joy.

THE CATHOLIC DIFFERENCE

The family in the modern world needs transformation that is fully human and divine, natural and supernatural, in order to fulfill its identity and mission as school of life and love or *domestic church*. Christian married couples must lead the way with an ever-new understanding, living out, and witness of their living, vibrant, personal relationship with Jesus Christ. Christian family life makes their children the first witness and followers, and parents both primary educators and "graduate students" in this school of sanctification. It takes a mother and father to raise a child, but it also takes a child to raise a mother and father to new heights of sanctity.

This noble reality of marriage and family life should set Christian marriage and families cosmologically apart from our secular neighbors. It calls us to a transformation of our mind, heart, and soul. We act in accord with who we think we are. Just so, Christian families will live their unique mission only when we embrace our unique *identity*. This identity compels us to live dynamically different together and in how we encounter the world. Much of this chapter will explore the identity of the family revealed and elevated by Christ and how it directly animates the mission of the family within itself and to the world at large. This mission will reveal itself in an authentic family spirituality that fosters intentional discipleship with Christ in the home that extends, with naturalness and ease, to the world.

WHAT DOES AN AUTHENTIC DOMESTIC-CHURCH-BASED FAMILY SPIRITUALITY LOOK LIKE?

An authentic family spirituality must begin with the "matter" of ordinary things in family life — the good, the bad, and the messy. In true liturgical form these are the ordinary things — *"fruit of the vine and work of human hands"*— that make up our offering to God. God receives them, breathes on and divinizes them, then gives them back to us *holy.* It is always easy to misjudge the value of our offerings. These *ordinary things* are too ordinary or unworthy for God. We think we need to "get our stuff together" for God or somehow make our offering "good" for him. For too long the ordinariness of family life, with its struggles, challenges, shame, doubts, disappointments, and "dysfunction," has been compared to more "holy" monastic, religious, clerical, or other ecclesial states of life. The path to holiness is out there, not here in our mess. But marriage and family life are primordial to humanity. They have been here from the beginning before the Church, far older and more fundamental to our human origin than the states of life formed by religious communities. Would not God have created from the beginning a means of human formation and flourishing along with our creation in his image and likeness? Are not monasteries, convents, and religious communities formed more like families than families like them? Doesn't the comparison alone confuse the distinct, unique, and complementary gifts of both family life and religious life in the universal call to holiness?

While holding a just reverence for the great and — rightly understood — *greater* vocation of celibacy for the sake of the kingdom, we have much to do to reclaim the great dignity of marriage and family life. In God's plan of salvation there is a primordial, sublime, and enduring place of honor bestowed on marriage and family life. This place of honor is not static or passive, but dynamic and powerful. Through its identity and mission gifted by God directly, the family is the place where God has chosen to reveal himself to us *personally*. He doesn't reveal himself to perfect families, but reveals himself to *perfect* families. It is *his* action. It is *his* gift to perfect in love whatever we offer him in love. That either includes all the small, ordinary things of family life, or it includes nothing at all.

FAMILIES BECOME WHAT YOU ARE

The family, this is the place where the theology of the body and the theology of love are interwoven. Pope Benedict XVI.

Marriage and family life are considered one of the few human universals. That's good and bad. The good is that we all have some experience with it. It's not something so completely unfamiliar that we must struggle to describe it. Even with all of the important historical expressions (monogamy, bigamy, concubinage, arranged marriages, etc.) we all come from a family, a mother and a father. That doesn't mean, of course, that we all come from a "good" family with nurturing relationships between parents and siblings, or that we even *know* our mother or father. But that absence or lack in those relationships is universally understood as a problem of brokenness that directly affects our ability to live and love as a friend, a lover, or in our own marriage and a family. The universal presence of marriage in human history speaks to a natural good, need, and reality deep in our humanity to love. And not just love, but to love and be loved in communion with others who truly know us. *We need to belong irreplaceably to someone else.*

Man cannot live without love. He remains a being that is incomprehensible for himself, his life is senseless, if love is not revealed to him, if he does not encounter love, if he does not experience it and make it his own, if he does not participate intimately in it. This, as has already been said, is why Christ the Redeemer "fully reveals man to himself." (Saint John Paul II, *Redemptor Hominis*, 10)

Without love, we don't even know who we are. Loved people love people. Hurt people hurt people. Love as a feeling or pleasure is not enough. We need to receive others as a gift and respond to them with a gift of our self. Love is self-gift. It is personal. Family life is the place where we first receive and accept God as the source of all Love. A husband and wife pledge to belong to each other bound by God's love. We accept the role of stewards of God's love, rejecting any idea or sense of being the owners or creators of love. Seeking God's will in all things, we "make love" (really make love *present*) by our mutual self-gift in all things, but uniquely in the marital embrace (not a euphemism, but a more descriptive term for the more biological sexual intercourse). Children are called into existence through this particular marital sexual act of self-gift love. Called and invited, not commanded or demanded as if we ourselves were "the Author and giver of Life." We are stewards, not owners. Stewards work for the mission of the owner in cheerful freedom and joyful gratitude for his lavish generosity. If it is the will of the true "Author and giver of Life," that moment of sexual intercourse expands our mission to "accept the children that God may bless you with and raise them in the knowledge of the Lord and His Church." From the moment a new human person "is" at conception, he or she is also becoming. Our humanity is, even as it is becoming. We are created in the image and likeness of God, and that immediately confers infinite dignity on our unique and unrepeatable self at conception. Yet it is God's love, revealed to us by others, that nourishes and flourishes us to become what we are. This is the beautiful, messy, ordinary, time-consuming role of the family — to build saints, not just good citizens. And, it pivots on our redemption of sex.

NOT JUST A ROLE OR TASK, BUT A *MUNUS*

The necessary transformation of our families in the modern world is both objective and subjective: informational and formational, conceptual and experiential, catechetical and evangelical. It is personal to each husband and wife, yet always ordered to what we know to be a *covenantal communion of marriage*. Matrimony is the true meaning of marriage. Matrimony is a *"munus* to motherhood" (*mater, monio*). It carries the reverence of being at once a task, role, mission, vocation, high office, honor, gift, and state of being that is raised in dignity by the greater authority (God) who chooses freely, confers undeservedly, empowers graciously, and entrusts lavishly.

Munus is a particularly Catholic ecclesial Latin term. Though unfamiliar, it is far from obscure. According to Dr. Janet Smith, the word munus is used 248 times in the documents of the Second Vatican Council (1962–1965), often translated to English as "task," or "role," or "mission," or "office." Twenty-four times in the seminal 1968 document *Humanae Vitae* ("Of Human Life"), and eighty-three in the 1981 *Familiaris Consortio* (even subtitled, "On the Role *(munera)* of the Christian Family in the Modern World"). But there is much more dignity than these simple translations of "task," "mission," or "role" convey. Jesus Christ, for example, has the triple *munera* of Priest, Prophet, and King as the Savior of the World. The Blessed Virgin Mary has the *munus* of being the Mother of God. Bishops in their fullness of ordained priesthood have the triple *munera* to teach (*munus docendi*), govern/pastor (*munus regendi*), and sanctify (*munus sanctificandi*).

Munus is a term that has power to elevate the dignity of marriage and family life. Christians aren't called to just *do*, even to just *do good*. Baptism changes who we are. Who we *are* changes what we do, how we act, and why we do it. Transforming all of this is the ineffable fact that God himself is the One who calls, wills, honors, and lavishes us with a share in his divine authority. We didn't earn this. We could never earn or make ourselves worthy of this. It is pure gift. It is divine mercy. By definition, neither gift nor mercy are deserved.

Matrimony has its complement in patrimony, or the *"munus* to fatherhood" that, drawing from the nature of conjugal love, gives marital love a particular realization in the new being of their children. Children as the fruit of their love and communion grow the matrix of relationships in the family where we can all experience being "irreplaceable" to one another. I am yours, and you are mine. Together "the family finds in the plan of God both what it *is* (a "community of life and love") and what it should *do* (expend its effort to *become* this "community of life and love").

We need a new marriage and family life *movement* that draws from the joy and zeal of rediscovering the God-ordained *munus* of matrimony and patrimony. It is informational in its content, formational in its norms, and joyful in its encounter. Such a movement can begin at any stage of marriage, but should begin with a focus on new marriages and families (first three to seven years) by nurturing friendship, fellowship, accompaniment, wisdom, confidence, encouragement, and relevance in helping to navigate the particular challenges they face in marriage and parenting. It is a privilege to enter into the love story of another couple. Often, young couples have not yet grown to value and honor their own story. But it is in their story that we come to know them and their desires for marriage, family, and life. What is their history, together and family of origin? What are they trying to make sense of? Can we help them see Christ in their past, present, and future? Can we share our own story of how we met and know Christ in a way that encourages and draws others to invite us into their lives?

What will connect us are our stories, our witness. For believers, it is the story of who we were before we met Christ, how we met him, and how Christ transformed our life. Knowing and sharing our witness to Christ is a profound gift to other couples. More powerfully than catechesis alone, witness stories cut to the heart of who Christ is and why he is the answer to the deepest longings of our heart. Sharing our own story is also an invitation to others to see how Christ is calling them to wholeness and holiness. When we hear and understand the questions others are asking in their life, marriage, or family, we can more naturally journey with them to Jesus.

As I heard so many years ago, there is nothing less credible than the answer to a question we are not asking. For Melanie and me, sharing our witness has been far more powerful these past twenty-six years than our zeal, study, and teaching of the beautiful "what's" of our faith. It is true: People don't care how much you know until they know how much you care. God came to Melanie and me at a crucial time in our young adult life. He met us far from the Church and faith of our childhood, in the hot mess of Berkeley, California, in 1989. What God has done for and with us should give every couple hope.

OUR STORY

When Melanie and I met, we were twenty-three-year-old graduate students at the University of California Berkeley. We both grew up in solid Catholic homes where our faith was an essential and expected part of life and identity. Melanie is one of eight children, the oldest girl, and has always tried to practice her faith, even as an undergraduate at the University of California at Santa Barbara. Still, college life and relationship in the 1980s took a toll on her. When we met as first-year graduate students at Berkeley, she was already deeply wounded and jaded in her search for love. I grew up on the other side of the country in New Jersey with my two sisters. We also grew up in a home where our Catholic faith was central to our family. Still, that was no match for the 1980s culture that formed my understanding of sex and what it means to be a man.

We are talking about the era that gave us HBO, MTV, Prince, Madonna, *The Love Boat,* and *Animal House.* So, when I entered my first year at Brown University in 1988, I may have technically been a virgin, but in my mind, *Animal House* was a documentary, and Prince was the soundtrack of college life. Within forty-eight hours of being on campus I was doing nearly everything I promised God I would never do five years earlier at my Confirmation retreat. By the time I would meet Melanie five years later, I would be just as broken, confused, and conflicted as she was. I'd still identify as Catholic if you asked me, but my faith had no power or authority over my identity or my life. When it came to relationships and sex, I knew I was living contrary to the faith. I knew it was "wrong," but I always planned to get things right *later,* when I was older and ready to get serious about life. For now, I was in college having fun. In my mind, the Church's idea of life, love, and happiness is the hard, joyless, adult work that would get me into Heaven *later.* For now, I have a few more years to enjoy life.

Then God brought me Melanie. From the moment I first met Melanie, I knew she was different. Or more honestly, she made me want to be different. Maybe not immediately, but if I were ready to begin the serious, non-fun, adult phase of my life, this is the woman I could see spending the rest of my life with. I remember the way she looked at me, and I remember wanting to be the man she saw. I really delighted in her delight with me. She was strong, yet fragile and vulnerable. I wanted to protect her. I loved the way she made me feel. I wanted to earn her love and be worthy of her respect. She was goodness, and I wanted to be good enough.

It was kind of a sweet agony with the joy of her attention and the constant reminder that I was not yet good enough to deserve to possess such a good. We began our relationship with that passionate, seeking love that Pope Benedict XVI describes as the marks of *eros*. *Eros* is an intoxicating kind of love, and when we are "under the influence" of *eros* we are powerfully drawn together. Melanie and I were sexually active and, in spite of the occasional twang of Catholic guilt, convinced that our love made everything right. The thing about *eros*, though, is that while it's powerful, it doesn't last long. *Eros* will come, and *eros* will go. *Eros* is a love that can show up at "first sight," and a love you can "fall in," but not a love that will last. Whether viewed biochemically with norepinephrine, dopamine, endorphins, or vasopressin, or spiritually as a drawing out of yourself to another, *eros* makes that interpersonal connection powerfully other-directed. If love is a weight or gravity as Saint Augustine proposed, *eros* is the gravitational pull into the orbit of another. There is a thrill when the passion of *eros* happens to you.

As Melanie and I drew closer together, a real friendship began to grow. I began to see Melanie as this fascinating person, not just attractive and fun. She didn't just delight me, I began to realize that she *is* a delight! There was so much I didn't know about her, but now wanted to. I wanted to know *her*. I still wanted the delight of being around her, but I also wanted to know everything about her. Saint John Paul II in his *Theology of the Body* describes this as moving from *how another person makes you feel* to *who the other person is*. It's an entrance into the mystery of the other person. And, that mystery is delightful.

Adam's delight, poetically described in Genesis 2, was not just an erotic delight in finding the helper fit for him, but in encountering another unique and unrepeatable "I" that is bone of his bone and flesh of his flesh. And yet, not him. The mystery of Eve, like all mysteries, is not a "do not enter," but an eternally new "come and see."

I remember the feeling of our *eros* giving way to *philia*. The passion of *eros* was giving way to willing Melanie's good, as my friend. I wanted the best for her. I didn't just want the good for her, I wanted the "goodest" good. I'm sure I still hoped that it would *earn* me a place in her heart and by her side, but I distinctly remember the shift in desiring her happiness more than my own. This was a different sweet agony. Now, the agony of knowing that I might not be with her was mixed with the sweetness of the beginning of a kind of *reverence*. Reverence, Saint John Paul II proposes in *Theology of the Body* (117b:4–5), is a spiritually mature form of the mutual fascination of the sexes: man for femininity, and woman for masculinity. What is still remarkable to me is that even in our objective state of sin, particularly sexual sin, we were not outside the reach of God and the power of love to woo us. *And he did woo us* — from *eros* to *phila*, and even to the *agape* pledge of marriage. But first, he was preparing our hearts for an unexpected conversation, crisis, and the first major conversion of our life together in Christ.

WHAT IF WE STOP HAVING SEX? THE ACCIDENTAL CONVERSION

I asked Melanie that question with no conscious expectation that it would begin the new era of our life together. I meant to be provocative, but had no intention of challenging or changing our perfect life together. As far as I was concerned, everything was just fine. My question was asked in the pretentious tone of an Ivy League educated graduate student who thinks he's already got the world figured out. I fully expected to have one of those graduate school latte conversations about how much our love trumped the idealistic rigid morality that others might need. But Melanie didn't answer me with words. She cried. What was "perfect" in my twenty-three-year-old boy-brain was an existential crisis in the heart of my beloved, Melanie. She had been asking herself that question for the previous months, and every likely scenario in her mind ended up with me leaving for any one of the twenty-thousand-plus other women at Berkeley. My "perfect" life was, for her, a "better-than-alone" compromise. After several hours of crying and pleading (she cried, I pleaded), we decided to stop having sex.

Part of me was furious and annoyed, but another part of me was strangely excited to be attempting something good and mature with someone I knew was worth it. We struggled. For months. Desperation brought us to a local parish priest in Oakland. We didn't know it then, but within a few weeks of meeting with that priest, Melanie and I stopped having sex and would not come back together sexually for another two-and-a-half years, until we were married. This was truly miraculous. Not merely two-and-a-half years, but the transformation of our relationship —with God and each other — during those years. As hard as it was for us to begin a new relationship in chastity, our intimacy deepened in ways I had neither experienced before nor imagined was possible with another person. I remember being able to see Melanie with such clarity and depth. Even the chastity that began as a renunciation of sex grew to become an expression and exercise of love—truly willing her good and wanting to suffer for it. I'm not sure I would have believed someone if they had told me this was going to happen, but after experiencing it we wanted to tell the world, *"You can have this joy, too! If we can do it, you can do it!"* As for our relationship, by the time I proposed marriage to Melanie, on Valentine's Day 1992, there was no doubt in either of our minds that we wanted to spend the rest of our lives together. God worked a miracle in our life together, and it filled us with hope. What else does he have in store for us? How much more can we love each other? I don't just want to be with you, I want to belong to you, forever!

THE CALL TO WITNESS

When we married in April 1993, our confidence was tempered by two years of passionate, chaste love, and animated by a renewed Catholic faith. We were on fire. We were compelled to share our story with the world. We designed our wedding to witness to what Christ was doing in us, and within months, we would be standing before engaged couples encouraging them to discover the joy that chastity could bring to their relationships. What we lacked in theological and doctrinal expertise, we overcompensated for with passionate, joyful witness. We had the *heat*. We told our good news story, and couples were convicted. Even as we were still trying to make sense of what God had done for us in our relationship, that witness alone had the power to capture the hearts and imaginations of our peers, who also longed for love that will last forever.

THE TRUTH AND MEANING OF SEX

We had experienced chastity not as a renunciation or repression, but an ordering of sex to love. Sex is good. God created it. It was the primordial blessing in the "beginning." But the truth and meaning of sex is unknowable outside of love. Not merely the passionate intoxication of *eros* that "happens to us" or drives us to act. But the more noble human loves of *philia* and *agape* that we choose, in freedom, to will the good of the other and to entrust ourselves to them. The purpose of sex is to express the truth of a particular type of love — *agape* love. The love that is pledged at the altar in marriage, and in celibacy "for the sake of the Kingdom." Agape love is the ultimate self-gift. The marital vow itself is a pledge of agape love. I am yours, and you are mine. The pledge of marriage is a pledge of belonging to each other made possible only by God's love. We freely pledge the total, faithful gift of ourselves and consent to serving the fruitfulness of that gift. We pledge to be a free, total, faithful, and fruitful self-gift at the altar, and we are married. We make the free, total, faithful, and fruitful self-gift in the sexual embrace. This is why it is a *marital act*. Sex is unknowable outside of love's order. The misuse or abuse of this God-given power of sexuality still retains its power. This power, disordered from life and love, now has the power to bring loneliness and death.

SO GOES THE WORLD

The dislocation or, rightly understood, disordering of sex from love is the hinge or tap root of every human evil in the world. Every. Human. Evil. Conversely, and more hopefully stated, reordering sex is the key and hinge to the redemption of the world. I hope that sounds ridiculously simplistic and overstated to you. Before our own conversion experience, I would've thought the same thing. But while our conversion experience redeeming our sexuality helped us to know in our hearts the truth, Saint John Paul II's *Theology of the Body* confirmed what, in our *particular* experience, is *universally* true. While not all of our particular, subjective experiences have universal, objective projections, sexuality is one of the few human universals that does. When we can move beyond our own partial perspectives to a truly comprehensive understanding of what it means to be a man or woman made in the image and likeness of God all, matter matters. Sex matters. Our actions matter. The body matters.

> The body, in fact, and only the body, is capable of making visible what is invisible: the spiritual and divine. It was created to transfer into the visible reality of the world, the mystery hidden … in God, and thus to be a sign of it. (*Theology of the Body*, 19:4)

SEX IN THE CITY

The world teaches us that sex is a verb — an action — some something that we *do*. The growing public pornographic display of sex in our movies, TV, and music is paradoxically set against the dogmatic principle that sex is a private affair. My sexual attractions, behaviors, and overall choices are right or wrong because I say so. This right to privacy was "discovered" hidden in the penumbra of our U.S. Constitution and has been the basis of deconstructing our culture's entire understanding of man, woman, marriage, pregnancy, motherhood, fatherhood, fertility, sexual morality, sexual duties, family, and the very dignity of human life. Sex is about *me* and my right to immediate sexual pleasure. Even with the very recent uproar of the #MeToo/#TimesUp movement, the dissension around even the highest moral value of consent is noteworthy.

What is consent in a world where the highest moral value is the expression of our own private desires in the pursuit of immediate sexual pleasure? One of the greatest social sins today is telling someone what they can or cannot do sexually. It seems we know that any prohibition presumes some kind of order, meaning, or right has been violated. What claims or demands can you make on the culture in a world of privatized sex? In this world sex has nothing to do with marriage or children unless you decide that it does. We have demanded and been promised that we can have sex without marriage or marriage without sex; sex without children or children without sex. In this world, babies don't come from sex but from the failure of contraception. The decision to have sex is not the decision to be a mother or father. Sex has very little to do with the future but everything to do with the present moment. Sex is about me and my fulfillment and satisfaction. Period. Responsible people protect themselves from their "partners" and any consequence that may burden them beyond this moment. It is fair to say that the dogmatic principal of modern sexual morality is that sexual pleasure is the right to life, liberty, and our pursuit of happiness.

This has had irrefutably destructive effects particularly in the last seventy years on individual men and women, marriage, children, families, communities, healthcare, economies, crime, and overall human happiness. It has fractured the Church, our human identity, and our relationship with God. We are not even sure what is *real*. Not even evidentiary sciences such as biology can save sex and gender from private meaning. Sexual brokenness has broken the world.

AMNESIA REQUIRES ANAMNESIS

This is not merely a crisis of morality. Our disordered actions and beliefs express a disordered identity: We have forgotten who we are. Ours is an *amnesia,* a radical forgetting of the foundational reality of being made in the image and likeness of God. This truth expressed in the biblical poetry of Genesis 1 is not foundational or primordial simply because it's stated in the first chapter of the first book of our family album, the Bible. It is foundational and primordial because it is the anthropological hinge that grounds our origin, history, and destiny in God himself. Anthropology is the study of the meaning of humanity. Where do we come from? What is universally true of the human person? In what cultures do we flourish? There are indeed many, many anthropologies demanding authority over us. More of us accept the premises or promises of one anthropology or another without knowing their bases or fuller assumptions. This is a frightening thought given the enormous importance of knowing the fullness and truth of who we are. If we don't know who we are or accept a false or partial identity, our actions and behaviors will be false. And they will bring us despair and sadness. But we were created for joy. Not fickle pleasure or fleeting happiness, but eternal joy. The antidote to this amnesia is not just morality.

We don't require just a radical change in behavior but a radical re-membering — an *anamnesis*. A change of mind or behavior implies introducing something foreign or new. A remembering speaks to a something that is already ours. This memory of our identity as sons and daughters of God the Father is neither conscious nor subconscious but a primordial memory. I love that word. It speaks to something so foundational and inalienable that it cannot be erased or ever fully forgotten. It is dormant. Not a memory to be recalled or something created from our own imagination, but a "heart" memory. It's something we *know* in our deepest being is true even before we have the words or confidence to articulate it. We *know* we exist, for example. It takes heavy PhD study to really begin questioning our own existence, and there are famous philosophers who have injected such thoughts into our public psyche. Outside of those circles, we have certainty of our own existence. Likewise, we know life is good. To be alive is good. Death is bad. Love is good. We long to be known and loved, to know and love someone. We long for peace, affection, and to belong. Jesus Christ promises all this and more. The Christian proposal is that all of the deepest longings of our heart — the most important and fundamental desires — can only be fulfilled by the Father who placed them there. We are created in the image and likeness of God who is Father, Son, and Holy Spirit. *Remember ...*

SEX IN THE SACRED CITY

Christianity, in a certain sense, is an initiation into this radical remembering. We remember who we are by accepting *whose* we are. Being made in the image and likeness of God makes him our Father and we his sons and daughters. To father is to engender life outside of yourself and to ensure it's good. God is Father and the origin of all fatherhood, because everything comes from him. Everything. We believe God exists and that he loves us because we have encountered and trust in Jesus Christ. Jesus Christ in himself reveals "God to man and man to himself." Through our relationship with him, he reveals to us who we are, whose we are, and why we are here. This is not just informational or even formational, but transformational. Jesus Christ makes it possible for us to remember who we are and to become what we are. We are sons and daughters made in the image and likeness of God, who is Love. We are created for joy, with a mission to love with God's own Love. The organic interdependence of this relationship between Christ, the Salvation Story, the Church, and the family is stated no better than in the Summary Statement of the 2015 World Meeting of Families catechesis *Love Is Our Mission: The Family Fully Alive*:

> The Church believes that God exists and that he loves us. We make this claim because we have encountered and trust Jesus Christ. This trust enables a relationship in which God's plan for all creation is revealed and disclosed. Confident in this plan, we are able to proclaim that each and every human being is created in the image of God. We believe that God creates us with a purpose and for a mission.
>
> We believe that in Jesus, God became man. We believe that in Jesus, God invites and summons the whole world to know him and live as his covenant people in the Church. We believe that God's love is visible and manifest in this covenant, which reveals that God is faithful even unto death, despite our infidelity and sinfulness. We believe that Jesus suffered, died, and rose from the dead, confirming the power and fidelity of God, giving us confidence that his way is true. We trust that as his covenant people, Jesus is now present with us sacramentally, and that ultimately, we will share his victory and heavenly communion.
>
> Sustained by the Holy Spirit and the sacraments of the Church, we seek this communion, which Jesus has promised is our destiny. We believe that all aspects of our lives — including our sexuality, fertility, and family life — are part of this mission to live and love as Jesus taught.
>
> We believe that in the Sacrament of Marriage, God has given us the gift of experiencing his covenant. In the marriage covenant, husband and wife live together in light of the covenant already established by God and Israel, Christ and the Church. We believe that marriage is the seedbed of a family, the nucleus

of the domestic church, which is itself an essential member of the wider universal Church.

We acknowledge that we are fallen, and that all manner of suffering, temptations, and sins can burden us and prevent us from becoming who we were created to be. But we trust that no matter what trials we face or wounds we inflict upon ourselves and others, God is faithful. His passion, crucifixion, and resurrection are the decisive evidence that he will not depart from his covenant. The Lord has shown that he is stronger than all our sins and that he conquers sin. In our life together, through the presence of Jesus and the Holy Spirit in our midst, we believe that God will bring to fruition the work which he has begun in us. Anticipating that day when Jesus comes again and fully establishes his Kingdom on earth, we believe it is our mission to testify to what God has done and is doing. We believe it is our mission to love God and neighbor as he has taught us.

We believe that love is our mission, and that this mission is the only way we can be fully alive and be who we were created to be. We believe that this love should be taught, shared, and communicated in and through the family, the domestic church. We believe that the family shares in the mission of the whole Church, and we devote this catechesis to explaining this vision of love in more detail. (*Love Is Our Mission: The Family Fully Alive* [Huntington, IN: Our Sunday Visitor Publishing, 2015])

This summary is an eloquent manifesto on the connection between sex and salvation that passes through the family. This is *by God's design*. Families that understand and embrace this identity will seek to live marriage and family life in a distinctly different way. Family life is a lived theology of love wherein we love one another in response to being loved by Love itself. We forgive because we have been forgiven. We are merciful because mercy has been lavished upon us. We seek understanding and wisdom from Our Father in Heaven because we trust him as a beloved daughter or son. We long to know his will and look for it in the small, ordinary things of our day. We see everything we have as a gift from

God to be shared. Money, time, children, work, friends, strangers, possessions, health, spouse, and even our own life — it is all gift from God to be shared.

In our families, this is not only an external ethic (what we do), but also an internal ethos (who we are). We form an ethical system (habits, norms, and structures) for our family to serve, foster, and express our heart's desire (ethos) to live like a son or daughter of God. We don't just want to do what Jesus would do, but to live as the body of Christ. Our goal is not to be good or moral, but to *become Christ*. Jesus Christ is the Head, and we are his body. But there is only one Christ.

Christ and his Church thus together make up the "whole Christ" (*Christus totus*). The Church is one with Christ. The saints are acutely aware of this unity:

> Let us rejoice then and give thanks that we have become not only Christians, but Christ himself. Do you understand and grasp, brethren, God's grace toward us? Marvel and rejoice: we have become Christ. For if he is the head, we are the members; he and we together are the whole man. ... The fullness of Christ then is the head and the members. But what does "head and members" mean? Christ and the Church.
>
> Our redeemer has shown himself to be one person with the holy Church whom he has taken to himself.
>
> Head and members form as it were one and the same mystical person. (*Catechism of the Catholic Church* 795)

This is what it means to be fully human — divinity. Everything in this material world has been created for our sanctification. The Church was created from the side of Christ on the cross. As Eve was taken from the side of Adam in our Creation account, so the Church was made from the side of Christ. Christ is the bridegroom and the Church is his bride, his betrothed, his spouse. This is the very definition of sacrament: a sign instituted by Christ to confer grace. The Church is no mere human organization or institution. The Church is a "she," a bride, whose bridegroom is Lord, God, and Only Begotten Son of God the Father. She is one, holy, catholic, and apostolic not because of her members, but in spite of us.

COMMUNION IS THE KEY

Communion is the interpretive key to understand everything in heaven and on earth. God himself is a perfect Communion of Father, Son, and Holy Spirit. Three distinct Persons in such union that they are One. The Father is God. The Son is God. And the Holy Spirit is God. But the Father is not the Son, the Son is not the Father; and neither is the Holy Spirit. Yet while the Father is God, the Son is God, and the Holy Spirit is God, there are not three gods, but one. The Father is God because everything comes from him. He is the origin and source of all fatherhood. To father is to engender life that can exist outside of you and to ensure it's good. But who can receive the totality of God? Not us! Only God can receive the totality of God. Jesus Christ, the only begotten Son, stands before the Father and receives all of him. Then the Son, completing this perfect self-gift, entrusts himself back to the Father, glorifying him with all of who he is. Outside of time, the Father and the Son are this eternal exchange of love. So perfect is this divine exchange of Father and Son, the very giving and receiving of the Father to the Son is so real *it is the Holy Spirit,* "the Author and Giver of life who proceeds from the Father and the Son." This is what we profess at Mass every Sunday within our Creed. God is Love because God is this Divine Trinitarian Communion of Persons. We don't just say God *has* love or that God *loves,* but God *is* Love. So perfect is their Communion that Jesus Christ has said, "If you have seen me, you have seen the Father" … "The Father and I are One." While the experiencing of this mystery will be the delight of our eternity, this delight and eternity can and should begin now.

This is the God in whose image and likeness we are made. He is not a solitude but a Communion of Persons. Man, made in the image and likeness of God, male and female, has this call to communion literally stamped into the body as sexuality. God created sex when he created us. As Dr. Peter Kreeft observes, masculinity and femininity are cosmological — seen throughout the cosmos as complementarity from molecules to the Milky Way. Man, within the cosmos, manifests masculinity and femininity as male and female. Seen as a whole and not merely parts, complementarity speaks to a communion not just *in Creation* but *of the Creator.* This again is why, "The body, in fact, and only the body, is capable of making visible what is invisible: the spiritual and divine. It was created to transfer into the visible reality of the world, the mystery hidden... in God, and thus to be a sign of it" (*Theology of the Body,* 19:4).

What is this mystery? The mystery of love as the Communion of Persons that manifests in Creation as the communion of persons. We are also not a solitude. We do not find fulfillment, flourishing, or joy in solitude as an end or destiny. *This is not who we are.* It is only in the gift of self, given to and received by other persons, that we can *"become what we are."*

> This likeness reveals that man, who is the only creature on earth which God willed for itself, cannot fully find himself except through a sincere gift of himself. (*Gaudium et Spes,* 24)

Communion is the interpretive key to understanding all of reality. The creation account in Genesis 1 is a story of how God creates new separation and communion, whether it's light from dark on day one. the waters above in the waters below, to between land and sea on day three, or in the crowning of creation in man, made male and female. Even in this objective account of creation from God's view to man, we can recognize this key of communion flowing from the creator to his creation.

"Let us make man in our image and likeness, male and female he created them and bless them and said be fruitful and multiply have dominion over the earth and subdue it" (Gn 1:27–28).

This theme of communion extends to the subjective account of creation in Genesis 2. This Creation account from man's view to God begins with the Lord God forming from the dust a body, then breathing his spirit into that body before the poet proclaims man as a living being. Our human personhood itself is in a certain sense a communion of body and soul, matter and spirit. We are not spiritual beings. We are not animals. We human beings — or, more precisely, human persons — are made up of the matter of the natural world and the spirit of the supernatural. So how does a creature like us prosper? Where do we thrive? In what environment, ecosystem, or culture does a human person flourish?

In communion. We are made for life and love through communion with God and one another.

Because God is love and God is life, we, made in his image and likeness, can only love and live to the limit of our communion with him. This is the theology of love: God is the Logos of Love.

LOVE IS SELF-GIFT

How do we love? Love is self-gift. But we cannot give what we do not have or possess. So, a gift of self requires a possession or mastery of our self through the virtues, those firm and habitual dispositions to do the good. But we similarly cannot possess what we do not *know*. Self-knowledge leads and calls us to a self-mastery or self-possession, which makes it possible for us to love as self-gift. Love or self-gift, though, deepens our self-knowledge. It is the experience of love that reveals the deepest mystery of the person as lover and beloved. His deeper self-knowledge calls us deeper into the virtues of self-mastery and self-possession in order to make a *more sincere* self-gift. Deepening our self-knowledge even further, the transformative power of love becomes clearer. Love is not merely an act — it changes us. It *forms* us. Into what? Saints! We become what we love. When we love like Christ, we *become* Christ. Isn't that the promise? Isn't that the hope?

AND MARRIAGE IS THE ICON

The sanctifying power of love has marriage as its icon and the family as its school. When Christ raised natural marriage to the dignity of a sacrament, the family also was raised to the dignity of a *domestic church*. Through the sacraments husband and wife are gifted particular graces of life and love that bear witness to the entire Salvation Story: Creation, Fall, and Redemption. The Sacraments of Eucharist and Baptism, Matrimony and Reconciliation renew and grow these graces throughout our marriage. We are ministers to the Sacrament of Matrimony and stewards of God's gift of life and love.

The moment we pledge ourselves to one another freely, totally, faithfully, and fruitfully, we are married. However, the marriage is not "sealed, perfected, and brought to completion" until the spouses "have performed between themselves in a human manner the conjugal act which is per se suitable for the generation of children" (*Code of Canon Law,* 1061). Sexual union *consummates* the marriage. Moreover, the sexual act is a marital act precisely because it speaks the marital vow in the "language" of the body. The man and the woman "speak" the *agape* love pledge: "I give myself to you freely, totally, faithfully, and fruitfully from this day forward." With this sense the marital act doesn't "make" love as much as it "makes love present." The sexual act is a promise, because it is the act that invites new life. As stewards, we do not create new life with the marital embrace. The Holy Spirit is the author and giver of life, not us. Life is a gift that only God can give. But with puzzling generosity, God called us to be co-Creators with him — "co-" not meaning "equal," but "with."

STEWARDSHIP OF SEXUALITY

In what might rightly be described as the heart of what makes Catholic families dynamically different from other families is this *stewardship of our sexuality.* We are neither owners nor bystanders. Our stewardship is active, dynamic, and a call to engage our intellect, emotion, will, memory, and imagination to do the Father's will. Living this stewardship of sex is alone powerful enough to set our marriages and families apart from the world. They will know we are Christians by our *stewardship.* The joyful stewardship of our sexuality is an act of reverence. Reverence for our sexual powers naturally flows from our reverence for God and what he has gifted us, and what we promise in the wedding vows at the altar.

As a couple we seek God's will for us together *in prayer.* We seek spiritual direction and sacramental strength from our priests. We seek fellowship and counsel from other couples also longing to do God's will. We study and understand not just the *biology* of our bodies related to reproduction and reproductive health, but the *theology* of our bodies for procreation and the right use of our sexual powers. The biology reveals the theology, and the theology give the deepest meaning of the biology. We seek natural and supernatural wisdom in order to live our stewardship with honor, freedom, and joy. The right ordering of our sexuality within marriage depends on our understanding of both the biology and theology of the body. Together these natural and supernatural sources of wisdom empower us as co-Creators to live our stewardship with generosity and faith. What we all pledge at the altar — "accept children lovingly from God and bring them up according to the law of Christ and his Church" — each family receives their own call to receive children. Though every act of marital intercourse renews and re-presents the marriage vows, not every act of intercourse can achieve pregnancy.

By its nature, the marital act is procreative, whether or not conception occurs. (Which is why infertile and post-menopausal couples still have valid, procreative marriages.) However, there is only a twelve- to twenty-four-hour period each menstrual cycle when conception is even possible. That's how long a woman's egg or ova can live after it is released at ovulation and before it disintegrates in the outer third of the fallopian tube. This is the one "window" of fertility in every woman's cycle of fertility that begins with menarche and ends with menopause. Clearly, if God wanted every act of intercourse to achieve pregnancy, he would have a larger window than twelve hours out of a typical thirty-day fertility cycle. While pregnancy is not possible with every act of intercourse, every marital act in the name of love must remain open to life. This means that any act before, during, or after the sexual act intended to render the sexual act sterile is not just an attack on the life-giving nature of the marital embrace, but also an attack on the marital love that it is meant to be renewing.

CONFRONTING CONTRACEPTION

Contraception, by definition, is any deliberate act before, during, or after the sexual act in order to render the act sterile. Contraception is a very specific type of birth control or family planning that tries to change the meaning of the marital act. It is important that couples not confuse contraception with the broader categories of birth control and family planning. Family planning, the broadest category, is not only moral but part of the promise we make in the marital vow to be co-Creators with him through our marriage. Within family planning there are more specific methods of birth control. Though the term "birth control" is used in condemnation by earlier Church documents (e.g., *Casti Connubii*), it can now be broadly understood to include both immoral acts of contraception, sterilization, and abortion *and* morally licit periodic continence or abstinence. One reliable way to "control birth" is to *not have sex.*

Contraception, however, is very specific in its definition as an attack on the nature of a specific marital act. This is why the moral condemnation of contraception can be so strong and definitively condemned as an *intrinsic* moral evil. Because of its specific attack on both life and love in the marital act, no good intention or circumstance can justify its use. In her infallible wisdom on this matter of faith and morals, the Church calls us to a "responsible parenthood" (*Humanae Vitae,* 10) that is exercised by either generously accepting a large number of children or, with grave ("weighty") reasons and due reverence for the natural law, postponing children for a definite or indeterminate time.

This teaching from *Humanae Vitae* has confused and angered Catholics since its release July 25, 1968. It has angered those on one side who embrace contraception and those who embrace a philosophy of total providence of God on the other. How can you be responsible with many children or with none at all? Why does it matter how we space or avoid children? And why does each and every marital act need to be open to life? While Pope Paul VI spoke definitively on the *what* (the grave evil of contraception), it would be another ten years before the compelling *why* would be part of the Church's teachings. Saint John Paul II's *Theology of the Body* was written specifically to provide the deeper and broader context of the truth and dignity of marriage and sex in God's plan.

Where Pope Paul VI's *Humanae Vitae* addressed the *moral* problem, the *Theology of the Body* grounded us in the *anthropology.* We act in accord with who we think we are. Identity shapes actions, and actions reveal who we think we are. In the thought of Saint John Paul II, modern man has accepted a partial, false, or *inadequate* anthropology based on our own limited life experiences and experiences of those around us. The dominant example of a false anthropology today is one evangelized by pornography. In this worldview, people are not made for love, but for my use. Your value is directly proportional to the pleasure I derive from you.

In stark contrast, an *adequate* anthropology is Christological. It is received from God the Father, Jesus Christ the Son, and the Holy Spirit who guides us in all wisdom and truth. Trusting in the dignity of creation, most especially our own experience as a body-person, it is possible to discern both the universal truth of our humanity *and* our particular call as a unique, unrepeatable creation in God's image and likeness. We can both "re-read the language of the body in truth" and discern our own experiences of our life to know and live God's plan for a joyful life. Our origin, history, and destiny are knowable by the grace of God, and his Church. Freely choosing to live that plan is a work of sanctification and salvation. As Saint Paul said, we *"work out our salvation in fear and trembling"* (Phil 2:12).

The natural marriage of Adam and Eve is our origin. Supernatural marriage of Christ the Bridegroom and the Church as the Bride is our destiny. And it is the Sacrament of Marriage — yours and mine — that is the hinge connecting Genesis to Revelation, our origin in the Garden of Eden to our destiny as Bride at the Wedding Feast of the Lamb (Eph 5).

THEY WILL KNOW WE ARE CHRISTIANS BY OUR JOY

For more than twenty-five years, my wife, Melanie, and I have tried to understand, live, and proclaim the goodness, truth, and beauty of marriage and family life faithful to Jesus Christ. The key word here is "tried." While we have not gotten it always right, through good times and bad, there has been joy. In the beautiful mess of our marriage and eight kids, the noble Catholic ideals of marriage have been a constant call to our hearts. We know that for too many families, these ideals feel more like burdens, rebukes, or accusations, but *something* has kept these unattainable perfections fresh and refreshing for us. Firm yet affirming. Heavy yet uplifting.

Since 1993, Melanie and I have had the gift of working with tens of thousands of couples preparing for marriage, learning natural family planning (NFP), struggling with difficult teachings on sex, or persevering difficult years of marriage or parenting. Working with other couples while struggling to navigate our own family life has had two unexpected benefits. First, it has kept the teachings of our faith (theology, philosophy, morality) fresh, present, and accessible. And second, we have been granted an intimate place in the lives of so many couples also longing for love, peace, and joy. This familiarity has not bred contempt, but awe, fascination, and wonder at what God has created with marriage and family.

This *ad-extra* ministry work, along with the *ad-intra*, first apostolate of our own marriage and family, has convinced us that there is something divine in the ordinariness of marriage and family life. More so when we intentionally order the ordinary things to God's plan, for sure, but even when we don't. I am reminded of the quote in *Les Miserables*, "what is hidden is divine." *("quid obscurum, quid divinum")*. That holiness remains in even in our world today. Even for Christian couples, it can be difficult to recognize the divine in the ordinary things of life, let alone in the messy realities of our own marriage and family. But there is real divinity there. How dynamically different will Catholic families live when the true meaning and purpose of and reverence for family life is known, lived, and revered? As in all things, we act in accord with who we think we are. There in the moments of hurt and anger, in the awkward silence, or the dirty kitchen, overflowing laundry baskets, chaos, the doubts and fears of being a husband or father or mother or wife, our actions reveal our identity and beliefs. There is something divine in the small ordinary things of life, probably more so than in the big, grand events. There, in the silence or the conflict, and agony or delight, we come face-to-face with our own weakness or lack. Reaching that boundary of our own inability forces us to look elsewhere. Even to God. Where we see failure or our own inability to get our stuff together, God only asks us for our stuff as an offering.

Everything matters to him because all matter matters. We are stewards, not owners. Stewards who worship God liturgically "live, and move, and have our being" differently than those who do not. Within the home, our spirituality is the fire of sacramental, liturgical stewardship. To the world, we witness by our joy. When Christian families blaze with this fire and joy, people will come from miles around to watch us burn. When our time on earth has ended, may we hear from God our Father, *"Well done, my good and faithful servant. Come, share my joy!"*

DISCUSSION QUESTIONS

1. When the Church describes your family as a "school of love," "domestic church," or "God's greatest masterpiece," what feelings, thoughts, or images does that conjure in you?

2. Do the lofty ideals of marriage and family inspire, puzzle, or discourage you in your own marriage and family life?

3. What is your "love story"? Can you recognize how Christ has been present throughout it? Do you share this story as a witness to others? If not, why not? If so, how was it received?

4. What are some "ordinary" things in your marriage and family you might now see as worthy of offering to God for thanksgiving?

5. What could this idea of *sexual stewardship* mean to you, your marriage, and your family?

Putting It All Together: A New Vision for Family Spirituality and Family Ministry

This final section offers a practical framework for continuing the conversation about what a domestic-church-based spirituality looks like in practice.

Drawing from the available research — and particularly the work of the various contributors to the Symposium on Catholic Family Life and Spirituality — the following section proposes an outline of the Liturgy of Domestic Church Life and the three "rites" that comprise this liturgy.

In the first chapter in this section, the Popcaks, along with their associate David McClow, unpack the practical significance of viewing family life though a liturgical lens. Specifically, that the liturgical view of family life allows family life, *itself*, to be seen as holy, not just for the time families spend in prayer or in service to others, but in their intentional efforts to bring Christ's sacrificial, transformative love to one another. They conclude this chapter by enumerating the three "rites" that, they suggest, make up the Liturgy of Domestic Church Life: the Rite of Relationship, the Rite of Rituals of Connection, and the Rite of Reaching Out. The Popcaks argue that these rites represent the primary and normative way God forms his children in the threefold mission of priest, prophet, and royal (respectively).

The remaining chapters explore each of the three rites in detail.

The Rite of Relationship is proposed as the primary and normative way God empowers Christian families to form his children in the priestly mission of Baptism. Through the conscious practice of sacrificial love in the home, parents-as-priests facilitate an encounter with God at home, work to make the common aspects of family life a little way of holiness, faciliate human integration/transformation, and make a true communion of persons possible.

The Rite of Rituals of Connection is proposed as the primary and normative way God empowers Christian families to form his children in the prophetic mission of Baptism. Strong family rituals for praying, working, talking, and praying together enable family members to prophetically model how a healthy Christian person must relate to prayer, work, relationship, and leisure.

The Rite of Reaching Out is proposed as the primary and normative way God empowers Christian families to form his children in the royal mission of Baptism. By exploring ways to serve each other, their community, and their parish *together*, families become the primary engines of evangelization and positive social change that they are meant to be.

Throughout each of these chapters, many practical, concrete suggestions for practicing these "rites" are offered, as well as specific recommendations for pastoral ministers who wish to help families fully celebrate the Liturgy of Domestic Church Life.

CHAPTER TWENTY

Come and Be Formed! The 3R's in the Liturgy of Domestic Church Life

---

GREGORY K. POPCAK, LISA A. POPCAK, DAVID McCLOW

Pastoral Solutions Institute

FIVE QUICK TAKES

1. Family life is holy, not only for the time families spend in prayer or service, but any time they intentionally seek to share the love of Christ in their relationships and service to one another.

2. The image of the family as an "Icon of the Trinity" is the basis for a renewed vision of family spirituality and family ministry.

3. Family life is liturgical in that it is instituted, not invented, conveys God's love and blessing in tangible ways, facilitates transformation and integration through grace, and enables the faithful to participate in the life of the Trinity.

4. The Liturgy of Domestic Church Life comprises three "rites": the Rite of Relationship, the Rite of Rituals of Connection, and the Rite of Reaching Out.

5. The three "rites" of the Liturgy of Domestic Church Life enable the family to offer ongoing formation in the priestly, prophetic, and royal mission of Baptism, respectively.

WHAT MAKES A FAMILY HOLY?

In our experience, some people tend to think that family life is only holy to the degree that a family spends time on its knees, while others tend to think that family life is only holy to the degree that a family spends its time in service to others.

It's true that both family prayer and charitable service are important components of a healthy family spirituality, but to limit it to these practices ignores at least 98 percent of the activities that make up family life. Is it really possible that only 2 percent of family life leads to holiness? Unfortunately, a lot of the people we speak with appear to think so.

In *Divine Likeness,* Cardinal Ouellet wrote, "Until recently the family was considered the terminal point, a field for applying … the Church's pastoral decisions. The post-Vatican II appreciation of the family as 'domestic church' … opens to it undreamed-of perspectives of participation in the salvific mission of the Church" (2006. Chap. 1, par. 3).

That's an exciting prospect. But because the wider Church primarily exercises its salvific mission through liturgy, if we truly want to unpack the family's potential to share in that mission, we have to question the degree to which the domestic church, itself, is liturgical — not just for what it does, but in its very nature.

The term "domestic church," resurrected by Vatican II, isn't meant to be a pet name by which the "real Church," (i.e., the institutional Church) refers to its inferior. As Evdokimov explains, when we speak of the domestic church, "It isn't merely a question of resembling the Church … the community of the spouses is an organic part of the ecclesial community: it is the Church" (357).

Likewise, in *Amoris Laetitia*, Pope Francis wrote, "the Church is a family of families, constantly enriched by the lives of all those domestic Churches" (87).

But if the domestic church *is* church, that suggests that relationships within the family must somehow also be liturgical, because Church life is inherently *liturgical* in nature. As Philip Mamalakis explains, "Families are not church only when they read scriptures, pray, study the faith, or help the needy. They are church in their (turning toward) love, and it is Christ's love that constitutes the church of the home" (Mamalakis 2013).

Building on arguments like this, it would appear that family life is liturgical; not just for the certain, specific activities in which it engages, but also in the nature and quality of the relationships that comprise Christian family life.

Of course, classically, "liturgy" is understood to be a "public act of worship." But how can changing diapers, paying bills, keeping house, negotiating conflicts, and all the rest be public acts of worship? The fact is, Christian families operate in the world; and in that sense, everything they do is "public" to at least some degree. Likewise, the *Catechism* tells us that worship of God "sets man free from turning in on himself." When Christian families are taught to bring the self-donative love of Christ to even the lowliest tasks associated with family life, these practices become public acts of worship, because they help us come outside of ourselves and enable us to communicate God's love first to the members of our household and then to the world. Rather than simply trying to "get credit for stuff families already have to do," the view that family life is liturgical — that is, it is a public act of worship — gives outward signs of the many ways God's grace operates to make the common holy.

But truly appreciating how even the most mundane aspects of family life can be liturgical must begin with the big-picture idea that the family is an "icon of the Trinity."

THE FAMILY IS THE "ICON OF THE TRINITY"

"It has been said, in a beautiful and profound way, that our God in his deepest mystery is not a solitude, but a family, since he has in himself fatherhood, sonship and the essence of the family, which is love" (Saint John Paul II, 1979). The Trinity *is* a family. The human family is an "icon of the Trinity" created in the image and likeness of the "Heavenly Family" that exists at the heart of God. This insight cuts right to the heart of our investigation into the basis for an authentic domestic-church-based spirituality. As Ouellet put it, "The supernatural participation in the Trinitarian communion is the ultimate basis of the family as an ecclesial reality."

In this view, the Christian family is Church — and therefore liturgical — because it is capable of imaging the inner life of God in a way that no other human institution can.

An icon isn't "just a picture"; it is meant to give us a window into a divine mystery. Saint Gregory the Great explained that by looking at an icon, "even the ignorant see what they ought to follow; in it, the illiterate read."

In some way, by saying that the family is an icon of the Trinity, the Church asserts that the family doesn't just symbolize the Trinity, but draws us up and into it. God intends the Christian family to facilitate, for all people, those who are both "literate and illiterate" of the Gospel, a meaningful and deeply phenomenological encounter with the inner life and love of God.

This phenomenological encounter — incarnated in the relational life of the Christian family — is the very essence of the term "the new evangelization." In our post-modern, post-Christian world, words mean nothing. In particular, Millennials and Gen Z have heard it all. Growing up in the third and fourth generations of the culture of divorce, today's young adults believe that "I love you," "You can count on me," "I'll always be here for you," and similar phrases are just empty sentiments (Marquardt 2006).

How do you evangelize a generation that believes that words don't mean anything and promises don't count? You have to *show* them that the love experienced in an intentionally Christian household is different than what they have experienced anywhere else, because it isn't rooted in human affection, but rather the deep love that flows from the heart of God.

Families can only be authentic outposts of evangelization and engines of positive social change if they live and bear witness to Trinitarian love in their relationships. Of course, this Trinitarian understanding of the family is inherently *liturgical* because, as the *Catechism* explains, liturgy is "the work of the Trinity" (*CCC* — P2, S1, C1, A1).

So what? What difference does any of this make to our effort to establish an authentic, domestic-church-based spirituality? Simply put, we believe that this idea points to at least four important things that liturgy and domestic church life have in common, each of which clarifies how God wishes to use simple families, like yours and ours, to touch hearts and change the world. Specifically, both liturgy and the domestic church:

1. are instituted, not invented
2. convey God's love and blessing in tangible ways
3. facilitate transformation and integration through grace
4. enable the faithful to participate in the life of the Trinity

Let's take a brief look at each of these.

1. INSTITUTED, NOT INVENTED

The first point of connection between liturgy and the domestic church is that both are instituted, not invented.

In *The Spirit of the Liturgy*, Ratzinger wrote, "*In any form, liturgy includes some kind of 'institution.' It cannot spring from imagination, our own creativity — for then it would remain ... mere self-affirmation."*

If we say that the domestic church is inherently liturgical, we have to accept that — like any other liturgy — the Christian understanding of the *form* of the human family (i.e., one woman, one man, and the children they form through the complementarity of their love) isn't merely a social construct that we're free to redesign as we see fit. Rather, it is a divinely revealed institution.

Saint John Paul II referred to marriage as *"the primordial sacrament."* The marriage of our First Parents stood at the center of the Original Unity that existed between God, man, and woman before the Fall; a union that Christ later sought to restore by instituting all the sacraments, including restoring the Father's original marriage.

Additionally, by having only chosen men as apostles, the Church teaches that Jesus meant to communicate that there is something about maleness that is essential to the office of the ministerial priesthood. If that's true, it would seem that we must also accept that by raising marriage to the dignity of a sacrament at the wedding feast of Cana, Jesus meant to assert that there was something unique about the lifelong union between one man and one woman that distinguished it from every other household arrangement. To put this in liturgical terms, we might say that Jesus chose man and woman to constitute the essential components of the Liturgy of Domestic Church Life.

Joseph Atkinson offers a comprehensive look at the revealed and instituted nature of God's vision for marriage and family life in his chapter in this volume and in his excellent book Biblical and Theological Foundations of the Family. But even from the two data points we've offered in this brief reflection, we can see that God has claimed an important stake in the life of the family, both from the beginning of time and at the beginning of his ministry on earth. If liturgy must be instituted rather than invented to be considered "liturgical," both Scripture and tradition demonstrate that the Catholic vision of the domestic church isn't merely a social construction, but a divinely revealed one.

2. CONVEYS GOD'S LOVE AND BLESSING

Second, both liturgy and the domestic church exist to convey God's love and blessing to the world.

The *Catechism* explains, "From the beginning until the end of time the whole of God's work is a *blessing*" (1079). As this passage suggests, it's liturgy's full-time job — so to speak — to convey God's love and blessing to his people. To say that domestic church life is liturgical, it must also fulfill this duty in some way.

Perhaps the most significant way that families convey God's love and blessing is through the hard work of "forming a communion of persons" through grace — the first of the four family tasks outlined in *Familiaris Consortio*.

As an illustration, in *Divine Likeness*, Ouellet, reflecting on Ephesians 3:14–21, asserts that the *human* relationship between parents and children directly images the *divine fatherhood* of God and is rooted and grounded in Christ's love. In short, the more a parent's love reflects the love that flows from God's heart, the more perfectly that interaction represents a liturgical encounter.

If something must convey the blessing and love of God in a tangible way in order to be considered liturgical, it's clear that domestic church life is directly ordered to participating in this sacred work.

3. FACILITATES TRANSFORMATION AND INTEGRATION

Third, both liturgy and the domestic church facilitate integration and transformation of the people who participate in them.

The *Catechism* tells us that the purpose of liturgy is "to make the saving work of Christ present and active by his transforming power" (1112). In light of this statement, we see that the domestic church functions *as liturgy* when it facilitates both *healthy human integration* and *the graceful transformation of its members* through the practice of self-donative love. This process enables families to form loving, responsible persons who are capable of entering into authentic communion with God, their family, and the world.

The domestic church fulfills this duty by "serving life," which is the second task identified in *Familiaris Consortio*. This task goes far beyond a willingness to have children. In the document *Family and Human Procreation,* the Pontifical Council for the Family observed that "serving life" also involves carefully attending to the developmental needs of every child at each age and stage. By doing this, parents can raise children to be whole persons through the process they called "integral procreation."

The document states, "Procreation is integral when the child is introduced into life in such a way that he develops totally." It goes on to say, "Saint Thomas describes these tasks of parents — who nourish and educate their children — using the image of the maternal uterus. For the child, his family, and home are comparable to a [spiritual womb]."

In other words, in its role as both "spiritual womb" and "school of love and virtue," the family becomes a conduit of grace by which God and parents co-create whole, integrated, mature persons. This clearly echoes the Muldoons' insight regarding *perichoresis*. Perichoretic love "is about making room for all members of the family to thrive." They also note that *perichoresis* is used to describe the inner relations of the Trinity. It is a *perichoretic* love that makes room for the other both in the life of the Trinity *and* in the life of the human family. The domestic church is liturgical in that it facilitates this tangible encounter with the power of God's transforming, perichoretic love as it flows through the life of the family.

4. FACILITATES PARTICIPATION IN THE LIFE OF THE TRINITY

Coming full circle, the fourth and — for the purposes of this discussion — final way that the domestic church functions as liturgy is that it allows families to participate in the life of the Trinity.

As Ratzinger notes, liturgy "not only saves mankind but is also meant to draw the whole of reality into communion with God." This corresponds with Ouellet's earlier assertion that "the supernatural participation in the Trinitarian communion is the ultimate basis of the family as an ecclesial reality."

How does the family participate in the life of the Trinity? Through mutually self-donative love. God is a family *and* God is love. The eternal, self-donative, loving communion of the Father, Son, and Holy Spirit creates the communion of persons, a family.

In the Lord's Prayer, Jesus indicates that his disciples should order their lives according to the Father's will "on earth as it is in heaven."

Striving to replicate this Trinitarian love in our our human relationships is the most direct way we can follow this command. Famlies bring this Trinitarian love to earth in a way that is "a great mystery" through the physical union of husband and wife (Eph 5:21–33). With their bodies, man and woman each make a *gift of self to* the other, and *each one receives* the other. When rightly ordered, this love brings forth new life, both in the form of the intimte bond that grows between the couple and sometimes also through the conception of children. This loving, embodied exchange serves as the liturgical foundation of the domestic church — a communion of persons that produces persons.

Of course, this mutually self-donative, Trinitarian love is also found on the psychological or conversational level of marriage and family relationships. Everything from a simple hello to a deep sharing of hopes, dreams, fears, and needs — and everything in between — is a making of a gift of self to the other that is always done in the hope of being received and returned. In every exchange, love received and returned brings new life in the form of a deeper communion: the giver is affirmed, and the movement of love is enacted or embodied both spiritually and physically in some way. Every interaction rooted in this mutual and simultaneous loving exchange is a participation in the life and love of the Trinity.

The giving and receiving structure of self-donative love can also be found in many other aspects of family life, like the gaze between a parent and child (including during diaper changes), cooking and cleaning, reading aloud, or a hug. And if every good conversation, gaze, act, and touch can be a participation in the giving and receiving of love in the Trinity, the floodgates are opened to practice a distinctly liturgical family spirituality the other "98 percent of the time" (i.e., when a family isn't specifically praying or serving others). Relationships are/become fundamentally liturgical, and every time families turn toward each other in Christ's love, no matter how silly or profound or mundane the exhange may be, they are growing in holiness.

Of course, this Trinitarian love is first experienced and lived out in the family, but it doesn't stop there. When God's love is experienced, it radiates out. It attracts and includes others. It is always generative or life-giving. The family who loves each other can function as a beacon for the world just by its very existence and nature, but the Christian family also actively reaches out to others in the world and draws them back into communion among its members and with God. In this way, families, through the Liturgy of Domestic Church Life, consecrate the world to Christ.

Again, because liturgy is the "work of the Trinity," the ability of the family to function as an "icon of the Trinity" is the basis for its liturgical identity, which, in turn, is the basis for developing a spirituality that is unique to domestic church life. As we conclude this reflection of the liturgical nature of the family, it appears clear that the family functions as liturgy in more than just an analogous or metaphorical way. If we can think of marriage as the "primordial sacrament," it naturally follows that the domestic church functions a primordial liturgy that — like all liturgy — was (1) instituted by God, (2) conveys God's love and blessing, (3) facilitates integration through grace, and (4) calls the world into communion with him, not just since the beginning of the Church, but from the beginning of time.

WHAT "RITES" COMPRISE THE LITURGY OF DOMESTIC CHURCH LIFE?

Of course, it's one thing to speak of the existence of a Liturgy of Domestic Church Life; it's another thing to define what that liturgy looks like in practice.

We're all aware that the Liturgy of the Eucharist comprises different rites (e.g., opening rite, penitential rite, communion rite, etc.) that make the Mass recognizable and relatable no matter where in the world we might celebrate it. Similarly, we suggest that the Liturgy of Domestic Church Life is also made up of specific "rites" that can enable the faithful to live the Catholic difference in family life, regardless of the context in which they find themselves.

THE 3R'S OF THE LITURGY OF DOMESTIC CHURCH LIFE

One of the many challenges of articulating the rites of the Liturgy of Domestic Church life is that every family is different — culturally, economically, demographically, and even structurally.

Psychology offers us two different paths for developing a template for an authentic, domestic-church-based spirituality. The first is to adopt a content-based (i.e., practice-based) approach. The second option is a more process-based approach (Held 1991).

Like it sounds, a *content-based* approach would require every Catholic family to engage in specific practices such as daily Mass, or the Rosary, or certain acts of charitable service in order to celebrate the Liturgy of Domestic Church Life to the fullest. Obviously, because of the uniqueness of every family and their circumstances, a strictly content-based approach is not possible, appropriate, or desireable.

By contrast, a *process-based* approach examines what research suggests about the general structures or processes that apply universally to a particular group, while still allowing for individual differences of expression. For instance, every religious order requires its members to make vows of poverty, chastity, and obedience. But how those vows are lived out can vary widely from one order to the next. These three, common vows provide a basic framework for Catholic religious life, but each family of religious is given a reasonable degree of latitude to determine the best way to live those vows in light of their context, charism, and mission.

Social science research — especially over the last thirty years — reveals that there are certain processes that every healthy, high-functioning family share regardless of that family's sociocultural, economic, or demographic context. Specifically, these processes include strength of attachment; the frequency, strength, and quality of family rituals; and the ability of a family to maintain cohesion while pro-socially engaging in the wider community. The way these processes are lived out vary widely from household to household, but the basic structures are still there.

In light of this, we propose using these three universal building blocks of healthy family functioning as the basis for articulating the "rites" that constitute the full celebration of the Liturgy of Domestic Church Life. We will also discuss how each of these "rites" provides ongoing formation in one of the three baptismal missions.

- **The Rite of Attachment** provides ongoing formation in the priestly mission of baptism.

- **The Rite of Rituals of Connection** provides ongoing formation in the prophetic mission of baptism.
- **The Rite of Reaching Out** provides ongoing formation in the royal mission of baptism.

We like to think of these proposed rites as the "3R's" of domestic church life. Drawing from Joseph White's chapter on the divine pedagogy in family life, we would argue that these "rites" represent the normative way God forms his children in the threefold baptismal mission.

In liturgical terms, these three rites might be said to constitute the *substantial components* of the Liturgy of Domestic Church Life. That is, the absence of any one of these "rites" wouldn't necessarily negate the validity or basic integrity of a particular domestic church, but could render it profoundly dysfunctional and unable to effectively serve as a "spiritual womb." Even so, while each healthy family includes these components, every family would be free to develop practices that allow them to celebrate these rites in a manner that respects their unique circumstances.

In the next few mini-chapters, we will explore the role that each of these "rites" plays in both the formation of God's people and the transformation of the world through grace.

DISCUSSION QUESTIONS

1. Beyond the theological value of the concept, what is the practical significance of viewing the family as an "icon of the Trinity"? How could this view challenge Catholic families to relate differently to each other than other families?

2. What is the practical significance of viewing family life as a liturgy? How does it change your understanding of family life to see that it is instituted, not invented; that it conveys God's grace and blessing; that it facilitates transformation through grace; and that it calls families to participate in the life of the Trinity?

3. What is one simple thing you could do to live this vision of family life more fully with your own family? What is one way you could promote this vision in your ministry work?

CHAPTER TWENTY-ONE

The Rite of Relationship/Attachment: A Formation Program in the Priestly Mission of Baptism

FIVE QUICK TAKES

1. The Rite of Relationships facilitates ongoing formation in the priestly mission of baptism by giving families the opportunity to practice the sacrificial, self-donative love that flows from the one priesthood of Christ. This is the normative way God forms his children in the common priesthood.

2. Through the exercise of this sacrifical, priestly love, families (1) transform the common tasks of family life into a "little way of holiness," (2) facilitate healthy human formation/integration, and (3) make a true communion of persons possible.

3. The closest human equivalent to the self-donative love that exists at the heart of the Trinity is known to psychologists as the love that facilitates "secure attachment."

4. Secure attachment between parents and caregivers is facilitated when family members respond promptly, generously, and consistently to each other's needs.

5. Human attachment styles consistently predict "God attachment" style for good or ill. Secure attachment is the psychological term for what the Church calls "human formation."

The first rite of the Liturgy of Domestic Church Life — and we would argue, the most foundational to an authentic, domestic-church-based spirituality — is the Rite of Attachment. This rite facilitates ongoing formation in the priestly mission of baptism. Reflecting on the principles of the divine pedagogy of family life as articulate by Joseph White in his chapter in this volume, we would argue that the Rite of Attachment represents the normative pathway God uses to form his children in the exercise of their common priesthood.

A priest's role is to engage in sacrifices that make the transcendent imminent and the common holy. In his explanation of the common priesthood, Bishop Robert Barron says, "A priest fosters holiness, precisely in the measure that he or she serves as a bridge between God and human beings. The reconciliation of divinity and humanity produces in human beings a wholeness or integration, a coming together of the often warring elements within the self."

Using Barron's framework, the parent as priest works to model a responsible, self-donative love that (1) transforms the common tasks of family life into a "little way of holiness" (as per Saint Thérèse of Lisieux), (2) facilitates healthy human formation/integration, and (3) makes a true communion of persons possible. The intimate family dynamic produced by this priestly-parental effort communicates the kind of transformative, integrating love that most accurately reflects the heart of the Trinity and allows the family to function as a "spiritual womb."

In converstions about family spirituality, there can be a strong temptation to limit the discussion to specific spiritual practices. But it makes little sense to speak of a family spirituality that is separate — in any way — from the *quality of the relationships* between family members. The chapters by Bengtson, Bartkus, and Narvaez in this volume speak to this reality at length. Drawing from their work, and other research like it, we note in *Discovering God Together: The Catholic Guide to Raising Faithful Kids* that children are much more likely to own their faith as adults if, growing up, "they have experienced the faith as the source of the warmth in their homes." This dynamic has profound ramfications for the church as a whole. As Pope Francis explains, "The experience of love in families is a perennial source of strength for the life of the Church."

In human terms, this mutually self-donative, healing, transforming, Trinitarian love of which we are speaking most closely resembles the dynamic psychologists refer to as **"secure attachment."**

Just to be clear, some readers may be familiar with the term "attachment parenting." Although we do promote attachment parenting practices in our popular work, we're not specifically talking about a particular parenting style in this context. Attachment parenting, per se, promotes a set of practices that are intended to encourage secure attachment, but these practices aren't the same thing as secure attachment.

In general, *secure attachment* results when parents respond *prompt-*

ly, generously, and consistently to the physical, emotional, relational, and spiritual needs of their child. This prompt, generous, and consistent attention results in the child naturally and spontaneously "turning toward" the parent, and viewing the attached caregiver as the primary source for acquiring the nurturance, resources, and guidance he or she needs to flourish.

Secure attachment is fostered when parents are generous with their affection, provide ample but sincere affirmation, foster strong family rituals, prioritize relationship time over activities, and adopt a loving-guidance approach to discipline (akin to Saint John Bosco's *Preventive System* of education). (See Bowlby [1988] and Ainsworth [2015] for a more comprehensive look at secure and insecure attachment.)

Both securely attached children and adults display healthy interdependence, strong empathy skills, a greater capacity for sound moral reasoning, good self-control, and high degrees of resilience. Likewise, they are comfortable needing others and being needed by others, giving and receiving appropriate affection, and capable of setting respectful boundaries so that healthy relationships can be cultivated and unhealthy relationships can be weeded out.

Of course, attachment is more than a psychological or spiritual reality. It is neurological as well. Research using functional imaging technology shows that consistent, healthy, parental-attachment behaviors literally stimulate growth in the child's "social brain," the neurological seat of relational, emotional, and moral reasoning. Other studies illustrate that poor parental attachment behaviors inhibit the development of the child's social brain; which, in turn, diminishes the child's capacity for intimacy, empathy, pro-social behavior, and healthy moral reasoning. As we argue in *Parenting with Grace*, the *Theology of the Body* allows us to see that God's design of our body offers strong evidence for how he wishes parents and children to love one another. God has literally wired the body in such a way that it requires secure attachment for optimal physical, psychological, moral, and spiritual functioning.

Daniel Siegel, distinguished fellow of the American Psychiatric Association, asserts that secure attachment is responsible for fostering the eight components of good mental health (see table 1).

Table 1.
Secure Attachment Facilitates the Eight Components of "Good Mental Health"

1. Body Regulation — the ability to keep the organs of the body and the autonomic nervous system (e.g., heart rate, respiration, body temperature) coordinated and balanced. Body regulation isn't just about physical health. Emotions begin as an embodied experience. For example, a racing heart and shallow respiration often precipitate feelings of panic/anxiety. Feelings of exhaustion or under-stimulation often precipitate depression.

2. Attuned Communication — the ability to pick up on the meaning of subtle, nonverbal, physical cues (facial expressions, tones of voice, posture) that indicate another person's emotional states and degree of well-being.

3. Emotional Balance — the ability to maintain optimal emotional functioning; that is, I know how to be emotionally stimulated enough to be aware and engaged in my circumstances and relationships, but not so emotionally stimulated that I am regularly flooded by my feelings and carried away by them.

4. Response Flexibility — the ability to pause before acting on my impulses and willfully change the direction of my actions if doing so suits me better than my initial impulses. People with ADHD, pathological anger, addictions, and other impulse-control problems struggle with this skill.

5. Fear Modulation — the ability to consciously reduce one's fear response. People with anxiety and panic disorders, especially, have a difficult time modulating the brain's fear responses. They become easily flooded with anxiety when others might just experience nervousness or even excitement.

6. Insight — the ability to reflect on my life experiences in

a way that links my past, present, and future in a coherent, cohesive, compassionate manner. Insight helps me make sense of both the things that have happened to me in the past and the things that are happening to me now.

7.   Empathy — Essentially, empathy is the ability to have insight (as defined above) into other people. Empathy is the ability to imagine what it is like to be another person, and to reflect on their experiences in a way that links their past, present, and future in a coherent, cohesive. compassionate manner. Empathy helps you make sense of other people's lives, the way they think, and their feelings.

8.   Morality — the ability to imagine, reason, and behave from the perspective of the greater good. Includes the ability to delay gratification and find ways to get my needs met while understanding and accommodating the needs of others. Darcia Narvaez's work explores this connection comprehensively.

The more securely attached a person is, the more he or she is able to demonstrate the eight social-brain-based skills that support good mental, relational, and spiritual health.

By contrast, the more insecurely attached a person is, the more he or she will struggle to consistently exhibit some or all of the eight foundational mental health skills. Insecure attachment results when parents, for whatever reason, struggle with or resist responding to their children's physical, emotional, relational, and/or spiritual needs.

There are two (basic) types of insecure attachment: anxious attachment and avoidant attachment. Anxious attachment results when parents respond in a habitually delayed, reluctant, or inconsistent manner to their child's bids to meet his or her needs. Anxiously attached people are at high risk for scrupulosity/neurotic guilt, codependency, fears of abandonment, struggles with basic trust, poor self-care, anxiety disorders, substance abuse (particularly opiods), and the inappropriate use of affection/sex as a strategy to foster relational security.

For its part, avoidant attachment, results from parents' miserly responses to their child's needs — especially emotional and relational needs. Parents of avoidantly attached children may not be — strictly speaking — abusive or neglectful, but they tend to be terminally disengaged, unaffectionate, intolerant of emotional displays, and allergic to anything that looks too much like "neediness."

Avoidantly attached people tend to be suspicious of relationships and exhibit an unhealthy sense of autonomy, poor insight, and impaired empathy. They tend to be workaholics who prefer chasing accomplishment over intimacy. They often display a selfish (e.g., "consumer" or "power-based") approach to sex. They are also prone to anger control problems, substance abuse (typically stimulants), and somatic complaints rooted in their inability to appropriately express needs and emotions.

Poor attachment should be of particular concern to pastoral ministers. Research shows that a person's human attachment style corresponds perfectly to their God attachment style. Anxious God attachment leads people to view God as a punishing parent, while avoidant God attachment makes people either highly resistant to any relationship with God, or relegates them to one that is rooted in duty and rules over intimacy (Clinton and Sibcy 2009; Clinton and Straub 2014).

Finally, because of its role in a host of mental and physical disorders, insecure attachment is a serious public health issue. A 2014 study by Princeton University found that 40 percent of children in the United States are insecurely attached (Moullin, Waldfogel, and Washbrook 2014). Other studies have found insecure attachment rates to be as high as 66 percent in countries like Germany that, culturally speaking, encourate low rates of parental affection and early childhood "independence" (Klaus and Karin Grossman et al. 1981, 1985). These studies powerfully illustrate Saint John Paul's famous warning that "as the family goes, so goes the nation, and so goes the world in which we live."

In sum, a person's *attachment style* represents their unconscious, neurologically based inclination to turn toward or away from both others and God. Without secure attachment, an individual's potential for achieving personal integration, healthy human relationships, and an honest, intimate, relationship with God are significantly compromised.

The Rite of Attachment represents the process by which the child's heart is turned toward the parent and the parent's heart is turned toward God, who reveals his face to the child through this dynamic, intimate communion. It is the Rite of Attachment that makes family discipleship possible.

PASTORAL RECOMMEDATION

To facilitate the Rite of Attachment, the Church must help families see that strong, intimate family relationships — rather than being incidental to family spirituality and faith formation — are primary, central, and foundational. We must encourage Catholic parents to take the cue for their parenting style not from the culture — or even from their own families of origin — but rather from the mutually self-donative relationships found in the life of the Trinity.

In order to cooperate with God's grace to transform the hearts of our household and of the world, it is not enough for Catholic parents to cling to the old chestnut, "I was raised in X manner and I turned out fine." Instead, Catholic parents must be encouraged to see that the ministry of parenting is not ordered to merely confirming what is comfortable and familiar. Rather, it must be ordered to the mission of becoming saints and raising up the next generation of saints by embracing those practices that equip both parents and children with the foundational physical, psychological, relational, and spiritual resources necessary to fully participate in the life of grace.

―――――――――

DISCUSSION

1. How does seeing the Rite of Attachment as the primary and normative way God forms his people in the common priesthood change your view of the importance of cultivating strong family relationships?

2. How do you think this view of family life compares/contrasts with secular and Protestant perspectives on family life that you are aware of?

3. How would striving to live out the Rite of Attachment enable a fam-

ily to more effectively witness to Christ's love in the home and in the world?

4. What is one simple thing you could do to strengthen the Rite of Attachment in your family? What is one simple way you could promote the Rite of Attachment in your ministry to families?

CHAPTER TWENTY-TWO

The Rite of Rituals of Connection: A Formation Program in the Prophetic Mission of Baptism

FIVE QUICK TAKES

1. The Rite of Rituals of Connection enables families to offer ongoing formation in the prophetic mission of baptism. This is the normative way God forms his children in this mission.
2. A prophet is committed to "the proclamation of Christ by word and the testimony of life" (*CCC* 905).
3. Strong family rituals around praying, working, talking, and playing together enable families to have healthy Christian relationships with essentially every type of human activity.
4. Family rituals facilitate a family's ability to create strong, visceral bonds and foster an education in lived faith.
5. Christian families must be encouraged to see family life as both a ministry and the most important "activity." They must be encouraged to schedule most other activities around family rituals, instead of vice versa.

The second rite in the Liturgy of Domestic Church Life is the Rite of Rituals of Connection. Through this rite, the "family school of love" provides ongoing formation in the prophetic mission of baptism. A prophet calls people to God and instructs them on how to live as disciples. As the *Catechism* puts it, a prophet is committed to "the proclamation of Christ by word and the testimony of life." For lay people, "this evangelization ... is accomplished in the ordinary circumstances of the world" (*CCC* 905).

The Rite of Rituals of Connection helps form parents and children in their prophetic mission by encouraging them to create meaninful rituals that enable all the members to develop a balanced, Christian perspective toward all the roles and activities that fill their daily lives. Building upon Joseph White's reflection on the divine pedagogy in family life, we would argue that the Rite of Rituals of Connection constitutes the normative pathway through which God forms his children in the exercise of their prophetic mission.

In *Amoris Laetitia*, Pope Francis wrote, "The spirituality of family love is made up of thousands of small but real gestures. In that variety of gifts and encounters which deepen communion, God has his dwelling place." These "gestures" to which Pope Francis refers are more than just "nice things that families sometimes do." They represent the family rituals that give a particular domestic church both structure and strength, and help families live a balanced, joyful, orderly, and godly life.

Family psychologist Barbara Fiese defines family rituals as "repeated patterns of behavior that facilitate family life, communicate family values, and augment family identity." Her research demonstrates that the stronger and more well-defined a family's rituals are, the healthier that family and its members will be. In her book, *Family Routines and Rituals* (New Haven, CT: Yale University Press, 2006), Fiese reports that families with strong rituals enjoy greater stability and relationship satisfaction, and children raised in such households exhibit better physical and emotional health, perform better academically, and are at lower risk for promiscuity, violence, and substance abuse.

Family rituals create a visceral bond between family members that transcends both reason and emotion. This ritual-based bond is what makes us long to reconnect with our families-of-origin, *even when we can't stand being around them!* Of course, in addition to this unconscious bonding power, strong rituals also give families concrete and conscious opportunities to model the way their beliefs and values are lived in the real world.

In our own writings, we promote four categories of "rituals of connection" that help families *pray, work, talk, and play together* on a daily and weekly basis (Popcak 2015). Because these four categories encompass virtually every type of human activity, in Christian households, strong family rituals model how faithful people cultivate healthy, life-giving attitudes toward prayer, work, communication, and play.

Let's briefly examine how each of these four sets of rituals facilitates formation in our *prophetic* mission of baptism.

PRAY, WORK, TALK, PLAY
Prayer Rituals

Family prayer rituals include meaningful spiritual practices such as gathering for morning or bedtime prayers, family blessings, grace at meals, Scripture reading, at-home praise and worship times, a family Rosary or chaplet, attending Mass as a family, and other similar activities. Rituals like these facilitate ongoing formation in the prophetic mission of baptism by inviting families to sit *together* at the feet of the Master and learn how to love each other, not with mere human affection, but with God's own love. As we argue in our book *Discovering God Together,* when it is done properly (that is, when a family is taught to go beyond viewing prayer as merely "saying words at God"), family prayer rituals invite God to become an actual member of the household and a participant in the daily life of the family (Popcak 2015).

Beyond the spiritual benefits a family can gain from family prayer, an article by the Institute for Family Studies argued that family prayer can promote family cohesion, improved communication, better conflict management skills, and deeper intimacy in the home (McGuire 2016).

Unfortunately, a 2015 survey by CARA (sponsored by Holy Cross Family Ministries) found that only about 17 percent of Catholic families regularly pray together (Gray 2015). That isn't necessarily surprising, in light of the fact that — to our knowledge — not a single popular marriage preparation program on the market currently teaches couples the basic steps of family prayer. Likewise, we are unaware of any parish renewal programs that spend any time teaching participants how to create "small faith groups" in their domestic churches. The lack of attention parish renewal efforts give to renewing the domestic church would appear to fly in the face of the divine pedagogical model presented by Joseph White in this volume as well as being an odd kind of rejection of Pope Francis's vision of the Church as a "family of families." How can we hope to authentically renew the Church if our efforts to do so completely ignore the domestic churches of which our Church is supposedly constructed?

Recommendation: As a Church, we need to promote the idea that praying together as a family is *expected, normative, and necessary.* If we want to foster an authentic, domestic-church-based spirituality, we need to teach couple prayer as a normal part of marriage preparation. We need to make sure that all efforts at parish renewal include ideas for renewing the domestic church participants both come from and live in. We should also seek to foster initiatives — especially around times of sacramental preparation — that actively teach families how to pray together. We need to instruct the faithful that, in a Christian household, family prayer can't simply be a *part* of family life. It must be the *heart* of family life.

Work Rituals

Next, we'll look at the prophetic role of family work rituals. Family work rituals enable parents and children to do simple chores and household maintenance tasks *simultaneously and together* (as opposed to the more common "divide and conquer approach" to chores). Strong family work rituals, such as cleaning up the kitchen together after dinner, putting away the toys together before bed, maintaining the yard together, or regularly doing simple household projects together help households create a sense of "solidarity" and foster an ethos of mutual self-donation. Likewise, strong family work rituals encourage family *stewardship* over the gifts God has given them and model the importance of caring for others in concrete ways.

Recommendation: We must actively teach families that chores are not just about "getting things done." They are an underappreciated opportunity to bond as a family and grow in virtue — particularly the virtues of solidarity and stewardship. As a Church, we must encourage families to create small, daily — and larger, weekly — opportunities to work side by side, practicing cheerful service in the home so that they can practice stewardship, authentically care for each other, and create a foundation for sharing this spirit of service to the parish and community.

Talk Rituals

Now let's look at how family talk rituals facilitate the prophetic mission of baptism. Strong family talk rituals include things like *meaningful* family dinners, regular one-on-one time with one's spouse and children, and thoughtful, dynamic conversations (not lectures) about faith and values, and similar activities. Talk rituals offer formation in our prophetic mission by reminding families to "choose the better part," taking time to connect with each other and build social communion.

In addition to affirming the dignity and personhood of each family member by prioritizing intimacy over activity, regular family talk rituals make it possible for families to have meaningful conversations about values, character, and faith formation that actually stick. Children intuit that the lessons gathered from these heartfelt discussions are not lectures, but true discipleship moments.

Perhaps the easiest way to promote family talk rituals is to emphasize the importance of regular family meals. The good news is that, according to CARA, about 80 percent of Catholic families already do eat some kind of family meal several times a week. About 50 percent have daily family meals. Unfortunately, only about 13 percent of Catholic families say grace before every meal, and fewer than 8 percent of Catholic familes have daily conversations about faith-related topics (Gray 2015). Likewise, it's important to note that meals that consist of shoveling in food as fast as we can so we can get the kids to practice in time don't bear much relational fruit.

Recommendations: As a Church, we need to provide encouragement and resources that can help families make mealtimes more meaningful from both a spiritual and relational point of view. Families need guidance and resources that can help them discuss the faith at home in a casual, natural way that takes advantage of the natural circumstances of family life. Families especially need guidance and resources to help them have conversations about how the faith can help them negotiate life and relationship challenges. As Bartkus notes in this volume, parents in particular need help creating a meaningful narrative describing how they lean on their faith for comfort, courage, and discernment in how to live abundantly. His research shows that these narratives play an important role in a parent's ability to effectively witness to his or her children. We must also help families identify other, simple ways to celebrate social communion. Examples include activities such as one-on-one dates between parents and children as well as spouses, and tips for speaking and listening in ways that open up lines of communication.

Play Rituals

Finally, let's looks at the prophetic role of family play rituals. Piaget believed that observing children at play, which is their "work," offered a window on how morals develop (Piaget 1932). In fact, play is serious business that provides an education in cooperation, social skills, virtue, and morals.

In a world that equates "fun" with "sin," strong family play rituals provide ongoing formation in the prophetic mission of baptism by proclaiming healthy ways the Christian can experience pleasure, enjoyment, humor, and connection — with a "side effect" of moral development.

Our counseling practice, CatholicCounselors.com, offers Catholic pastoral telecounseling services to clients around the world. In our work, we find that many faithful families struggle to play together. They often attend their children's activities and games, but they don't tend to make time to play *together*. It is disturbing to see how parents who had very close relationships with their younger children start to lose those chilren in adolescence as their teens start taking their friends' lead in making decisions about the type of activities that constitute "fun." By contrast, we have observed that families with strong play rituals like game nights, movie nights, a weekly "family day," frequent family celebrations, and holiday traditions do a much better job of retaining their connection and ability to mentor their teens and young adults.

Of course, equally important is the fact that strong family play rituals (e.g., game nights, movie nights, "family days," and various family and religious celebrations) teach family members to see one another as a source of joy. Play rituals facilitate intimacy by encouraging families to, as Pope Francis put it, "waste time together."

Recommendations: As a Church, we need to teach our families the importance of prioritizing regular family fun times over organized sports, lessons, and other scheduled activities. The Archdiocese of Detroit recently took the bold step of banning Catholic school participation in Sunday athletic events (*CNA*, 2019). We need more of this kind of leadership.

We also need to develop programs and resources that help families have more meaningful family celebrations, religious celebrations, and holiday traditions. With our abundance of feast days, Catholics have a special opportunity to help families to create fun, joyful connections around religious celebrations year-round, with various foods and traditions. That said, we would offer one qualification. There are several popular websites and resources that do offer different suggestions for ways families can celebrate feast days and other holy days at home. The problem is that many of the projects offered by these sites are quite time and labor intensive. Others are very pious, but not particularly engaging. It is difficult to imagine how relationship-building many of these activities are. As we develop other resources for families, it will be important to make sure that the projects, games, and ideas we suggest for encouraging family celebrations are less about helping parents increase their social credit on Pinterest and more about actually creating connection between parents and children in ways that allow the faith to be experienced as the source of the warmth in the home.

CONCLUSION

As we conclude our look at the Rite of Rituals of Connection, we hope the takeaway will be that the Church must help families see rituals for praying, working, talking, and playing together as "sacred rites of the domestic church." We need to encourage families to set family rituals on the calendar first, scheduling all other activities around them (instead of vice versa) so that family life can be seen as the most important activity on the docket.

DISCUSSION

1. How does seeing the Rite of Rituals of Connection as the primary and normative way God forms his people in the prophetic mission of baptism change your view of the importance of cultivating strong family rituals for praying, working, talking, and playing together?

2. How do you think this view of family life compares/contrasts with secular and Protestant perspectives on family life that you are aware of?

3. How would striving to live out the Rite of Rituals of Connection en-

able a family to more effectively witness to Christ's love in the home and in the world?

4. What is one simple thing you could do to strengthen the Rite of Rituals of Connection in your family? What is one simple way you could promote the Rite of Rituals of Connection in your ministry to families?

CHAPTER TWENTY-THREE

The Rite of Reaching Out: Ongoing Formation in the Royal Mission of Baptism

---

FIVE QUICK TAKES

1. The Rite of Reaching Out gives families opportunities to provide ongoing formation in the royal mission of baptism. This is the normative way God forms his children in this royal mission.

2. "The People of God fulfills its royal dignity by a life in keeping with its vocation to serve with Christ."

3. The Rite of Reaching Out enables families to fulfill their potential to be the primary engines of evangelization and positive social change.

4. The four ways families can engage in the Rite of Reaching Out are by (1) serving one another at home, (2) thinking about others while being a family-at-home, (3) being godly families in the world, and (4) serving *together* in parish/community ministry.

5. The Liturgy of Domestic Church Life is liturgy to which the common priesthood is inextricably tied. It is the primary means by which the common priesthood consecrates the world to Christ.

The third and final rite of the Liturgy of Domestic Church Life is the Rite of Reaching Out. The Rite of Reaching Out provides ongoing formation in the royal mission of baptism.

If the Christian family is to model itself after the Trinity, then the loving communion it creates in the home must be shared with the wider community. Trinitarian love is always generative. In the Liturgy of Domestic Church Life, love is cultivated in the Rite of Attachment, shaped through rituals of connection, and then directed to reaching out. Saint Teresa of Calcutta says it this way: "Love begins at home." Experiencing this generative love at home enables us to "love naturally … First in our own home, [then with our] next door neighbor, [then] in the country we live, [and] in the whole world" (Saint Teresa of Calcutta).

As the *Catechism* puts it, "The People of God fulfills its royal dignity by a life in keeping with its vocation to serve with Christ" (*CCC* 786). The Rite of Reaching Out enables family members to promote the gospel of life by working for the common good of their parish and community. Building upon Joseph White's reflection on the divine pedagogy in family life, we would argue that the Rite of Reaching Out represents the normative pathway by which God forms his children in the royal mission of baptism. Likewise, the Rite of Reaching Out empowers families to fulfill the third and fourth tasks enumerated in *Familiaris Consortio:* participating in the development of society, and sharing in the life and mission of the Church. It is ultimately this rite that empowers families to be the outposts of evangelization and positive social change that the "new evangelization" calls them to be. As Saint John Paul put it, "In the future, evangelism will depend largely on the domestic church."

As well as being good for the community, family service also promotes family well-being. For instance, a study by Indiana University found that family service projects yielded ten distinct benefits to family life ranging from a sense of increased togetherness, to higher levels of gratitude, and an increase in pro-social behavior and attitudes, to name a few. Other research has found similar benefits (Friedman 2019).

The Rite of Reaching Out plays an important role in fostering an authentic family spirituality and affording families the opportunities to be primary outposts of evangelization and engines of positice social change. Both in her chapter in this volume and in her book *Family Ethics,* Julie Rubio shares many examples of how simple family practices like the ones we will briefly discuss here can enable families to participate in the salvific mission of the Church.

We suggest four general categories of activities families can employ to exercise the Rite of Reaching Out:

- serving one another at home
- thinking about others while being a family-at-home
- being godly families in the world
- serving *together* in parish/community ministry

1. SERVING ONE ANOTHER AT HOME

The first way families can celebrate the Rite of Reaching Out is by *encouraging cheerful, generous service in the home*. Most adults are concerned with making sure *children* learn the value of chores and other acts of service; but, in our experience, *parents* often underestimate the spiritual value of the mundane tasks they do each day.

When our oldest child was in second grade, we were preparing him for his first Holy Communion. As part of his lessons, Lisa was reviewing the Corporal Works of Mercy with him: feeding the hungry, giving drink to the thirsty, clothing the naked, etc. When Lisa was done with the list, he looked up and said, "You do those things all the time. They should call them the 'corporal works of mommy.'" His observation became the basis for one of our books on family spirituality, *The Corporal Works of Mommy (and Daddy Too)* (Popcak 2016).

Service in the home isn't wasted spiritual effort, no matter how much we might feel after washing the millionth dish, putting away the billionth sock, or paying the trillionth bill. When families are mindful about serving one another lovingly, generously, and (as much as possible) cheerfully, they are walking the little way of holiness and learning the steps of mutual self-donation.

As a Church, we must help families discover the everyday saint-making potential of the Corporal and Spiritual works of mommy and daddy — and brother and sister, too (Popcak 2016).

2. THINKING ABOUT OTHERS WHILE BEING A FAMILY AT HOME

The second way families celebrate the Rite of Reaching Out is by *being mindful of others while being a family at home*. This category includes practices like working *together* as a family to make extra meals for a pregnant, sick, or elderly neighbor, working *together* as a family to gather food, clothing, or toys for the local mission, or other home-based, family activities done for the benefit of others. In order to gain the full spiritual, relational, and missional benefits afforded by this category of practices, it is important that children play an active role in these activities alongside their parents instead of parents doing these activities on their own in the name of the family or sending children to do these things by themselves.

Julie Rubio offers additional suggestions along these lines in her contribution to this volume and in her book, *Family Ethics.*

3. BEING GODLY FAMILIES IN THE WORLD

The third way families celebrate the *Rite of Reaching Out* is by *being godly families in the world.* It's hard to overestimate the evangelistic impact a family can have just going out to dinner together, *if* they do things like unashamedly pausing to say grace, willingly putting down their electronic devices and talking together, enjoying one another's company, engaging in respectful humor, being polite to the restaurant staff, saying "please and thank you," and tipping appropriately to show gratitude for services rendered.

Pope Francis has noted the power of simple acts like these in *Amoris Laetitia.* It would be helpful to remind families that more than "being nice," intentional acts like these are a spiritual exercise in the virtue of kindness.

4. FAMILIES SERVING TOGETHER IN PARISH/COMMUNITY MINISTRY PROJECTS

Finally, the fourth way families celebrate the Rite of Reaching Out is by looking for simple ways to serve their parish or community *together.*

Instead of letting parish service divide families, parents should ask the parish to schedule their family to serve, read, sing, etc. at the Mass they usually attend *together as a family.*

Similarly, we need to give families more opportunities to engage in parish and community service projects *that enable them to serve together.* The website doinggoodtogether.org offers many ideas that allow families — even families with small children — to serve others together. That said, it is important to remember that family service must be unifying. Emphasizing charitable service to the parish or community *to the point that it jeopardizes a family's rituals or their experience of togetherness* can be seriously detrimental to family well-being.

Recommendations: For many families, parish life becomes one more thing that divides them. Families don't go to Mass together because they are scheduled for different ministries at different times. Likewise, the men's, women's, and youth groups may do service projects, but parishes offer few opportunities to serve together. What's worse is that these various opportunities to serve the parish often unintentionally undermine a family's ability to get family time. As a result, the most active members of a parish often find their family life suffering *because* of their parish involvement. This seems counterproductive to promoting the vision of a parish as a family of families. As an alternative, we would suggest that parishes should adopt a Titus 2 model of parish service; that is, parishes should look for opportunities for parents to bring their children to help in age-appropriate ways with the setup for parish events or other parish and community ministry projects.

Additionally, the Church must provide guidance and resources to help families understand the spiritual, relational, and missional benefits of serving one another at home and being families in their world. The Rite of Reaching Out allows families to exercise their royal mission and use the Liturgy of Domestic Church Life to consecrate the world to Christ through their loving witness and self-donative service.

CONCLUSION

As we've outlined it, our proposed Liturgy of Domestic Church Life comprises the rites of attachment, rituals, and reaching out, and offers a possible structure for an authentic, ecological, domestic-church-based spirituality as well as a more systematic way to appreciate how the common priesthood of the laity complements the ministerial priesthood and the Liturgy of the Eucharist.

David Fagerberg points to this complementarity when he writes:

> The common priesthood of the laity is directed toward the cure of this now corrupted structure of the world, and the ministerial priesthood is at the service of the common priesthood to equip them for their lay apostolate. ... Therefore, "though they differ from one another in essence and not only in degree, the common priesthood of the faithful and the ministerial ... priesthood are nonetheless interrelated: each of them in its own special way is a participation in the one priesthood of Christ."

It's inherent to the nature of priesthood to preside over liturgy. For instance, that's why the Church celebrates the institution of both the Eucharist and the ministerial priesthood on Holy Thursday. The two are inextricably tied. It's impossible to speak of priesthood without simultaneously referencing the liturgy over which the priest presides. The ministerial priesthood consecrates the bread and wine into the Body and Blood of Christ through the Liturgy of the Eucharist. In a sense, the common priesthood consecrates the world to Christ through the Liturgy of Domestic Church Life.

Perhaps our understanding of the value and dignity of the "common priesthood of the laity" has suffered for so long because we've been attempting to talk about it without adequately defining the Liturgy of Domestic Church Life to which it is inextricably attached. Building the kingdom of God doesn't necessarily require us to "do great things for Jesus" like building hospitals and converting entire nations to Christ. For most of us, building the kingdom of God simply requires cooperating with grace to heal the way sin ruptured our relationships with one another and God. The common priesthood facilitates this healing through all three rites of the Liturgy of Domestic Church Life. Seen through this lens, creating strong families isn't just a nice thing to do. It is the primary way the common priesthood of the laity participates in the salvific mission of the Church.

Similar to the way that the ministerial and common priesthoods represent distinct yet complementary means of participating in the one priesthood of Christ, the Liturgy of Domestic Church Life could be thought of as a true liturgy that is distinct from yet complementary to the Liturgy of the Eucharist. Of course, the relationship between these two liturgies is enhanced by the fact that they are the only two liturgies where love itself becomes incarnate in flesh and blood — the former through the conception of children and the latter through the Precious Body and Blood.

If the concluding cry of the Liturgy of the Eucharist is, *"Ite! Missa est"* ("Go! You are sent"), perhaps the opening, complementary call of the Liturgy of Domestic Church Life would be, "Come and be formed!"

We hope that this analysis will jumpstart a renewed effort to help families participate more fully in God's plan for calling the whole world to him. In this way, Pope Francis's vision in *Amoris Laetitia* could be realized, and the Church could truly become "a family of families, constantly enriched by the lives of all those domestic churches."

DISCUSSION

1. How does seeing the Rite of Reaching Out as the primary and normative way God forms his people in the royal mission of baptism change your view of the importance of family working together to serve each other inside and outside the home?

2. How do you think this view of family life compares/contrasts with secular and Protestant perspectives on family life that you are aware of?

3. What is one simple thing you could do to strengthen the Rite of Rituals of Connection in your family? What is one simple way you could promote the Rite of Relationship in your ministry to families?

4. What do you think of the idea that the Liturgy of Domestic Church Life is the liturgy to which the common priesthood is essentially connected? How would accepting this view change your idea of the role the domestic church is meant to play in God's plan for the salvation of the world?

REFERENCES

Agishtein, Peryl and Claudia Brumbaugh. "Cultural Variation in Adult Attachment: The Impact of Ethnicity, Collectivism, and Country of Origin." *Journal of Social, Evolutionary, and Cultural Psychology* 7, no. 4 (December 2013).

Ainsworth, Mary D. Salter. *Patterns of Attachment: A Psychological Study of the Strange Situation.* London: Psychology Press, 2015.

Atkinson, Joseph C. *Biblical and Theological Foundations of the Family: The Domestic Church.* Washington, DC: Catholic University of America Press, 2014.

Barron, Bishop Robert. "Priests Prophets, Kings." *Word on Fire,* February 14, 2014, https://www.wordonfire.org/resources/article

/priests-prophets-kings/.

Bowlby, John. *A Secure Base: Parent-Child Attachment and Healthy Human Development.* New York: Basic Books, 1988.

Catechism of the Catholic Church: Second Edition. New York: Doubleday, 2003.

Catholic News Agency. "Detroit Archdiocese Cancels Sporting Events on Sundays." Catholic News Agency, May 16, 2019, https://www.catholicnewsagency.com/news/detroit-archdiocese-cancels-sporting-events-on-sundays-45730.

Clinton, Tim, and Gary Sibcy. *Attachments: Why You Love, Feel, and Act the Way You Do.* Nashville: Thomas Nelson, 2002.

Clinton, Tim and Joshua Straub. *"God Attachment: Why You Believe, Act, and Feel The Way You Do About God."* Brentwood, TN: Howard Books, 2010.

Crouan, Denis and Michael Miller. *The History and the Future of the Roman Liturgy.* San Francisco: Ignatius Press, 2005.

Evdokimov, P. Ecclesia Domestica. *L'Anneau d'Or: Cahiers de spiritualite conjugale et familiale.* (1962).

Fiese, Barbara H. *Family Rituals and Routines.* New Haven, CT: Yale University Press, 2006.

Fagerberg, David W. (2004). *Theologia Prima: What Is Liturgical Theology?* Mundelein, IL: Hillenbrand Books, 2007.

Pope Francis. *Amoris Laetitia,* https://w2.vatican.va/content/dam/francesco/pdf/apost_exhortations/documents/papa-francesco_esortazione-ap_20160319_amoris-laetitia_en.pdf.

Friedman, J. (2019). *Benefits of family volunteering.* DoingGoodTogether.org

Gray, Mark M. *The Catholic Family: 21ˢᵗ Century Challenges in the United States.* Center for Applied Research in the Apostolate. Georgetown. June 2015, https://cara.georgetown.edu/staff/webpages/CatholicFamilyResearch.pdf.

Gregory the Great. "Epistle to Bishop Serenus of Marseilles." *NPNF 2,* vol. XIII, p. 53), http://www.ccel.org/ccel/schaff/npnf213.ii.v.xliv.html.

Held, Barbara S. "The Process/Content Distinction in Psychotherapy Revisited." *Psychotherapy: Theory, Research, Practice, Training* 28, no. 2 (Summer 1991): 207–217.

Saint John Paul II. *Apostolic Journey to the Dominican Republic, Mexico and the Bahamas. Homily of His Holiness John Paul II.* January 28, 1979, http://w2.vatican.va/content/john-paul-ii/en /homilies/1979/documents/hf_jp-ii_hom_19790128_messi-co-puebla-seminario.html.

Saint John Paul II. *Address of John Paul II to the Members of the Foyes Des Equipes des Notre-Dame.* September 23, 1982, https:// w2.vatican.va/content/john-paul-ii/en/speeches/1982/september /documents/hf_jp-ii_spe_19820923_foyers-equipes -notre-dame.html.

Saint John Paul II. *Familiaris Consortio*, http://w2.vatican.va/content/john-paul-ii/en/apost_exhortations/documents/hf_jp-ii _exh_19811122_familiaris-consortio.html.

Littlepage, Laura. *Family Volunteering: An Exploratory Study of the Impact on Families*, https://archives.iupui.edu/bitstream /handle/2450/438/31_03-C05_Family_Volunteering.pdf ?sequence=1.

Mamalakis, P. M. "Eastern Christian Perspectives on the Church of the Home." In *The Household of God and Local Households: Revisiting the Domestic Church.* Leuven, Belgium: Peeters Publishing, 2013: 146.

Marquardt, Elizabeth. *Between Two Worlds: The Inner Lives of Children of Divorce.* New York: Crown Publishing Group, 2015.

McGuire, Ashley. "Does the Family that Prays Together Really Stay Together?" *Institute for Family Studies*, April 20, 2016.

Saint Teresa of Calcutta. *Mother Teresa. Noble Prize Acceptance Speech.* December 10, 1979, https://www.nobelprize.org/prizes/peace/1979 /teresa/26200-mother-teresa-acceptance-speech-1979/.

Moullin, Sophie, Jane Waldfogel, and Elizabeth Washbrook. *Baby Bonds: Parenting, Attachment and a Secure Base for Children*, https://www.suttontrust.com/wp-content/uploads/2014/03 /baby-bonds-final.pdf.

Narvaez, Darcia. *Neurobiology and the Development of Human Morality:*

Evolution, Culture, and Wisdom. New York: W. W. Norton & Co., 2014.

Ouellet, Marc Cardinal. *Divine Likeness: Toward a Trinitarian Anthropology of the Family*. Grand Rapids, MI: William B. Eerdmans Publishing Co., 2006.

Pontifical Council for the Family. *Family and Human Procreation*, http://archive.wf-f.org/FamilyandHumanProcreation.html.

Popcak, Greg, and Lisa Popcak. *Discovering God Together: The Catholic Guide to Raising Faithful Kids*. Bedford, NH: Sophia Institute Press, 2015.

Popcak, Greg, and Lisa Popcak. *The Corporal Works of Mommy (and Daddy Too)*. Huntington, IN: Our Sunday Visitor, 2016.

Ratzinger, Joseph Cardinal. *The Spirit of the Liturgy*. San Francisco: Ignatius Press, 2000.

Rubio, Julie Hanlon. *Family Ethics: Practices for Christians*. Washington, DC: Georgetown University Press, 2010.

Seigel, Daniel. *Pocket Guide to Interpersonal Neurobiology: An Integratie Handbook of the Mind*. New York: W. W. Norton & Co., 2012.

Van Ijzendoorn, Marinus H., and Pieter M. Kroonenberg. "Cross-Cultural Patterns of Attachment: A Meta-Analysis of the Strange Situation." *Child Development* 59, no. 1 (1988): 147–156.